The
Christian History
DEVOTIONAL

The Christian History
DEVOTIONAL

365 Readings and Prayers to
Deepen and Inspire Your Faith

J. STEPHEN LANG

THOMAS NELSON
Since 1798

NASHVILLE   DALLAS   MEXICO CITY   RIO DE JANEIRO

Published in Nashville, Tennessee, by Thomas Nelson. Thomas Nelson is a registered trademark of Thomas Nelson, Inc.

Published in association with the literary agency of Mark Sweeney & Associates, Bonita Springs, Florida 34135.

Thomas Nelson, Inc., titles may be purchased in bulk for educational, business, fund-raising, or sales promotional use. For information, please e-mail SpecialMarkets@ThomasNelson.com.

All Scripture quotations, unless otherwise noted, are taken from the Holy Bible, New International Version. Copyright © 1973, 1978, 1984 Biblica. Used by permission of Zondervan. All rights reserved.

Scripture quotations marked ESV are from *The Holy Bible, English Standard Version*, copyright © 2001 by Crossway Bibles, a division of Good News Publishers. Used by permission. All rights reserved.

Scripture quotations marked NKJV are from *The New King James Version*. Copyright © 1979, 1980, 1982, Thomas Nelson, Inc., Publishers.

Scripture quotations marked KJV are taken from the King James Version of the Bible.

Library of Congress Cataloging-in-Publication Data

Lang, J. Stephen.
  The Christian history devotional : 365 readings and prayers to deepen and inspire your faith / J. Stephen Lang.
     p. cm.
  Includes bibliographical references and index.
  ISBN 978-1-4002-0433-5 (alk. paper)
  1. Church history--Miscellanea. 2. Devotional calendars. I. Title.
  BR150.L25 2012
  270--dc23

2012022476

Printed in the United States of America

12 13 14 15 16 QG 6 5 4 3 2 1

Introduction · HISTORY WITH A HEART

Say the word "history" and many people immediately think of the word "boring." Why is this so, when the past is a vast and colorful world full of fascinating people and events? And many of these people are our ancestors, spiritually speaking, as much a part of our religious heritage as the people of the Bible are. And so I present this book to you, so that for a few minutes each day you can look into Christian history with the same motive as reading the Bible: to enlarge your spiritual family and find more friends for the soul.

Many of the names here will be familiar to you: Martin Luther, John Wesley, Billy Graham, Augustine, John Bunyan, Francis of Assisi, Mother Teresa, C. S. Lewis, John Stott, Corrie ten Boom, Dietrich Bonhoeffer. But much of the pleasure in writing this book came from writing about lesser-known figures, some of them from fields we normally think of as secular. Some were athletes, such as Olympic runner Eric Liddell and cricket star C. T. Studd--both of whom became missionaries. Some were scientists, such as astronomer Johannes Kepler, botanist Gregor Mendel, and chemist Robert Boyle—all committed Christians who saw no conflict between science and faith. Some were politicians, such as British prime minister William Gladstone, America's William Jennings Bryan, and France's king Louis IX—men whose politics and faith could not be separated. And some—many—were martyrs, believers who fulfilled Jesus' prophecy that his followers would be persecuted in this world. One of the recurring themes in this book is that it isn't easy to be a Christian. But it is supremely rewarding. The history of Christianity has countless examples of well-lived lives, saints who were often distressed and depressed, who coped with frets and dreads, and who triumphed over obstacles because of their whole-souled commitment to one who promised he had overcome the world. Some of these heroes would do anything possible—and impossible—for the Lord. Of such people we need reminding. People like these are good company on the road to God.

I have tried to accentuate the positive, focusing on people who can serve as role models of faith. But it was impossible to avoid looking at people who were *bad* examples—and sometimes the contrast is striking, as in the case of Alexander VI, a thoroughly vile man who happened to be pope, and who ordered the execution of the saintly reformer Savonarola. A picture of the godly Savonarola would not be complete without contrasting him with the worldly and corrupt Alexander. The church has never been completely pure (as we see in

Paul's letters in the New Testament), but we can learn lessons both from those who followed Christ faithfully and from those who did not.

As I scroll through this completed book, I realize what a delightfully diverse group of believers are presented here: evangelist Billy Sunday, the former baseball player full of fizzing vitality; martyr William Tyndale, who gave us the Bible in English; missionary Gladys Aylward, who faced many trials in China; Bill Bright, founder of Campus Crusade for Christ; John Newton, the former slave trader who became a pastor and author of "Amazing Grace"; scientist Georges Lemaitre, who gave the world the Big Bang theory; the artists Rembrandt, Michelangelo, Durer, and Tintoretto; the poets John Milton, Anne Bradstreet, and Dante; journalists Malcolm Muggeridge and Robert Novak, whose disillusionment with the world led them to Christ; religious freedom pioneers William Penn and Roger Williams; soldiers Thomas "Stonewall" Jackson, Oliver Cromwell, and Charles "Chinese" Gordon; hymnwriters Charles Wesley, Fanny Crosby, and Isaac Watts; George Washington Carver, born a slave but renowned as a scientist; social reformers William Wilberforce and Josephine Butler, who proved that "otherworldly" Christians do great things in this world; department store mogul John Wanamaker, who ran his business on Christian principles; Sundar Singh, the Indian Sikh who became a lone guru for Christ; TV personality Fulton Sheen, the bishop whose weekly program reached millions; composers Bach and Handel; authors Dorothy Sayers, G. K. Chesterton, Daniel Defoe, and Fedor Dostoevsky. These and many others will be your companions in this year's worth of devotions, with each day of the calendar tied to a key event of that day—the birth or death of a notable person, the beginning of a new ministry, the ending of a wave of persecution, a Supreme Court decision that had far-reaching effects on religion. Here is a year's worth of history, history with a heart. See if you can commit five minutes each day to fellowship with your enormous spiritual family.

JANUARY

Do not be overcome by evil, but overcome evil with good.

ROMANS 12:21

404: Blood flowed, men died, crowds cheered—such was the "entertainment" enjoyed by the ancient Romans, which is familiar to us thanks to movies such as *Gladiator* and *Spartacus*. In the gladiatorial contests, combatants greeted the emperors by shouting, "We who are about to die salute you!" The loser in each contest was usually stabbed through the throat, while the crowds roared. The bloody sand was raked over, and a new contest would begin. Such bloodbaths were not just for the dregs of society but for everyone, including the emperors.

Constantine, the first Christian emperor, ended the gladiator spectacles in 313—but apparently the ban was not enforced for long, for the games were revived later. The emperors, even though they were Christians, feared to take away something that gave the masses such pleasure.

The early Christians lamented the evil of Roman public amusements. One Christian author called the games "cannibal banquets for the soul." Other Christians claimed that the public shedding of blood for sport encouraged crime and a general disdain for human life. Even though many gladiators were convicted criminals under a death sentence, sensitive souls grieved that citizens enjoyed watching the butchery. Churches refused baptism to a gladiator unless he changed professions. Pastors taught their flocks that Christ's people had no business attending such spectacles, and some congregations refused holy communion to Christians who did.

One Christian tried a more drastic approach. In the year 400, Telemachus leapt into the arena to stop a gladiatorial contest. The mob (composed mostly of citizens who were nominally Christian) stoned him to death. The emperor eventually ordered the contests stopped permanently. The last gladiator contests were held January 1, 404. They did not end solely because of Telemachus's martyrdom. They ended because enough Christians, and people influenced by Christians, saw the games as the vulgar, inhumane outrages that they were. Faith in the Prince of Peace had triumphed over the spirit of cruelty.

Prayer: Lord of life, make us beacons of light in a dark world. Amen.

The weapons we fight with are not the weapons of the world.

2 CORINTHIANS 10:4

1924: How did a man with fifteen children ever find time to write hymns—or write anything, for that matter? An ordinary man could not, but Sabine Baring-Gould was no ordinary man, for his mind ranged over so many things—Christianity, folk songs, ghosts and werewolves, and archaeology.

Born in 1834, he studied at Cambridge and was ordained in the Church of England. In forty-eight years of marriage, his wife, Grace, bore him fifteen children. While pastoring a church, he found time to collect and publish English folk songs. Appropriately for a pastor, he was fascinated by Christian history, and he wrote a sixteen-volume *Lives of the Saints*. He also wrote books on ghosts, werewolves, and superstitions. He was an amateur archaeologist, often digging in prehistoric ruins.

Sabine Baring-Gould is mostly remembered as the author of one of the church's greatest hymns—which he wrote in about fifteen minutes. This was "Onward, Christian Soldiers," written for a church parade of children held on Pentecost in 1864. His title for the hymn was "Hymn for Procession with Cross and Banners." For the music he lifted a melody line from a symphony by Joseph Haydn. The hymn might have been forgotten had not the composer Arthur Sullivan in 1871 written the rousing tune that is so familiar. (Sullivan would later become famous for the music in the comical Gilbert and Sullivan operettas.) Not surprisingly, it was often used by the street bands of the Salvation Army.

The song has nothing to do with actual combat—the war is a spiritual one, between God's "Christian soldiers" united in faith against the forces of darkness. Sadly, this superb hymn has been criticized and even dropped from some hymnals for its "militarism," even though its mentions of war, battle, and army are obviously spiritual.

Sabine Baring-Gould died on January 2, 1924, the author of dozens of books—and remembered for a stirring hymn he dashed off in fifteen minutes.

Prayer: Father, thank you for hymns that stir the soul and deepen faith. Amen.

January 3 · MISSIONARY MAID

Do not be dismayed, for I am your God. I will strengthen you and help you.

ISAIAH 41:10

1970: In a movie titled *The Inn of the Sixth Happiness*, the strikingly beautiful actress Ingrid Bergman portrayed an English missionary named Gladys Aylward. The real Gladys was not beautiful on the outside, but everyone who met her knew her to be beautiful within.

Born in London in 1902, Gladys worked as a maid but aspired to be a missionary. The China Inland Mission turned her down, saying she did not have enough education. Not one to be thwarted, Gladys saved enough money to pay for her own passage to China in 1930, which required a ponderous train trip across Russia, a voyage to Japan, then to China, then a trek by mule to a mission station north of Beijing, where she and an older missionary woman turned their home into an inn, a stopping point for trade caravans passing through. The "entertainment" the women provided was telling stories about Jesus, and in time they made many converts. Gladys gradually perfected her use of Chinese and began dressing as a native.

Gladys took in an orphan, then another, until in time there were a hundred. Japan invaded China in 1938, and Gladys and the band of orphans had to flee, journeying on foot for twelve days, sleeping some nights in the open. When they reached the Yellow River, there was no way to cross, all boat traffic having stopped due to the war, but Gladys and the children began to pray and sing hymns. A Chinese officer heard them and arranged for safe passage. Having found a safe home for the orphans, she started a church and later worked in a home for lepers.

Gritty though she was, Gladys's health was broken by the war years, and in 1947 she returned to England for medical treatment. For the rest of her life she preached and lectured on her China adventures. She died on January 3, 1970, respected as a woman of deep faith and boundless courage.

Prayer: Lord, as we face obstacles and adversities, remind us of your unfailing love. Amen.

January 4 · PRAYING IN THE POWER PIT

Be still, and know that I am God; I will be exalted among the nations.

PSALM 46:10

1947: What would you say if you had two minutes to address a room full of the most powerful politicians in America? That question must have occurred many times to Peter Marshall, one of the most-quoted preachers of his day.

Born in 1902 in Scotland, Peter arrived in America when he was twenty-four. He made friends at a church who financed his education at a seminary in Atlanta, was ordained, and served a small church. He moved back to Atlanta to pastor another church and met his future wife, Catherine Wood (who, as Catherine Marshall, became a noted Christian author). In 1937 he was called to be the pastor of the "power church," New York Avenue Presbyterian in Washington, with its pews full of political VIPs. Marshall's sermons drew crowds and were often reprinted in *Reader's Digest* and *The New Yorker*.

The U.S. Senate asked Marshall to serve as its chaplain, a position he assumed on January 4, 1947. The chaplaincy was mostly ceremonial, consisting of the chaplain opening each day's session with a prayer. Marshall saw this mere formality as a means of speaking truth to the powerful. In one of his first prayers in the Senate chamber, he prayed, "We are at cross-purposes with each other. Take us by the hand and help us see things from Thy viewpoint." Marshall's prayers were collected and published as *Mr. Jones, Meet the Master*.

Peter, with his Scots accent, oozed charm and warmth. He had a contagious zest for life, which helped to draw young people to his church. He packed a great deal of living and life-changing influence into a few years. Peter had a heart attack, then a second, and he died January 26, 1949, at the age of forty-six. His widow published his story as *A Man Called Peter*.

Prayer: Father, let our faith in you be a life-affirming thing that draws others to you. Amen.

January 5 · FREED TO THINK—AND SERVE

He made the earth by his power; he founded the world by his wisdom.

JEREMIAH 51:15

1943: A noted scientist who died on this date saw no conflict at all between science and faith. On the contrary, he was certain that "without God to draw aside the curtain, I would be helpless." His name was George Washington Carver, and few people ever started life with more handicaps. Born about 1864 in Missouri, he was the son of illiterate slaves, though all slaves were legally freed while he was still a toddler. A white couple whose last name was Carver were his owners, then guardians, and he referred to Mrs. Carver as "Aunt Susan." The Carvers saw a lively intellect in the child, as did all who met him. He attended Simpson College in Iowa (one of the few colleges of the time that would admit blacks), but due to his knack for growing plants, he transferred to Iowa's agricultural college.

In 1896 Booker T. Washington invited him to teach agriculture at Tuskegee Institute in Alabama. He taught there till his death, while conducting research into the uses of soil-enriching crops like peanuts and sweet potatoes and urging farmers of all races to diversify their crops instead of relying on cotton, notorious for exhausting the soil. In the last years of his life, Carver was an international celebrity, meeting with three U.S. presidents and writing a syndicated column, "Professor Carver's Advice." Carver's fame increased when Southern farmers began growing peanuts after their cotton was devastated by the boll weevil.

Carver was certain that it was God who gave him success. He had become a Christian at age ten and read the Bible constantly. While teaching agriculture at Tuskegee, he also modeled character development, and for years he taught a Sunday Bible class. He firmly believed that nature was one means by which God spoke to man, and though he enjoyed and encouraged reading, he believed his discoveries arose from communing with God.

Prayer: Lord, bless all those who study your creation and use their knowledge to benefit others. Amen.

How many are your works, O LORD! In wisdom you made them all.

PSALM 104:24

1884: Are religion and science opposed to each other? Gregor Mendel, who died on this date, did not think so. He is known as the father of genetics, but when he died, very few people knew of his scientific work, though many knew him as the head of a monastery in the Austrian Empire. It wasn't until many years after his death that the world saw the significance of his work.

Born in 1822, Mendel grew up on a farm and learned to cultivate plants and tend bees, two skills that would prove useful years later. He joined a monastery in 1843, and the abbot there shared Mendel's interest in science and gave him leave to study at the University of Vienna. In the monastery's garden Mendel cultivated thousands of pca plants and maintained bee hives and through experimentation in making hybrids, formulated Mendel's Laws of Inheritance. Scientists had always assumed that inherited characteristics blend, but Mendel discovered that heredity is affected by the interplay of *dominant* and *recessive* genes. He wrote up his findings in a paper presented to several scientific societies, but at the time no one really understood the importance of Mendel's Laws.

Mendel became abbot of his monastery in 1868, and his administrative duties gave him little time for scientific pursuits. When he died in 1884, he was beloved by all who knew him and admired him as a Christian but were barely aware of his being a scientist. It would have amazed this gentle man that in the following century scientists and Christians would see each other as enemies.

Sometimes fame comes after death. There is a Mendel University in the Czech Republic, and the monastery where he lived and died has a Mendel Museum that includes his garden. These places honor a man who was a sincere Christian in his own time and an honored scientist afterward.

Prayer: Creator God, we give you thanks for your beautiful and intricate world, and for minds that understand it. Amen.

January 7 · Knocked Down, Never Out

I call on the LORD in my distress, and he answers me.

PSALM 120:1

1676: The great Reformation leader Martin Luther insisted that people needed the Bible and hymns in their own language. So Luther not only translated the Bible into German but also wrote several hymns, and he insisted that hymns be an important part of Protestant worship. He started the rich tradition of hymn singing and composing in Lutheran churches.

A follower in that tradition was Paul Gerhardt, born in 1607. He studied at the University of Wittenberg, the very spot where Luther had launched the Reformation years earlier. Gerhardt became a pastor in Berlin, where he and composer Johann Cruger collaborated in writing hymns. Gerhardt's preaching and songs attracted many people, and in a time when denominational differences mattered, Gerhardt, a Lutheran, reached out to other Protestants. Sadly, he lost his post due to a conflict with the local ruler, Elector Friedrich Wilhelm. He could not even hold services in his home. In the meantime, his wife died, as did four of their five children. Having lived through the turbulent Thirty Years' War, in which a third of Europe's population died, Gerhardt had seen his share of suffering.

Sustained in all this sadness by his faith in God, Gerhardt wrote some great hymns, 123 in all. They were written in German, of course, but many of them have been translated into English. John Wesley, founder of Methodism, rendered one of Gerhardt's hymns into the English "Jesus, Thy Boundless Love to Me," a song Wesley had heard onboard ship as he sailed to America. Wesley also translated Gerhardt's "Give to the Winds Thy Fears," and both these hymns are found in most English-language hymnals.

Paul Gerhardt died on January 7, 1676, having witnessed much sadness in his life but also having experienced the sustaining love of the Lord.

Prayer: Almighty God, you give us hope through our many trials. Teach us patience, and give us strength to endure whatever this world does to us. Amen.

"My kingdom is from another place."

JOHN 18:36

1198: How much earthly power should a spiritual leader possess? In the Middle Ages most of the popes would have said, "As much as possible." For centuries the popes were not only the heads of the Roman Catholic Church but also ruled over a large part of central Italy (a region known as the Papal States). Possessing the power to excommunicate anyone, a pope held great power over even the mightiest of kings. Not surprisingly, the office of pope attracted many ambitious, unscrupulous men. And yet, the most powerful pope of all was a reasonably moral man, though definitely an ambitious one.

That man was Innocent III, whose reign began on January 8, 1198. Many high officials in the church were corrupt, but Innocent (true to his name) had led a scandal-free life. Taking office at the age of thirty-seven, he had no qualms about using his power to bring some of Europe's wayward rulers into line. One example: Innocent appointed a man to the office of archbishop of Canterbury, head of the church in England. King John of England had his own candidate for the post, and when John resisted, Innocent excommunicated John and put England under an interdict, meaning that, technically, the whole country was "outside the church." John, fearing a rebellion, gave in and accepted Innocent's appointee.

In one of his writings, Innocent stated that the power of the pope and the power of a king were like the sun and the moon, meaning that the sun (the pope) was a greater light since the moon (a king) only reflected the light of the sun.

Despite the great impression Innocent made on his contemporaries and on historians, he has never been officially made a saint, nor was he ever referred to as "Innocent the Great." Perhaps the church has never been quite comfortable with the awesome amount of worldly power Innocent wielded, given that Jesus said his kingdom was "not of this world."

Prayer: Lord, keep us from the lust for worldly power and let us rely on you. Amen.

Where the Spirit of the Lord is, there is freedom.

2 Corinthians 3:17

1724: Isaac Backus, born on this date in Connecticut, was a firm believer in the separation of church and state. At the time of his birth, the colony had an established church, and all citizens had to pay taxes to support it. Isaac studied for the ministry, pastored a Separatist church, and in 1749 refused to pay the church tax, though a friend paid it for him. He took the case to the Connecticut assembly and reminded them that their ancestors had left England to escape a state church and be free to worship as they please—and support any church that they pleased. He did not change the assembly's mind.

Backus joined the Baptists, who were at the time a new and small denomination in America. He spent much of his life in the saddle, traveling and preaching to a large circuit of Baptist churches. In 1777 there were 119 Baptist churches in America; by 1795 there were 325. He supported the founding of Rhode Island College, later known as Brown University. And he continued to press for the disestablishment of churches in America, freeing people from having to pay taxes to support a state church they did not attend.

Something called the American Revolution settled the issue. England, the mother country, had a long tradition of a state church, but a new country was emerging. Baptists backed the American side in the war, hoping there would be no established churches in it. They were disappointed—in Massachusetts, anyway, which kept its established church for several decades. But in the south and west of the new United States, there were no established churches, and the Baptists flourished there. In time there would be no established church anywhere in the United States.

The driving force of Isaac Backus's life was not the issue of an established church: like most preachers of his day, he wanted to save souls. But his beliefs about established churches had a profound effect on the new nation.

Prayer: Lord, we praise you for freeing us from sin and empowering us to live for you under any political system. Amen.

January 10 · FULL HOUSE

Sons are a heritage from the LORD, children a reward from him.

PSALM 127:3

1863: Harriet Beecher Stowe, author of *Uncle Tom's Cabin*, recalled that the home she grew up in was "full of moral oxygen and intellectual energy" due to the personality of her father, Lyman Beecher, one of the great American preachers of the 1800s. The home was full of moral energy as well, for Lyman Beecher had pronounced opinions on every issue of the time: some he opposed (dueling, slavery, liberalism, drunkenness); some he supported (religious revivals, higher education, Bible societies, women's rights). Born in 1775, Lyman Beecher was in a sense born with the nation, and like many people of the time, he had great reverence for the Founding Fathers. He was one of a generation of preachers who had no qualms about discussing politics and culture from the pulpit. In fact, in a day with no mass communications except newspapers, Christians expected their pastors to be zealous, biblically astute, knowledgeable about the world—and opinionated.

Raised in New England, Beecher later joined many fellow Americans in the move west and became president of Lane Theological Seminary in Cincinnati. When his students found out that he favored a gradual (as opposed to immediate) emancipation of slaves, most of the students departed. Beecher spent the last years of his life as pastor of a Presbyterian church in Cincinnati.

Lyman Beecher died on January 10, 1863, in the middle of a war that had split his country in two. Friends said that he believed his ministry had been a failure. But he had overlooked something: from his three marriages he had thirteen children and an impressive brood they were, not only novelist Harriet Beecher Stowe, but renowned (and controversial) preacher Henry Ward Beecher, preacher and abolitionist Edward Beecher, and women's rights activist Isabella Beecher, just to name the most famous. No wonder historians have called Lyman Beecher "the father of more brains than any man in America."

Prayer: Lord, bless all fathers and mothers who raise their children to love you and to do good in the world. Amen.

January 11 · A Voice in the Crowd

He had compassion on them, because they were like sheep without a shepherd.

MARK 6:34

1740: If colonial America had a "superstar" that everyone wanted to see, it was George Whitefield, the most famous preacher of his time, not only in America but in his native England as well. It was on this date that he began his great preaching tour of the American colonies.

Whitefield, born in 1714, was a friend of John and Charles Wesley and a member of their "Holy Club" at Oxford. Like them, he was ordained in the Church of England, but despised the spiritual deadness in that Church. Despite being cross-eyed (as all his portraits attest), he was not shy about speaking in public, and the greatest actor of the time, David Garrick, was in awe of Whitefield's speaking voice.

Americans turned out in droves to hear that voice. When Whitefield preached in Philadelphia, young Benjamin Franklin estimated that Whitefield's voice was audible to the very back of a crowd of twenty thousand. But there was more to Whitefield than his voice. The message was the key: man needs salvation and attending church (or even being a clergyman) does not assure salvation, for there must be a change in the heart with the sinner in a warm, personal relationship with God. This was not a message people often heard in English churches, especially the Church of England. Many clergymen barred Whitefield from their pulpits, but this was a moot point, since the enormous crowds required him to preach outdoors. His preaching not only led to many conversions but to the founding of numerous charities and schools.

The spiritual revival known as the Great Awakening would not have been the same without this amazing man. Some historians credit Whitefield's interdenominational revival with uniting the thirteen colonies spiritually, paving the way for the political union that would result in the American Revolution that began shortly after Whitefield's death in Massachusetts in 1770.

Prayer: Merciful Father, we thank you for those who preach your word faithfully, who call for a revolution of the heart. Amen.

January 12 · THE STORM-WATCHER

They were looking for a better country—a heavenly one.

HEBREWS 11:16

1729: Edmund Burke, born on this date, was that rare combination of deep thinker and practical politician. In his lifetime he watched two world-changing political revolutions unfold, and he saw a place for religion in this new world that was taking shape.

Burke was born in Ireland to a Protestant father and Catholic mother, and this interfaith marriage taught him an early lesson about different denominations living peacefully together. Like many future politicians, he studied law, though he preferred to make his living by writing. In 1765 he was elected to Parliament, and his maiden speech impressed everyone who heard it. Within a few years one of the great issues before Parliament was the matter of the American colonies revolting. In Burke's view, the colonies' grievances were legitimate, and he opposed the use of force to put down the rebellion.

It was another revolution in that century that brought out Burke's eloquence and also his devotion to religion. The French Revolution broke out in 1789, and Burke soon realized that this revolution that claimed to support the "rights of man" was executing thousands of people, all in the name of creating a new world order. Burke's *Reflections on the Revolution in France* laid out his view of politics: not all change is good; radical revolutions are dangerous, especially those led by atheists who have no God to hold them accountable; slow and gradual change rooted in tradition is best. Burke understood that political revolutions are rooted in the desire to create a heaven on earth—yet they always fail and often make matters worse. He would not have been surprised that in the twentieth century atheist governments in Russia and China were cruel and repressive. He understood that mankind had advanced in science and technology but not in morality, for the moral teachings of Christianity could not be improved or updated. God has given us all we need to know about living the good life.

Prayer: Lord, we thank you that our citizenship is in heaven, and that we may see clearly the limitations of this world's politics. Amen.

January 13 · LIGHT-MINDED

"I am sending you to them to open their eyes and turn them from darkness to light."

ACTS 26:17–18

1691: William Penn, the founder of Pennsylvania, was a member of the Society of Friends, better known as Quakers. According to Penn, George Fox, the founder of the Quakers, "in all things acquitted himself like a man, yea, a strong man, a new and heavenlyminded man." Fox made a similar impression on almost everyone he met.

Born into a devout working-class home, George Fox was serious about religion from his youth, and he had no use for "professors," his name for superficial believers. Like many people of his time, he found the state church, the Church of England, to be full of "professors," so although he felt called by God to minister, it would not be within the Church of England—nor any other. None of the existing sects satisfied him.

Wandering about England, he began to attract people who responded to his talk of the "Inner Light" that can guide the Christian's steps. His followers were called "Friends of Truth," then simply "Friends." The name "Quaker" arose when Fox, seen as a troublemaker, found himself before a judge whom Fox told to "tremble at the word of the Lord." This judge, and many other Englishmen, looked askance at these people with their talk of "Inner Light," fearing they were dangerous radicals. More than once Fox found himself in prison. The Quakers were persecuted by the Church of England, but during the short rule of Oliver Cromwell in the 1650s, they were tolerated.

Never one to keep still, Fox took his message all over Britain, to America, and to the Caribbean islands. He preached peace, abolition of slavery, and simplicity of dress and manners. The Quaker meetings had no clergy, rituals, or music. Rather, members would wait in silence for the Spirit to move one of the members to speak a word from the Lord.

Fox died on January 13, 1691, leaving behind his fascinating journal, the spiritual record of a truly unique man.

Prayer: Lord, help us to be sincere and zealous in our faith, not mere "professors" of religion. Amen.

January 14 · UNITING THE TWO-BIBLE NATION

Your word is a lamp to my feet and a light for my path.

PSALM 119:105

1604: The King James Version of the Bible was the result of a conference that met on this date at Hampton Court palace in England. The new king, James I, agreed to meet with the Puritans, those members of the Church of England pushing for more reform than the previous ruler, Elizabeth I, had allowed. James saw the Puritans as troublemakers and had no intention of giving them an inch.

But one of the Puritans, John Reynolds, made an interesting proposal: a new version of the Bible. England at the time was a two-Bible nation: most people read the popular Geneva Bible at home while the church used the "official" version known as the Bishops' Bible, which no one liked much. Since the Geneva Bible had been the official Bible of Scotland, James's home country, Reynolds hoped James would approve it for England. But James claimed he thought the Geneva was the worst translation ever. In fact, he claimed he had only seen one once—which was a blatant lie, since the Geneva was read in all churches in Scotland. Instead of giving his approval to the Geneva, he commissioned a new version, with the work farmed out to committees of scholars. The conceited king would have been pleased to know that centuries later many people still read the version named for him.

The most important thing to know about the KJV is that it was *not* a translation. It was a revision of previous versions, and much of it resembles the Geneva Bible—and much of it is, word for word, like the translation William Tyndale did in the 1520s. When it was finally published in 1611, it was criticized by many and ignored by others, and many people went on reading their Geneva Bibles. But in time the goal of the Puritans at Hampton Court was achieved: one Bible read in both church and home. And no English Bible has ever been so widely quoted and loved.

Prayer: Lord, we praise you for all who have labored to bring to life your Book of Life. Amen.

January 15 · Repenting for Hysteria

Do not follow the crowd in doing wrong.

EXODUS 23:2

1697: One of the black marks in the history of Christianity is the church's treatment of those who were accused of being witches in Salem, Massachusetts, in 1692. People hostile to Christianity point to this episode as an example of Christianity's cruelty and intolerance. The executions are indeed part of the Christian story—but not the whole story, for the follow-up to the 1692 incidents is, sadly, forgotten.

Samuel Parris, a minister in Salem, was like most Christians in Europe and America at that time: he believed that witches were real. Several adolescent girls in Salem, including Parris's own daughter and niece, claimed they had been bewitched by Tituba, the Parris family's black slave woman. The girls also accused two old women of the town of being witches. By the summer of 1692, the jail was filled with people the girls had accused of witchcraft, the "evidence" being that the girls went into convulsions in their presence, or that the girls had seen an "apparition" of the accused person.

But not all the accused were executed. Most, finding themselves in the difficult situation of either having to confess to something they did not do or be killed, confessed to witchcraft and said they were repentant. These were released. But by September, nineteen of those who would not admit to practicing witchcraft were executed by hanging. While many supported the trials and executions, there were many Christians in Salem and elsewhere who protested the way the trials were conducted. (Note that no one was executed by *burning*, a common accusation made against Christians.)

Now for the part of the story that is seldom told: the Massachusetts legislature declared January 15, 1697, to be a day of public penance and fasting, expressing remorse for what had happened in 1692. The judge and jurors all confessed their errors, Samuel Parris was expelled from Salem, and some of the families of the victims were given compensation. The Salem witch trials are indeed a shameful episode in America's Christian history, but the remorse and confession are also part of the record.

Prayer: Lord, none of us is sinless. Fix our gaze on our own failings, not those of others. Amen.

January 16 · A Mission to Run

I run in the path of your commands, for you have set my heart free.

Psalm 119:32

1902: Thanks to the 1981 movie *Chariots of Fire*, audiences became familiar with a great Christian athlete, the Scotsman Eric Liddell, born on this date. His birthplace was not Scotland but China, where his parents were missionaries. At age five he was sent to a boarding school in England, where he was an outstanding athlete, excelling not only in track but in cricket and rugby also. The headmaster of his school remarked that young Liddell was "entirely without vanity."

Active as an athlete, Liddell was also involved with Christian student groups and often witnessed to his deep faith. He continued in his Christian work and in sports when he enrolled at the University of Edinburgh, Scotland.

As seen in *Chariots of Fire*, Liddell represented Great Britain in the 1924 Olympics, held in Paris. Although he excelled in 100-meter races, he would not compete in the Olympic 100-meter since it was held on a Sunday. However, he did compete in the 400-meter and won the gold medal, and he also won the bronze medal in the 200-meter.

After his Olympic wins Liddell returned to his real life's work, the mission field in China. Teaching at a school for Chinese boys, Liddell found that boys around the world were more likely to listen to a message from a renowned athlete, so his fame aided his success as a missionary.

As a result of Japanese aggression in World War II, Liddell and his family found themselves working as medical missionaries among poor Chinese. The Japanese took over the mission and put Liddell and his family in a prison camp. He died of a brain tumor in the camp in February 1945, to the last deeply impressing the other prisoners with his warmth, humility, and wideness of heart. No one who met the "Flying Scotsman" could ever forget him.

Prayer: Almighty God, teach us to be faithful witnesses for you, no matter what the circumstances. Amen.

"Do not worry about your life, what you will eat or drink; or about your body, what you will wear."

MATTHEW 6:25

356 : What is the key to living to the age of 105? An Egyptian Christian named Anthony would have said, "Faith." Born in the year 251 into a well-to-do Christian family, Anthony was deeply affected by a sermon on Matthew 19:21: "If you would be perfect, go, sell what you possess and give to the poor." These were Jesus' words to the rich young ruler, but Anthony believed they were meant for him. He sold his family property, gave the money to the poor, and retired to the desert.

He was walking a familiar path. Since Emperor Constantine had made Christianity the favored religion of the empire, it was no longer risky to be a Christian. Being martyred for the faith was no longer possible, so Christians with heroic hearts opted for a life of self-denial and solitude, forsaking the comforts of civilization.

But solitude was the one thing Anthony did not get. Like many of these desert-dwelling saints, Anthony gained a reputation as a fount of wisdom, and many people sought out "Abba" ("Father") Anthony. For twenty years he lived in an abandoned fort, subsisting on bread, salt, and water, and sleeping on the bare ground. When too many people sought him out at the fort, he moved even farther into the wilderness, but to no avail. His location was always discovered. People found him wise—and, surprisingly, they found him cheerful also. There are no portraits of him, but considering his meager diet, never bathing, and having a wardrobe of one garment, he must have been quite a sight. And yet something about him impressed all who met him, all the more as he lived to, and beyond, the age of one hundred. A life such as his reminded Christians that material possessions are not so important. He died on January 17, 356, one of the most respected men of his time.

Prayer: Father, teach us to rely on your love, and free us from the worries about material goods. Amen.

January 18 · ARM IN ARM WITH THE LORD

Draw near to God and He will draw near to you.

JAMES 4:8 (NKJV)

1917: One of the pleasures in reading the history of Christianity is discovering how multinational and multiethnic the body of Christ is. Consider the case of Andrew Murray: ethnically, he was a Scot but he served as a missionary in the Dutch Reformed church and was born in (and ministered to) South Africa. Born the sons of missionaries, Andrew and his brother were university-trained in Scotland and the Netherlands. At this time, the 1840s, the Dutch church was going through a spiritual dry spell, but Andrew and his brother were active in a revival movement, calling on believers to make their religion a matter of heart as well as head.

The two brothers were ordained and returned to South Africa, where both were key players in the South African Revival of 1860. Andrew was active in missionary work to both black and white residents of South Africa. Like many Christian workers in this bilingual nation, Murray was fluent in both Dutch and English.

But Andrew Murray's chief claim to fame is as a devotional writer. Considering how much time he gave to preaching and missions, it is amazing that he wrote more than two hundred books. Probably the most-loved of these is *Abide in Christ*, consisting of thirty-one meditations of what Jesus meant in John 15:4 when he told his disciples, "Abide in me." Murray understood that most Christians see Jesus as someone to obey or to pray to in times of need, but the truly pleasurable life is one in which every moment the believer feels the closeness of Christ. Christians live "divided lives," setting aside moments to read the Bible or devotional books, when in fact Christ desires all of us, all the time.

Murray died, aged eighty-nine, on January 18, 1917, but his writings live on, touching those who desire a closer walk with God.

Prayer: Lord Jesus, we acknowledge you as Savior and King, but we also acknowledge you as Friend and Companion, desiring our fellowship every moment. Amen.

January 19 · CRUEL CHANGE

You saw my affliction and knew the anguish of my soul.

PSALM 31:7

1918: The Russian Revolution is remembered as being aggressively antireligion. Curiously, it did not begin that way. When the government of Tsar Nicholas II collapsed in 1917, the new government made up of moderates gave the Russian Orthodox Church freedom, even allowing it to restore the office of patriarch, chief bishop in the church. A man named Tikhon was appointed to the post. He was in for a rough ride.

The hard-line Communists edged out the government's moderates. In December 1917, the government decreed that all land was government property, including church land. The government took control of all schools, including seminaries, and religious instruction was forbidden. Marriages were to be civil unions, not religious ones, and registration of births and deaths, formerly handled by the church, were now civil matters. Technically, people had religious freedom—so long as it did not "interfere with public order."

Patriarch Tikhon was horrified at these changes. On January 19, 1918, he publicly denounced the government's acts, including the murder of the tsar and his family. He called on Christians to resist the state—and the state responded by throwing resisters in prison or, more often, shooting them without trial. While killing off adult Christians, the government stepped up anti-Christian propaganda among the youth. Restrictions were tightened, and no professed Christian could teach school. Thousands of clergy and laity were sentenced to slave labor in cold Siberia. Beautiful cathedrals were turned into museums of atheism. The Communists broke Tikhon—or so it seemed. After serving a year in prison, he emerged to tell the Orthodox Christians they should *not* resist the government. Was he playing along, hoping that by his seeming cooperative the government might ease its pressure on Christians? No one is quite sure. The Orthodox continued to respect him, and still do today. He died in 1925 while celebrating Communion, his last words being, "Glory to you, O Lord, glory to you."

Prayer: Father, we ask your blessing on all those who suffer for their faith under cruel governments. Amen.

January 20 · THE PURGE

"I know that you have little strength, yet you have kept my word and have not denied my name."

REVELATION 3:8

250: The Roman emperor Decius reigned only two years, but in a short time he did a lot of killing. Previous emperors had persecuted the Christians, but those persecutions had been limited in area and duration. Under Decius, persecution took place systematically and over the whole empire.

In early January 250 he issued an edict: all citizens had to perform a sacrifice to the pagan gods in the presence of an imperial official. Those who did so were given certificates to prove they had complied. Christians reacted to this edict in different ways. Some made the sacrifice, despite knowing that in doing so they were denying Christ. Others would not make the sacrifice but bribed the officials to give them a certificate. But, to their great credit, many Christians refused to make the sacrifice. Rounding up all these might have been impossible, for there were so many, so Decius directed his wrath at the leaders. On January 20, 250, Fabian, bishop of Rome, was executed, and later the bishops of Jerusalem and Antioch were killed. Others were arrested, and some of these were tortured, others killed. By early 251 the persecution eased up, for the pagans were beginning to sympathize with the Christians.

The persecution raised an important question for the church: Should the Christians who offered the pagan sacrifice still be considered worthy members of the fellowship? These were referred to as the *lapsi*, the "lapsed ones," and many Christians believed that such people who denied Christ had no right to call themselves Christians. Hadn't Jesus himself said that he would deny those who denied him? Others took a more lenient view—after all, which of us knows what we would do in such a situation? And didn't Jesus himself forgive Peter who denied him three times?

One thing they could all agree on: despite losing friends and family members in the persecution, it had strengthened the church instead of weakening it.

Prayer: Father, strengthen our feeble hearts so that we will never be ashamed of being your children. Amen.

"Whoever believes and is baptized will be saved."

MARK 16:16

1525: In the 1500s having the wrong opinion about baptism could be deadly. For centuries the church had been baptizing infants, and few people questioned the practice. When the Protestants began breaking away from the Catholic Church in the Reformation period, they dropped many Catholic practices—but not infant baptism. The few who did choose to abandon that practice got into deep trouble.

The first were a group of men in Zurich, Switzerland, who approved of the reforms taking place under the pastor Ulrich Zwingli. But they didn't think Zwingli was moving fast enough, or far enough, toward creating a church based on the New Testament. On January 17, 1525, one of the men, Conrad Grebel, debated baptism publicly with Zwingli. The church sided with Zwingli: infant baptism would continue, *and* no one would be allowed to question it further. On January 25 Grebel and the others met together—and baptized each other. Since they had all been baptized as infants, this was considered *anabaptism*—"baptism again." In less than a week, thirty-five others were baptized, and the first Anabaptist congregation was formed.

The Anabaptists practiced *believer's baptism*, meaning baptism only of those who made a voluntary choice to join the church—which, of course, ruled out baptism of infants. This belief would lead to trouble, and they were heartily persecuted by Protestants as well as Catholics. Many of the Anabaptists were working-class or poor folk (which was also true of the first Christians), and this made them suspicious in the eyes of authorities.

On January 25, 1527, one of the Anabaptists, Felix Manz, a former priest, was executed—the first Protestant executed by other Protestants. He was drowned, which his executioners thought appropriate for one who had sought a second baptism.

Most of the Anabaptists were decent, law-abiding folk who took the Bible seriously. Their persecution by people claiming to be Christian is impossible to excuse, just as their courage is impossible to ignore.

Prayer: Lord, rid us of cruelty and intolerance, which have no place in the lives of your people. Amen.

January 22 · THE MORAL BOMBSHELL

I am setting before you the way of life and the way of death.

JEREMIAH 21:8

1973: Is America a Christian nation? Prior to the turbulent 1960s, everyone (even non-Christians) assumed it was. Certainly the Supreme Court did, handing down rulings that referred to America as a "Christian" or "religious" nation. Then came the 1963 ruling against mandatory prayer and Bible reading in public schools. Was the Court becoming antireligion? That question was asked even louder after January 22, 1973, when the Court, in the infamous *Roe v. Wade* case, claimed that no state or locality could restrict a woman's "right" to an abortion. Most liberals, especially feminists, cheered the ruling. Conservatives wondered why this "right" had never been noticed by previous courts. The country found itself dividing into "pro-choice" (approving the Court's decision) and "pro-life" (opposing the decision). One side claimed to speak for women, the other for unborn children—and for the morality that had long protected the unborn.

The division created some curious alliances. For many years Catholics and evangelical Protestants thought they had little in common, but now they found themselves joining hands on the pro-life side. New and extremely active organizations came into being, such as the Moral Majority. The pro-choice side depicted the pro-life movement as dangerous reactionaries, trying to put women "back in the kitchen" and roll back the sexual revolution. The pro-life side depicted the pro-choicers as selfish hedonists who were furthering the moral breakdown of the country.

The pro-lifers had an unexpected ally: science, which was advancing in showing the unborn child in the womb and in keeping premature babies alive, even performing surgery on unborn children. The pro-choicers continued to use the term *fetus*, but sonograms made it clear enough to pregnant women that it was most definitely a *child* in the womb.

Pro-lifers regard *Roe v. Wade* as a horrible mistake. The mistake has proven to be an opportunity for believers to take a stand for the cause of life.

Prayer: Lord of life, watch over the unborn and bless the labors of those who strive to protect innocent lives. Amen.

January 23 · God's Samurai

The people walking in darkness have seen a great light.

ISAIAH 9:2

1890: For many years Japan chose to seal itself off from the rest of the world. Citizens were not permitted to travel abroad without government permission, and permission was seldom given. Yuzuru Neesima, a young man of samurai stock, was fascinated by America, science, and Christianity, and in 1864 he talked an American captain into letting him stow away on his ship. Had Yuzuru been caught, the Japanese government could have had him executed, but he kept a low profile and arrived safely. Since the ship captain's last name was Hardy, Yuzuru took the name Joseph Hardy Neesima.

On reaching America, he found some eager sponsors: a Christian couple in Massachusetts who paid for his education at a prep school and then Amherst College. Along the way he embraced Christianity and was baptized. After finishing at Amherst, he graduated from a seminary and was ordained. He was the first Japanese to graduate from an American college and the first to be ordained a Protestant minister.

Japan had opened itself to the world in the years Neesima was in America, with the old edict banning Christianity being revoked in 1873. Neesima returned to Japan in 1875. Assisted by a Canadian missionary, he established Doshisha University, the first Christian university in Japan. The name Doshisha means "one purpose society," and it was established in Kyoto, a stronghold of Buddhism. In time, Kyoto became the center of Christianity in Japan.

Neesima took his faith seriously, and he aimed for the university to combine the best of Western academics with biblical teachings. Christianity had always had a difficult time in Japan, but Neesima believed that in the modern world, the Japanese could find their fulfillment in the Christian faith.

Neesima's health had always been fragile, and he died on January 23, 1890, only forty-six years old, having used himself up in the cause of introducing his people to a faith that in centuries past would have led to execution.

Prayer: Lord, you are a God of many surprises, and we are inspired by the stories of your apostles in unexpected places. Amen.

January 24 · SLANDERED SHEPHERD

The LORD detests lying lips, but he delights in men who are truthful.

PROVERBS 12:22

1534: If you are part of an organization desperately in need of reform, do you break from it or try to change it from within? That was the question that confronted many faithful Christians in the 1500s after Martin Luther launched the Reformation. Many of the devout threw in their lot with Luther and the other Reformers, but a handful of saintly men stayed within the Catholic Church and tried to set an example of Christian living. One of these was Guillaume Briçonnet.

Guillaume was born about 1472 into a wealthy and devout family, and he became bishop of the French city of Meaux in 1516—the year before Luther began the Reformation. He shared Luther's desire to clean up a corrupt church, and as bishop he disciplined lax clergymen and worked to raise the standard of education and morals. Though some of the immoral priests and monks became his enemies, he attracted reform-minded Catholics who became known as the Circle of Meaux, and they met for Bible study and prayer. Like Luther and the other Protestants, Briçonnet and his friends found their spiritual lives changed by the close study of Paul's letters.

Briçonnet became a spiritual advisor to Margaret, sister of King Francis I, but despite having this friend in high places, he came under suspicion, for he was living in an age when any sort of reformer was suspected of being a "heretic," meaning Protestant. Some of the lax clergy he had disciplined ran a smear campaign to depict the bishop as a heretic, and he was called before the national assembly to affirm his loyalty to the Catholic Church and assure the authorities that he was no heretic. A cloud of suspicion hung over him the rest of his life, however, and soon he had to disband the Circle of Meaux. He died on January 24, 1534, a good man who was frustrated because he served a church that looked upon reform as heresy.

Prayer: Father, when we are slandered and misunderstood, be with us and be our righteous Judge. Amen.

Great are the works of the LORD; they are pondered by all who delight in them.

PSALM 111:2

1627: A man born on this date was living proof that science and religion do not have to be in conflict. He was Robert Boyle who formulated Boyle's law, familiar to every student of physics and chemistry. He also endowed the Boyle Lectures, aimed at defending the truths of Christianity against skeptics.

Born into a wealthy family in Ireland, Boyle as a young man toured Europe and met some noted scientists, including the elderly Galileo. While living in England he became part of a group known as the Invisible College, later known as the Royal Society for the Improvement of Natural Knowledge.

When Boyle was born, chemistry was still in the dark ages. For centuries men dabbled in alchemy, a fruitless effort to change cheap metals like iron and copper into gold. Thanks to Boyle and his contemporaries, chemistry grounded in hard science began.

Boyle lived through the turbulent period of England's Civil Wars, when religious controversies were very prevalent. Like many believers, he wanted to see an end to Christians arguing over petty matters. He hoped they would turn their energy to the real enemies, skepticism and atheism. This is why he left money in his will to establish the Boyle Lectures. His will stipulated that the lectures should never be used to promote quarrels among Christians.

Throughout his life, Boyle contributed to the support of missionaries and the translation of the Bible into the languages of the lands the missionaries served. Having grown up in Ireland, he backed a translation of the Bible into the native Gaelic language of the Irish since many of the Irish of his day spoke no English.

The man sometimes called the "Father of Chemistry" was friends with another great scientist, Isaac Newton, who was also a Christian. Newton agreed with Boyle that science was God's "second book," supporting faith as surely as the "first book," the Bible.

Prayer: Lord, let our pleasure in your creation draw us nearer to you, the Creator. Amen.

January 26 · BOLDNESS TO THE NTH DEGREE

The LORD is my light and my salvation—whom shall I fear?

PSALM 27:1

1885: In the spring of 1862, a British soldier stationed in China contracted smallpox. In a letter to his sister he stated that "I am glad to say that this disease has brought me back to my Savior." He was Charles Gordon, nicknamed "Chinese" Gordon after he molded a horde of native riffraff and peasants into a model army that fought on the British side during a brief war with Chinese rebels. Gordon returned to England as the hero of the day but was so modest that he declined dinner invitations from aristocrats and politicians.

His reward for his service in China was the governorship of the Sudan, at that time under British control. It was not a plum assignment, for the Sudan, south of Egypt, was the site of constant tribal warfare and a slave trade that horrified Gordon, who wrote his family that *he* had an "Almighty God to direct and guide [him]." Protecting Europeans in these lands was no easy task, but in any battle Gordon could be found in the most dangerous spot, confident that he would not die until it was God's will.

Gordon left the military life behind in 1882 and gave himself up to study of the Bible and touring Palestine, where he identified the site he was sure was Golgotha (a site still pointed out to tourists as "Gordon's Calvary"). But Gordon's country called him back to action. A crazed character calling himself the Mahdi, the "expected one" of Islam, launched a jihad against Europeans in the Sudan. Gordon reached the city of Khartoum in 1884 and evacuated two thousand women, children, and sick. He was wounded before the Mahdi's army closed in. Gordon and his native troops held out against the Mahdi until January 26, 1885, when Gordon, fearless and fighting to the end, was killed. All Britain mourned him. Gordon, the small, wiry man who seemed to fear nothing, had entered a more peaceful world.

Prayer: Lord, teach us to master our fears and recognize you as the power that cannot be defeated. Amen.

The Lord is at your right hand; he will crush kings on the day of his wrath.

PSALM 110:5

1547: King Henry VIII of England is famous for having had six wives—two of whom he divorced, two he ordered beheaded, one who died after giving birth, and the last who outlived him. The stories of his marriages intertwine with the course of the Reformation in England.

In his youth Henry wrote a book condemning Martin Luther. Probably the book was ghostwritten by a bishop, but it bore Henry's name. For taking this stand against Protestantism, the pope bestowed the title "Defender of the Faith" on Henry, and every English ruler after him has borne that title. Henry's first wife was Catherine of Aragon, the daughter of the famous Isabella and Ferdinand of Spain. After Catherine bore him a daughter and endured several stillbirths and miscarriages, Henry became convinced Catherine would never bear a son to succeed him and sought to end the marriage. The pope would not grant Henry a divorce, so Henry broke England away from Rome and established the Church of England. His new archbishop of Canterbury (chief bishop in England) gave Henry the divorce he wanted, enabling him to marry Anne Boleyn—who bore a daughter and no sons, was framed for adultery and beheaded. Henry's third wife, Jane Seymour, bore him a son—and then died.

During all these marital muddles, Henry shut down the monasteries and convents, leaving thousands of monks and nuns homeless and giving their lands to his cronies. The Protestants in Europe applauded this, just as they applauded Henry giving his approval to a Bible in English. He seemed to be acting Protestant, but then he decreed that clergy could not marry and that laymen must cease reading the Bible.

In Germany, Martin Luther sized up the situation accurately: the power-loving Henry was not only head of England's government but its church also.

Henry was by no means an admirable or devout man. But his key achievement was to break England away from the Catholic Church, ensuring that it—and, later, America—would be Protestant.

Prayer: Lord, you alone are the righteous King and Judge, and to you alone we owe our ultimate loyalty. Amen.

January 28 · EMPEROR UNDER GOD

Love and faithfulness keep a king safe.

PROVERBS 20:28

814: Here is a truth that bears repeating: it is very hard for a politician to live as a Christian. One who tried and (more or less) succeeded was the imposing Charles the Great, or Charlemagne, the ruler of a wide European empire until his death on January 28, 814. The empire included all of what is today France, the Netherlands, and Belgium, and large parts of Germany, Italy, and Spain. Charlemagne's official title for many years was "king of the Franks," but then something remarkable happened on Christmas Day, 800: he was in Rome, praying at the tomb of Peter, when Pope Leo III entered and crowned Charlemagne as "great and peace-giving emperor of the Romans." Historians debate whether Charlemagne was genuinely surprised or if this was a piece of "political theatre" planned by him and the pope. Whatever it was, for the rest of his reign he was known as *emperor*, not *king*, and the church regarded him as its protector and as the chief Christian ruler in Europe.

Did the Christian emperor behave as a Christian? In many ways, no. He could be cruel in battle, and he had concubines and illegitimate children. Yet in other ways he ruled as a Christian: In dealing with other nations he generally spoke honestly. He was concerned for the welfare of Christians in other countries and often aided them, either through diplomacy or with ransom money. He regarded Christian morality as binding on all officials, both clergy and laymen, and his letters are full of Bible quotations that he applied to his servants. He had no patience with corruption, and his officials known as the *missi dominici* traveled throughout his realm to report abuses.

For some politicians, religion is little more than a pose, but with Charlemagne it was the guiding principle for the empire he governed. If he was not the perfect Christian king, he was better than most who came before and after him.

Prayer: Father, touch the hearts and minds of those who govern and endow them with wisdom and fairness. Amen.

January 29 · A New Pentecost

If anyone does not have the Spirit of Christ, he does not belong to Christ.

ROMANS 8:9

1929: What does it mean to "have the Holy Spirit"? In 1900, Charles Parham, head of a Bible college in Topeka, Kansas, asked his students to study the Bible and come up with an answer to that question. On January 1, 1901, at a New Year's "watch night" service, student Agnes Ozman requested prayer and laying on of hands from Parham. Then she began speaking in tongues. Two days later, Parham and other students also began speaking in tongues. Parham came to believe that this was evidence of the baptism of the Spirit, and he made this belief a pillar of his Apostolic Faith movement. He began a ministry of evangelism and healing, and a 1903 revival in Galena, Kansas, sparked wide interest in the movement.

It also provoked ridicule, not only from unbelievers but from many Christians. To many people, worship was supposed to be a dignified, solemn experience. So where did speaking in a language that was like no earthly language fit in? Parham's followers based their belief on the New Testament, where Paul, in 1 Corinthians, wrote at great length on speaking in tongues and said that he himself did so. Acts 2 shows that on the day of Pentecost all the apostles were filled with the Spirit and spoke in tongues. (This is the root of "Pentecostal," referring to Christians being filled with the Spirit.) Parham believed that one of the reasons for the spiritual deadness of so many churches was that Christians were not filled with the Spirit—nor did they even know that this was something they should pray for.

Parham's Apostolic Faith movement spread, and many new churches were established. Many regard him as the father of the modern Pentecostal movement. Parham died on January 29, 1929—while showing slides from a trip to the Holy Land.

Prayer: Holy Spirit, fill us and empower us to be valiant witnesses in the world. Amen.

January 30 · SHELTERING MINDS

See to it that no one takes you captive through hollow and deceptive philosophy.

COLOSSIANS 2:8

1912: For people who were in their teens or twenties in the 1970s, one of the most familiar Christian faces was Francis Schaeffer, with his white goatee, receding hairline, and bulbous nose. (He also had a habit of wearing knickers.) Schaeffer did not look like a typical Christian author but more like a secular professor—which is curious, because his popular books were intended to save young people from some of the wackier ideas of intellectuals.

Born in 1912 in Philadelphia, Schaeffer pastored several churches before moving with his family to Europe, answering a call to establish new churches on the war-ravaged continent. Wanting to understand the secular mind, Schaeffer immersed himself in modern philosophy, theology, and art, hoping to discover what turned people away from God and traditional morality. In 1955 he and his wife, Edith, established L'Abri, a youth center in a French-speaking part of Switzerland. The name is French for "the shelter," and indeed it became a shelter for college students wrestling with questions about God and the purpose of life.

Word of Schaeffer's ministry with young people spread, and in the 1960s he began lecturing at American colleges. Some of his lectures were published as the books *The God Who Is There* and *Escape from Reason*, which made a case for Christianity and against the hollow philosophies college students were exposed to. *How Should We Then Live?* was both a book and film series that looked at how culture had abandoned its Christian foundations. Schaeffer's 1981 book *A Christian Manifesto* was a concise summing-up of a Christian approach to politics and culture. Schaeffer, like most evangelical Christians, took a strong stand against abortion and euthanasia, subjects addressed in his book *Whatever Happened to the Human Race?*

Schaeffer died in May 1984, a loved and respected figure, a man that many Christian students regarded as an intellectual mentor.

Prayer: Lord, you gave us minds to glorify you and to serve others. Keep us in the way of wisdom. Amen.

All the ends of the earth will see the salvation of our God.

ISAIAH 52:10

1955: "The evangelization of the world in this generation" was a phrase coined by a man not afraid to dream big, John R. Mott. He was influenced by evangelist D. L. Moody, by the YMCA (in the days when it was about faith, not just physical fitness), and by English cricket player J. K. Studd, a devout Christian. The world needed saving, and while much progress had been made in the 1800s, Mott and many others saw the dawning twentieth century as the Great Age of Faith.

Mott became a globetrotting spokesman for the Student Volunteer Movement for Foreign Missions (SVM), founded in 1888. When he spoke on college campuses, he drew thousands, and some of the wild enthusiasm that we today associate with college sports was then channeled into organizations like the SVM. The salvation of souls was the main goal, but the SVM also saw evangelism and missions as a means to civilize the entire world. Both liberal and conservative Christians agreed that Christianizing the globe was the grand goal of the new century.

Mott stuck to his motto that "no movement can be adequately led from an office chair," so he traveled constantly on behalf of the SVM, witnessing firsthand some of the horrors of World War I. His travels convinced him that the real battle was not abroad but on the campuses of America's colleges. If Christians could win a substantial part of the college population to Christ, they were well on their way to conquering the world.

Mott chaired the 1910 World Missionary Conference held in Edinburgh, Scotland. In 1946 he received the Nobel Peace Prize for his tireless work in promoting Christian missions. He stuck with his great cause, missions, and turned down offers to become the ambassador to China and the U.S. secretary of state. When he died at age ninety on January 31, 1955, the Christian world lost one of its most devoted servants.

Prayer: Lord, ignite in us the fire that motivated the tireless missionaries of days past. Amen.

FEBRUARY

Your word is a lamp to my feet and a light for my path.

PSALM 119:105

1516: The Dutchman named Desiderius Erasmus did not have a promising beginning in life: he was the illegitimate son of a priest. Born in 1466, he did have the good fortune to be schooled by the Christian group known as the Brethren of the Common Life. From them he absorbed the belief that the main point of studying the Bible and theology was to live a godly life, not to engage in academic debate.

Erasmus was ordained a priest, but he did not have the heart for ministry, for all he really desired in life was to study and write. He became a wandering scholar, and in 1501 published the book *Enchiridion Militis Christiani* ("Handbook for the Christian Soldier"), encouraging people to live by the teachings of the Bible. The problem was the Bible was in Latin, a language only scholars understood. Erasmus believed it should be translated into the languages people actually spoke—but first the translators had to have access to the original Greek text of the New Testament. On February 1, 1516, Erasmus published his version of the Greek New Testament. In its preface he expressed his hope that in time the farmer and the housewife might be familiar with the Bible in their own language. The task of doing that he left to others.

The Protestant Reformation began the following year, and one of its key aims was to get the Bible into the people's languages. Martin Luther translated the Bible into German and could not have done so without Erasmus's Greek New Testament. In fact, it was a common saying that "Erasmus laid the egg that Luther hatched." Erasmus shared the Protestants' desire to make the Bible available and to reform a church that had become wealthy and corrupt. But Erasmus was a scholar not someone who would rock the boat, and he never broke from the Catholic Church. Even so, the Reformation might not have happened without him.

Prayer: Father, we thank you for endowing your servants with different gifts that are used for your glory.

February 2 · A "Character" for God

We are fools for Christ's sake.

1 Corinthians 4:10 (nkjv)

1834: The 1850 U.S. census showed a curious development: "Lorenzo" was one of the most popular names for boys, even though it had never been common among English-speaking people. The only explanation is that many families were impressed by one of the most colorful and eccentric preachers of the day, Lorenzo Dow.

Lorenzo was born in Connecticut in 1777 and at an early age was very religious. He joined with the Methodists and for a while was one of their circuit-riding preachers on the frontier. He preached in New England and New York State then at the beginning of the new century traveled in England and Ireland, where people turned out to see this "character" from the American wilderness.

Dow dressed shabbily, owning only one suit of clothes at a time. When those wore out, some admirer would purchase him new ones. He cultivated a "hippie" look with long and unkempt hair and beard. (People said that he "never met a comb.")

His preaching style matched his appearance: he was a true "performer," often shouting and gesturing, sometimes wildly. While his main message was the call to conversion, he spoke out against the "-isms" of his day, such as atheism, deism, and universalism. The great crowds he attracted were not all admirers, and like many preachers of his time he was sometimes pelted with eggs, rocks, and rotten tomatoes. He was not, to put it mildly, easy to intimidate. Though he sometimes preached in churches, he was more likely to preach in a barn, a town hall, or an open field.

He severed his official connection to the Methodists—not surprising, for mavericks do not fit well into organizations. He regarded the whole country as his parish, also preaching in Canada and the Caribbean. His autobiography became a bestseller, and Dow gave the earnings to the poor. He died on February 2, 1834, ending a colorful career that touched thousands of hearts.

Prayer: Father, endow us with some of the divine energy that empowered the preachers of your word. Amen.

February 3 · PRESSING GOD'S WORD

The unfolding of your words gives light.

PSALM 119:130

1468: As we move further into the twenty-first century, we wonder if books will always exist. More and more books are being purchased in electronic format, and more books from libraries are being digitalized. We may forget all about Johann Gutenberg and the radical change his invention caused in the world.

Actually, no one person invented the printing press, though Gutenberg is given most of the credit. The basic idea seems so obvious: cut letters in small pieces of metal, run ink over the pieces, and print a book—then reuse the metal pieces, since they are set in small trays. Prior to this, the only way of copying something was by hand—a tedious and laborious process and often done with errors. Books produced this way were rare and expensive, and since there was so little material to read, many people were illiterate. This was an unfortunate situation in regard to the Bible since Christians were expected to know the Word of God, but all that most of them knew were snippets they might hear read in church.

In August 1456 Gutenberg's press in Mainz, Germany, produced the first (and, some would say, most beautiful) Bible. This was the Latin version, the Vulgate. It had no page numbers, but it did have beautiful (though hard-to-read) type. More important than its appearance was this: *it could be mass-produced*. Mass-production meant cheaper production, so more people would have a motivation to learn to read—especially Christians. It is no coincidence that the Protestant Reformation occurred not long after the invention of printing. The writings of Martin Luther and John Calvin could be distributed quickly and cheaply—and so could the responses of their opponents. The Word of God could be widely spread—and so could much nonsense and rubbish. Nonetheless, Gutenberg should be honored by Christians. We wonder if when he died on February 3, 1468, he knew he had changed the world.

Prayer: Lord, you have entrusted your Word to us to share with the world. Give us energy for the task. Amen.

February 4 · THE MYSTERIOUS "MATTHEW"

You are my refuge and my shield; I have put my hope in your word.

PSALM 119:114

1555: On this date a saintly man died cheerfully with his wife and eleven children nearby giving him comfort . . . as he was being burnt at the stake. His name was John Rogers, and he was the first of many English Protestants who were martyred during the reign of Queen Mary I, who during her short reign turned England Catholic again and executed those who resisted the change.

But John Rogers's chief claim to fame is his role in the English Bible. In the 1520s Rogers lived in Europe, the chaplain to a group of English merchants. He met William Tyndale, who was translating the Bible into English and who converted Rogers to Protestantism. When Tyndale died in 1536, executed as a heretic, he had translated the entire New Testament and the Old Testament from Genesis to 2 Chronicles, but his Old Testament books had never been published. The manuscripts came into Rogers's possession, and in 1537 he published a complete Bible with the fictitious name "Thomas Matthew" on the title page. Rogers did not put his own name on the Bible because the English church officials wanted nothing to do with William Tyndale or any of his friends.

This version is known as the "Matthew's Bible." It included everything Tyndale had translated (the New Testament and the Old from Genesis to 2 Chronicles) with the rest of the Old Testament being the work of pastor Miles Coverdale, who did not know Hebrew, so from Ezra to Malachi he translated from Martin Luther's German Bible. The Matthew's Bible had the approval of King Henry VIII, and it put Tyndale's fine Old Testament translation into circulation; afterward all English Bibles worked from that translation. When we read the King James Version of the Old Testament, most of it is the work of Tyndale, thankfully preserved by John Rogers.

Prayer: Lord, let us never forget those who sacrificed much to preserve and publish your sacred Word. Amen.

February 5 · WHO WILL CONVERT THE CONVERTERS?

"These people honor me with their lips, but their hearts are far from me."

MATTHEW 15:8

1703: One of the key themes of the Bible is that people often seem religious on the outside even though their hearts are not right. So Jesus spoke out often against the Pharisees, the religious Jews of his day, and even though the Pharisees ceased to exist long ago, the Pharisee mentality never died.

"On the Danger of an Unconverted Ministry" was the title of a famous sermon preached by a minister born on this date. He was Gilbert Tennent, the son of pastor William Tennent and a graduate of his father's "log college," a humble academy in Pennsylvania for training preachers. It consisted of one log building with an attic where some of the students slept, while others boarded with the Tennent family. William had graduated from the University of Edinburgh, so his denomination, the Presbyterians, gave him their stamp of approval, but the graduates of William's log college were looked on with disdain by the Presbyterian authorities. Even so, the log college graduates passed (with flying colors) the exams used to screen ministerial candidates. The great evangelist George Whitefield visited the log college and called it a "school of the prophets."

Both Tennents believed education itself was not enough to make an effective preacher. A pastor needed a personal relationship with God if he was to convert others through his preaching. No college could bestow that. So in 1740 Gilbert preached his "Unconverted Ministry" sermon, comparing unconverted clergy to the Pharisees of the Gospels. Such sermons led to Tennent becoming one of the chief preachers in the Great Awakening of the American colonies. They also led to a split in his denomination—the "New Side" emphasized conversion experiences and revival-style preaching, and the "Old Side" scorned the "enthusiasm" of preachers like Tennent. The two sides split in 1741, not the first or last time a denomination would split over the issue of emotion in preaching. The New Side had one clear advantage: its churches grew.

Prayer: Lord, give your global church zealous servants whose hearts chime in with their words. Amen.

February 6 · BISHOPS AND KINGS

God is not a God of disorder but of peace.

1 CORINTHIANS 14:33

1685: One of the problems with a national church is that those who don't conform to it get into trouble. One who did so happened to be the king. He was James II, who became king of England on this date after the death of his brother, Charles II, a notorious philanderer who fathered many children—none of them legitimate. Charles had wanted to extend toleration to Catholics and Dissenters (Protestants outside the Church of England), but Parliament wouldn't let him, and many Dissenters and Catholics suffered during his reign.

James II had also been wild and promiscuous in his youth, but then he married a beautiful and virtuous Italian princess and saw Catholicism as the one true religion. He began his reign with a great deal of good will, and for awhile the English seemed not to mind his being Catholic. In 1687 he issued a Declaration of Indulgence, granting liberty of conscience to Dissenters and Catholics. This was joyous news to these two groups, but not to the Church of England establishment, which was also disturbed that James was appointing his Catholic friends to high government posts—and making Catholics leaders of a large standing army. The church's bishops feared a Catholic takeover and became even more fearful after James's wife gave birth to a son, a son James intended to raise as a Catholic.

Fearing that James was establishing a Catholic dynasty, the church leaders prodded some of the English noblemen to invite William, a Dutch Protestant prince (married to Mary, James's Protestant daughter from his first marriage), to come to England and rule. William landed in England with an army, James fled the country, and William became the new king, ruling jointly with his wife. Parliament ruled that no Catholic could ever again rule in England, but also ruled that Dissenters would be tolerated. A long era of religious persecution and turbulence had ended.

Prayer: Lord, give all your children the desire to live peacefully together as brothers and sisters in Christ. Amen.

February 7 · MORE DEFIANT

Judgment without mercy will be shown to anyone who has not been merciful.

JAMES 2:13

1478: Thomas More, one of the great figures in English history, was born on this date. In his lifetime he wore many hats: writer of anti-Protestant propaganda, right-hand man of King Henry VIII, author of *Utopia*, and Catholic martyr.

More was a highly intelligent and devout child. He studied law, married, and became a devoted husband and father, head of probably the best-educated household in England. He eventually came to serve Henry VIII and was Henry's "hit man" in the religious arena, writing books against Martin Luther and Bible translator William Tyndale. Religious propaganda then was a "claws-out" affair, and in condemning Protestants, More could be thoroughly nasty. What a pity that More and Tyndale, both good and decent men, should have been enemies instead of friends.

In 1529 Henry made More lord chancellor of England, the highest civilian post. More used his power to keep Protestant books from being smuggled into England and had a network of spies to monitor Protestants. Several Protestants were burned at the stake with his approval.

But More's devotion to the Catholic cause proved his undoing. Wanting to divorce his wife Catherine, Henry could not get the pope's approval, so he broke England away from the Catholic Church. All subjects had to swear that Henry's first marriage had been invalid and that his daughter by that marriage was illegitimate. More would not do this since Henry's first marriage had been approved by the pope himself. More's loyalty to the Catholic Church outweighed his loyalty to the king. As Henry saw it, his chief official was a disloyal traitor. On July 6, 1535, More was beheaded with an ax, his head fixed on a bridge so the public could see what became of traitors. In 1935, four centuries after his death, the Catholic Church declared him a saint. In 2000 Pope John Paul II declared him the patron saint of politicians.

Prayer: Lord, in this world of cruelty and malice, guide us in the paths of mercy and compassion. Amen.

February 8 · MYTH MAKING

The sinful mind is hostile to God.

ROMANS 8:7

1874: Was Jesus the divine Son of God—or just a very inspiring teacher? That was one of the great questions of the 1800s, a century of religious vitality but also a century of doubt. One of the best-known skeptics, a kind of "evangelist of doubt," was German author David Friedrich Strauss, who died on this date.

Strauss was born in 1808 and attended seminary to prepare for the ministry. He had highly intelligent teachers who knew the classics of ancient literature, including the Bible. Unfortunately, they seemed to regard the Bible the same way as they regarded Homer's *Iliad* or Plato's *Apology*—interesting literature, full of good thoughts, but of purely human origin. Later Strauss came under the influence of theologian Friedrich Schleiermacher, who was also skeptical about the Bible.

In 1835 Strauss published *The Life of Jesus, Critically Examined.* In it he took the position that the miracles in the Gospels never happened. Christians had long insisted they did happen, and skeptics had said they *appeared* to happen but could be explained rationally. Strauss put forward a third alternative: the miracle stories were just myths which the writers attached to the story of a man they admired. He did not think of himself as working to destroy Christianity but to make it more truthful.

He hoped the book would excite people, and it did—both critics and admirers. The novelist George Eliot (the pen name of Mary Ann Evans) translated the book into English, so the book generated international controversy. One reviewer said it taught "Iscariotism," not Christianity. In 1840 Strauss published *Christian Doctrine* in which he moved even further away from Christianity, and in 1872 he published *The Old and the New Faith* in which he said he was putting his faith in science, not a nonexistent God. Like so many intellectuals in the 1800s, Strauss had convinced himself that science and religion were at war and that religion was bound to lose.

Prayer: Father, in this hostile and skeptical world, feed our faith and draw us closer to your Son. Amen.

February 9 · THE ROBE ISSUE

You are a chosen people, a royal priesthood, a holy nation.

1 PETER 2:9

1555: Does it matter what the pastor wears in church? It did in England in the 1500s. England changed from Catholic to Protestant under King Henry VIII, and some of the Protestants insisted that the elegant robes worn by the clergy were a holdover from the Catholic past. Protestants, following Martin Luther, believed in the priesthood of all believers, and wearing robes made the clergy appear to be a distinct order from the laymen. John Hooper, an English pastor, had spent time in Zurich, Switzerland, where the Protestants had done away with clergy robes, and he wanted England to follow suit. This quarrel is known as the *vestiarian* controversy, and while it strikes many people as unimportant, Hooper did not see it that way. When the Church of England offered to make him a bishop, he refused—unless he was allowed to *not* wear a robe. The Church gave in, and Hooper was made bishop.

Hooper may sound nitpicky, but, in fact, he was a fine bishop who took his duties seriously. Visiting the churches under his supervision, he was appalled at the ignorance of the clergy: many could not even recite the Lord's Prayer or the Ten Commandments. This was the result of many centuries when the Bible was not available in English, and though in theory the clergy could read the Latin Bible, many barely knew Latin. In other words, England had many pastors who had never read the Bible.

Hooper hoped to change this situation but never had the opportunity. In 1553, Henry VIII's daughter Mary became queen and made England Catholic once again. Hooper, as one of the best-known Protestant leaders in the nation, was doomed. He was thrown in prison, convicted of being a heretic, and on February 9, 1555, burned at the stake, meeting his fate with courage—one of many good men to be martyred in this violent and intolerant century.

Prayer: Lord, when the hour of trial comes, be with us and give us courage. Amen.

February 10 · DAWN MASSACRE

Stand still, and see the salvation of the LORD.

EXODUS 14:13 (NKJV)

1676: On this date "came the Indians with great numbers upon Lancaster." So opens one of America's first bestsellers *The Sovereignty and Goodness of God, Together with the Faithfulness of His Promises Displayed*, published in 1682. It is more often known by its subtitle, *The Captivity and Restoration of Mrs. Mary Rowlandson*. She was the wife of a minister in Lancaster, Massachusetts, and her husband was away in Boston on the fateful day that the Indians made a dawn attack on Lancaster, killing most of the residents and carrying off the others as captives. Mary Rowlandson watched in horror as houses went up in smoke and small children were killed brutally.

"It is a solemn sight to see so many Christians lying in their blood, some here, some there, like a company of sheep torn by wolves." It was by no means solemn to the attackers who, according to Mrs. Rowlandson, behaved as if the massacre was a delightful game. "Yet the Lord by His almighty power preserved a number of us from death." The rest of the narrative tells of the tense weeks that followed with the captives given almost no food and kept constantly on the move as the Indians feared being tracked down by the colonial militia. Finally, in May of that year, women of Boston collected enough money to ransom Mary Rowlandson and her three children.

It is an exciting story, but more importantly, an inspiring one, which is reflected in her book's title. For her, the whole ordeal was a working out of God's purposes, and scarcely a paragraph of her book is without some relevant quotation from the Bible. The Puritans who settled New England knew their Bible intimately, not only as letters on paper but as something living, showing what God did in the past but also showing what he still does for his servants. This confidence in God was one of the finest traits of the Puritans.

Prayer: Lord, in the most trying of our ordeals, keep our hearts fixed on you. Amen.

February 11 · STANDARD REJECTION

The grass withers and the flowers fall, but the word of our God stands forever.

ISAIAH 40:8

1946: Could the beloved KJV (King James Version) of the Bible be improved? Over centuries many attempts were made, but none ever came close to winning over the reading public. Most people clung to their KJVs, even after an English Revised Version was published in 1881 and a similar American Standard Version in 1901. Everyone agreed that much of the language in the KJV was difficult for modern readers. But how to replace it with something readers would embrace?

On February 11, 1946, the New Testament of the RSV (Revised Standard Version) was published. Having been widely publicized, it sold well, and people awaited the full RSV Bible, which was published in September 1952.

On the RSV title page was this notice: "The version set forth A.D. 1611, revised 1881-1885 and 1901, compared with the most ancient authorities and revised 1952." In other words, it was based on the 1611 KJV and revised versions of 1881 and 1901. (The "ancient authorities" referred to were some very old Bible manuscripts that the KJV revisers did not possess.) This title page notice was intended to assure readers that this new version was *based on the KJV* and not something radically new.

Even so, the RSV generated intense hate. Some pastors publicly burned the new Bible, citing disturbing changes from the KJV—notably Isaiah 7:14, where the KJV had "a virgin will conceive" while the RSV had "maiden." Critics said the RSV was denying the virgin birth of Jesus. Others were disturbed that in John 3:16 the KJV's "only begotten Son" was changed to "only Son." Entire books were written on the many imperfections of the RSV. There was nothing new in this—when the KJV was published, many people claimed it was full of flaws. No translation of the Bible is perfect, and no version will ever please everyone. Yet the truths God intended us to have still shine through in the multitude of translations.

Prayer: Father, keep us grounded in your Word that we may live by its precepts. Amen.

February 12 · MUDDLING GENESIS

The mocker seeks wisdom and finds none, but knowledge comes easily to the discerning.

PROVERBS 14:6

1809: "My theology is a muddle." So wrote Charles Darwin in 1870. Curiously, when he went to Cambridge University in his youth, he considered becoming a clergyman. Instead he became a scientist whose writings have done so much to muddle other people's theology.

Born on this date, Darwin wrote two world-changing books: *The Origin of Species* (1859) and *The Descent of Man* (1871). Though it was not his aim to destroy faith, that is how things have turned out. In his writings Darwin described evolution, including the evolution of man from simpler primates. He wasn't sure if God was involved in the process or not—hence his statement that his theology was a muddle. But many of Darwin's followers *were* sure there was no God. Darwin had, they thought, explained nature and man scientifically.

From the beginning there were critics—including many scientists. The great Louis Pasteur, who was a Christian, was horrified by Darwin's ideas, which he believed to be unscientific. Robert Fitzroy, captain of the ship that carried Darwin on his scientific voyages, wrote one of many anti-Darwin books. The writer George Bernard Shaw, no friend to Christianity, thought that if Darwin's ideas were true, all the beauty and honor of human life went out the window.

The world Darwin described was certainly a cruel place where only the "fittest" survived—and, he said, this is way things *should* be. According to him, man is not really different from animals—and just as breeders took care to see that only the healthiest cattle and horses bred, so humans should keep "inferiors" from reproducing. Darwin thought that care for invalids, retarded people, and the chronically ill was a waste of time. Darwin himself was a quiet, gentle man, but in the next century, the governments of Nazi Germany and Soviet Russia were not so gentle in exterminating the "unfit." What a pity that a scientific theory has been used by people to do such harm.

Prayer: Creator God, your word has withstood many assaults. Keep our minds and affections fixed on you. Amen.

Whatever you do, do it all for the glory of God.

1 CORINTHIANS 10:31

1728: The term *Puritan* is often used to refer to someone narrow-minded, but in looking at the life of one of the most famous Puritans, we see just how wide the Puritan mind could be. His name is Cotton Mather, and he died on this date after a life devoted to his faith but also to every branch of human knowledge. His intellect isn't surprising, given his descent from two of the brilliant founding families of colonial Massachusetts, the Mathers and the Cottons (which explains his unique name). Born in 1663 in Boston, a graduate of Harvard, he joined his famous father, Increase Mather, in the ministry at Second Church in Boston in 1685.

Naturally he was fascinated by the Bible and theology but, typical of so many men of his age, by science also. He collected data about natural science and published it in the book *Curiosa Americana*. Learning that scientists had developed a vaccine for smallpox, he urged all citizens to submit to this healthful procedure. The young Benjamin Franklin knew Mather and admired his scientific curiosity and his obsession with hard work and making the most of his gifts.

Mather's most famous book was *Magnalia Christi Americana*, a history of New England from its beginnings, a story that Mather saw as the unfolding of God's purpose in planting Christian communities in America, far from the corrupt churches and kings of Europe.

In all, Mather published more than four hundred and fifty books. He adapted his style to his audience, quoting Latin and Greek in his intellectual works, but assuming a simpler style in his *Winter Meditations* and *Essays to Do Good*. He prepared his sermons not only for the pulpit but also for publication. No matter what he wrote about—the Bible, theology, botany, history, biography, politics—he saw God's hand in the subject and wrote everything for the glory of God.

Prayer: Lord, keep our eyes and our minds open to see in all things your handiwork and to do all things for your glory. Amen.

February 14 · WORD BROTHERS

The Sovereign LORD has given me an instructed tongue, to know the word that sustains the weary.

ISAIAH 50:4

869: Where the Bible goes, literacy goes, because Christians have always insisted that believers be able to read the Bible in their own language. Thus many missionaries become language experts, and some have had to invent alphabets for languages that did not possess them. Such was the case of the most famous missionary brothers in Christian history, Cyril and Methodius, both born in Thessalonica in Greece. Both were intelligent and devout, and in 861 the Roman emperor sent the two brothers to evangelize the Moravian people in eastern Europe. Before departing, the two created an alphabet for the Moravians' language, Slavonic, an alphabet (based on Greek) that came to be known as Cyrillic. They also began translating the Gospels into Slavonic.

In Moravia they encountered opposition from German missionaries who insisted that the only proper languages for use in churches were Hebrew, Greek, and Latin. The two brothers went to Rome to ask the pope to intervene, and he gave his approval for their use of Slavonic for the Bible and church rituals.

Cyril died on February 14, 869, and the Catholic Church honors both brothers on February 14. Methodius continued as a missionary to the Slavs, and despite the jealousy and scheming of the rival Germans (who at one point threw him in prison), he made great progress evangelizing the Slavs and also continued his work on the Bible in Slavonic. He died in 884, and Catholics and Eastern Orthodox Christians regard both brothers as Apostles of the Slavs. The Czechs, Croats, Serbs, and Bulgars all honor the brothers, and Cyril's name lives on in the alphabet that has been used for centuries by the Russians, Serbs, Bulgarians, and Ukrainians. The creation of the alphabet spurred the writings of a rich Slavonic literature, and even today many Eastern Orthodox Christians study Slavonic so they can read this literature, and some churches still use it in worship.

Prayer: Father, let us never forget the patient work of missionaries and translators who spread your divine Word to all the globe. Amen.

February 15 · TAKING LIBERTIES

Proclaim liberty throughout the land to all its inhabitants.

LEVITICUS 25:10

1723: While the American Revolution was raging, some people in Europe called it a "Presbyterian rebellion." The Presbyterians in America were mostly of Scotch heritage, and the Scots had a tradition of loving freedom in both politics and religion. The English Civil War in the 1640s actually started because the king, Charles I, tried to dictate rules to the Scottish church the way he did to the English. Scottish settlers in northern Ireland were frequently harassed and persecuted by their English overlords, which is why so many Scotch-Irish settled in America. In short, Presbyterians took both their freedoms and their faith seriously.

On this day was born John Witherspoon, one of the signers of the Declaration of Independence. He was the only clergyman to sign it, and, not surprisingly, he was a Presbyterian, born in Scotland. Well-educated and devout, he encountered two Americans who persuaded him to immigrate and become president of a Presbyterian school, the College of New Jersey—later to be known as Princeton. So in 1768 he and his family came to America. At Princeton he was not only president but also professor. Among his students were two future notables, James Madison and Aaron Burr. Historians have called Princeton during this period a "nest of revolutionaries."

When the American Revolution began, it surprised no one that Witherspoon took the side of the rebels against the king. New Jersey sent him as a delegate to the Continental Congress, and he served as its chaplain. While some delegates were hesitant to break away from England, Witherspoon was not. He endured a sort of punishment during the war, for the British did some damage in Princeton, but after the war he helped the school rebuild.

Historians remember Witherspoon for his role in the Revolution, but in fact his greatest legacy was encouraging his Princeton students to combine clear thinking and wide reading with a sense of duty to God and one's neighbor.

Prayer: Father, we bless the memory of those who fought and died for freedom's sake. Amen.

February 16 · SMALL MAN, BROAD MIND

Be of one mind, live in peace.

2 CORINTHIANS 13:11

1497: Martin Luther referred to his friend and supporter Philipp Melanchthon, born on this day, as a "shrimp," and indeed Melanchthon was scrawny and ugly, as all his portraits attest. Nonetheless, it is impossible to imagine the Reformation without Melanchthon, whose peaceful and conciliatory nature helped balance Luther's roughness and temper.

Melanchthon and Luther met in 1518, when both were teaching at the University of Wittenberg in Germany. Melanchthon was a widely read Greek scholar, and he proved useful to Luther as a theologian, penning the 1521 book *Loci Communes*, the first thorough statement of Lutheran beliefs. With his skill in Greek, he was useful to Luther in his translation of the German Bible, and he was the main contributor to the 1530 Augsburg Confession, the chief statement of faith for Lutherans.

Though he adored Luther, Melanchthon was more of a peacemaker—or, his critics said, a compromiser. Melanchthon subscribed to the idea of *adiaphora*, Greek for "things indifferent." For him, some things were not negotiable: for example, all Christians had to believe in salvation through the cross. But some other matters (*adiaphora*) might be less important: for example, the matter of the Lord's Supper, where Luther absolutely insisted that the bread and wine *were* the body and blood of Jesus, other Protestants insisted they only *symbolized* the body and blood. Melanchthon would have compromised on this issue, as he would on some other issues that separated Protestants from Catholics, mostly matters of rituals in worship.

Some of Luther's followers accused Melanchthon of being willing to betray the beliefs Luther had fought for. But Luther never forsook his faithful friend, and after Luther's death in 1546, Melanchthon was the most important man in the Lutheran movement. Like Luther, he insisted that the Reformation was not a matter of "new" doctrines and practices but of returning to the things taught in the New Testament. In Melanchthon's words, "We will test everything by the touchstone of the gospel and the fire of Paul."

Prayer: Lord, give us wisdom to know when, and when not, to compromise. Amen.

They will fight against you but will not overcome you.

JEREMIAH 1:19

1878: If there were a prize for Christian Group That Has Been Persecuted the Longest, the Waldensians would win it. Their story begins in 1173 when Peter Waldo, a wealthy merchant in Lyons, France, began to take his faith seriously. He sold his estate and gave the money to the poor then had two priests translate the Bible from Latin into French and began to memorize passages. He began to attract followers who wanted to know the Bible, preach it, and put it into practice. His followers called themselves the Poor in Spirit, and they went about in pairs, preaching in the marketplaces. Their lives of poverty and service were an obvious contrast with the wealth and immorality of the church's officials. Despite the fact that they were doing nothing wrong, they were branded as heretics and excommunicated. In the Middle Ages, thinking outside the box was dangerous.

The Poor in Spirit—or, to use the more familiar name, the Waldensians—were active in the Piedmont, the region where France, Italy, and Switzerland meet. In this isolated, mountainous area they found shelter from persecution—but never for long because now and then a ruler, with the approval of the pope, would launch a crusade against these Bible-centered people. In 1487 the pope decreed that anyone killing a Waldensian could receive pardon for all sins and confiscate the dead man's property.

In the 1500s the Waldensians joined forces with the Protestants—after all, Waldo and his followers had been ahead of the curve in emphasizing the Bible as a guide to life. But since they lived in an area that was technically Catholic, persecution continued. King Louis XIV of France detested the Waldensians and in 1685 ordered his cousin who ruled the region to exterminate them.

Finally, on February 17, 1848, came the Edict of Toleration, issued by Charles Albert, king of Piedmont. The Waldensians could finally live and worship in peace.

Prayer: God of mercy, give heart and hope to those who suffer in your name. Amen.

You are awesome, O God, in your sanctuary.

PSALM 68:35

1564: Think of David or Moses and your mind will probably conjure up images like those of Michelangelo's sculptures of these biblical heroes. Michelangelo is probably the greatest Christian sculptor of all time and also one of the greatest Christian painters.

Born in 1475, Michelangelo joked that he had absorbed marble dust as a child growing up near a marble quarry. He began sculpting at an early age and produced many biblical figures, his first masterpiece being his *Pieta*, showing the dead Christ held by his mother. The famous *David*, almost fourteen feet high, was unveiled in 1504 and may well be the most famous statue in the world. In 1516 he unveiled the great *Moses*, showing him holding the tablets with the Ten Commandments.

He was also a superb painter, and the pope commissioned him to paint the ceiling of the Sistine Chapel with figures from Genesis, including the familiar image of the naked Adam stretching forth his hand to God. The artist spent years lying on his back to complete the awesome project.

The human body and face fascinated Michelangelo. While most artists produced landscape or still-life pictures, Michelangelo never did. Scenery did not interest him—human beings did, and God did.

Artists were not known for their high morality, and many were flagrantly immoral. They did religious work for the obvious reason: it paid well, for the popes had lots of money to spend. But Michelangelo over time became very devout—and no wonder, since his contact with the popes made him aware of the church's wealth and corruption.

Appropriately, his final masterpiece was *The Last Judgment*, on a 48-by 44-foot wall, showing the saints entering heaven and the damned entering hell. When it was unveiled in 1541, people gasped, and many tourists still do.

Michelangelo was at work on another sculpture when he took sick and died, aged eighty-eight, on February 18, 1564. Then and now, many people consider him the greatest artist ever.

Prayer: Father, let the awe that great artists felt for your saints fill our hearts. Amen.

February 19 · TROPICAL HARVEST

Let us not become weary in doing good, for at the proper time we will reap a harvest if we do not give up.

GALATIANS 6:9

1812: "I am not easily dissuaded" was the theme of Adoniram Judson's life. Born in Massachusetts in 1788, Judson resolved to take the gospel to Asia, with its millions who did not know Christ. On February 5, 1812, he married and the following day was ordained as a missionary. He and his wife, Anne, sailed for India on February 19. When they arrived in Calcutta in June, they learned that the British government did not want missionaries evangelizing Hindus—and the War of 1812 was being waged, so no Americans were welcome in British territory. Not to be dissuaded, the Judsons moved on to the Buddhist nation of Burma (today called Myanmar). They immersed themselves in studying the Burmese language, despite being warned that the Burmese were almost impossible to convert. Adoniram completed his translation of the book of Matthew in 1817, but it was not until 1819 that the first convert was baptized.

War between Britain and Burma erupted in 1824, and Adoniram, suspected as a spy, spent months in a Burmese prison, sometimes suspended by his feet or tortured in other ways. Kept on starvation rations, most prisoners died. Ann worked constantly to have her husband freed, but sadly, she died in the year of his release, 1826.

While converting the Burmese did prove to be difficult, the Judsons did make converts among the Karens, a minority dwelling in the hills. An ancient Karen prophecy held that a "Golden Book" would be returned to them by a white man, and some saw Judson with his Bible as a fulfillment of the prophecy.

Adoniram died in 1850, having made thousands of converts. His perseverance in learning a difficult language and translating the entire Bible was remarkable, as was his endurance of the torture he received in prison. He and Ann had set a high standard for the patience and toughness of missionary couples.

Prayer: Lord, we praise you for the persevering ones who inspire us all. Amen.

Worship the LORD with gladness; come before him with joyful songs.

PSALM 100:2

1991: Grammy Awards were handed out on this date, and a new sub-category had been added to the gospel category: "rock/contemporary." The Christian rock group Petra took home the first Grammy for Best Rock/Contemporary Gospel Album. At the 1994 Grammys different awards were given for "pop/contemporary gospel" and "rock gospel." Things had changed dramatically since the days when preachers warned against the dangers of rock music.

What had happened? For one thing, America had grown comfortable with rock music and no longer saw it as threatening. For another thing, many people born after 1960 found traditional church music unappealing. Hymns written two centuries ago, sung to the accompaniment of an organ or piano, had lost much of their appeal, particularly in churches where congregational singing bordered on the comatose.

New categories had not only entered the Grammy Award list but the churches as well. Sunday worship in many churches began, in the late 1980s, to involve "contemporary Christian music" (or "CCM"), also called "praise and worship" music. Instead of an organ or piano, music was provided by guitars, drums, and electronic keyboards. Instead of traditional hymnals, there were video projectors displaying the words to the songs—either new songs, or old ones with new (and livelier) music. Projectors freed up a congregations' hands to clap and sway. Many churches began holding two Sunday services, one "traditional," one "contemporary."

Entire books have been written against CCM, with claims that it turns worship into more of a "show" than a religious service. Many churches who switch to or add CCM find themselves growing, while others try CCM and eventually go back to strictly traditional music. Many churches have settled for having two different worship services, while others drop the traditional completely.

Fizzing vitality or reverent dignity? Which pleases God most? The debate goes on, and a common answer is, "Why not both?"

Prayer: Father, whatever form of music we use, let it be for your glory, and let it express the joy that should be the mark of all believers. Amen.

February 21 · GOD'S MAN VERSUS CAIN'S MAN

"The greatest among you will be your servant."

MATTHEW 23:11

1076: Who had more power—the pope or an emperor? Gregory VII, whose reign began in 1073, had no doubt it was the pope. He published the decree *Dictatus Papae*, stating that the pope owed his power to God alone and that all Christians must obey him. The pope could, if necessary, depose kings and emperors. Gregory believed that the power of kings originated in murderers and thugs (which was partly true) and that secular government originated with Cain but spiritual power was given by God.

Did anyone believe this besides Gregory? Henry IV, Holy Roman Emperor, was the most powerful secular ruler in Europe, and he saw things differently. The emperors had been in the habit of appointing bishops within the empire. The pope said this had to stop—only popes could appoint bishops. Henry was told to obey or be deposed. Henry sent an insulting letter to Gregory, insisting that the emperor also owed his office to God alone. On February 21, 1076, Gregory declared Henry deposed and excommunicated, and citizens of the empire were released from their obligation to obey him.

Finding himself isolated with his enemies plotting to install a new emperor that Gregory would approve, Henry caved. He traveled to Canossa, Italy, where the pope was a guest in a castle. Henry stood, barefoot and dressed in rags, in the snow outside the castle for three days, pleading for the pope's forgiveness. Gregory gave it, with Henry swearing to be an obedient servant of the church—an oath he had no intention of keeping. Within a year Gregory deposed him again. Henry responded by installing a rival pope in Rome. Gregory fled and died in exile the following year.

This story has no hero. Gregory accomplished some good things as pope, but he was obsessed with power, which is more shameful in a pope than in an emperor. Here is a textbook case of men with ambition and vigor wasting their talents in a pointless battle of wills.

Prayer: Father, train us to pursue spiritual power only to be used in the service of others. Amen.

February 22 · CHURCH CLEANING

Create in me a pure heart, O God, and renew a steadfast spirit within me.

PSALM 51:10

1072: One of the curiosities of Christian history is that a man who has a reputation as a holy hermit is often called to a task that involves frequent interaction with others. One such man was Peter Damian, born in Italy in 1007. At a young age he devoted himself to a life of solitary prayer and self-denial. He was called to head a community of hermit monks in 1043 and gained such a reputation as a strict reformer that the pope made him a cardinal, a post he was very reluctant to accept.

The typical cardinal of those days lived in splendor and often led an immoral life. Peter was a distinct exception—he was hard on himself and hard on others, for he thought all Christians should take their faith seriously and live as people who had their sights on heaven. He did not hesitate to scold worldly clergymen, and it goes without saying that he made enemies. He wrote an entire book on the clergy's sexual immorality, which was widespread. Most people of the time took it for granted that clergy would cohabit with women, father children by them, and then find church positions for these "nephews." Peter insisted on a higher standard for priests, monks, and nuns: no marriage, no cohabiting, and no sex—period. He was equally harsh in denouncing simony, the use of bribery to obtain lucrative positions in the church.

If Peter sounds like a joyless scold, this was not the case. Like many people of deep faith, he knew there was a time to denounce sin in a loud voice but also a time to listen to the still small voice of God. Peter's righteous anger could be intimidating, yet he seems to have had a warm relationship with God throughout his life, and his preaching of reform was a natural outgrowth of the desire to have a spiritually pure church that would please God.

Prayer: Lord, when we go astray, guide us back to the path of righteousness. Amen.

"If a man remains in me and I in him, he will bear much fruit."

John 15:5

156: Marcus Aurelius was one of the better Roman emperors, a much more decent and responsible ruler than most of the rogues who held the throne. Unfortunately, he persecuted Christians, and among those martyred during his reign was the elderly Polycarp, the bishop of Smyrna. Polycarp had known the apostle John, and he may have been the last survivor of those who had known eyewitnesses of the life of Jesus.

The story of Polycarp's death was written down in great detail by a witness. In the amphitheater in Smyrna, the Roman official in charge tried to talk the aged man into renouncing his faith. He told Polycarp, "Respect your years!" By swearing reverence to the emperor and renouncing the Christians, Polycarp could live. The official told him to point to the Christians and say, "Away with the godless!" Polycarp spoke the words—but did so while pointing to the pagans in the stands—they, not the Christians, were the godless ones. The official pressed further: "Curse Christ and I will set you free." Polycarp replied, "Eighty-six years have I served him, and he has never done me wrong. How can I blaspheme my King who saved me?"

The official threatened to have him torn apart by wild beasts or burnt. Polycarp answered that fire in the arena was only temporary while the fire of God's judgment was eternal. "Why do you hesitate?" Polycarp asked. "Do what you want." The official announced, "Polycarp has confessed he is a Christian!" The people rushed from their seats and piled up wood to burn the aged saint. In his final prayer Polycarp praised God for counting him worthy to die for the faith.

The name Polycarp is Greek for "much fruit." The martyrdoms of godly men and women did bear much fruit. The Christians outlived and out-died their pagan adversaries, and every martyred saint meant more people were drawn to the faith.

Prayer: Father, endow us with your strength when we are mocked or persecuted for your sake. Amen.

February 24 · IMITATION FIXATION

Remember your leaders. . . . Consider the outcome of their way of life and imitate their faith.

HEBREWS 13:7

1946: One of the world's best-selling novels owed its sales not just to popularity but to an accident. Its author, Charles M. Sheldon, died on this date and is remembered for *In His Steps*, a novel that grew out of a sermon series Sheldon preached on the question "What would Jesus do?" which is the novel's subtitle.

In the novel, published in 1897, pastor Henry Maxwell turns away a jobless man who appears at his door. The following Sunday the same man walks into the church and confronts the people about their lack of compassion. The next Sunday the pastor poses a challenge to his congregation: for an entire year they will not do anything without first asking, "What would Jesus do?" The rest of the novel follows various members of the congregation as they rise to the pastor's challenge.

The book sold well when published, but afterward the publisher realized a serious mistake had been made: the copyright had not been filed correctly, so the book could be copied and published by other companies without paying a cent to the author or the original publisher. Needless to say, publishers took advantage of this, and numerous editions of the book were published, which did not make any money for Sheldon but did increase the book's sales since it was available at low prices. Probably 30 million copies of the book were sold.

And what about the author? Sheldon was a Congregational pastor in Topeka, Kansas, when he wrote his novel and was a tireless crusader for prohibition and women's rights. He believed that true Christianity consisted of modeling one's behavior on Jesus. As we might put it today, he was more concerned with "walking the walk" than with "talking the talk." All who knew Sheldon agreed that he "walked the walk" and never asked his congregation to do anything he was not willing to do himself.

Prayer: Lord, in all our acts, great or small, help us remember and honor your Son. Amen.

February 25 · Mel's Passion

He was pierced for our transgressions, he was crushed for our iniquities.

Isaiah 53:5

2004: Mel Gibson chose this date to premiere his long-awaited movie. It was Ash Wednesday, a holy day observed by many Christians, the beginning of the Lent season leading up to Good Friday and Easter. The date was a wise choice—but many people believed Gibson had been very *un*wise to make a movie with unknown actors and with all the dialogue in ancient languages. In fact, no Hollywood studio would back the effort, so Gibson produced the movie himself. His confidence in the project paid off: *The Passion of the Christ* was one of the biggest money-makers of 2004.

Profitable movies based on the Bible were nothing new, of course, but the world was more secular in 2004 than it was in the 1950s, the decade of *The Ten Commandments* and *David and Bathsheba*. Yet audiences flocked to see *The Passion*, many of them people who hadn't entered a movie theater in years.

Not everyone was pleased. Critics accused it of being anti-Semitic—a charge that has been made about every movie about Jesus' crucifixion. Critics also lambasted the movie's graphic violence—in fact, many Christians stayed away, claiming they would not pay to see violent movies. These people missed the whole point: Jesus' flogging and crucifixion were genuinely horrible. Movies in the past had Jesus showing little pain and not much blood flowed. Gibson understood that what Jesus endured really was disgusting. Anyone who saw *The Passion* will likely find it hard to watch older movies like *The Greatest Story Ever Told* where Jesus seems to be barely suffering.

A few years after the movie's release, Gibson's private life became, to put it mildly, a mess. But there's no doubt that when he was making the movie, it was a genuine labor of love. And he succeeded in his aim: once people saw *The Passion*, they could never forget just what a sacrifice Jesus made.

Prayer: Father, thank you for the sacrifice of your Son who suffered so that we might have loving fellowship with you. Amen.

You were once darkness, but now you are light in the Lord.

EPHESIANS 5:8

1931: Would a Christian title his autobiography *The Prince of Darkness*? One did: political journalist Robert Novak, who converted to Christianity in 1998 and published his memoirs in 2007. Novak had a long career as a newspaperman then became a familiar face to viewers of cable news. "Prince of Darkness" was a nickname his fellow journalists bestowed on him due to his tough-minded approach to covering the news.

Like many people in public life, Novak became cynical—*very* cynical—about politics and celebrities. In his memoirs the rare politician that he describes as "nice" he also describes as incompetent. He discovered early on that politicians who make their honesty a key issue are often the worst deceivers of all. One of the key messages of his book is "love your country—but never trust your government."

Born to working-class Jewish parents on February 26, 1931, Novak grew up in a thoroughly secular home and for most of his life he had no religious convictions. That began to change when his wife became strongly pro-life. He recalls that George H. W. Bush was bothered by pro-lifers who showed up at his appearances carrying signs. Bush asked, "How do I get rid of the people?" Novak replied, "Change your position." Bush did.

Seeking a spiritual home, Novak and his wife attended a Unitarian church a few times but found the services "uninspiring." Reflecting on that church years later, he thought its problem was "the absence of God." He and his wife both became Catholics in 1998. In the cynical world of Washington, politicians often join churches to gain votes, but journalists feel no such pressure, so many of Novak's acquaintances wondered what had made him become a Christian. His reply: "The Holy Spirit." Though still cynical about politics and fame, Novak had found a place to rest his heart. He died in August 2009 and, we trust, is at rest in the Lord.

Prayer: Father, keep our hearts focused on your kingdom, a kingdom that will never pass away. Amen.

Blessed is the nation whose God is the LORD.

PSALM 33:12

380: Christianity went from being a persecuted religion to state religion in less than a century. The man who made it the official religion of the Roman Empire was emperor Theodosius I, known as "the Great" because he was both a victorious general and a zealous Christian. Born around 346, Theodosius became the ruler of the eastern half of the empire in 379. On February 27, 380, he and Gratian, the ruler of the western half of the empire, proclaimed that all subjects of the empire should embrace the Christian faith. All other religions and all heresies were described as "insane" and were banned.

Theodosius backed up the edict with force. Most of the remaining pagan temples were torn down, closed, or converted to churches. These included the famous Serapeum in Alexandria, Egypt, the temple of the god Serapis. It is said that when a blow was struck at the statue of Serapis, a swarm of rats came running out, which many took as a sign of how rotten paganism had become. Pagan sacrifices were banned, as were witchcraft and conjuring.

He summoned the Council of Constantinople in 381 to settle some disputes over doctrine, and the creed published by the council, known as the Nicene Creed, is considered one of the classic statements of Christian belief. Unlike the older Apostles' Creed, it gives more attention to the Holy Spirit, defining him as "the Lord, the giver of life, who proceeds from the Father, who with the Father and Son together is worshipped and glorified; who spoke by the prophets."

Theodosius was neither cruel nor fanatical. His laws were aimed at banning *public* practices of paganism, not ferreting out and prosecuting individual pagans. If individuals still privately believed in the old gods, that was not the government's concern. He achieved his main aim, making it clear that the only religion worthy of the government's support was Christianity, the faith that had been illegal and persecuted when the century began.

Prayer: Lord, thank you for government officials who bring their faith into the public arena. Amen.

February 28 · REVOLUTION V. REVIVAL

Oh, the depth of the riches of the wisdom and knowledge of God!

ROMANS 11:33

1764: Europeans who were in their twenties when the French Revolution broke out in the 1780s felt a thrill of exhilaration. For most of them it wore off once they saw how much blood—mostly innocent blood—was shed. Robert Haldane, born February 28, 1764, to Scottish parents living in London, was of the Revolutionary generation, and like so many of that generation he became disillusioned with the idea that political restructuring could create a perfect world. He looked elsewhere for his, and the world's, salvation.

Born to wealth, he decided in 1796 to finance a Christian mission to India, but the British East India Company would not sanction it. Unable to spread the gospel abroad, he chose to spread it in Scotland. He sold his family's castle, broke from the state Church of Scotland, and traveled the country preaching, helping to build "chapels" and "tabernacles" for Christians outside the Church of Scotland. (Technically, only the state church had "churches," so outsiders had to use another name for their meeting places.) He also financed the training of three hundred young men for the ministry. While other men of wealth were living lives of idleness and luxury, Haldane was spending a fortune to further the gospel.

In 1816 he visited Geneva, Switzerland, where a curious thing happened: sitting on a park bench by Lake Geneva, he chatted with some theology students who clearly did not take their faith very seriously and knew little of the Bible and basic Christian beliefs. In a short time they were visiting Haldane in his rented rooms and studying Paul's letter to the Romans, and several of the young men experienced genuine conversions. The men's professors were appalled that this "amateur" was teaching their students—and even more appalled that the students responded with enthusiasm.

Haldane died in 1842, having touched many lives, and continues to do so through his fine commentary on Romans.

Prayer: Lord, give us opportunities to witness to your truths and transform lives. Amen.

MARCH

March 1 · GOING NATIVE

I have become all things to all men so that by all possible means I might save some.

1 CORINTHIANS 9:22

1854: "God's work done in God's way will never lack God's supplies." So said Hudson Taylor who on this date entered China as a missionary. He would spend fifty-one years there, doing God's work God's way.

Born in England in 1832, Taylor prepared for his mission by learning the Mandarin Chinese language and also Greek and Hebrew, and he also read books on China. He apprenticed himself to a doctor to learn the basics of medicine. With experience in languages, medicine, and preaching, he offered his services to the China Evangelization Society. Taylor was twenty-two when he landed in China on March 1, 1854.

He decided that to evangelize the people he needed to seem like one of them, so he adopted Chinese dress, which shocked other missionaries. Taylor insisted that God did not require his preachers to dress like Europeans. He lived among the Chinese, growing more proficient in the language, translating the Bible, and running a clinic. Feeling constrained by the Chinese Evangelization Society, he started the China Inland Mission, which, not surprisingly, asked its missionaries to dress as Chinese—as Taylor put it, "Let us in everything not sinful become like the Chinese, that we may by all means save some." The mission accepted people from different denominations and those who had no college education. It never solicited for funds but relied on faith and prayer. "The Lord will provide" became the byword for the organization, and by 1914 it had a staff of more than a thousand, proof that relying on the Lord was a wise policy. Hudson kept control of the mission in China, not faraway Europe or America, for he understood that the on-site people knew more about running it than bureaucrats a thousand miles away.

Taylor died in 1905 and was buried near the Yangtze River. In time the China Inland Mission became the largest missionary organization in the world.

Prayer: Father, keep us open to opportunities for mission wherever we may be. Amen.

March 2 · EXECUTIVE ENLIGHTENMENT

Let justice roll on like a river, righteousness like a never-failing stream!

AMOS 5:24

1807: Thomas Jefferson considered himself a Christian—by his own definition, someone who tried to live by the teachings of Jesus. Jefferson's enemies branded him an "infidel" since he did not believe the miracles of the Bible (including the supreme miracle, the resurrection of Jesus) nor did he believe Jesus was the Son of God. Nonetheless, Jefferson sometimes attended Christian worship services in the U.S. Capitol and contributed money to churches, missions, and Bible societies and sent his daughters to a Catholic school. The "infidel" seemed comfortable living in a nation that was predominantly Christian.

The 1700s are known as the age of Enlightenment with its emphasis on being guided by reason, not revelation—the human mind, not the Bible and Christian belief. Jefferson imbibed Enlightenment philosophy, but he recognized that in one respect the "enlightened" people lagged behind Christians: their attitude toward slavery. The Enlightenment philosophers accepted slavery as part of a world where some people were meant to rule over others. But Christians in the 1700s had grown less and less comfortable with slavery, and many American Christians insisted that a nation founded on the concept of liberty could not continue to tolerate slavery.

Jefferson was raised on a plantation staffed by slaves, and he owned them as an adult. He detested slavery yet was unsure of how to deal with slaves if they were freed all at once.

On March 2, 1807, Congress presented Jefferson with a bill to sign: the Slave Importation Bill which would not abolish slavery in America but would at least end the slave trade with other nations, a trade in which thousands of slaves died in tightly packed "death ships" crossing from Africa to America. The following day Jefferson signed the bill into law. The man who had penned the Declaration of Independence, the man who considered himself both "enlightened" and Christian, finally struck a blow against slavery.

Prayer: Father, in our lives of comfort, let us not forget those who are oppressed and persecuted. Amen.

March 3 · SAVING MEMORIES

How can a young man keep his way pure? By living according to your word.

PSALM 119:9

1933: When the U.S.S. *West Virginia* was sunk at Pearl Harbor in 1941, many of its crew went home to heaven, and of those, many had been converted through the ministry known as the Navigators, founded on March 3, 1933, by Dawson Trotman. True to its name, the organization originally focused on sailors, then other branches of the military, and today it is probably best-known for its ministry to college students. Always the emphasis has been on one-on-one contacts, individual Christians leading friends and associates to faith. Thousands of people have stored up Scripture verses in their minds thanks to the Navigators' popular Topical Memory System.

Trotman was converted at age eighteen from a very worldly young man to a devoted believer, thanks to his wooing of Lila Clayton, a Christian girl whom he would later marry. He believed that the memorizing of Bible verses, a practice at Lila's church, had played a key role in his conversion, just as it played a role when he witnessed to a sailor who became a convert. It is not surprising that memorizing scripture has always been an emphasis of the Navigators.

Trotman, known as "Daws" to his friends, was close to Billy Graham who enlisted Daws's help in discipling the people converted at Graham's crusades. Daws gave the name "B Rations" ("B" for Bible) to the instructional materials he devised for Graham's converts.

In June 1956 Daws went boating with some friends, one of them a girl who could not swim. When the boat bounced on a wave, both he and the girl fell into the lake. Daws saved the girl—but was drowned himself. Graham preached at Daws's funeral, lamenting the loss of a man who "had personally touched more lives than anyone I have ever known." His death was in keeping with his life, for, as Graham put it, "he lived to save others."

Prayer: Heavenly Father, fill up our minds and hearts with your saving words, and let our deeds chime in. Amen.

Watch out for those who cause divisions and put obstacles in your way that are contrary to the teaching you have learned.

ROMANS 16:17

1866 : "Campbellites" used to be a common name for members of the Churches of Christ, the name coming from their founder, Alexander Campbell, who died on this date. Born in northern Ireland, of Scotch Presbyterian heritage, Alexander followed his minister father Thomas to America, where both father and son were disturbed by the often spiteful rivalry among denominations. They severed their connection to the Presbyterians, partly because they ceased to believe in infant baptism. They wished to be Christians of no denomination, and their motto was this: "Where the Scriptures speak, we speak; where the Scriptures are silent, we are silent"—meaning, their sole model for the church was the church of the Bible, and no doctrines or practices from outside the Bible mattered.

In practice, "no denomination" meant "new denomination." In time the Campbells' followers merged with those of revival preacher Barton Stone, and the new denomination was called the Disciples of Christ ("disciples" being a biblical name, unlike other denominations' names). Despite the Campbells' distaste for denominational quarreling, the Disciples could be just as contentious as the Baptists, Methodists, Presbyterians, and others as they competed for members. Sad as it is to read about the "denomination wars" of the 1800s, the competition probably had a positive effect, leading Americans to think seriously about religious matters.

Following the New Testament, the Disciples had holy communion at each worship service, baptized only believers (not infants), and had no musical accompaniment for their singing. They did not use theological terms (such as Trinity) that were not found in the Bible.

In time the Disciples' leadership became somewhat liberal, and members uncomfortable with this development split in 1906 to become the Churches of Christ, the "Campbellites" of the southern states, dedicated to maintaining churches based strictly on the New Testament.

Prayer: Lord, give us a gentle spirit as we seek to live by your Word and deal in a loving way with those who hold different views. Amen.

March 5 · BLOOD ISLAND

He has rescued us from the dominion of darkness and brought us into the kingdom of the Son he loves.

COLOSSIANS 1:13

1797: Tahiti has always impressed visitors as an idyllic tropical paradise. The first European visitors saw something else: barbarism that curdled the blood, people mired in violence, theft, drunkenness, and superstition. War was almost constant, and a defeated foe was often pounded into pulp and his flattened body worn as a sort of poncho. Foes not killed in battle were often sacrificed to the gods. If a man thought he sinned against the gods, he would sacrifice a pig or chicken, but if he sinned in a big way, he would sacrifice a human being. Infants were commonly tossed into volcanoes or to the sharks to curry favor with the gods. The elderly or sick were often buried alive.

An English brick-layer, Henry Nott, arrived as a missionary on March 5, 1797, and saw that the Tahitians desperately needed the light of the gospel. They constantly extorted gifts from the missionaries (clothing, tools, cookware), and when the gifts were not given freely, the natives stole. Despite the missionaries living in fear, they preached the Bible, speaking through two dissolute sailors who had learned the native language. The king, named Pomare, was a violent man, yet, to Nott's surprise, he seemed open to the missionaries' "Book of God," and he was especially impressed by John 3:16. As Nott taught himself the Tahitian language, this was the first Bible verse he translated.

It would be pleasant to report that Nott quickly made converts. In fact, more than twenty years would pass before any conversions. Finally, a new king, Pomare's son, converted and agreed to live by a Christian code drawn up by Nott. In the intervening years most of Nott's missionary companions had been killed or gave up in frustration. Over time, thanks to Nott's commitment, the inhabitants of the Pacific paradise began to behave less like beasts and more like children of God.

Prayer: Lord, let us not forget that no individual and no land are beyond the reach of your saving love. Amen.

March 6 · PLANTING VILLAGES FOR THE LORD

Make straight in the wilderness a highway for our God.

ISAIAH 40:3

1609: Imagine a Christian community deep in the heart of South America where clergymen live among the native people and treat them as equals instead of exploiting them, guide them into building homes, planting crops, manufacturing, and trading, and try to persuade them, gently, to accept the Christian faith. Amazingly, there were many such communities, lasting from 1609 to 1767 until they were abandoned due to colonists' greed. These communities were known as the *reducciones* and were built and managed by the Jesuit order. King Philip III of Spain admired the Jesuits and took a great interest in the welfare of the native Indians, and his decree of March 6, 1609, mandated that "the Indians should be as free as the Spaniards." The decree did not apply to areas already settled, but it opened the way for the founding of the *reducciones*.

These communities were colonialism at its best. Scattered throughout what is today Paraguay, the thirty-two *reducciones* were staffed by Jesuits from Spain who learned the native language of the Guarani people and taught them how to read and speak Spanish. The people farmed in communal fields and worked at handicrafts. The Indians who were lazy usually left, so the remaining people were productive. Far away in Europe the French writer Voltaire, who was no friend of Christianity, admitted that the *reducciones* were living proof that sometimes Christianity bore real fruit. In time, more than 100,000 natives lived in the *reducciones*.

Sadly, every happy community has enemies. The Portuguese who settled Brazil had fathered children with native women, and these children, known as the Mamelucos, were notorious for capturing native people and selling them as slaves. Worse, greedy colonists coveted the lands of the *reducciones* and persuaded the king of Spain to expel the Jesuits from South America in 1767. The prosperous and vibrant communities were abandoned and soon overgrown by the jungle.

Prayer: Father, help us to honor the blessed memories of those who traveled far to plant communities of faith in the wilderness. Amen.

March 7 · God's Ox

Test me, O Lord, and try me, examine my heart and my mind.

Psalm 26:2

1274: Before his death on this date, a man known as the "Dumb Ox" by his acquaintances requested that all his writings be destroyed once he was dead. They did not honor his request because they agreed that the numerous volumes written by Thomas Aquinas were worth preserving. His multivolume *Summa Theologica* was never completed because he received a vision telling him not to continue work on it. But even in its unfinished state it has fascinated theologians for centuries.

Thomas was born around 1225 in the town of Aquino in Italy to a wealthy family. When he told them he wanted to join the Dominican religious order, they had him kidnapped and held in a castle, hoping he would change his mind. He didn't. He joined the Dominicans and became an outstanding theologian and teacher. Though fat, slow-moving, and quiet—hence his name "Dumb Ox"—Thomas was brilliant, absorbing not only the Bible and theology but also the philosophical writings of the Greeks. One of his aims was to show that human reason could prove most of the beliefs of Christianity as sure as theology could.

He began *Summa Theologica* with these words: "Is there a God? Apparently not." He was not denying God's existence but saying that, judging simply from what we see around us, there is no hard evidence of God. But he went on to show that God's existence is evident not only from the Bible but from the use of man's reason.

Thomas's attempts to merge Christian theology with the writings of the Greek philosopher Aristotle disturbed many people—including, perhaps, himself, hence his decision near the end of his life to cease writing theology. At the time he died, no one would have predicted that centuries later (in 1879, in fact) his theology would be accepted as official Catholic teaching.

On the personal side, Thomas was warm and humble, and everyone who knew him loved him. Would that all theologians were so Christlike in their behavior.

Prayer: Lord, train us to use our minds for your glory. Amen.

March 8 · SEPARATION SYNDROME

When we are persecuted, we endure it; when we are slandered, we answer kindly.

1 CORINTHIANS 4:12–13

1948: An atheist named Vashti McCollum believed that justice was served on this day. The U.S. Supreme Court ruled in her favor in the case *McCollum v. Board of Education*, and the ruling had a powerful effect not just on her but on all who took their faith—and the Constitution—seriously. McCollum's son had been enrolled in a public school in Champaign, Illinois, and the school allowed weekly sessions of religious instruction by Protestant, Catholic, and Jewish clergy on school property. Students could choose whether to attend or not, but McCollum said her son was "ostracized" for not participating and that he and other nonparticipants felt "coerced." She asked the school board to terminate the classes, and when they did not, she sued the board, but the board was supported by the Illinois supreme court.

The U.S. Supreme Court ruled in her favor, agreeing with her that the classes violated the First Amendment, which prohibits establishment of religion: "The First Amendment rests upon the premise that both religion and government can best work to achieve their lofty aims if each is left free from the other within its respective sphere." The Court insisted that there was no "governmental hostility to religion or religious teaching" in refusing to allow religious teaching in the public schools. Only one of the nine justices dissented.

In May 1945, *Time* magazine ran an article on McCollum's suit at the state level. In the article it is fairly obvious that McCollum was posing as a noble defender of the First Amendment, when in fact the affair was a case of an angry atheist crusader working to strike a blow at religion. She succeeded, and in years to come the Supreme Court would tilt even further in the direction of keeping faith out of public life.

Prayer: Father, you alone administer true justice, and you alone deserve our ultimate loyalty. Amen.

March 9 · FAITH TOWN ON LAKE MICHIGAN

Do not be yoked together with unbelievers. For what do righteousness and wickedness have in common?

2 CORINTHIANS 6:14

1907: Zion was built by a Scot who immigrated to the United States from Australia. He was John Alexander Dowie, born in 1847, a preacher who had a healing ministry in Australia before coming to America in 1888. In 1896 in Chicago, he founded a new denomination, the Christian Catholic church. In 1900 he and five thousand followers built Zion City, north of Chicago, site of his eight-thousand-seat tabernacle. Since Dowie technically owned the entire city, he was able to lay down laws against drinking and smoking and to prohibit the opening of theaters and dance halls—and doctors' offices and pharmacies, since he believed Christians should rely on the Lord to heal. It was a one-church town since Dowie regarded other denominations as "apostates." Dowie gave the streets biblical names—Antioch, Berea, Damascus, Galilee, Bethel, etc.

Zion was one of the first planned cities in America, well laid-out with ample parkland. It prospered, and the people, sometimes called Doweyites or Zionites, were generally happy with Dowie, who had the title First Apostle. Although he stressed healing as part of the church's life, he was not a Pentecostal, since he flatly opposed speaking in tongues. After his death, however, many of his followers became influential in Pentecostal churches and approved of speaking in tongues.

Dowie became eccentric in his later years, dressing in ornate robes modeled after those of the high priests of Israel. With the community prospering, Dowie lived lavishly in Shiloh House, a mansion with twenty-five rooms. After experiencing some health problems, he handed over control of the city and denomination to another man temporarily—but "temporarily" turned into "permanently," and Dowie lost control of all the enterprises he had founded. He died on March 9, 1907, but Zion continued on as a Christian city, though numbers dwindled. Like so many other places planned as Christian cities, it prospered awhile but was never the same without its founder.

Prayer: Father, in this sinful world, help us to find fellowship and community with people of deep faith. Amen.

March 10 · UNWAVERING RELIANCE

"If you believe, you will receive whatever you ask for in prayer."

MATTHEW 21:21

1898: No one who knew George Müller in his youth would have predicted he would live a life of Christian service. Born in Germany in 1805, the son of a tax collector, George was a notorious drinker, gambler, and thief, even pilfering government funds from his own father. Curiously, his father decided George should enter the ministry—not because he was suited for it but because a pastor in the state church had a secure job. Something surprising happened: while preparing for the ministry at the University of Halle, George was actually converted to Christ. He immediately reformed and, in time, settled in Bristol, England, where he pastored a small church. He and his wife started numerous other ministries, including day schools for poor children.

Then in 1836 he began the work he is most famous for: orphanages. He and his wife turned their house into a home for thirty orphan girls. Over time they purchased and built new homes, eventually housing thousands of children. The orphans received an education, training for proper employment, and, of course, instruction in the Bible and Christian beliefs. The novel *Oliver Twist* by Charles Dickens paints an ugly picture of orphanages, but in fact most orphanages, including Müller's, gave excellent care to the children.

The remarkable thing about Müller's orphanages is the funding: never once did he solicit people for donations. He prayed and counted on God to provide what was needed. God always came through. People testified to how, in big and small things, God provided for Müller. No doubt part of the secret of his prayer life was that none of his prayers were selfish in nature but always for the ministries. His operation on the "faith principle" has been imitated by many other ministries.

George Müller died on March 10, 1898, having blessed thousands through his orphanages and having set an example of total reliance on the Lord.

Prayer: Father, train us to pray without doubting and to rely utterly upon you. Amen.

Be strong and take heart, all you who hope in the LORD.

PSALM 31:24

2011: Few nations take their religion as seriously as Saudi Arabia, which is not surprising, since Arabia was the birthplace of Islam. Although Arabia had numerous Christians and Jews centuries before Muhammad lived, Islam is regarded as the final revelation of God to man, and Arabia has shown zero toleration of religious minorities.

On March 11, 2011, two Christian men from India, employed in Saudi Arabia, were arrested for proselytizing. Typically, they were beaten severely at the time of arrest and their apartment was ransacked for evangelistic literature. (Observers of the global scene are aware that in situations like these, illegal drugs are often "planted" in homes of offenders, though that did not occur in this case.) Both men were finally released from prison in July 2011 and deported back to India.

The Saudi government needs foreign workers to do various jobs in the country, but, to the government's chagrin, some of these workers are Christians, and though there are no churches in the country, informal house churches exist. The two men from India were probably arrested not for proselytizing but for participating in Christian worship, even though this was done in private. The men could have escaped deportation had they converted to Islam, but they refused.

In America and Europe, tolerance and multiculturalism are highly valued. This is clearly not so in the rest of the world, particularly in Muslim nations. The intensity of persecution varies according to who is in power at a particular moment. King Abdullah came to power in Saudi Arabia in 2005 and has been a zealous persecutor of Christians. The country's Commission for Promotion of Virtue and Prevention of Vice is active in enforcing the law against any Muslim converting to another faith, and the government monitors Internet use in the country, watching for anything critical of Islam. Despite having a cordial meeting with the pope in 2007, the king continues the centuries-old legacy of hatred for "infidels."

Prayer: Lord, bless all who live under the threat of persecution and fill their hearts with peace. Amen.

March 12 · THE FINAL SOLUTION

Be faithful, even to the point of death, and I will give you the crown of life.

REVELATION 2:10

303: Despite great hostility, Christianity spread throughout the Roman Empire. In the year 298 pagan priests officiating at a sacrifice claimed they were unable to read omens because the Christians present were making the sign of the cross, which offended the gods. The emperor at this time was Diocletian, a pagan who seemed to have sincerely believed in the old gods and feared for the empire's welfare if the gods were neglected.

On February 23, 303, Diocletian decreed that copies of the Scriptures should be surrendered and burned, churches closed, and all Christian meetings banned. After two fires in one of his palaces were blamed on Christians, he ordered the arrest of all clergy, who would be released if they made sacrifices. Some did and were released. Others did not and were killed.

In the spring of 304, another edict ordered all people in the empire to sacrifice to the gods. This led to widespread martyrdom, as it put all Christians in the position of having to deny Christ and make a sacrifice to gods they knew did not exist. As would happen in all the imperial persecutions of the faith, the steadfastness of the martyrs led to more conversions to the faith. As the Christian writer Tertullian said, "The blood of the martyrs is the seed of the church."

A surprising thing happened on March 12, 303: three officials in Diocletian's own household were executed. The faith had spread to the point that Christians were even serving on the emperor's staff.

Diocletian abdicated in May 305, worn out by a hectic life. The persecution conducted during his reign was the most comprehensive that had ever occurred. Could he have known that the only reason he would be remembered was because he persecuted Christians—and that the faith he tried to exterminate lived on? Could he have imagined that in a mere eight years a Christian would rule as emperor?

Prayer: Heavenly King, earthly rulers come and go, but you remain, filling us with hope. Amen.

March 13 · A New Home for Exiles

If it is possible, as far as it depends on you, live at peace with everyone.

ROMANS 12:18

1741: One of the finest rulers in the 1700s was born on this date: Joseph II, ruling over Austria, Hungary, and other regions. These lands were mostly Catholic, and the Protestants in them had either immigrated or endured persecution. For several years Joseph was coruler with his mother, Empress Maria Teresa, who was a devout Catholic. After her death, Joseph was able to do something he'd wanted to do for years: grant toleration to non-Catholics. In October 1781 he issued the Patent of Toleration, granting freedom of worship to all Christians.

Joseph was a wise politician, and he understood that he still ruled a predominantly Catholic country. So he allowed Protestants to build churches and worship in them—so long as they did not *look* like churches, which meant no steeples or crosses outside. His Catholic subjects could take some satisfaction in having the only churches that looked like churches.

Joseph's toleration of non-Catholics was partly rooted in his own generous personality, but it had another motive, a practical one: Europe had thousands of Protestants who were respectable and industrious citizens, yet they were persecuted in their homelands. By granting them toleration, Joseph was encouraging them to settle in his country and contribute to its prosperity and stability. His ancestors on the throne of Austria had persecuted Protestants and driven thousands of them away; Joseph was beckoning them to return. He gave toleration; they gave their industry and good behavior.

Most rulers of the 1700s were shameless in their private lives, but Joseph was genuinely devout, and his life was untouched by scandal. Few kings have ever worked harder, and few were more humane, for Joseph was a great reformer of law, abolishing torture and curtailing the use of the death penalty. It is to his credit that though he was devoted to the Catholic Church, he granted other Christians the right to live inpeace.

Prayer: Lord, give us wise and compassionate people to govern us. Amen.

March 14 · CROSS AND SWASTIKA

Wake up! Strengthen what remains and is about to die.

REVELATION 3:2

1937: In the 1930s, Germany had become a prosperous nation and at the same time it was embracing a horrible ideology that had no respect for human life—or God. Christians have been accused of not reacting strongly to Hitler and the Nazis, but the record shows this was not the case.

On March 10, 1937, Pope Pius XI sent out an encyclical (official statement) to be read from the pulpit of every German Catholic church the following Sunday, March 14, which was Palm Sunday. Printed copies were distributed to those attending. Normally an encyclical is known by its Latin title, but this encyclical's title was in German, and for a good reason: it was targeted specifically at Germans and required a title that would hit them directly. The title was *Mit brennender Sorge*—"with burning concern."

The document spoke of "God-given rights" that all human beings possess. It spoke of the pagan nature of Nazism and the danger of exalting one nationality or race over others. The Nazis had a faulty conception of God and, because of their contempt for Jews, rejected the Old Testament completely. No race, ethnic group, or nation had the right to set itself up as something to be worshipped.

The pope knew the encyclical would stir up trouble, so it was distributed stealthily. The following day newspapers, censored by the Nazis, did not even mention the encyclical. The Gestapo, the German police, confiscated every copy they could find. Printers who had printed the encyclical were shut down. Hitler swore to punish the Catholic Church in Germany—not by making martyrs but by framing priests and monks for crimes they did not commit.

Did the encyclical do any good? It did harm in the sense of stepping up anti-Christian activity by the Nazis. Yet the pope had done his sacred duty. A vile ideology was at work, and the Catholics of Germany had been warned.

Prayer: Father, give us strength to denounce evil when we see it and wisdom to heed the warnings of the wise. Amen.

March 15 · MINING THE SOUTHWEST'S TREASURES

Those who hope in the LORD *will renew their strength. . . . They will run and not grow weary, they will walk and not be faint.*

ISAIAH 40:31

1711: Eusebio Kino might be called a well-memorialized man: a statue of him in the U.S. Capital building represents the state of Arizona, and another statue of him sits near the Arizona capitol in Phoenix. Mexico also has numerous monuments to this tireless missionary saint.

Born in 1645 in Austria, his birth name was Eusebius Kaehn. During a long illness he vowed to devote his life to missions. Like many committed Catholic men of that day, he joined the Society of Jesus (also called the Jesuits), and he was sent to Mexico. He is usually known by the Spanish form of his name, Kino. He was told to plant missions on the large "island" off the western coast of Mexico—though he discovered that the "island" was instead the long Baja Peninsula that runs south of California. He established the first Spanish mission there in 1683.

Like most missionaries, Kino was disturbed that the Spanish settlers saw the colonies as places to exploit for their mineral wealth, when the true "treasure" was the mass of people who had never heard the gospel. Dealings with the natives were not always pleasant, and there were many occasions of Apaches and other tribes raiding missions and killing the inhabitants, both whites and Indian converts. But Kino's love for the people was unwavering, and as he traveled about founding new missions, he was the first to bring the faith to what would someday be the states of Arizona and New Mexico.

Kino left his colorful life story to posterity in his book *Favores Celestiales,* *"Heavenly Favors."* He died on March 15, 1711, having ridden eight thousand miles on horseback, confident to the end that all the Americas would one day be Christian.

Prayer: Father, in our lives of comfort let us not forget those who loved much and sacrificed much to spread your gospel. Amen.

March 16 · MESSIAH MESSENGER

They could not stand up against his wisdom or the Spirit by whom he spoke.

ACTS 6:10

1889: Most Jews rejected the Christian message. This was true in A.D. 30, true in later times, and true today. But it is also true that when Jews do convert, they become, like the apostle Paul, seriously committed. One modern Jew who committed his awesome intellectual resources to Christ was Alfred Edersheim, born to a wealthy, cultured Jewish family in Vienna in 1825. In this cosmopolitan home, young Alfred learned English at an early age, and his knowledge of English would have a powerful effect on his later life.

He was teaching foreign languages in Hungary when he came under the influence of a Church of Scotland minister, who converted him to Christianity. Edersheim accompanied the pastor back to Scotland, studied theology there, married a Scottish woman, and became a pastor in the Free Church of Scotland. Health problems limited his active ministry but did not limit his research and writing, and Edersheim wrote several books on the New Testament and the early history of Christianity. His greatest book, still widely read, is the awesome *Life and Times of Jesus the Messiah*, published in two volumes in 1883.

It is the story of Jesus as only a Jew could write it, for Edersheim's background and study were all put to use in this rich and detailed depiction of Jesus the Jew, followed by Jewish disciples and persecuted by a Jewish religious bureaucracy. The curious thing about the book is that, far from being dull or dry, it is history written with pleasure and can be read with pleasure. Edersheim had a way with words, describing the Jews of Jesus' time as "industrious, sober, pushing." He could explain Hebrew and Greek terms without sounding "professorish." He could make the reader feel he was reading about real people, not words.

Edersheim died on March 16, 1889, an example of an intense intellect put to use in the cause of the Messiah.

Prayer: Father, let all who put their faith in your Son use whatever gifts they possess to spread the message of salvation. Amen.

March 17 · WISE, BOLD, AND VIGOROUS

Come with me and see my zeal for the LORD.

2 KINGS 10:16

1780: Scotland has contributed a multitude of heroes to the history of Christianity, none more heroic than Thomas Chalmers, born on this date. Raised in a large family, Chalmers was blessed with a quick mind, boundless vitality, and a genuine love for people. While pastoring two Church of Scotland parishes in Glasgow, he was renowned not only for his preaching but for his work with the city's poor. Later he taught religion, philosophy, political science, economics, math, and chemistry at the universities of Edinburgh and St. Andrews. In short, he was a man fascinated by, and knowledgeable about, the world. In 1831 he was elected head of the Church of Scotland, which surprised no one given that he was one of the most admired men in the country.

Then came the Great Disruption. On May 18, 1843, Chalmers was among the two hundred pastors and elders who walked out of the Church of Scotland's assembly and formed the Free Church of Scotland, subject to no control by king, Parliament, or any governmental body. Small denominations had done this in the past, but the 1843 Disruption involved 474 of 1,200 pastors leaving the state Church of Scotland. In severing their ties to the state church, they were giving up all claim to government aid and to the right to worship in Church of Scotland buildings or live in its parsonages. "Free" meant not only "no government interference" but also meant "self-supporting."

Chalmers was elected head of this new Free Church. With his usual vigor, he pitched in to help the new denomination build churches and create a vital organization with no aid from the state. Forming a new church from scratch was a colossal task, but Chalmers rose to the occasion. He and the other seceders understood that a church, if it is truly Christian, has to be something beside a department of the government.

Chalmers died in 1847, having contributed immeasurably to the life of the church and the life of Scotland.

Prayer: Lord, send us pastors with wisdom, zeal, and genuine love. Amen.

March 18 · The Voice of London

So many gathered that there was no room left, not even outside the door, and he preached the word to them.

Mark 2:2

1861: "Over the water to Charlie" was a familiar call in London in the 1800s. Men who ran ferryboats on the Thames River made money getting people across the river to the enormous Metropolitan Tabernacle, which opened on this date. "Charlie" was the greatest preacher of Victorian England, the remarkable Charles H. Spurgeon, known in his day and after as the "Prince of the Pulpiteers."

Spurgeon was born in 1834 and converted at age sixteen. At eighteen he began preaching at a small Baptist church, and word of the "boy preacher's" direct and homey sermons spread. At nineteen he was called to New Park Street Chapel, a large church with many empty pews. Eighty people were present at Spurgeon's first sermon there, but soon the church overflowed and had to rent a concert hall that held four thousand. The church's new location, the Metropolitan Tabernacle, held six thousand, a "megachurch" of its time.

Spurgeon had thousands of admirers—and a few enemies. Preachers who served dwindling congregations were sure that Spurgeon's secret was "vulgarizing" the gospel. The press attacked Spurgeon after seven people died when some troublemakers caused a panic by yelling "Fire!" in a packed hall.

But the crowds kept coming. Spurgeon published his sermons (which filled fifty volumes) and also commentaries and devotional books. With so many people attracted by the star preacher, the church opened a preaching college, which graduated over nine hundred men before Spurgeon's death in 1892. The church also ran an orphanage and other ministries.

One of Spurgeon's books was *John Ploughman's Talks*, with the subtitle *Plain Advice for Plain People*, which is a good summary of Spurgeon's approach. He did not preach eloquently or intellectually but plainly, with ample warmth, sincerity, and humor to attract the working class as well as the elite. In short, he preached like Christ.

Prayer: Lord, we thank you for voices of truth that draw people yearning to hear the word of life. Amen.

March 19 · CROWN OF OPULENCE

Here now is the man who did not make God his stronghold but trusted in his great wealth.

PSALM 52:7

1513: A man born into wealth and power became even wealthier and more powerful on this date. He was Giovanni de Medici of the renowned Medici family of Italy, and on this date he became pope, taking the name Leo X. He was the supreme head over every Christian in western Europe and in the new colonies in America. He would be the last pope to rule over so many Christians, for during his reign the Reformation launched by Martin Luther would change things forever.

Leo X was not the man to deal constructively with the Reformation. He had been made a cardinal at age thirteen and saw the church as a means to live in opulence, not to minister to the spiritual needs of millions of people. If sophistication was the road to salvation, then Leo would surely have been saved, for his court in Rome patronized artists and poets. Raphael, one of the greatest of artists, was a close friend. Leo was not only at home in the world of wealth but in the world of crime and corruption too, and when he learned some cardinals were plotting to poison him, he tortured and executed the ringleader and imprisoned the others. Under Leo any man could become a bishop or cardinal—for a price. These bribes helped pay for Leo's extravagant court—and so did the sale of indulgences, which promised that the buyers would be released from years in purgatory. As it happened, the indulgences were what prompted Luther to launch the Reformation.

Leo and his court were thoroughly unspiritual, with no desire for reforming the church. Leo excommunicated Luther as a heretic in January 1521, but he hardly took Luther seriously and assumed Luther's "heresy" would come to nothing. Leo died in December 1521, one of the most spiritually blind men to ever hold the office of pope.

Prayer: Father, teach us to walk humbly with you and to pursue spiritual richness. Amen.

March 20 · A Mind for God

By wisdom the LORD laid the earth's foundations, by understanding he set the heavens in place.

PROVERBS 3:19

1727: The more science, the less faith—that is the usual understanding today. One of the world's greatest scientists, who died on this date, would not have agreed. In Isaac Newton's mind religion and science coexisted very well—in fact, one seemed to support the other.

When Newton was born in 1642, the scientific revolution was well underway and due to him would progress even further. Newton grew up on a farm in northern England and at an early age found creation fascinating. While studying at Cambridge University, he underwent a conversion and decided that the goal of his life was to understand the Bible. He saw science as a "garden" that God intended him to cultivate, and he believed that his many discoveries in science were communicated to him by the Holy Spirit.

Newton's discoveries of the laws of gravitation were path-breaking, as were his writings on optics and calculus. His book *Principia Mathematica* explained the movements of the heavens and laid the foundation for modern science. In the years when Newton was changing the face of science, he was also active in Christian work, helping to distribute Bibles to the poor.

Queen Anne knighted Newton in 1705, the first time the honor had been bestowed on a scientist. Formerly the men knighted were those who distinguished themselves in war. The world had changed, and men of ideas had become important.

Newton's contemporaries regarded him as a devout Christian, which he was, but they were not aware of just how much writing he did on the subject of religion. In fact, his religious writings fill up several volumes, and not all have been published.

Sir Isaac died on March 20, 1727. He would no doubt be distressed to learn that people would come to regard faith and science as incompatible. Newton had written that science "cannot explain who set the planets in motion. God governs all things."

Prayer: God of majesty, open our eyes to the wonders of your handiwork. Amen.

Sing to him a new song; play skillfully, and shout for joy.

PSALM 33:3

1685: In the small German town of Eisenach, Johann Sebastian Bach was born into a family already renowned as musicians and composers. He would outshine his ancestors and also his several sons who became famous in their own right.

In his productive years—from about 1700 to 1750—he composed what many music experts (and millions of music lovers) regard as some of the finest music ever written. And while much of it is secular—the great *Brandenburg Concertos*, the *Goldberg Variations*, *The Art of Fugue*, *The Well-Tempered Clavier*, and countless other masterworks—much of what Bach wrote was for performance in churches. Most composers of his day wrote religious music—after all, churches paid composers well. There were plenty of church musicians and church artists whose lives were not even remotely Christian.

But Bach genuinely was a sincere Christian, thoroughly devoted to his faith. For him, composing cantatas and anthems for church services was never "just a job." According to Bach, "The purpose of music can be nothing but the glory of God and the restoration of the heart. Where this is not the case there is no real music but only a demonic noise." Bach's library included the works of Martin Luther, commentaries on the Bible, and numerous devotional writings. Some of his music manuscripts have inscriptions like "To the greater glory of God" and "To God alone be the glory."

When Bach died in 1750, his music was considered old-fashioned. But in 1829 German composer Felix Mendelssohn conducted Bach's great oratorio, the *St. Matthew Passion*, and a Bach revival began. Since then the great man's music has never ceased to be popular, though one wonders if secular audiences appreciate the composer's conviction that all his music—secular or religious—was for "the greater glory of God."

Prayer: Father, thank you for the inspiring works of music and art that draw us nearer to you, and thank you especially for those who lives were in keeping with the divine works they produced. Amen.

March 22 · THE AFFECTION ADVOCATE

Fix these words of mine in your hearts and minds.

DEUTERONOMY 11:18

1758: Jonathan Edwards, one of the great preachers of colonial America, is remembered for his famous hellfire sermon, "Sinners in the Hands of an Angry God." This is unfortunate, for he preached and wrote more about God's love than his wrath—although he believed firmly in both.

Edwards was born in 1703, the son and grandson of Puritan pastors and the only son in a family with ten sisters. Fascinated with science as well as theology, he studied and taught at Yale and made a happy marriage that produced eleven children. In the 1730s his sermons contributed to the revival known as the Great Awakening. Edwards wrote about the revival in his book *Faithful Narrative of the Surprising Work of God*, which showed him to be psychologist as well as theologian. The Awakening also led Edwards to write his *Treatise on Religious Affections*. In those days "affections" was used the way we use "emotions." The Puritans have been accused of making faith too much a matter of the head, not the heart. This was not the case at all, and Edwards insisted that "true religion, in great part, consists in holy affections."

Edwards's contemporaries, especially the skeptics who hated religion, taught the importance of man's reason. Edward could use reason in writing theology but understood that it had its limits. If man was not emotionally engaged with God, nothing mattered. Edwards engaged in a war of words with Charles Chauncy, a pompous Boston pastor who mocked the revival and said it was all meaningless emotion. Edwards replied that for some people the emotions did not run deep, and some conversions were even faked—but that did not negate the lives that were genuinely changed by the revivals.

In 1757 he became president of the College of New Jersey (later called Princeton) and was vaccinated for smallpox. On March 22, 1758, he died from the vaccination. He was one of the great minds—and hearts—of the American story.

Prayer: Lord, engage both our hearts and minds so that we live in whole-souled fellowship with you. Amen.

March 23 · BISHOP ON FOOT

"I am among you as one who serves."

LUKE 22:27

1606: We cannot help but admire people who are born into wealth and comfort but who give up security as they attempt great things for God. Consider Toribio de Mogrovejo, born in Spain in 1538. His family was well-off, and he had a secure position teaching law at the University of Salamanca. The Spanish king Phillip II admired him and made him a judge but later asked him to do something requiring great courage: sail to America and become archbishop of the Spanish colony of Peru. Toribio arrived in Peru in 1581 and traveled six hundred miles—on foot—to the city of Lima.

"Time is not our own, and we must give a strict account of it," said the archbishop. Certainly he made full use of his time and abilities, and between his arrival in Peru and his death in 1606, he is said to have traveled eighteen thousand miles, mostly on foot, often alone, always unarmed, and frequently in poor health. Many bishops in Europe lived in luxury, but the archbishop of Peru did not, for he saw himself engaging in the same work as Christ's apostles. He founded the first seminary in the Americas, which opened in Lima in 1591. He supervised the building of roads, schools, hospitals, churches, and convents, and it is believed he baptized almost half a million people. Preferring to preach without an interpreter, he learned some of the Indian languages, and he constantly urged the Spanish colonists to treat the native people with compassion. He also had to remind the colonists that as Christians they had to behave like followers of Christ so as to set an example to new converts.

Like many Europeans who settled in America, Toribio succumbed to disease, though he was active to the very end. Before dying on March 23, 1606, he repeated the familiar words of Jesus on the cross: "Into your hand I commit my spirit."

Prayer: Father, let the stories of those who lit up the world with their faith encourage us to love and to serve. Amen.

I will turn the darkness into light before them.

ISAIAH 42:16

1820: Frances Jane Crosby was born on this date, and, thanks to a doctor's negligence, six weeks later an eye inflammation caused her permanent blindness. Despite this handicap, her education was not neglected, and she was writing poetry by age eight, as well as learning a great deal of the Bible by heart. She was given music lessons and became a pupil, and later teacher, at the New York Institution for the Blind.

Fanny Crosby, the name most people know her by, wrote poetry throughout her life, and she began writing songs with a composer named George Root. These were the romantic, sentimental "parlor songs" of the era. She also wrote political campaign songs and some pro-Union songs during the Civil War. But Fanny was destined to make her name as a hymn-writer. Between 1864 and her death in 1915, Fanny wrote almost nine thousand hymns. She was such a prolific writer that her publishers sometimes used pen names on her hymns, wanting to disguise just how productive this amazing woman was. Though she made money from her hymns (albeit not much), she claimed the money meant little, that her hope was that her songs would help win people to Christ.

Fanny wrote only the words with several composers providing the music. One of these was the great Ira Sankey, the music director for evangelist Dwight L. Moody. The use of Fanny's songs in Moody's crusades spread their popularity. Anyone browsing through an American hymnal is bound to uncover many Crosby hymns, including "Blessed Assurance, Jesus Is Mine," whose lyrics she spoke almost immediately after hearing the tune for the first time. Other Crosby classics are "To God Be the Glory," "Jesus Is Tenderly Calling," "Redeemed, How I Love to Proclaim It," "Jesus, Keep Me Near the Cross," and the song that reflects Fanny's concern for the poor, "Rescue the Perishing." Fanny was a truly amazing and richly talented woman.

Prayer: Lord who brings light out of darkness, you give gifts to all your children, if they will only labor to use them. Amen.

March 25 · A Life Brief and Focused

The world and its desires pass away, but the man who does the will of God lives forever.

1 John 2:17

1843: "Live near to God and all things will appear little to you in comparison with eternal realities." So said Robert Murray M'Cheyne, who did live near to God, although only for thirty years in this world. For one who lived such a short time, he made an indelible impression.

Born in Scotland in 1813, M'Cheyne (whose name is pronounced like McCheyne, and sometimes is spelled that way) was a highly intelligent child who taught himself the Greek alphabet when he was only four. He had a phenomenal memory and could quote long passages from Scripture.

After graduating from the University of Edinburgh at age twenty-two, he was ordained in the Church of Scotland, the state church, which had far too many spiritually indifferent pastors. M'Cheyne was not that kind of pastor. He visited his parishioners, prepared his sermons faithfully, prayed, meditated, and studied the Bible. His sermons blended intellectual solidness with an emotional appeal to turn to God. A contemporary said that M'Cheyne preached "with eternity stamped on his brow." In his six years as a pastor, his church in Dundee, Scotland, grew to over a thousand members, which for the time was enormous. Today he is probably best remembered for his plan for reading through the entire Bible in a year.

In 1839, M'Cheyne took a sabbatical from his church and traveled to the Holy Land, hoping in the future to be active in missions to the Jews. He prayed for his church while away, and when he returned found his prayers answered with the church even more lively than before.

Like many pastors of his day, M'Cheyne wrote hymns, and appropriately one of them is "When This Passing World Is Done." He was a vigorous force for good during his brief life, and he never forgot that this world was a preparation for the next.

Prayer: Father, put us to work for you, use us up in your service, and never let us forget our destination. Amen.

March 26 · FREE TO SERVE

We were all baptized by one Spirit into one body—whether Jews or Greeks, slave or free.

1 CORINTHIANS 12:13

1831: A new independent nation was born in 1776, and in 1777, a slave found a kind of spiritual independence when he became a Christian. He was Richard Allen, born the child of slave parents in 1760. As it happened, his conversion had a powerful effect on his owner who became a Christian himself and quickly saw that Christians had no business owning slaves. He allowed Allen to earn money doing odd jobs, and in 1783—the same year America's war of independence ended—Allen purchased his freedom. He resolved to show his gratitude to God by preaching the gospel.

Allen settled in Philadelphia, joining a Methodist church where he taught classes and led prayer meetings. Although Allen was respected by white Christians, America at this stage of history was simply not a place where the races mingled in churches. If blacks attended a white church, they had to sit in a separate section (often a balcony), or the church would allow blacks to hold their own separate services very early on Sundays. It was almost impossible for blacks to hold any positions of authority in white churches. So, with the blessing of Francis Asbury, the head of the Methodists in America, Allen and two other black men from his church founded a new congregation, Bethel, for blacks. Though relations with white Methodists were cordial, Allen and his followers never felt fully accepted by the denomination, so in 1816 he and other black pastors founded a new denomination, the African Methodist Episcopal Church. Allen was elected its first bishop.

Though he was a dutiful pastor and bishop, he wore many hats, running successful businesses and acting as a labor contractor who found jobs for blacks in Philadelphia. When he died on March 26, 1831, he was respected as a diligent and devout man who helped his fellow blacks spiritually and materially.

Prayer: Father, teach us to use our freedom to serve others, for in serving them we glorify you. Amen.

Light is shed upon the righteous and joy on the upright in heart.

PSALM 97:11

1842: One of the greatest Christian hymns was the result of blindness, a broken engagement, and a marriage. Its author, George Matheson, was born in Scotland on this date, and he attended the University of Glasgow to prepare for the ministry. There was an obstacle: he discovered he was going blind. He determined to go into the ministry anyway, but his other plan—marriage—was scuttled, for when he told his fiancée he was going blind, she informed him she could not go through with the marriage.

Matheson never married, but he became a respected parish minister in Scotland and on one occasion preached before Queen Victoria. He wrote prolifically on theology and on the place of Christianity in the modern world. The University of Edinburgh awarded him an honorary doctorate.

In June 1882 his beloved sister was preparing to marry. Matheson recalled his own broken engagement years earlier, and on June 6, the day before his sister's wedding, he wrote "O Love That Wilt Not Let Me Go." He recalled later that "the whole work was completed in five minutes. . . . All the other verses I have written are manufactured articles. This came like a dayspring from on high." He suffered "extreme mental distress, and the hymn was the fruit of that pain." Curiously, Albert Peace, who wrote the music two years later, recalled that "I wrote the tune straight off, and may say that the ink of the first note was hardly dry when I finished the tune." Clearly there was something emotionally raw but beautiful: *O Love that wilt not let me go. . . . O Joy that seekest me through pain.* And for this blind man, *O Light that followest all my way* had special meaning. Human life has its sorrows; human love is fickle; earthly joys are fleeting. God alone gives eternal love, joy, and light.

Prayer: Lord, light our way through the dark times, and keep our hearts fixed on eternal pleasures. Amen.

March 28 · CHURCHLESS CHURCH

"Where two or three are gathered together in my name, there am I in the midst of them."

MATTHEW 18:20 (KJV)

1930: We see in Acts and the letters of Paul that there were no church buildings in Christianity's early days. Believers generally met in homes, and there were no tightly organized bureaucracies. In fact, bureaucracies tend to "quench the Spirit," so Christians have often reverted to the New Testament model, meeting in house churches and small groups.

One strong advocate of "non-church Christianity" was Uchimura Kanzo of Japan. Born in 1861, he attended an American-run agricultural college and was led to faith by one of its founders, a committed lay missionary who introduced Uchimura to a nondenominational Christianity based on a covenant made by a small group of believers.

Uchimura went to the United States to study both science and theology. He found seminary disappointing and regarded many of the pastoral students as frivolous and at times even blasphemous. (Sadly, many foreign students studying in U.S. seminaries have had similar experiences.) This increased his distaste for institutional Christianity.

He returned to Japan in 1888 and published a magazine, *Seisho no Kenkyu* ("Biblical Studies"), and also lectured on the Bible. He was regarded as the leader of the *Mukyokai* ("non-church") movement. It was by no means a "lone wolf" form of faith, for Uchimura knew that true Christianity requires fellowship. He insisted that Mukyokai groups study the Bible closely, subscribe to a creed of core beliefs, and pray for and encourage each other. He knew that the New Testament word *ekklesia* meant "gathering" or "assembly," though it is always translated "church." He saw no need for ordained clergy, and was aware that, in the Bible, religious establishments usually existed to maintain themselves, not spread the faith. He called Mukyokai "the church for those who have no church" and said that "there is no church in heaven."

Uchimura died March 28, 1930, a unique spirit whose teachings continue to have an influence.

Prayer: Lord, help us find genuine spiritual fellowship, reaching out to others who gather together in your name. Amen.

March 29 · FARMER SOWS THE WORD

The Lord stood at my side and gave me strength, so that through me the message might be fully proclaimed.

2 TIMOTHY 4:17

1824: Norway today is very much a "post-Christian" nation, but in the past Christianity was very much alive. One of the greatest figures in Norwegian Christianity, Hans Hauge, died on this date after leading an amazing revival movement in his country.

Hauge was born in 1771 on a farm, one of ten children. In 1796 in a field, he experienced a conversion to Christ. He began preaching, and although he was never ordained, in less than ten years he traveled ten thousand miles, much of the time on foot, preaching almost every day. He preached the need for a new birth in Christ, and his message touched people who found no real satisfaction in Norway's state church with its emphasis on correct belief and rituals. Hauge criticized the church for its spiritual deadness, and, not surprisingly, he found himself in trouble: in 1804 he was arrested for unlicensed preaching and was confined to prison for ten years. Many of his followers were also persecuted since religious gatherings outside the church were illegal.

If the story sounds familiar, it is because it is the story of the first Christians, one that repeats itself over the centuries: devout laymen preach the message of a personal relationship with God, and the religious establishment feels threatened and tries to stamp out the new movement. The movement Hauge launched was impossible to stamp out, for even while he languished in prison, the books he wrote were widely read, and many of his converts turned to lay preaching even though they risked going to prison for it. His followers were often called *Leser*, Norwegian for "readers," those whose lives were changed by reading the Bible and Hauge's writings. Ironically, Norway's church benefited greatly from Hauge and his followers, for over time church attendance increased dramatically. A simple farmer with little education had, against all odds, worked a miracle in his nation.

Prayer: Father, bless all who proclaim your message of salvation. Amen.

---

*Though you have made me see troubles, many and bitter, you will restore
my life again.*

PSALM 71:20

1533: Every Sunday around the globe, millions of people recite words written
by Thomas Cranmer, although most of them are not aware of it. Cranmer was
England's first Protestant archbishop of Canterbury, a post he assumed on this
date. Cranmer was the chief author of the Book of Common Prayer, the worship
book used in all services in the Church of England and its daughter churches,
including the Episcopal Church in the United States. He also became a martyr.

Cranmer, born in 1489, was one of the first clergy in England to be sympathetic to the Reformation. He might have remained an unknown, except that
he was drafted into the service of King Henry VIII who wanted to divorce his
wife Catherine (who had not borne him sons) and marry Anne Boleyn. The pope
would not grant Henry a divorce, and when the old archbishop of Canterbury
died, Henry put Cranmer in his place, and Cranmer granted the divorce. Henry
broke the English church away from Rome, and from that point on Cranmer did
not answer to the pope but to Henry. In this position, Cranmer was able to push
through the Reformation in England, although Henry (still Catholic at heart)
nixed some of the reforms. As a Protestant, Cranmer wanted clergy to be able
to marry. Henry would not allow this, yet he overlooked the fact that Cranmer
himself was married.

During the brief reign of Henry's son, Edward VI, Cranmer was able to
reform the English church further. His Book of Common Prayer was introduced
in 1549, and though modified over the years, much of it remains as Cranmer
wrote it.

Edward died in 1553, and his half sister Mary Tudor became queen. She
restored Catholicism in England and removed Cranmer from his post. As the
chief promoter of Protestantism in England, he was burned at the stake in 1556,
meeting death bravely. The man Mary saw as a heretic was seen by English
Protestants as a martyr.

Prayer: Lord, give your martyrs courage and confidence in you. Amen.

March 31 · HARDY-HEARTED MEN

Our light and momentary troubles are achieving for us an eternal glory.

2 CORINTHIANS 4:17

1816: During his lifetime Francis Asbury was one of the most famous men in America. He once received a letter from England that was addressed to "The Rev'd Bishop Asbury, North America." The sender knew that someone as well-known as Asbury could be located.

He did not have a fixed address. In his long career preaching and supervising Methodist churches in America, Asbury traveled 300,000 miles on horseback. His aim was to grow the church, and he did—from about 5,000 Methodists at the time of the American Revolution to more than 200,000 at the end of his life in 1816.

Asbury was born in England in 1745. He joined the Methodists at fourteen. When he showed an eagerness to go to America, Methodist leader John Wesley sent him off. Later Wesley conferred the title "superintendent" on Asbury, although American Methodists referred to him as "bishop." The title was not important but the willingness to do without home, wife, or any form of earthly comfort was. Asbury's diary is almost a catalog of health problems, yet he gritted through his ailments, depression, and doubts, not to mention foul weather and sleeping in barns and woodsheds. The circuit-riding preachers he supervised were tough men too, but many married and settled down—they called it "locating." Asbury himself never married nor even seems to have considered it. God had given him a task. He did it.

Thousands of people on the fringes of civilization came to Christ thanks to Asbury and the steelyspined men he supervised. The genteel Presbyterian and Congregational parsons in their brick homes on the Atlantic coast lived comfortable lives that were nothing like the lives of the apostles—or the Methodist circuit-riders. It took men like Asbury—who described himself accurately as "steadfast as a wall of brass"—to create and sustain vital communities of faith on the American frontier.

Having preached more than sixteen thousand sermons, Asbury died on March 31, 1816, meeting the God he had served with distinction.

Prayer: Lord, create in us the steely resolve of your hardy servants. Amen.

APRIL

———

April 1 · FROM GODLESS TO GOD

By smooth talk and flattery they deceive the minds of naive people.

ROMANS 16:18

1901: Would you believe that the man who translated the delightful children's book *Bambi* into English had been a Communist spy—and, later, a committed Christian and anti-Communist? He was Whittaker Chambers, born on this date, whose religious life is a kind of panorama of religion in the modern world.

Chambers was by nature a religious person, meaning he wanted to believe in something that gave life purpose and meaning. Like many intellectuals of his time, he was drawn to Communism since it was "scientific" while religion was not. However, Chambers grew disillusioned with Communism. One day he and a fellow Communist encountered a shivering derelict asking for a handout. Chambers's friend ignored the man, which Communists were supposed to do, since charity was believed to "dull the revolutionary spirit of the masses." Chambers also noticed that while Communists were committed people, they were neither happy nor loving.

"Every sincere break with Communism is a religious experience," wrote Chambers in his memoir, *Witness.* He turned from a godless religion to the religion of God. Making amends for his days of spying, he testified to Congress about Communist spies working in the Truman administration, and he named names. One name was Alger Hiss, an Ivy League sophisticate who had passed on state secrets to the Russians. The media rallied behind Hiss, who denied everything and looked better on camera than the pudgy Chambers. But in 1950 Hiss was convicted of perjury, and everything Chambers said about him proved true.

For Chambers, the Hiss episode was more than just a matter of Communist spies in America. He saw a bigger battle: godless materialism versus Christianity. Communism had its roots in what the serpent whispered to Eve: "Ye shall be as gods." The godless world was an unhappy, oppressive place, as the Russians and Chinese learned. Chambers found peace with God and prayed his memoirs would alert others to the dangers of a godless religion.

Prayer: Lord, we praise you, for you alone can give us lives rich with meaning. Amen.

April 2 · SPIRITED GROWTH

We have not received the spirit of the world but the Spirit who is from God.

1 CORINTHIANS 2:12

1914: When the twentieth century began, few people had ever heard the word *Pentecostal*. When the century ended, Pentecostals were a vibrant global presence, and there were dozens of Pentecostal denominations, including the largest, founded on this date, the Assemblies of God. At a gathering in Hot Springs, Arkansas, the foundations were laid for a denomination that would pass the 3 million mark in membership by 2010, an amazing achievement, particularly at a time when many denominations were losing membership not gaining.

Why has it grown? For the same reason that most Pentecostal churches have grown: an openness to the working of the Holy Spirit, the "missing person" of the Trinity. Worship at Pentecostal churches tends to be lively and enthusiastic, and members attribute this to the encouraging of spiritual gifts, including healing and speaking in tongues. In the early 1900s the expression of these gifts, especially tongues, led to divisions in congregations and even in entire denominations. Some of the "splinter" groups became larger than the "boards" they splintered from.

A word about this denomination's name: in the New Testament the Greek word that is usually translated "church" is *ekklesia*, literally "assembly" or "group called together." *Ekklesia* did not refer to a building nor to a bureaucracy but to a fellowship of people called together by the Lord. Although people often speak of an "Assembly of God church," the proper designation is simply "Assembly of God." This was a wise choice on the group's part since many people have a negative view of "church." Some other denominations and independent churches have taken a similar approach, calling themselves "fellowships" or "Christian centers." The term used is not important, of course. What matters is that the people who gather together see themselves not as a building or as an organization on paper but as an *ekklesia*, a warm and worshipful gathering of God's people.

Prayer: Father, we thank you for the working of your Spirit, uniting people worldwide in a growing fellowship of love. Amen.

April 3 · A Tale of Two Brothers

Let us draw near to God with a sincere heart.

Hebrews 10:22

1593: The English writers George and Edward Herbert had the same parents and the same upbringing, but religiously they were poles apart. Edward was known in his lifetime, and later, as the great defender of Deism, which had a great influence on intellectuals in the 1700s, including some of America's Founding Fathers. Disgusted with all the religious discord in Europe and with Christians executing each other for heresy, Edward decided that the way to bring such strife to an end was to discard Christianity and practice a simple religion based on reason, not revelation. He believed that God exists but does not interfere in human affairs, and people should treat their fellow man well, but beyond these basic beliefs nothing is essential. Edward had let his intellectual pride lead him away from the God of the Bible.

His younger brother, George Herbert, born on April 3, 1593, was a different sort altogether. George imbibed his mother's warm devotion to the Christian faith. He became a minister, and early in life he decided that he would let other poets write about their favorite subject of man and woman while he would write of a greater subject, the Christian and God.

George Herbert published no poetry in his lifetime, though some of his poems circulated among friends. In his lifetime he did gain fame as a pastor who took his duties seriously, and he wrote a book about pastoral care, *The Priest to the Temple*. As he lay dying in 1633, Herbert gave his poems to a friend, who published them under the title *The Temple*. They are some of the finest Christian poems ever written, a record of Herbert's own spiritual life with its highs and lows. Like the best religious poets, he makes the life of faith seem appealing not burdensome. Unlike his Deist brother, George knew that a religion based on cold reason and a distant God could never satisfy the mass of people.

Prayer: Father, thank you for the great saints of the past, whose writings still comfort and inspire us. Amen.

April 4 · THE FAST TRACK BISHOP

Each one should use whatever gift he has received to serve others.

1 PETER 4:10

397: Some people feel God calling them to ministry and spend years preparing for it. Less often, someone finds himself hastily "drafted" into the ministry by public demand. Such was the case with Ambrose of Milan. Born about 340, Ambrose was raised in a religious home and trained to be a lawyer. Like many lawyers, he became a politician, serving as governor of one of the provinces of Italy, with his home in the city of Milan.

Ambrose received his call when the bishop of Milan died, and two different factions fought to have their candidate be the new bishop. As governor, Ambrose showed up to restore order, and suddenly people were calling out, "Ambrose for bishop!" At this point, Ambrose was not even a full member of the church. In a period of eight days he was baptized, ordained a priest, then consecrated bishop.

The people had made a wise choice, for Ambrose's political skills made him a fine bishop. He was admired for his generosity to the poor and his spotless character. He had a certain amount of catching up to do in terms of learning the Bible and theology, but he proved a fast learner. He was noted as a fine preacher and also a writer of hymns.

In Ambrose's time the Roman Empire was officially Christian, though paganism still lingered. Some pagans wanted to set up an altar to the old Roman goddess Victoria in the Senate, but Ambrose used his influence to prevent this. In fact, he had such influence that he could even bring the emperor himself to heel. The emperor, Theodosius, had ordered the massacre of some civilians in Greece. Ambrose ordered Theodosius to do public penance before he could be received back into the church. This established a precedent: church officials demanding that politicians of the Christian empire *act like Christians.*

Ambrose died on April 4, 397, one of the most respected men of his age.

Prayer: Lord, in a world where power is so often abused, we thank you for those who wield their power for good. Amen.

April 5 · A Mother to Outcasts

He raises the poor from the dust and lifts the needy from the ash heap.

PSALM 113:7

1922: The word *pundit,* used so often in political circles, is from the Sanskrit Indian word *pandit,* meaning "learned one." Pandita Ramabai of India was true to her name, well educated by her father who was a wise Hindu teacher and also a rare one, for he thought women should be educated as well as men. Pandita married a lawyer, who died six months after the birth of their daughter. She found a copy of Luke's gospel among her husband's books and began to study it. Although she had amazed people by memorizing thousands of lines of the Hindu scriptures, she found no satisfaction in Hinduism. Later she went to study in England and, while there, converted to Christianity. She toured America, lecturing on the status of women in India, and supporters formed a Ramabai Foundation to help her in her pursuit to improve the quality of life for women and girls. She returned to India, determined to put her new faith to work.

Indian society is divided into *castes* (classes), and Pandita was from the highest caste, the Brahmins. This was an advantage in her ministry since Indians respect the Brahmins as intellectuals and leaders. In 1889, aided by the Ramabai Foundation, she opened the Mukti Mission as a home for child widows, of which there were many in India. These girls were held in low esteem since it was believed they were responsible for their husbands' deaths, and neither their own families nor their husbands' would take them in. Some worked as slaves; others worked as temple prostitutes. The Mukti Mission provided a home for them, and many converted to Christianity under Pandita's influence. Appropriately, the word *mukti* is Sanskrit for "salvation."

"A life totally committed to God has nothing to fear, nothing to lose, nothing to regret." So said this brave, wise, patient, and tireless woman, who died on April 5, 1922.

Prayer: Lord, we see in your saints' lives a wisdom that expresses itself through compassion. Fill us with the desire to reach the downtrodden. Amen.

April 6 · HANDS, PRAYING AND CREATING

Blessed are those who have learned to acclaim you, who walk in the light of your presence, O LORD.

PSALM 89:15

1528: You know the familiar image of the *Praying Hands* and you have no doubt seen it displayed in many homes. German artist Albrecht Durer, who died on this date, created the original which he titled *Hands of an Apostle*. Durer was a child prodigy, and his self-portrait done at age thirteen is an amazing work for one so young. Durer excelled in everything he tried—oil painting, watercolor, and engraving. Born just a few years after the invention of the printing press, he was the first great artist to see his works printed in book form. He also created some sublime Christian art.

Like most artists of the time, Durer did familiar subjects—Adam and Eve, Mary with the infant Jesus, the crucifixion, the nativity. But his most famous biblical images are the sixteen engravings he did for the book of Revelation, especially the famous image of the four horsemen of the Apocalypse. The stark image in black and white is truly horrifying, showing the four riders literally treading mankind under their horses' hooves. *Michael Fighting the Dragon* shows the angel and a gruesome Satan grappling in midair. These and the other illustrations from Revelation made Durer famous throughout Europe since the pictures were mass-produced via the printing press.

His 1523 painting *Four Apostles* shows John, Peter, Mark, and Paul, all very individualized. *Hands of an Apostle* was a "study" (preliminary drawing) for an altar painting of the apostles. Such drawings were usually tossed aside once the painting was done, but *Hands* was preserved and reproduced more than any drawing ever made.

Durer was fascinated by the human form, especially faces, but he was inspired by nature as well, and his watercolor of a young hare shows astounding detail. In all his images—portraits, landscapes, saints, animals—we sense that Durer was in awe of the Great Artist, God.

Prayer: Lord, let the works of great artists deepen our reverence for you, the Supreme Artist. Amen.

April 7 · THE TEACHERS' TEACHER

Let the word of Christ dwell in you richly as you teach and admonish one another with all wisdom.

COLOSSIANS 3:16

1719: "Be driven by the love of God" was the motto of a man who died on this date after a lifetime of devotion to education, both spiritual and mental. He was Jean Baptiste de La Salle, a French priest whom some historians have called the "Father of Modern Education." Born the eldest son in a large family, Jean had to delay his own seminary education, for when his father died he had to take charge of his younger brothers and sisters for a time not only providing financial support but overseeing their educations. This proved to be excellent preparation for his life's work, overseeing the education of youth and their teachers.

A little background is in order to understand his achievement: there were no public schools at the time and many children, especially the poor, had no opportunity for schooling at all. There were no special schools for training teachers, and most instruction (especially in Catholic countries) was in Latin not the vernacular. Most teachers were priests or monks, and though some of these were capable, few of them saw teaching as their main vocation, and even fewer felt a call to teach poor children.

Jean changed all this in 1682 when he founded the Brothers of the Christian Schools, an order of men whose sole vocation was the education of young people, especially those from poorer families. They saw their main goal as training children to believe and behave as Christians, but they also taught literacy, literature, history, and science.

By the time of Jean's death in 1719, the order had 274 brothers teaching over nine thousand pupils. His supervision of the brothers extended beyond his death, for he wrote a manual for education, *Conduct of Christian Schools*, that was published after his death. The Catholic Church regards him as the patron saint of education.

Prayer: Lord, raise up men and women of wisdom and devotion to train our children for this world and the next. Amen.

April 8 · GOD IS *Not* DEAD!

The fool says in his heart, "There is no God."

PSALM 14:1

1966: Any American alive on this date remembers the *Time* magazine cover, three words in blood-red on a stark black background: Is God Dead? *Time*'s editor hoped the cover would sell issues—it did.

The cover story, titled "Toward a Hidden God," looked at some of the trendy theology of the day, especially the writing of a religion professor named Thomas Altizer who had published the book *The Gospel of Christian Atheism*. Altizer and others suggested that theology could exist even though God did not. Most readers, whatever their religious persuasion, did not agree.

Time and Altizer received tons of mail, most of it critical, some of it threatening. Whether *Time* intended it or not, the cover question got Americans talking about just what religion should be like in an increasingly secular world. The 1960s were years of startling social change in America, and many children who were raised in church turned into young people experimenting with sex, drugs, Eastern religions, and communal living. Some denominations (especially the more liberal ones) lost members. To many people's surprise the more conservative churches, firmly rooted in the Bible and traditional beliefs, actually grew—perhaps not so surprising, since people need spiritual anchors in a world dizzy with change.

In the wake of the *Time* cover, cars began sporting bumper stickers that read, "God is real, I talked with him today" and "If your God is dead, try mine." As far as we know, no bumper stickers supported the "Christian atheism" discussed in the *Time* story, and the whole movement proved to be a passing thing, a trend that somehow bubbled up from seminaries into the wider culture. Doubts about God and religion continued—as they have since ancient times—but so did belief, and in a rapidly changing world people found more life-affirming comfort in God than in the pessimistic and pointless "death of God theology."

Prayer: Lord, you are our anchor in this changeable and confusing world. Keep our hearts and minds close to you. Amen.

I know where you live—where Satan has his throne.

REVELATION 2:13

1945: When fourteen-year-old Dietrich Bonhoeffer told his family he wanted to be a minister, they were horrified. Born into a well-to-do German family, he was an excellent pianist and tennis player, and he could have pursued a music career or followed his father and become a psychiatrist. When Dietrich's brother spoke of what a waste of time the boring church would be, Dietrich said, "If it is so bad, I will reform it."

He was such a brilliant theology student that he received a doctorate when he was twenty-one, and was ordained just as the Nazis were coming to power. Bonhoeffer feared Hitler and said so in a radio broadcast—which was "accidentally" cut off. He watched with horror as the German Protestant churches cravenly rallied behind Hitler and would not criticize his regime, largely due to pro-Nazi pastors being put in key positions. Bonhoeffer and others formed the breakaway Confessing Church which did not toe the Nazi party line. He was branded an "enemy of the state," and his teaching license was revoked. Contrary to what his brother predicted, serving the church was *not* boring.

Bonhoeffer became involved in a failed plot to assassinate Hitler. In April 1943 he was thrown in prison, and on April 8, 1945, he was condemned to death as a traitor, without trial. At dawn the next day he was stripped naked and hanged with wire.

He impressed all who knew him as a supremely lovable and Christlike man, but his involvement in the assassination plot has disturbed some Christians who question whether a believer should ever resist evil, even such a monstrous evil as the Nazi regime. His legacy to the world are his books, *Letters and Papers from Prison* and *The Cost of Discipleship* which contains the line, "When Christ calls a man, he bids him come and die."

Prayer: Lord, thank you for seeing us through the darkest of times when evil seems to have the upper hand. Amen.

April 10 · CITY GRIT

"Whatever you did for one of the least of these brothers of mine, you did for me."

MATTHEW 25:40

1829: We are so accustomed to the Salvation Army that we forget how radical it seemed when it first appeared. Its founder was William Booth, born on this date. His father apprenticed him to a pawnbroker, a profession that gave him a look at the life of the poor. Booth became a Methodist preacher, but the ministry he had in mind for his native England required him to start his own unique organization. He wanted to spread the gospel in England's industrial cities, so naturally he was drawn to London.

In 1865 he and his wife, Catherine, opened the Christian Mission—in a tent, to begin with—in one of the worst slums. By 1878 the mission was known as the Salvation Army. Many mocked it, thinking the brass bands the Army used in its open-air preaching services looked ridiculous. Some Army workers were arrested for disturbing the peace, and others were assaulted. Buildings owned by the Army were vandalized and destroyed. Brewers and saloon owners harassed the Army—a backhanded compliment to the Army's success in reforming drunkards. Many clergymen thought the Army was "undignified"—and indeed it was, because Booth realized the "dignified" churches were not reaching the masses of people crowded into the unsanitary cities.

Over time the critics grew quieter. There was no doubt that Booth was a man with a heart for God—and for England's outcasts. Booth saw that the core problem was the core of man: convert the soul and a person's life would change for the better. But physical needs were not neglected. The Army provided cheap meals for the hungry, cheap coal for heating, shelters for the homeless, rescue homes for reformed prostitutes, and halfway houses for released prisoners.

Booth, known as "General," ruled the organization as a benevolent autocrat. By the time he died in 1912, he was one of England's—and the world's—honored citizens.

Prayer: Lord, let us never forget "the least of these" that Christ commanded us to serve. Amen.

April 11 · A Fresh Wind of Freedom

How good and pleasant it is when brothers live together in unity!

PSALM 133:1

1689: Do political freedom and religious freedom go hand in hand? It certainly seemed that way in 1689 when England's new rulers, William III and Mary II, husband and wife, issued a Bill of Rights guaranteeing political freedom and signed a Toleration Act granting religious freedom. Their coronation on April 11 began a new era in England.

A bit of background is essential here: churches that were not part of the Church of England, the state church, were referred to as "Dissenters" or "Nonconformists." For the previous century, these people—Baptists, Quakers, Presbyterians, Congregationalists, Separatists, and others—suffered sometimes mild, sometimes severe persecution. Their houses of worship were occasionally shut down, or their preachers silenced or imprisoned. The 1650s, when Oliver Cromwell and the Puritans were in control, were years of toleration for Dissenters—no doubt because *they* were Dissenters. But persecution of Dissenters returned under King Charles II, partly because Dissenters were blamed for the removal and execution of his father, Charles I. Even in times when persecution was mild, Dissenters were not allowed to hold public office or attend a university.

The Toleration Act of 1689 ended, for all time, real persecution of Dissenters in England. They still had to pay taxes to support the Church of England, and they had to swear an oath of allegiance to the rulers, but the restrictions on worship and preaching were gone. People loyal to the Church of England still regarded Dissenters with mild suspicion, but they were no longer regarded as dangerous. The old idea of "one nation, one church" had been a long time in dying. After many turbulent years, the English would finally realize that different denominations could exist peacefully together. Across the Atlantic the American colonies were learning the same lesson, and in time would decide that a nation did not even need a state church.

Prayer: Father, we thank you for the freedoms we possess, freedoms our ancestors too often were not granted. Their faith during times of intolerance is an inspiration to us. Amen.

The trouble he causes recoils on himself.

PSALM 7:16

1630: Never did a king and a church leader work better together than Charles I of England and William Laud, archbishop of Canterbury. They both believed the king had a divine right to rule as he pleased and that all Christians in the country should worship exactly the same way. Both ended up being beheaded by people who did not agree with them.

King Charles's reign began in 1625 and like his father, James I, he had a lofty view of kingship. One of his faithful servants was William Laud who moved up the career ladder by agreeing with the king. Laud believed in the policy of "Thorough"—he wanted all churches in England to use the same form of worship with no unlicensed church meetings. He hated the Puritans in England, fearing that their "meetings" and "lectureships" might lead to trouble. He submitted to the king a list of all the clergy in England—labeling them with an "O" for "orthodox" and "P" for "Puritan." To be a "P" was to be on the king's black list.

The Puritans liked serious exposition of the Bible in preaching. Laud thought worship was more a visual matter—stained glass, beautiful robes for clergy, incense, etc. To the Puritans, all this was mere fluff.

On April 12, 1630, Charles made Laud head of Oxford University. A few years later Charles made Laud archbishop of Canterbury, head of the English church, and Laud used his power to harass the Puritans. He went too far when he tried to make the Church of Scotland use the same ritual as the Church of England. A riot ensued, igniting the English Civil War. Before it was over, Charles and Laud were convicted of treason and beheaded.

England's Civil War might never have taken place if Laud and Charles had tolerated the Puritans and not pressured churches into ritualistic worship. For the sake of conformity and ritual, a country was torn apart.

Prayer: Lord, make us instruments of peace and compassion in a world of strife and persecution. Amen.

April 13 · The Great Hallelujah

I will praise God's name in song.

Psalm 69:30

1742: The most-loved classical music work of all time premiered on this date: George Frederick Handel's *Messiah*, performed as a charitable benefit in Dublin, Ireland. The composer, known as a fast worker, completed the work in twenty-four days and created something that is destined to live forever.

In his younger days Handel's main claim to fame was composing operas—a German, living in England, writing operas with Italian words. Later in life he turned to writing oratorios—choral works in which soloists sang the parts of people from the Bible. His oratorios include *Saul, Israel in Egypt, Solomon, Esther*, and *Samson*. Their rhyming lyrics were not always of high quality. But the words of *Messiah* are inspired, literally, for they are all taken directly from the Bible. Handel's collaborator, Charles Jennens, arranged verses from the Old and New Testaments to tell the story of Christ's birth, death, resurrection, and triumph at the end of time.

When penning the music for the great "Hallelujah Chorus" (with words from Revelation), Handel was so caught up in emotion that he thought he saw heaven open and the face of God himself. When an English earl told Handel that the audience found *Messiah* to be "a fine entertainment," Handel replied, "My lord, I did not mean to entertain them, I meant to make them better men and women." Whether he accomplished this is open to debate, but certainly many believers have had their faith deepened by Handel's masterpiece. Handel's age, like our own, was one in which it was fashionable to mock religion, yet people continue to be drawn to a faith that can produce such powerful works as *Messiah*.

England's King George II attended a performance of *Messiah* and stood during the "Hallelujah Chorus," a tradition that continues to this day. Perhaps the king sensed there was something sublime in such words and music that deserved such a gesture of respect and awe.

Prayer: Almighty God, thank you for the power of music to draw us nearer to you. Amen.

April 14 · PENTECOST II

"No one can enter the kingdom of God unless he is born of water and the Spirit."

JOHN 3:5

1906: The *Los Angeles Times* ran a story, "Weird Babel of Tongues," reporting on a strange phenomenon that began on this date: "Meetings are held in a tumbledown shack on Azusa Street, and the devotees of the weird doctrines practice the most fanatical rites, preach the wildest theories, and work themselves into a state of mad excitement." What the *Times* described in such derogatory terms is regarded by Christians, particularly Pentecostals, much more favorably, for the so-called Azusa Street Revival is considered the beginning of the modern Pentecostal movement.

The meetings at the "shack" (actually a large two-story building) were led by William J. Seymour, a black Holiness preacher recently arrived from Houston, calling on believers to be "sanctified" and "baptized in the Holy Spirit." Sitting on benches made of planks, the congregation at 312 Azusa Street prayed, spoke in tongues, testified, wept, and sang. The meetings were not advertised, and yet (perhaps aided by the publicity given by the *L.A. Times*) more and more people flocked to the meetings. The congregation finally took on a name, Apostolic Faith Gospel Mission, and its revival continued for three years with people from across the United States and even from overseas joining in the Spirit-led worship. The Mission launched a newspaper, *Apostolic Faith*, with the first headline reading "Pentecost Has Come."

Great things have humble beginnings. William Seymour was the son of slaves, and 312 Azusa Street was a former warehouse with bare wood floors and nothing remotely church-like, not even a pulpit. And yet the Spirit was moving, and by May 1906 more than 1,500 people were crowding in—white, black, Asians, Hispanics. To the *L.A. Times* this was the "newest religious sect" with "strange utterances" and "a creed which no sane mortal could understand." The *Times* was behind the times—the Spirit was moving, and churches in every corner of the globe would be affected by what began on Azusa Street.

Prayer: Father, thank you for your Spirit and for his awesome works in revitalizing your church worldwide. Amen.

When I called, you answered me; you made me bold and stouthearted.

PSALM 138:3

1892/1983: By an interesting coincidence, one of the most-read Christian authors of the twentieth century was born and died on the same date, April 15. This was Cornelia ten Boom, better known as "Corrie," a remarkable and heroic woman.

Born in Amsterdam in the Netherlands, Corrie witnessed Nazi Germany's takeover of her country in 1940. The Nazis were bent on the total extermination of the Jews, and many Jews from the Netherlands disappeared into the Nazis' concentration camps and death chambers. Corrie's family took in numerous Jews, hiding them from the Nazis. Corrie's father, Casper ten Boom, told one Jewish refugee, "In this household, God's people are always welcome." The family also sheltered members of the Dutch resistance movement. As more refugees were taken in by the ten Booms, the family constructed a secret room in the upstairs, in case the Nazis ever raided the home. Building the room required the family to sneak bricks and other material into the house in briefcases and shopping bags. The Nazis raided the house in 1944, and six people were able to hide in the secret room.

The entire ten Boom family was arrested in February 1944, some sent to prison, others to a concentration camp. Corrie's father and one sister died before release. Corrie herself was eventually released, due to a clerical error—or, as she knew, the hand of God. Shortly after she left the camp, the other women prisoners were all killed.

Corrie's remarkable story was told in the popular books *The Hiding Place* and *Tramp for the Lord*. It was a story not only of the war years but the aftermath, including an encounter with a Nazi guard she knew from the concentration camp, in which she was able to forgive this man who had seemed the embodiment of evil. Her story reminds us that confronting great evil is the Christian's opportunity to do great good.

Prayer: Lord, give us the courage to resist evil, and to see difficulties as opportunities to do good. Amen.

April 16 · FUNERAL MASSACRE

The enemy has a sword, and there is terror on every side.

JEREMIAH 6:25

1925: For many centuries it was understood among Christians that churches were sacred spaces that had to be respected. It was wrong to assault, murder, rape, or steal in any place, but to do such things in a house of God was not only a crime but a sacrilege. The pagan Vikings in the Middle Ages had no scruples, so they often looted churches and killed the clergy, but as Europe became more Christianized, most people looked upon churches as "crime-free zones."

That changed radically with a new ideology called Communism. The Communists did not believe in God, and they regarded all religions as foolish superstitions that stood in the way of human progress. They had no qualms about harming churches—or the people inside them.

In April 1925 in Bulgaria, a Communist had assassinated General Konstantin Georgiev. The general's funeral was planned for April 16—which was Maundy Thursday that year—at St. Nedelya church in Sofia, Bulgaria's capital. The Communists smuggled in fifty-five pounds of explosives. At the funeral the church was packed with government officials paying their last respects. Shortly after the service began, the explosives were detonated. The church's dome collapsed, burying the people inside. About 123—many from the upper echelons of Bulgaria's government—were killed, about 400 wounded.

More deaths followed when the government declared martial law and executed suspected conspirators. As the Communists had hoped, their act of violence provoked a government response of violence—giving the Communists justification for more crimes. Most of the conspirators found refuge in the Soviet Union which had earlier given its approval to the plot. A new age of barbarism and terrorism, conducted on an international scale, had arrived. At the end of World War II, Bulgaria found itself a satellite of the Soviet Union, its government run by Communists, and the centuries-old Bulgarian Orthodox church barely tolerated. In this new world no place and no person were sacred.

Prayer: Father, give your people steadfast minds and quiet hearts in this world of violence. Amen.

April 17 · A Slave of God

"The Son of Man did not come to be served, but to serve, and to give his life as a ransom for many."

Matthew 20:28

1625: "The worst enemies of the Church are her unworthy priests." So said Vincent de Paul who proved himself a friend of the church by being a *worthy* priest, one whose life story was colorful enough for him to be the subject of an important French film, *Monsieur Vincent*.

Vincent was born around 1580 to a family of French farmers. He became a priest, but in 1605 a ship he was traveling on was raided by Muslim pirates who sold him into slavery in Tunis, North Africa. For a time he endured the horrors of being a galley slave, chained to an oar in a Muslim ship. He escaped in 1607 after converting his Muslim owner to Christianity. Back in France he became chaplain to the queen, Marguerite, a cultured but promiscuous woman whom the king eventually divorced.

Having ministered at the immoral court, Vincent found his true calling in a much different area. On April 17, 1625, he founded the Congregation of the Mission, an order of priests ministering to poor country folk. The order is generally known as the Vincentians in his honor. DePaul University in Chicago is one of several schools run by the Vincentians.

As one who knew the horrors of slavery, Vincent also devoted much of his energy to ransoming the Christian slaves of Muslims, especially the galley slaves. Distressed by the low moral and intellectual levels of so many priests, he helped establish seminaries to train more worthy men. Within a century, a third of all French priests had been trained at Vincentian schools. He also founded the Sisters of Charity, an order of nuns dedicated to nursing. They and the Vincentians both ministered to the many victims of the Thirty Years' War in the 1600s.

Dying at the age of eighty, Vincent had accomplished much. In 1885 the Catholic Church declared him the patron saint of all charitable societies.

Prayer: Lord, animate our hands and feet and wills with a passion to serve others. Amen.

"A time is coming when anyone who kills you will think he is offering a service to God."

JOHN 16:2

1587: Martyrdom, or the threat of it, was something John Foxe knew about first-hand. In the 1540s he began writing a book about Christian martyrs in England, and in 1553 he and his wife fled England and went to live in Europe, because as Protestants they feared persecution under the new Catholic queen, Mary I. Among the Protestants executed by Mary was Foxe's old friend Nicholas Ridley, whose martyrdom would be recorded in Foxe's 1563 book *Acts and Monuments of These Latter and Perilous Days*, which quickly became known as *The Book of Martyrs*. A big book adorned with illustrations, it became a bestseller, and every Protestant home was sure to have two books: the Bible and Foxe's book.

Like the authors of the Bible, Foxe was writing history with a purpose—that is, he was writing to inspire, but he was obsessive about getting the facts right, and over time he revised his book, adding new material and making corrections. Foxe understood that the glory days of the faith did not end with the New Testament, for there were still holy people willing to make the ultimate sacrifice for their faith. Foxe had a way with words and could make a saint's death scene very moving. Nowhere was this more true than his account of the burning of his friend Nicholas Ridley who was executed along with Hugh Latimer, whose words have been often quoted: "Be of good cheer, Master Ridley, and play the man, for we shall this day light such a candle in England as I trust by God's grace shall never be put out."

Foxe was a saintly man, one who tried to intervene to prevent both Protestants and Catholics from being executed by Queen Elizabeth I. When he died on April 15, 1587, he left behind many admirers and a book loved by English-speaking people around the world.

Prayer: Lord, in this dark and fallen world we thank you for the light given by the lives of your saints. Amen.

April 19 · Feast of Barbarians

"In this world you will have trouble. But take heart! I have overcome the world."

JOHN 16:33

1012: Denmark has been a peaceful nation for many years, but it certainly wasn't in the Middle Ages when the Danes were notorious raiders of coastal towns throughout Europe, pillaging, looting, killing the men, and raping the women. As pagans, they had no respect for Christians, and many a church was looted by these fearsome people.

One who suffered at their hands was Alphege, born around 954, a holy hermit who was so renowned for his sanctity that he was made head of a monastery at Bath, England. He became the bishop of Winchester, and it fell to his lot to confirm a converted Viking, Olaf Tryggvason, into the faith. In the future his relations with the Scandinavians would be less pleasant.

In 1006 Alphege was made archbishop of Canterbury, the head of the English church. Five years later the Danes raided Canterbury, looted the city, burned the cathedral, and held Alphege captive for seven months. The Danes assumed that the English would pay a hefty ransom to get their archbishop released, but Alphege himself would not hear of it, believing his people had endured enough hardship already. On April 19, 1012, the Danes, very drunk with wine, tied him to a stake and began pelting him with the bones of cattle—in effect, stoning him. One Dane, named Thrum, a convert to Christianity, took pity on the bleeding man and brought him to a quick and merciful end with the stroke of an ax. Alphege was the first, though not the last, archbishop of Canterbury to die a violent death.

A curious thing happened a few years later: Canute, a Christian and king of both England and Denmark, had Alphege's body moved from his place of martyrdom back to an honored grave in Canterbury. When most of the Danes became Christian, they, like Canute, honored Alphege as a saint, a compensation for the abominable behavior of their ancestors.

Prayer: Holy God, our lives are in your hands. Be with us as we face an often hostile world. Amen.

Send forth your light and your truth, let them guide me.

PSALM 43:3

1939: In the 1800s science seemed to be on the rise and faith on the wane. The Book that people had regarded for centuries as divinely inspired was being doubted in every way, sometimes by the clergy who in times past worked to build up faith, not tear it down. But the new science of archaeology proved to be an ally of faith, not the enemy. The Bible spoke of a people called the Hittites, and no evidence had been found that they ever existed—until, amazingly, archaeologists discovered there really were Hittites.

One of the greatest archaeologists, William Ramsay of Scotland, died on this date. He had studied religion at German universities, which in the 1800s were hotbeds of doubt. But in the late 1800s, as he spent time digging in ancient ruins in the Middle East, Ramsay grew less and less skeptical about the Bible. In 1893 he published *The Church in the Roman Empire Before A.D. 170* and in 1895 his best-known book, *St. Paul the Traveler and Roman Citizen*, one of the great books on the apostle. The German universities had taught Ramsay that the book of Acts had little real history in it and that it was written around the year 150, more than a century after the events it describes, but Ramsay's archaeological findings taught him otherwise.

Ramsay for years was a professor of archaeology at Oxford, and, strictly speaking, he was not a specialist in the Bible. But his research into the world that the apostles inhabited influenced a new generation of Bible scholars who were learning to take the Bible seriously as history. So highly regarded was his work that in 1906 King Edward VII knighted him, making him Sir William.

Before he became Sir William, a more important change occurred in Ramsay's life: he had been an atheist but became a Christian. Science led him to embrace the Bible, not reject it.

Prayer: Father, in this confused and confusing world, anchor us in your truth. Amen.

In all these things we are more than conquerors through him who loved us.

ROMANS 8:37

341: Iran, also called Persia, has been Muslim for so many centuries that people forget that it once had a large Christian population. We learn from the Old Testament books of Daniel, Ezra, Nehemiah, and Esther about the Jews who lived in exile in Persia, and when Christianity began to spread from Jerusalem, inevitably it reached some of these Persian Jews. Persia's native religion was called Zoroastrianism with its belief in one good God, a Satan-like evil spirit, and heaven and hell. Clearly it had some similarities to both the Jewish and Christian religions, so many of the people converted to Christianity.

The story of Christianity in Persia is not all rosy, however. Persia was on the eastern border of the Roman Empire, and the two mighty empires often clashed. A curious pattern developed: when Christians were being persecuted in the Roman Empire, they were treated well in Persia. When the Romans eased up on the persecution, the Persians treated Christians badly. There were always people in Persia who eyed the Christians with suspicion, especially when Rome and Persia were at war, for Christians were suspected of being loyal to Rome.

The big change came when Constantine legalized Christianity in the Roman Empire in 313. As time passed, Christianity became more and more the majority religion of the Romans—and thus was more and more frowned upon in Persia. The great Persian persecutor was King Shapur II who reigned until his death in 379. Shapur tolerated no religion except Zoroastrianism, so Christians had three choices: convert to Zoroastrianism, flee the country, or die. Thousands were executed, many by crucifixion, a form of execution the Persians had invented. The saintly bishop Simeon Barsabae was falsely accused of corresponding with the Roman emperor, and on April 21, 341, Simeon was one of thousands of Christians tortured, then beheaded. Centuries later, the Zoroastrian religion would itself face persecution by Muslims.

Prayer: Lord, your martyrs shame us by their steadfastness. Let us never forget them. Amen.

April 22 · Opportunity Missed

Let us put aside the deeds of darkness and put on the armor of light.

ROMANS 13:12

1418: The church, since it is made up of human beings, sometimes does bad and foolish things. Sometimes it tries but fails to correct itself.

Consider the situation of Europe in 1414: there was not one pope, but three, each claiming to be the legitimate one (a situation known as the Great Schism). Sigismund, ruler of Germany, decided to end this embarrassing situation by calling a council of church officials from all over Europe, and the council assembled in Constance in southern Germany in November of 1414. One pope, John XXIII, agreed to step aside if the other two would—but another, Benedict XIII, refused, so the council deposed him. Meanwhile, John XXIII fled the council and declared it had no authority without him, but the council decreed its authority was from God and did not need a pope to approve its decrees. It deposed John, then the third pope, Gregory XII, abdicated willingly. A new pope, Martin V, was elected

The council established the rule that councils of the church were to be called regularly to deal with issues—a worthy rule that was, alas, not adhered to. The council did two things that reform-minded Christians were horrified by: condemned and burned the reformer John Huss of Bohemia, and condemned, several years after his death, the English reformer John Wycliffe. In other words, a large council called to reform the church ended up accomplishing little except condemning two sincere reformers as heretics. The only worthy accomplishments of the Council of Constance which wrapped up on April 22, 1418, were ending the Great Schism and putting one man, a fairly decent one, on the pope's throne. A century later, reform would come—not from a council but from Martin Luther and his followers breaking away from a corrupt church. The message of the Council of Constance was that the church was not going to correct its own abuses.

Prayer: Father, when your children stumble, set them again on the path of righteousness. Amen.

April 23 · LIGHTING UP JAPAN

"Whoever wants to become great among you must be your servant."

MARK 10:43

1960: Christianity has always had a difficult time in Japan, but one benefit of this is that very few Japanese Christians have been lukewarm. One of the most zealous believers to come from that nation died on this date after a life of selfless service and frequent harassment. Toyohiko Kagawa was born in Kobe, Japan, in 1888, the son of a promiscuous businessman and a concubine. Both parents died when he was young, and he was taken in by two American missionaries who taught him English and converted him to Christianity.

While studying at a seminary, he became disgusted with the endless debates over minor points of theology. He was convinced that the goal of Christianity was to serve others, not to quibble over theology. After studying in the United States awhile, he returned to Japan, living in slums and serving as both missionary and social worker. His activism led to more than one arrest, but he made a deep impression in 1923 while ministering to victims of an earthquake. Working with labor unions, he was disturbed at the role of Communism in the unions, and he and his followers formed the Kingdom of God Movement, rooted in the Bible not in any political ideology.

He and his associates worked to give all Japanese men the right to vote, then later extended the vote to women. When Japan occupied China in 1940, his criticism of the Japanese government landed him in jail again. After his release he went to the United States in a futile attempt to prevent war between the United States and Japan. Amazingly, in his very busy life he managed to write one hundred and fifty books.

Kagawa wrote, "I read in a book that a man called Christ went about doing good." Kagawa himself had no intention of "just going about." All who knew him knew that he, like Christ, dedicated himself totally to doing good.

Prayer: Father, teach us to go about doing good, to use ourselves up in service to you and to our neighbors. Amen.

April 24 · GOD BETWEEN THE LINES

Whatever you do, work at it with all your heart, as working for the Lord.

COLOSSIANS 3:23

1731: One of the world's most famous books happens to be a *Christian* book, though most people think of it as an adventure story. It is *Robinson Crusoe* by Daniel Defoe, published in 1719. The many "adaptations" of the book for children leave out the religious parts, so few people are aware that in the story of a shipwrecked English sailor, God is one of the main characters. As Crusoe narrates his story, he reveals that he had been a worldly man, but after being stranded alone on an island, he finds that his Bible becomes his most treasured possession, and he studies it daily, while he finds that the money he salvages from his ship now has no value to him at all. Later in the book he encounters the cannibal whom he names Friday and whom in time he converts to Christianity. Though it is indeed a fine adventure story, it is also the story of a man whose adversities teach him to rely on God. Religious conversions are prominent in some of Defoe's other novels as well.

Daniel Defoe's family were Dissenters—Christians who were not members of the Church of England—and since Dissenters could not attend the British universities, Defoe was schooled at one of the Dissenting academies. He was an avid supporter of King William III who ended the persecution of Dissenters. After William's death, the next ruler, Queen Anne, took a hard line against Dissenters. Defoe wrote a satirical pamphlet titled *The Shortest Way with Dissenters*, mocking the way the Church of England looked down on and harassed Dissenting Christians. It made him money—and also got him into trouble with the law, and for the first, but not the last, time in his life he went to prison.

Defoe died April 24, 1731, after a life in commerce, writing—and prison. Though a man of the world, he saw the world through Christian eyes, and this affected everything he wrote.

Prayer: Lord, whatever we do, we dedicate to you. Amen.

April 25 · A New Wave of Preaching

Their voice goes out into all the earth, their words to the ends of the world.

PSALM 19:4

1887: When Charles E. Fuller was born on this date, radio did not exist—nor motion pictures or television. In the 1880s "mass communications" meant speaking to a large crowd, like some of the noted evangelists of the day, D. L. Moody being one, who drew huge crowds. Radio changed everything, beginning in 1921 when Paul Rader began preaching by radio in Chicago. A few years later a newly ordained Baptist minister in the Los Angeles area wondered if he too could reach more people via radio. That was Fuller, who in 1930 began broadcasting the Sunday evening services from his church. In October 1937 he began broadcasting *The Old-Fashioned Revival Hour* in front of a studio audience—an audience that eventually outgrew the studio, requiring the show to be moved to a municipal auditorium. As part of the Mutual radio network, the show was heard nationwide. No one could have predicted in 1937 that the show would air until 1968, the year Fuller died.

Fuller had entered the ministry by a curious route: he taught a Bible class in a Presbyterian church, and it drew so many people that it had to be moved from the church to the city hall. Feeling the call of God, Fuller was ordained (switching denominations first) and pastored a Baptist church for eight years before going into full-time radio ministry. Thanks to radio, God had given him a much larger parish than he had ever expected. Response to the broadcasts eventually required him to establish the Fuller Evangelistic Association. Fuller hoped to train new ministers, and in 1947 Fuller Theological Seminary opened, destined to become one of the leading evangelical training grounds.

Listeners loved Fuller's folksy sermons and the show's music, and recordings were made of both. Thanks to the advent of the Internet, a communications medium Fuller did not foresee, *The Old-Fashioned Revival Hour* has found a new life as Internet audio.

Prayer: Father, thank you for everything that helps to spread your word. Amen.

April 26 · STEELY DEDICATION

Come, my children, listen to me; I will teach you the fear of the LORD.

PSALM 34:11

1806: Shipwrecks and missionaries seem to go together, beginning with the book of Acts where Paul survives a shipwreck on his way to Rome. Scotch missionary Alexander Duff, born on this date, lived through not one but two shipwrecks. When he was twenty-three, he and his bride were sailing to India when their ship was wrecked off the coast of South Africa. They survived with no possessions except a Bible and Psalm book. Lost were the many books Duff intended to use in his missionary work. They set forth again, survived another shipwreck, and finally reached India in 1830, where they opened a school in the teeming city of Calcutta. India was, and still is, a nation of hundreds of different languages. In his school Duff instituted a simple and sensible rule: make English the common language of all pupils.

Some missionaries begin by preaching the gospel and trying to make converts. Duff tried a different approach: teach the normal subjects that would be taught in school from a Christian viewpoint—and pray that in time some students will be drawn to convert. Schools like Duff's, known as the "Scots colleges," were respected for their high academic standards and were seen as a civilizing influence. Unfortunately, the conversions that Duff hoped for were few and far between. Hindus seemed to gladly absorb a European education without embracing the Europeans' religion.

Duff represented a new type of missionary, not so much evangelist as teacher. Such people did (and still do) a great deal of good in the world, and many fine schools in Asia, Africa, and South America were originally founded by missionaries. Whether Christians should engage in such work or concentrate on evangelism is open to debate. What is not open to debate is the gritty dedication and self-sacrifice of people like Alexander Duff.

Prayer: Lord, we praise and thank you for those who spread the joys of learning. Amen.

April 27 · THE MORAVIAN CONNECTION

He was a good man, full of the Holy Spirit and faith.

ACTS 11:24

1775: "Preach faith till you have it; and then, because you have it, preach faith." Peter Böhler spoke these words to John Wesley, a minister of the Church of England who was uncertain about his own spiritual condition. Böhler, born in Germany, was a minister of the Moravian church and a close friend of the Moravians' founder, Count Zinzendorf. In 1738 Böhler was in London preparing to sail as a missionary to America, and he met Wesley who had just spent two years in America. The two became friends, and Wesley admired Böhler's sincere faith. While Wesley was helping Böhler to learn English, the two men had conversations on the nature of faith. Böhler sensed that Wesley hadn't fully grasped the key belief that salvation was through faith, not works, and no man could earn his salvation. The chats with Böhler prepared the way for Wesley's famous Aldersgate experience in which his heart was "strangely warmed," and he was sure he was a saved man.

Böhler also influenced the other Wesley, Charles. Very sick and fearing he was about to die, Charles conversed with Böhler who asked him, "For what reason do you hope to be saved?" Charles replied, "Because I have used my best endeavors to serve God." Böhler shook his head: no, salvation was from faith, not from our "best endeavors." Charles did not die of his illness, but he did soon begin a new life, assured of his salvation.

Böhler took the gospel to Georgia and the Carolinas, preaching to the white settlers, slaves, and native Indians. The Georgia officials booted the Moravians out, and they settled in more tolerant Pennsylvania. Böhler was renowned as both a preacher and spiritual counselor, and in time he became the bishop of all Moravian churches in England and America. The Moravians honor Böhler as a church-planter, and Methodists honor him for his role in the Wesleys' lives. All Christians should honor him as a true saint.

Prayer: Lord, increase our faith and give us power to move mountains. Amen.

Let us meet together at the place of judgment.

ISAIAH 41:1

1952: "We are a religious people whose institutions presuppose a Supreme Being." That sentiment was voiced by the U.S. Supreme Court on this date, ruling on the case *Zorach v. Clauson*. The issue: New York City was allowing public school students release time, during school hours, to participate in religious instruction off campus. The Supreme Court ruled that this practice could continue, for it did not establish a religion nor violate the principle of separation of church and state. The Court affirmed that there is "no constitutional requirement which makes it necessary for government to be hostile to religion."

Most people of faith would support the Court's ruling in this case. The reference to "religious people" who believe in a "Supreme Being" is interesting, for earlier Court decisions went further: as recently as 1931, in *U.S. v. Macintosh*, the Court had stated that "we are a Christian people . . . acknowledging with reverence the duty of obedience to the will of God." What happened between 1931 and 1952? Were there more non-Christians in America in 1952? (Probably.) Was the Court in 1952 less certain that Americans were "a Christian people"? (How could anyone know for certain?)

Change continued to be reflected in the 1965 case *U.S. v. Seeger*. In its ruling, the Court broke with all precedent and stated that young men claiming to be conscientious objectors to the draft did not have to believe in God. Their objector status could be based on a "sincere and meaningful belief," which "parallels" belief in God. Prior to this, most conscientious objectors were members of "peace churches," such as Quakers and Mennonites which for centuries had required their members to abstain from war.

In 1931 we were "a Christian people." In 1952 we shared a belief in a "Supreme Being." In 1965 any "sincere and meaningful belief" was as acceptable as belief in God. It seems there was a slide into secularism. We have yet to see where the continual slide will lead.

Prayer: Father, we put our destiny in your hands, certain that you will keep us safe no matter what laws we live under. Amen.

April 29 · LOVE AND BOLDNESS

Never be lacking in zeal, but keep your spiritual fervor, serving the Lord.

ROMANS 12:11

1380: People think of the Middle Ages as a time when the entire church was wealthy, powerful, corrupt, and oppressive with the Inquisition eager to persecute suspected heretics. This is far from the whole truth, for there was no shortage of saints who believed it was their calling to be imitators of Christ.

Consider Catherine of Siena, who died on this date. Born into a wealthy Italian family in 1347, she was deeply religious from an early age, and much of her youth was spent in solitary meditation and prayer. She emerged from her solitude and began an active life of service. An epidemic of the bubonic plague, the "Black Death," had caused thousands of deaths in Siena, and she ministered to the dying and bereaved, and—according to witnesses—at times performed miracles of healing. She also ministered to prisoners and on one occasion converted a man about to be executed.

She was highly regarded as a spiritual counselor, and she put her counsel into letters, some going to humble folk, others to statesmen and high officials in the church, including the pope himself. The pope at the time, Gregory XI, was as much politician as pope, and more than once Catherine advised him to end his wars and begin living like a true Christian. Instead of being offended—or throwing her in prison—Gregory treated her well.

Catherine lived in a time of factional fighting. The Great Schism occurred, the scandalous situation of having two rival popes—one in Rome, one in the French city of Avignon. Catherine journeyed to Rome, hoping to end this quandary. She died in the city at the tender age of thirty-two.

Catherine's short life was a curious mixture of solitary prayer and meditation, ministering to the sick and prisoners, and laboring as a peacemaker in religion and politics. How many people have accomplished so much in so short a time?

Prayer: Father, in this world of suffering and conflict, send us forth armed with compassion and a zeal for peace. Amen.

April 30 · BEHOLD THE MAN

They will see his face, and his name will be on their foreheads.

REVELATION 22:4

1892: How odd that some of the best-known art of the last century was done by a little-known artist. That artist, Warner Sallman, did not mind, for he had the satisfaction of knowing that reproductions of his *Head of Christ* hung in millions of homes, churches, and Sunday school rooms and that his visual image of Jesus was, for so many people, *the* image of Jesus.

Sallman was born of Swedish parents on this date in Chicago, and like many devout Swedish Americans he grew up in the Evangelical Covenant Church. He trained in painting and drawing at the Art Institute of Chicago, later becoming the protégé of a newspaper illustrator.

In 1924 his denomination's magazine, *Covenant Companion*, featured on its cover a charcoal picture of Christ by Sallman, and in 1940 his oil painting of Jesus attracted the attention of the publishing arm of the Church of God, based in Anderson, Indiana, which began the mass-marketing of Sallman's *Head of Christ* and other works. During World War II numerous American servicemen received pocket-sized versions of the picture, distributed by the Salvation Army and YMCA. Baptist Bookstores, operated by the Southern Baptist Convention, helped popularize framed versions of the image to hang in the home. Other Sallman images sold well—*Christ in Gethsemane, The Lord Is My Shepherd*, and *Christ at Heart's Door.* But his *Head of Christ* was a genuine phenomenon, an image that satisfied many people's idea of what Christ must have looked like.

Sallman did not use an actual man as his model. The image came from his own mind, influenced by a friend's statement that the Jesus of the Gospels was a thoroughly masculine man, gentle but also strong, radiating both confidence and compassion. Sallman's Christ appears to be someone who could preach the Sermon on the Mount—and also chastise the Pharisees and endure scourging and crucifixion—Lamb of God, but also King of kings.

Prayer: Lord, steep us in your Word so that we will see more clearly the face of your Son. Amen.

MAY

We know that our old self was crucified with him.

ROMANS 6:6

1911: "The greatest burden we have to carry in life is self," according to Hannah Whitall Smith who died on this date after a productive life speaking and writing. Hannah's autobiography is titled *The Unselfishness of God and How I Discovered It*, although she is better known for another book.

Hannah and her husband, Robert Pearsall Smith, had both been reared in the Quaker faith, but neither found satisfaction in it. After both were converted in a revival meeting in 1858, they sought a fellowship that would bring them closer to the Lord and found their new home in the Holiness movement. Husband and wife both became sought-after speakers at Holiness gatherings, and they even encouraged the forming of Holiness groups in the Quaker churches.

The Holiness movement was a transatlantic phenomenon, and both the Smiths spoke at Holiness conferences in Britain. The Keswick Higher Life conferences, meeting annually in England's lovely Lake District, were the direct outgrowth of the Smiths' speaking engagements.

In a time when most Christian gatherings were dominated by male speakers, the Holiness movement was very open to women as speakers. The Smiths, having grown up among Quakers, were familiar with women speakers since their childhoods because the Quakers allowed women to preach.

Hannah's chief claim to fame is her authorship of *The Christian's Secret of a Happy Life*, published in 1875 and read by millions worldwide. In a sense the book is a commentary on Hannah's favorite verse, Romans 6:6, in which Paul speaks of crucifying the old self. Many readers who agree with Hannah that the greatest burden in life is the self have found release and satisfaction through a closer walk with God. William James, the noted psychologist of religion, was intrigued by the book and said that if he ever became a Christian, he would be the type that Hannah describes in her book. Many people have embraced Hannah's message and become happy Christians.

Prayer: Father, relieve us of the burden of selfishness and teach us to give ourselves up for you and our neighbors. Amen.

May 2 · BISHOP IN TRANSIT

What you have heard from me, keep as the pattern of sound teaching.

2 TIMOTHY 1:13

373: "Now you see him, now you don't" might serve as the title of a biography of the great bishop and theologian Athanasius of Alexandria whose career was filled with exiles and recalls. He was a deacon in the Egyptian city of Alexandria and in 328 became its bishop, meaning he was one of the most high-profile churchmen in the Roman Empire. He was present at the Council of Nicea in 325, which ruled that Christ was of "the same substance" as the Father, not of "similar substance." The second option, ruled a heresy, was called the Arian position. Athanasius strongly opposed Arianism, but several of the Roman emperors supported it, so Athanasius found himself exiled five times by Arian emperors, including one stretch in the Egyptian desert. For the Arians, he was the Great Enemy. For the orthodox, he was Saint and Hero.

Athanasius wrote two great theological books. *Contra Gentiles* (Against the Pagans) is a defense of Christianity, dealing with the criticisms of the pagans. *On the Incarnation* is his explanation of why God became a man and contains his famous statement that God "became what we are that he might make us what he is"—that is, the divine became human so that humans, through salvation, could become divine.

Controversy makes some people mellow, while others become combative. Athanasius became a crotchety, opinionated character, more respected as a defender of the faith than as a Christlike personality. Even so, his services to the church were enormous.

On Easter 367 he sent out an epistle to his flock, and in it he listed the twenty-seven writings that make up the New Testament (Matthew to Revelation). Athanasius's approval aided the acceptance of Revelation, James, 2 Peter, 2 and 3 John, and Jude as being inspired Scripture.

Athanasius died on May 2, 373, an honored leader and a survivor of turbulent times.

Prayer: Father, thank you for those who take a stand for the truth and do not waver. Amen.

May 3 · A Flea for God

Always give yourselves fully to the work of the Lord.

1 Corinthians 15:58

1814: John Wesley, the founder of Methodism, was one of a kind, but when he died in 1791, someone had to take charge of the movement, and for awhile that someone was Thomas Coke. Born in Wales in 1747, Coke was ordained in the Church of England. When he became a follower of Wesley, his irate parishioners booted him out of his church. He was made one of Wesley's chief aides, and in 1780 Wesley put him in charge of the Methodist societies in London. In 1784 Wesley consecrated Coke as "superintendent" of American Methodists, and Coke sailed for New York. At Christmas that year the Americans formed their own denomination, the Methodist Episcopal Church, and Coke and Francis Asbury were named its first bishops. Technically, the Americans were no longer one body with the Methodists in Britain, but spiritually the tie was not broken. Coke crossed the Atlantic several times and after Wesley's death was head of British Methodism for a time.

Coke was widely respected in America, and he met George Washington who invited him to preach before Congress. Coke also traveled to the Caribbean islands, where he was horrified at the living conditions of the slaves. He was constantly preaching wherever he went—the United States, Canada, England, Scotland, France, and Africa. He married a wealthy woman who helped fund the Methodist missions. Methodism had become a truly global phenomenon. In December 1813 Coke set sail for the island of Ceylon (now called Sri Lanka) in Asia. He never reached his destination, dying on May 3, 1814.

Very short (five foot one) and heavy, Coke was called "the flea" by Wesley because of his constant movement from one mission to another. Coke was a worthy successor to Wesley, and it is hard to imagine the history of Methodism without him. His contemporaries remember him as a devout man of God and a true gentleman.

Prayer: Lord, give us the same zeal and the holy energy that the great preachers and missionaries used in your service. Amen.

May 4 · HELL IN PARADISE

I will turn their mourning into gladness; I will give them comfort and joy instead of sorrow.

JEREMIAH 31:13

1873: The Hawaiian Islands are some of the most beautiful places on the earth, but for many years one island, Molokai, looked like the setting for a horror movie—not because of the scenery but because of the inhabitants, who were lepers.

The most famous resident of the Molokai leper colony was born Jozef De Veuster in 1840 in Belgium. Brought up in a devout family, he studied to become a priest and took the name Father Damien. He went as a missionary to Hawaii in 1864, at a time when the islands were still an independent kingdom. Sailors had brought diseases to the islands, including leprosy. Fearing the spread of the dreaded disease, the king confined all lepers to Molokai. Though the government provided food and some supplies, conditions on Molokai were horrible. The church asked for volunteers to minister to the lepers, letting them know that the mission would probably be a death sentence. On May 4, 1873, Damien volunteered.

Conditions were worse than he imagined. The lepers were not only rotting away but had reverted to barbarism with men raping girls and stronger lepers throwing the weaker out of the shelters, which stank horribly. Even after his eyes and nose began to adjust to the lepers, he found them apathetic about everything, unwilling to work to provide clean shelters and fresh water. But in time he won them over, helping them build new huts, laying out a cemetery for proper burials, organizing schools and farms, and reminding them that they were humans, not beasts. And as he had hoped, he led many to Christ.

The inevitable happened: he contracted the disease. Instead of despairing, he stepped up his activity, hoping to do as much as possible before he died. The handsome young man who had arrived there in 1873 was ravaged by the disease, yet when he died in 1889, he was deeply loved. The Catholic Church declared him a saint in 2009.

Prayer: Lord, we praise you for your committed ones whose love knows no boundaries. Amen.

May 5 · Beneath the Veneer

All a man's ways seem right to him, but the Lord *weighs the heart.*

Proverbs 21:2

1813: If you lived in a nation where everyone was a Christian, would you be happy? One who answered "No!" to that question was Søren Kierkegaard, born on this date in Denmark, a small nation in which everyone was (in theory) a Christian. Denmark had a state church which was Lutheran, and people were baptized, confirmed, married, and buried in that church. If you said yes to the basic doctrines of the church, it was assumed you were saved.

Kierkegaard disagreed. In his reading of the New Testament, he saw that being a Christian was a radical step to take. It meant a big choice: Christ or the world—the great *Either/Or*, which was the title of one of his books. Looking at the church in Denmark, Kierkegaard saw a religion that asked little of people and involved no real relationship with God. God was like a professor who stated a set of beliefs and asked people to nod their heads in agreement. Kierkegaard did not believe this was the God of the Bible, the Almighty, the loving Father.

When he was a child, Kierkegaard admired Jacob Mynster, the chief bishop in Denmark, but as he grew older, he saw Mynster as just a government official, a worldly man with no real feeling for the gospel. When Mynster died in 1854, Kierkegaard wrote an article titled "Was Bishop Mynster a Witness for the Truth?" to which the answer was "Definitely not!"

Kierkegaard studied theology for years but was never ordained. He got engaged but broke it off and never married. In his brief life of forty-two years, this troubled but insightful man wrote prolifically, criticizing the church in Denmark but also criticizing the philosophies that fascinated the intellectuals. He died in 1855, unknown outside of Denmark, but in the twentieth century people rediscovered his writings and were moved by his plea to make Christianity a life-changing thing and his exhortations to redeemed sinners to develop an intense relationship with the Lord.

Prayer: Father, let us not be satisfied with lukewarm faith, but only with a burning, Christ-centered faith. Amen.

In the last days scoffers will come, scoffing and following their own evil desires.

2 PETER 3:3

1856: "Only a few patients are worth the trouble we spend on them." So said psychiatrist Sigmund Freud to one of his colleagues. To read a biography of Freud is to discover how much he detested people, yet he wanted to be seen as the scientific savior of mankind.

Freud, born on this date, was raised in a Jewish home but ceased to believe in God at an early age. He described religion as a "neurosis," "poison," and an "illusion" that needed to be exterminated, while he would be the founder of a "new religion of science." There was nothing scientific in his methods, however. Based on no evidence at all, he said it was "obvious" that children were sexual beings from birth. He took the old Greek myth of Oedipus, a man who killed his father and married his own mother, and said that all men, everywhere, secretly wish to do as Oedipus did. Despite having numerous patients—and making a great deal of money from them—there is no evidence he ever cured anyone.

And yet, this vain, confused cocaine addict's ideas changed the world. Obsessed with sex, he made it respectable to talk about sex—and to separate it from emotion, since he described it as nothing but the union of the reproductive organs. He gave people an escape from responsibility—if they were neurotic or confused, it was their parents' fault. In his ideal world an intelligent, "scientific" person would toss aside religion and devotion to parents and would separate sex from love. We might say that Freud created the modern mind.

Freud did not destroy religion, as he had hoped, but he did it a great deal of harm. We wonder what he would make of surveys that show religious people to be happier than those with no religion. The word *poison* he applied to religion seems to apply more to his own twisted, toxic ideas.

Prayer: Father, in a world of destructive ideologies, let our hearts repose in you. Amen.

May 7 · Doubt and Distortion

Even from your own number men will arise and distort the truth.

ACTS 20:30

1851: A man born on this date was considered by some to be an enemy of the gospel—and by others to be the man who kept the gospel relevant for the modern world. He was Adolf von Harnack, the son of a German professor of religion, but the son became far more famous than the father, writing a seven-volume history of Christian doctrine as well as books on Luke, Acts, and the sayings of Jesus. Few people had studied the New Testament more thoroughly or were more familiar with the world in which Jesus and the apostles moved.

Unfortunately, like so many scholars of religion, Harnack's familiarity with the Bible made him respect it *less*. In 1901 he published his most famous—or infamous—book, *What Is Christianity?* A new century was beginning, and Harnack thought the world needed a new interpretation of Christianity. According to him, Jesus and the apostles were products of their own time. Most of the teachings of the New Testament were "timebound" and no longer meaningful for modern man. They were the "husk" that needed to be tossed aside, but there was a "kernel" of truth that was still valid. For Harnack, the kernel was the belief in God as Father and the infinite worth of the human soul. This was the original gospel, the "red thread" that could be traced running through all the "timebound" words of the New Testament.

Understandably, the book horrified many Christians, who were being told the writings they valued and loved were mostly "husk," that miracles were not possible, and that the gospel of John—probably the most loved of the four—had no historical value. Sadly, in his teaching post at the University of Berlin, Harnack influenced a whole generation of pastors. The success of *What Is Christianity?* was kind of an omen of the new century's doubts about the Bible—doubt voiced not by outsiders but by those within the church itself.

Prayer: Father, keep us grounded in your Word and give us discerning minds. Amen.

May 8 · EMMYFIED BISHOP

The Lord announced the word, and great was the company of those who proclaimed it.

PSALM 68:11

1895: A man born on this date won an Emmy award in 1953 for Outstanding Television Personality. He was a Catholic priest whose "act" consisted of standing in front of a chalkboard and speaking to a live audience about the human soul facing the perils of the modern world. Fulton J. Sheen, whom *Time* magazine called "golden-voiced," had hosted *The Catholic Hour* on radio from 1930 to 1950. Beginning in 1950 he took his position at the blackboard as host of the TV series *Life Is Worth Living*—which aired at the same time as Milton Berle's popular show. In the Cold War years, Berle distracted audiences by using riotous comedy, while Sheen didn't hesitate to discuss Communism and the other dangerous "-isms" of the age, but his primary message was more basic: human beings are sinners and need salvation. After winning his Emmy, Sheen quipped that he owed a lot to his four writers—Matthew, Mark, Luke, and John. (Berle quipped that Sheen used "old material.")

Hosting his TV series until 1968, Sheen somehow found the time to write seventy-three books—and to make several high-profile converts, including the writer-politician Clare Boothe Luce.

Television is often a frivolous, shallow form of communication. The popularity of Sheen's programs proved this did not have to be so. As preachers have found throughout the ages, if you speak seriously and clearly to people and act as if they have the power to comprehend great moral matters, you will always find an audience. Sheen's ability as a communicator is remarkable in light of the fact that he was trained to be a professor of philosophy. How many professors have ever communicated so clearly to such huge audiences?

Sheen died in 1979, but his television ministry lives on, for his programs from the 1950s and '60s continue to be shown on several cable channels.

Prayer: Father, your words are weighty and powerful, and we thank you for messengers who spread your gospel with the seriousness and earnestness it deserves. Amen.

May 9 · COMMITTED COUNT

Whoever sows generously will also reap generously.

2 CORINTHIANS 9:6

1760: Aristocrats have usually not been keen on religion, but a handful have used their wealth and influence to grow the faith. Count Nicholas von Zinzendorf was one of these. Born into an upperclass but devout Lutheran home in Germany, Nicholas as a young man purchased an estate called Berthelsdorf which he made into a faith community based on the devotional writings of the Pietists. These were members of the Lutheran church who emphasized a richer, more heartfelt faith, held meetings of small groups for prayer and Bible study, and advocated outreach to the poor.

Most Pietists stayed within the Lutheran church, but Nicholas was one of the many who chose to break free of the state church and form his own denomination. This began when he took in religious refugees from Moravia and Bohemia (today part of the Czech Republic) and allowed them to form a community called Herrnhut on his estate. Most of the people signed his Brotherly Agreement in 1727, and this document is considered the beginning of the Moravian church. Not long after, some immigrated to America and formed communities based on the Agreement in Salem, North Carolina, and Bethlehem, Pennsylvania.

Zinzendorf heard a freed slave speak of the horrible conditions on the Caribbean islands, and in 1732 his community began sending out missionaries to the islands. Some of the missionaries were abused by the islands' plantation owners, which impressed the slaves, who saw the missionaries as embodying the love of Christ. Zinzendorf visited his missionaries in the Caribbean as well as the Moravian communities in the American colonies, laying the groundwork for missions to the Indians. He was unfailingly generous in supporting all his ministries.

Being an aristocrat gave Zinzendorf entry into the halls of power, and his friends included kings, Catholic cardinals, and many other notables. Rarely has a Christian known and influenced so many people of so many nationalities, religions, and social classes. His death on May 9, 1760, was mourned by thousands.

Prayer: Lord, bless those who use their influence and power in the service of others. Amen.

Stand firm in the faith; be men of courage; be strong.

1 CORINTHIANS 16:13

1863: "Arm of Stonewall Jackson, May 3, 1863." So reads a small granite marker in a Virginia cemetery. The marker is a reminder of the reverence that many people felt for the devout and eccentric Confederate general Thomas J. Jackson.

On May 2, 1863, Jackson led his troops to a smashing victory at a site called Chancellorsville. Then, around twilight, Jackson and some aides rode out to reconnoiter the Union army's position. Some Confederate lookouts mistakenly fired on the party, thinking they were Union men. Jackson was struck with three bullets and was taken to a nearby farm. The next day his wounded left arm was amputated. An admirer of Jackson reverently buried the arm. Confederate general Robert E. Lee, hearing of the incident, said of Jackson, "He has lost his left arm, but I have lost my right arm."

Jackson lingered for several days, often delirious from infection. Southerners thought back on the general's quirks, such as his obsession with diet and exercise, his hypochondria, his off-key singing voice, his humorlessness. They thought about his fearlessness and steadfastness in battle, which earned him the nickname "Stonewall." And they thought about his unwavering devotion to his faith, his unquestioning belief that the New Testament was to be obeyed fully. Jackson held a place in people's affections because he was not only devout but a general who won battles, and a real "character" to boot. In two years of Civil War fighting, he had made a reputation for himself. As he lay prostrated with fever, thousands of Southerners prayed for his recovery, knowing his death would be a blow to Confederate morale.

On May 10, 1863, Jackson was mumbling deliriously. Suddenly he spoke clearly: "Let us cross over the river and rest under the shade of the trees." He was dead at age thirty-nine, but no one doubted he had "crossed over the river" to a better place.

Prayer: Lord, give us the boldness and confidence that the true saints possess. Amen.

As the body without the spirit is dead, so faith without deeds is dead.

JAMES 2:26

1621: Nothing is more dangerous to faith than to turn it into something academic. This has happened again and again in Christianity, and it was occurring in the late 1500s among Germany's Lutherans. Martin Luther himself had been a deeply emotional man with both heart and head devoted to God. The second and third generations of Lutherans were finding themselves stuck in a dull orthodoxy—believing much but feeling little.

Johann Arndt, born in 1555, was a graduate of the same University of Wittenberg where Luther once taught. Like Luther, he was fond of an anonymous devotional book from the Middle Ages, *Theologica Germanica*. Arndt wrote his own devotional classic, published in 1606, known in English as *True Christianity*.

In Arndt's lifetime many Christians had come to believe that what made Christianity "true" were the correct beliefs about God, Christ, the Holy Spirit, salvation, heaven and hell, etc. Arndt agreed that correct beliefs were important—but they did not by themselves lead to the rich spiritual life that the New Testament promised. In fact, Arndt said the churches were full of "formal Christians" who had been made members of the church by being baptized as infants and who claimed they believed the basic teachings of Christianity but who showed by their lives that they had never had a conversion experience. If a person did not show by his behavior that he was at least making an effort to model his life on Christ, his religion was a sham. The theologians were correct to talk about what Christ had done *for* Christians. Arndt's book shifted the emphasis to what Christ could do *in* Christians.

Arndt spoke of the believer being "enriched in God," but this could not occur until he realized he was a "stranger and pilgrim in this world." Arndt's earthly pilgrimage ended on May 11, 1621, after he had lived the life he recommended to others.

Prayer: Lord, draw us to a richer life with you, with our eyes fixed on Christ. Amen.

May 12 · HOLY PURSUIT

You uphold me and set me in your presence forever.

PSALM 41:12

1963: One of the Christian classics of the twentieth century is *The Pursuit of God*, written by A. W. Tozer, who died on this date. Tozer, born in 1897, was a pastor in the Christian and Missionary Alliance, a man with no formal theological training yet one of the most-read pastors of the past century. Tozer was a man of simple lifestyle, and though he gained fame from his writings, he and his wife never even owned a car, doing their traveling by bus or train.

Tozer saw a serious need for reform among his fellow evangelicals. Too many of them were leaving their churches on Sunday feeling a vague dissatisfaction. In Tozer's words, "the Presence of God" was not present in most worship services. It disturbed him to "see God's children starving while they were seated at the Father's table." Evangelicals prided themselves on holding to the correct Bible-based beliefs about God, Christ, salvation, and the afterlife, but right belief was not enough to give the Christian life its vitality. Tozer observed that "the devil is a better theologian than any of us," but his knowledge of theology is not *saving* knowledge.

There was more to Tozer's writings than just scolding Christians for their shortcomings. Like any true prophet, he could scold but also inspire. He encouraged readers: "Refuse to be average. Let your heart soar as high as it will." Christians were right to go to church, but Tozer observed that "you can see God from anywhere if your mind is set to love and obey him."

Tozer was known for his preaching as well as his books. He counseled preachers to remember in their sermons that they were speaking on behalf of God. A sermon is not designed to show off the preacher's learning, wit, or eloquence but to change hearts.

This influential but modest man has a simple tombstone: "A. W. Tozer—A Man of God."

Prayer: Father, let your presence be the greatest joy in our lives, now and forever. Amen.

"Blessed are the merciful, for they will be shown mercy."

MATTHEW 5:7

1981: The world was stunned on this date: a Turk named Mehmet Ali Agca fired a semiautomatic pistol in St. Peter's Square in Rome. The target: Pope John Paul II, who took four bullets, two in the abdomen. His bleeding was so profuse that he lost three-fourths of his blood. He eventually recovered after a three-week hospital stay.

The gunman was apprehended quickly by spectators and Vatican security. At thirty-three years old, Mehmet Ali Agca had led a wasted life of petty crime and violence. He had shot a journalist in Turkey in 1979 and been given a life sentence but escaped after only six months. He and a Turkish accomplice entered Rome on May 10 with the intention of killing the pope. Following his attempt on the pope's life, Agca was given a life sentence in an Italian prison.

Shortly after his recovery, the pope asked people to pray for his assassin, whom he had already forgiven in his heart. On December 27, 1983, the pope met privately for twenty minutes with Agca in prison, a gesture of mercy and reconciliation that is truly Christlike. In the coming years the pope also met with Agca's mother and brother.

An assassination attempt of a world figure naturally raises questions about conspiracies. Agca was questioned many times and gave contradictory information, and his motive is still unclear. All that is known for certain is that he had some connection with Bulgaria, a Communist nation at the time. Many people suspected that the KGB, the Russian secret police, had a hand in the plot.

Agca claimed in 2007 that he had converted to Christianity, but many of his statements reveal a severely disturbed man whose word cannot be relied on. We may never fathom what motivated him, but we can fathom John Paul II stretching out a merciful hand to the man who had sworn to kill him.

Prayer: Lord, as Christ on the cross forgave his executioners, so let us forgive whatever our enemies dole out to us. Amen.

May 14 · APOSTLE IN ACADEMIA

"You will know the truth, and the truth will set you free."

JOHN 8:32

1752: Yale University was, long ago, a very religious place. From 1795 until 1817 its president was Timothy Dwight, the grandson of colonial preacher and theologian Jonathan Edwards. As president, Dwight did not sit in his office dictating memos but was often preaching to his students, sometimes on doctrine and ethics but often on the need to repent. Rarely has one man combined so well the roles of academic administrator and revival preacher.

Sin in the human heart is always the key problem that needs addressing. Dwight preached against sin but also spoke out against some of the dangerous "-isms" of the time, such as deism and skepticism. When Dwight was born in 1752, deism was very much the philosophy of many intellectuals in America, including Thomas Jefferson whom Dwight referred to as an "infidel." The French Revolution and the anti-Christian violence it unleashed revealed all too clearly where deism led. (Jefferson himself was horrified at all the violence in France.) For Dwight, religious skepticism and the desire for a political solution to life's problems led to disaster. Democracy in America seemed to be working well enough, and Dwight did not want to see it destroyed by radicals. He was active in both pulpit and politics, one of the key figures in Connecticut's Federalist Party, and also the head of the Congregational church in Connecticut.

In Dwight's day, most college presidents in America and elsewhere were ordained clergy. The idea that a college was a "values-neutral" place was unknown. It was expected that college graduates would be Christian—perhaps in name only, but also, as Dwight hoped, in beliefs and behavior.

If he sounds like a stiff and solemn man, it is worth noting that he was also part of a group called the "Hartford Wits." Even devout men can enjoy times of mirth.

He died in 1817, having influenced hundreds of American preachers and scholars.

Prayer: Father, thank you for outstanding leaders who unite deep knowledge with deep faith. Amen.

May 15 · THE VOICE OF A CENTURY

Boldly and without hindrance he preached the kingdom of God and taught about the Lord Jesus Christ.

ACTS 28:31

1957: On this day the first service in evangelist Billy Graham's sixteen-week New York crusade was held at Madison Square Garden with 18,000 in attendance. Months of planning involved the training of 9,000 counselors and a 1,500-voice choir. Between May 15 and the last service on September 1, the crusade was profiled on all major networks and most major magazines with live radio broadcasts of most services.

June 1, 1957, was a landmark: the first live television broadcast of a Graham crusade, which reached about 6.4 million viewers, convincing Graham that television had great potential in his ministry. Interestingly, he had earlier run his *Hour of Decision* program on ABC for three years with little success, but clearly Graham was not at his best in this studio-bound format. Part of his success on television was that, unlike the typical televangelist, Graham was not seen daily or even weekly, so his face and style did not suffer from overexposure.

Graham became a beloved fixture in American culture, a preacher with a commanding yet likable presence, who was also the friend of presidents from both parties. (Richard Nixon appeared on the podium at a Graham crusade in 1970, but his friendship with Graham was strained as the Watergate scandal unfolded.) In the 1980s when several high-profile evangelicals were the subjects of scandal, Graham maintained his clean image and, indeed, not a hint of scandal has ever attached to him.

His crusades have taken him not just across America but across the world. In 1992 in Moscow, Graham drew a crowd of 150,000, a fourth of which responded to his altar calls—in a country that had been under the thumb of atheism for more than seventy years.

Graham, in failing health, held his last crusade in 2006, though he has appeared at crusades of his son, Franklin. One can only imagine the number of lives he has touched.

Prayer: Father, we honor your messengers just as we honor and embrace your message. Amen.

May 16 · MAID OF HEAVEN

God chose the weak things of the world to shame the strong.

1 CORINTHIANS 1:27

1920: Sometimes the church corrects itself. One correction occurred on this date when the Catholic Church declared that Joan of Arc, who had been burned at the stake for heresy and witchcraft in 1431, was a saint.

Joan's story is proof that truth really is stranger than fiction. In the early 1400s France and England were locked in a conflict called the Hundred Years' War. Because of the intermarrying between royal families in Europe, England's king, Henry V, claimed the French crown and led an English army to conquer France. When he died in 1422, his infant son, Henry VI, was king of both France and England—in theory. In fact, the English only controlled part of France; the French controlled the rest. The French king, the spineless, pleasure-loving Charles VII, showed no sign that he would boot the English out of the entire country.

Enter Joan, a thirteen-year-old farm girl, who told the French court that voices from heaven told her to put on knight's attire and lead the French armies. A panel of theologians examined Joan and declared that she was not a fraud. Joan was able to do what Charles could not, rally the French army and defeat the English. She was at his side when he was crowned.

Joan, alas, was captured by the English and put on trial as a witch. She was told the voices she heard were from Satan, not God. She was tricked into signing a confession but then changed her mind and put her armor back on. The church authorities then treated her as a relapsed heretic and burned her at the stake.

What do we make of Joan? Did she really hear voices from heaven? Does she deserve sainthood? The only certainty is that she was a unique individual who fought for what she believed in with a great deal of courage and conviction.

Prayer: Lord, the courage of Joan gives us all hope that, in you, nothing is impossible. Amen.

Will you not revive us again, that your people may rejoice in you?

PSALM 85:6

1808: Those who have researched their genealogy are aware that in the 1700s and 1800s married couples had *lots* of children. One reason they had so many was that often children died young. In a family where six children lived to adulthood, there were likely two or three who did not make it to age twelve. Families had lots of births—and lots of burials.

Consider the case of Jacob Albright, born in Pennsylvania to German immigrants in 1758 and a veteran of the Revolutionary War. He and his wife had nine children, but in a short span of time, three died. This was not unusual for the times, but it led Jacob to a spiritual crisis, for the Lutheran faith he was raised in brought him no comfort. He found some consolation in a nearby meeting of Methodists, and before long he became an active and powerful lay preacher among other German immigrants. Within a few years he had, without meaning to, converted enough people to form a new denomination which took the informal name "Albright's People." In 1807 the group named Albright its first bishop, although, being a humble man, he disliked the title. Albright died on May 17, 1858, fifty years old, having brought many German Americans into a closer walk with the Lord.

Here was a familiar pattern: a man is raised in one faith, finds it lacking in spiritual vigor, and begins a new reform/revival group that eventually becomes a new denomination.

A few years after his death, Albright's People renamed themselves the Evangelical Association and set down in writing a principle that reflected Albright's aim: "a friendly union of such persons as not merely wish to have the form of godliness, but strive to possess also the power and substance thereof"—in other words, Christians whose faith is a matter of living hourly in relationship with God, not merely showing up for church.

Prayer: Lord, when our faith seems dry and lifeless, revive us inwardly. Amen.

May 18 · Mission to the Heartland

Let the peace of Christ rule in your hearts.

1675: Jacques Marquette, who died on this date, left a deep impression on the American Midwest, for there are towns named Marquette in Wisconsin, Michigan, Illinois, and Iowa. He is remembered as one of the earlier explorers of America's interior, but his goal was not to explore but to carry the gospel to the native Indians.

Born in France, Marquette went as a missionary to Quebec where he showed skill in learning native languages. He traveled to the Great Lakes region where Indians told him of a mighty river, a river so long that none of the Indians knew where it ended. Accompanied by explorer Louis Jolliet, he found the Mississippi in June 1673, and they became the first white men to see this great American waterway. As they traveled south on the river, they realized its great potential for transportation through the interior, both for trade and for evangelism.

Marquette established several mission stations, including one at Sault Ste. Marie in Michigan, the first European settlement in that state. His relations with the Indians were mostly peaceful, and the Illinois Indians in particular were open to the gospel. When he and Jolliet traveled south on the Mississippi, they began to encounter Indians with guns, a sign that the Indians had been dealing with other Europeans, probably the Spanish. Sadly, the rivalries of the European nations that settled America were a hindrance to missionary work.

Perhaps the most interesting aspect of Marquette's story is that he had vowed he would never let fear or anxiety get the better of him, and this was a promise he kept—a remarkable thing for a man in a vast wilderness with few comforts, where natives were unpredictable and often threatening. When he died at the age of thirty-seven, he had made few converts, but his explorations opened up the way for other preachers of the gospel.

Prayer: Lord, your servants endure many trials in this world. Thank you for the peace of heart that allows them to persevere. Amen.

May 19 · God's G.O.M. in Britain

Speak up and judge fairly; defend the rights of the poor and needy.

PROVERBS 31:9

1898: Is it possible to be a Christian while holding high political office? Difficult—but not impossible. The man who died on this date, William Gladstone, was for many years the prime minister of Great Britain. He was a Christian in both his public and private life. In his youth he wished to become a clergyman, but his father persuaded him to enter politics—a choice that greatly benefited his country.

Gladstone was a faithful member of the official state-supported Church of England. Though he was a committed Protestant, he worked to remove some of the restrictions on Catholics in the British Empire. He also labored to grant a measure of self-government to the Catholic Irish but Parliament would not allow it.

In the 1800s the Turkish Empire staged several massacres of its Christian subjects, including the Bulgarians and Armenians. Gladstone spoke out boldly against these atrocities and would not let the public forget that Christians in other lands were being persecuted. He also spoke out against slavery and was glad when it was finally outlawed in the British Empire.

No British politician ever showed more concern for working-class people, and portraits of the G.O.M ("Grand Old Man") were found in many humble homes. He did whatever he could to lower taxes and decrease government spending. Queen Victoria disliked Gladstone who never flattered her as other politicians did, and the upper classes were uncomfortable with his high moral tone, but for most of the British he was the supreme figure in the politics of the 1800s. Despite having many political enemies, he was never accused of bribery, corruption, or dishonesty. When he died, aged eighty-eight, he was given a state funeral, with crowds of mourners paying their respects to this man who combined energy and integrity.

Prayer: Lord, in a world where power is abused so freely, we thank you for men and women of integrity who are able to put their faith to work for the public good. Amen.

May 20 · THE VOWEL COUNCIL

Have nothing to do with foolish, ignorant controversies; you know that they breed quarrels.

2 TIMOTHY 2:23 (ESV)

325: One of the biggest theological battles in the history of Christianity was over a vowel. Is the Son of God of "similar substance" to the Father (the Greek word *homoiousios*) or the "same substance" as the Father (*homoousios*)? That was the critical question at a gathering called the Council of Nicea which began on this date.

The Roman emperor Constantine had made Christianity legal. He had become a Christian himself, and he believed his religion would lead to unity in the empire. He had no use for a divided Christianity, so in 325 he called the chief bishops in the church together at the city of Nicea, not far from his capital, Constantinople.

The debate was over the nature of the Son of God. An Egyptian pastor named Arius held that only God could be God—and so Christ, the Son of God, could not be of the "same substance" as God the Father but was of "like substance." Arius's bishop believed that only God could save mankind from sin, so the Son had to be of the "same substance" as God. This sounds to us like useless nitpicking. All Christians agreed that Christ was the divine Son of God and the Savior of man. Why was it important to determine if he was "like" or "same as" God? Had it only been a theological matter, Constantine could have ignored it. But there were actually fights breaking out between the supporters and opponents of Arius's view.

Hearing the arguments for both sides, the council decided that the Son was the "same substance" (*homoousios*) as the Father. Arius and his supporters were sent into exile. An important precedent had been set: when a major theological dispute arose, the emperor would convene a council to decide things, trusting in the collective wisdom of the church's leaders. Another precedent: the state gave itself the authority to punish people it considered heretics.

Prayer: Father, give us wisdom to determine which battles are worth fighting. Amen.

May 21 · ENLARGED HEART

May the groans of the prisoners come before you; by the strength of your arm preserve those condemned to die.

PSALM 79:11

1780: "Since my heart was touched at seventeen, I believe I have never awakened from sleep, in sickness or in health, by day or by night, without my first waking thought being how best I might serve my Lord." So said the "angel of the prisons," the amazing woman Elizabeth Fry, born on this date to a wealthy Quaker family in England. Her marriage produced eleven children, and despite this overflowing household, she involved herself in ministering to prisoners and working to reform a notoriously inhumane system.

Visiting Newgate Prison, Fry found women and children sleeping on straw in overcrowded cells. Newgate, like most prisons, did not separate violent offenders from the nonviolent, and prisoners included not only those convicted of crimes but those awaiting trial. Many prisoners were "criminals" only in that they had been unable to pay off their debts. Fry published books on her findings and opened England's eyes to the deplorable conditions. She organized groups of women who visited the prisons, read the Bible to prisoners, brought them decent clothing, and taught them to sew.

She and other Christians pressured Parliament to shorten the long list of offenses that could lead to the death penalty. Helping her was her brother-in-law, Thomas Buxton, a Christian member of Parliament. Fry became the first woman to present evidence to Parliament when she spoke of the need for radical change in the prison system.

Fry had many admirers, among them Queen Victoria who met with her several times and gave money to her charities. Robert Peel, who organized London's police force (the "bobbies" are named in his honor), was another admirer.

Although England has become a secular country in recent times, Elizabeth Fry has been honored by having her image on Britain's five-pound note. A more secular world remembers her only as a social reformer, which she definitely was, but Fry herself believed that her charitable work was a way of serving and honoring God.

Prayer: Lord, bless all those who show kindness and love to society's outcasts. Amen.

May 22 · Empathy Empire

Let us not love with words or tongue but with actions and in truth.

1 John 3:18

1786: America in the early 1800s had a network of charitable organizations known as the "benevolent empire," active in such causes as Bible distribution, temperance, missions, and, last but not least, abolition of slavery. One of the prominent men in the benevolent empire was Arthur Tappan, born on this date into a devout Massachusetts family. He and his brother, Lewis, made a fortune in exporting silk, lost the fortune, made another fortune in finance, and they never forgot that God intended people of great wealth to do great things for mankind. There were few noble causes of the 1800s that the Tappan brothers were not associated with.

It is said that slavery is a stain on American history, something that never should have endured in a land where people honored Thomas Jefferson's words about all men being created equal. While this is true, it is also true that at no point did all Americans condone slavery, and many Christians opposed it on religious grounds. Both Tappans were active in the American Anti-Slavery Society, which some Americans regarded as extreme, and at one point Lewis Tappan's home was vandalized. The Tappan brothers understood that it was inevitable that, in time, a Christian nation would abolish slavery. Sadly, it took a bloody war to bring it about, but emancipation did come, and Arthur Tappan died in July 1865, having lived to see emancipation and the end of the war.

The brothers Tappan were more than social activists, for they were supporters of noted evangelist Charles Finney and helped build his enormous Broadway Tabernacle in New York. Finney shared their abolitionist views, as well as their belief that support for evangelism and missions did not exclude support for social change. While their critics sometimes mocked them as meddlesome do-gooders, the members of the "benevolent empire" deserve honor, especially those who, like the Tappan brothers, put their vast wealth to good use.

Prayer: Lord, whatever we possess is from you. Give us opportunities to use it for the glory of your kingdom. Amen.

May 23 · A Sparrow Among the Peacocks

The power of the wicked will be broken, but the LORD upholds the righteous.

PSALM 37:17

1498: Imagine this confrontation: a devout Christian who owns no worldly goods and keeps his vow of chastity versus a wealthy, corrupt, pleasure-loving philanderer—who happens to be the pope.

The setting of this confrontation was Florence, Italy, during the Renaissance. The city was sophisticated, home to some of the greatest art ever produced, but also full of corruption and materialism. Into the city came a preacher, the monk named Girolamo Savonarola, who did not hesitate to tell the people of Florence that the Christianity they professed was a sham. The pious man's words began to hit home, and the city booted out its corrupt ruler and put Savonarola in charge of things. The people put aside their costly clothing and threw their gambling materials and pornographic books and pictures into "bonfires of the vanities." Rich bankers and merchants even returned money they had wrongly earned.

Savonarola's fatal mistake was speaking out against the pope, Alexander VI. No one worse ever held the office of pope, for the money-loving, bribe-taking Alexander was notorious for sleeping with other men's wives and for bestowing church funds on his illegitimate children. In 1495 he ordered Savonarola to stop preaching. A year later the pope lifted the ban, and Savonarola began criticizing him again. Furious, the pope excommunicated him in 1497, but the people of Florence rallied behind their reforming preacher for a time.

But the city's moral reformation had not put down deep roots, and the people returned to their lives of pleasure. An opposition party removed Savonarola from power and handed him over to ambassadors from the pope. On May 23, 1498, he and two associates were burned in the city square. Savonarola, an embodiment of Christianity at its best, had been destroyed by Alexander VI, an embodiment of Christianity at its worst. When the Protestant Reformation began nineteen years later, the Reformers looked back to Savonarola as a saint and martyr.

Prayer: Lord, teach us to see the world through your eyes, to look upon the heart and not on material goods. Amen.

May 24 · A Heart Strangely Warmed

It is with your heart that you believe and are justified, and it is with your mouth that you confess and are saved.

Romans 10:10

1738: On this date John Wesley, an earnest minister in the Church of England, went to a religious meeting in Aldersgate Street in London. According to Wesley's journal, a man at the meeting was reading aloud from Martin Luther's introduction to Paul's letter to the Romans, and as the man was "describing the change which God works in the heart through faith in Christ, I felt my heart strangely warmed. I felt I did trust in Christ, Christ alone, for my salvation." The man who had been frustrated and unhappy in his ministry for many years now realized something crucial: he could touch people's hearts only if his own heart was touched.

Wesley's "heartwarming" is considered the beginning of the Methodist movement, and many Methodist churches today still celebrate Aldersgate Sunday, the Sunday nearest May 24. Following his Aldersgate experience, Wesley and his disciples took the gospel to the fields and factories of England and the frontier of the American colonies. The established Church of England seemed spiritually dead to many people, especially the working classes, but these people responded enthusiastically to the heartfelt preaching of John Wesley and his cohorts.

In the course of his long life, Wesley traveled a quarter-million miles, much of it on horseback, and preached probably forty thousand sermons. He once claimed that "the world is my parish," and indeed his entire life was proof that the gospel is too great a thing to be confined within the walls of any church building. In his long career, Wesley generated much love and admiration—and also hatred and scorn and even some attempts on his life because, like Jesus and the first Christians, his work upset the religious establishment of his day.

Prayer: Lord, thank you for John Wesley and the many others who have felt their hearts warmed by you, who used themselves up in opening up the hearts of others to the message of salvation. Amen.

May 25 · Lighting a Fire in Wales

Our competence comes from God. He has made us competent as ministers of a new covenant.

2 Corinthians 3:5–6

1735: A Welsh schoolmaster was taking communion in his church on this day which was Pentecost Sunday. He felt his heart filled with "the fire of the love of God." Pretty soon he was preaching—not in churches, since he was not ordained, but in private homes. His name was Howell Harris, and his conversion is remembered as the beginning of the great Welsh Revival.

Wales belonged to England, and Harris tried more than once to be ordained in the Church of England, which refused him, considering him too "enthusiastic," meaning too emotional (a charge also leveled at John Wesley). Not to be held back, Harris continued on as a lay preacher for the rest of his life. One who encouraged him to preach was the greatest preacher of the age, the globe-trotting George Whitefield. Possessing a powerful voice and great charisma, Harris drew listeners with his simple, Bible-based sermons. They were also drawn to his emphasis on assurance, the conviction that they were genuinely saved and in a right relation with God. His preaching must have been superb, for when Whitefield toured America, Harris filled in for him at Whitefield's London church. When he was in Wales as a traveling evangelist, he sometimes preached six sermons a day.

In 1750 Harris formed a religious community at his home in Trevecca, Wales, and was known as the "father" of this spiritual family of more than a hundred. Since he and his followers were outside the Church of England's system (meaning they could not be trained at English universities nor ordained), he founded training schools for preachers, aided by the devout Selina Hastings, the Countess of Huntingdon.

When Harris died in 1773, twenty thousand people attended his funeral. He and other Welsh preachers of his time were largely responsible for making Wales the religious country that it remained until well into the twentieth century.

Prayer: Lord, bless the memory of those who preached your word with vigor and boldness. Amen.

One generation will commend your works to another.

PSALM 145:4

735: "My chief delight has always been in study, teaching, and writing." So said a British monk named Bede who died on this date. He was born on the lands of the monastery at Jarrow in northern England, was schooled by the monks there, then became one himself. In the course of his life he read and wrote, and he penned one of the few books from the Middle Ages that is still a joy to read, *History of the English Church and People*. One reason it is such a great book is that Bede seems to have known everything there was to know at the time he lived, and yet he was living at the very fringe of civilization. Respect for his wide knowledge is the reason he is always referred to as the Venerable Bede.

When he came to write his *History*, he wrote it with the same motivation as the writers of the Bible: not just to record facts (although he was fanatical about accuracy) but to show the workings of God in men's lives. He wrote that "if history records good things of good men, the thoughtful hearer is encouraged to imitate what is good. Or if it records evil of wicked men, the religious listener or reader is encouraged to avoid all that is sinful and perverse and to follow what he knows to be good and pleasing to God."

The many stories in his *History* are still engaging. He tells of a bishop named Aidan who traveled about the island on foot, and if he met a pagan, he tried to lead him to Christ, and if he met a Christian, he would speak to him to give him encouragement in the walk of faith.

At the very end of his life, Bede was translating the gospel of John from Latin into Anglo-Saxon. The story goes that he dictated its last chapter lying on his deathbed, dying on May 26, 735.

Prayer: Lord, train our minds to read history and see your hand in its unfolding. Amen.

May 27 · Preaching Pleasure

You have made known to me the path of life; you will fill me with joy in your presence.

PSALM 16:11

1564: "There is not one blade of grass, there is no color in this world that is not intended to make men rejoice." So wrote theologian John Calvin who is remembered as the man who believed in predestination and whose theology was severe and pleasureless. The real man was better than his reputation.

Born in 1509 in France, Calvin studied at the University of Paris where the students' day began at 4 a.m. For the rest of his life, Calvin rose before sunup, worked hard, and pushed himself to the limit. His intense work accounts for his many illnesses and likely for his dying relatively young.

Sometime around 1530 Calvin had a conversion to the Protestant religion. France was hostile to Protestants, so Calvin settled in Geneva, which is today part of Switzerland but then was an independent city-state. Calvin took charge of church reform there, and under his influence Geneva was a magnet for Protestants from all over Europe.

Before he was thirty, Calvin published *Institutes of the Christian Religion*, a masterpiece of theology that has influenced Protestants for almost five centuries. The first chapter begins with a simple but profound idea: to know ourselves, we must know God. When we see that we need salvation and embrace Christ, we find joy and peace in God's presence. It is true that Calvin insisted on high moral standards for Christians. But his theology is far from joyless. In all his many sermons, Bible commentaries, and theological writings, Calvin preached pleasure—the joy of being in loving fellowship with God.

Calvin, who died on May 27, 1564, had ordered that he be buried in a plain wood coffin in an unmarked grave. Though possibly the most famous theologian in the world, he had no interest in being the center of a Calvin cult. His monuments were his writings, composed to lead men to love and enjoy God.

Prayer: Lord, we thank you for the pleasures you give, remembering that the greatest pleasure is you. Amen.

We must obey God rather than men!

ACTS 5:29

1663: Joseph Alleine wrote a bestseller, but he never knew it, since it was published four years after his death. He died in 1668, thirty-four years old, having served two prison terms for being a renegade against the state Church of England. Like many devout pastors in this period of time, he found that obeying God and preaching the gospel often meant persecution—not by atheists or pagans but by church authorities.

Born in 1634, Alleine attended Oxford University where he was such a distinguished scholar that he was offered several high-paying government positions, but he turned down these offers and served as a pastor in southwest England. His parishioners loved him for his learning and his warmth. The Church of England detested the Puritans within its ranks and in 1662 passed the Act of Uniformity, which had the effect of booting more than two thousand Puritan pastors, including Joseph Alleine, out of their pulpits. This episode is known as the Great Ejection, and it was a tremendous loss to the church, depriving it of some of its most committed men. Like some of the others, Alleine, finding himself barred from the pulpit, took to the road as an evangelist, and for unlicensed preaching he was sent to prison on May 28, 1663, enduring a year of abuse. Released in 1664 and certain God wanted him to spread the gospel, he began preaching again and in 1665 again found himself in prison. This second prison term broke his health, and he died in November 1668.

Alleine's posthumous bestseller, published in 1672, was *Alarm to the Unconverted*. Like his contemporary, John Bunyan, Alleine did not let prison turn him into a bitter man, but, on the contrary, prison drew him closer to God, and both men's experiences led them to write books that inspired others. What a pity that their persecutors were men holding high office in the church, men who foolishly thought they were doing the will of God.

Prayer: Lord, many brave hearts have obeyed you no matter what the cost. Let us always honor them and seek to be like them. Amen.

May 29 · Stuffed with Humor and Wisdom

This is the day that the LORD has made; let us rejoice and be glad in it.

PSALM 118:24 (ESV)

1874: People who think Christians are gloomy killjoys should look at English author G. K. Chesterton, born on this date. Chesterton was tall (6′4″), fat (almost 300 pounds), addicted to cigars, and almost always in a good mood with a laugh that could be heard several blocks away. He could be friends with radical thinkers like playwright George Bernard Shaw yet maintain his own commitment to his faith. Shaw, who described Chesterton as "a man of colossal genius," was notoriously thin (he ate little and was a strict vegetarian), and on one occasion Chesterton said to him, "From the looks of you, there must've been a famine." Shaw replied, "From the looks of you, you caused it." Chesterton described a character in one of his books as "a man stuffed with humor," a fitting description of himself.

Chesterton had his serious side, thankfully, and two of the best Christian books of the twentieth century are his *Orthodoxy* and *The Everlasting Man*, which were both admired by C. S. Lewis. Even in books that were not explicitly religious, his faith shines through, such as the popular Father Brown detective stories.

Chesterton was raised in the Church of England, but like many people of his time, he found no spiritual nourishment there, and in 1922 he converted to Catholicism. Though his writings are popular among Catholics, he is equally popular among evangelicals, and many readers with no religious convictions at all enjoy his fiction. He was a respected literary critic and also a cultural critic who could wittily demolish the foolish ideologies of the modern world. Though he held to the Christian view that all men are sinful and that the key problem in the world is human sin, he was not a gloomy pessimist. Though life in the world had many sorrows, Chesterton could write that "the supreme adventure is being born" and "each day is a special gift; something that might not have been."

Prayer: Lord of life, teach us to treasure each day as a gift from you. Amen.

May 30 · CROSSING CHINA

I have made you a watchman for the house of Israel; so hear the word I speak and give them warning from me.

EZEKIEL 3:17

1972: Nee Shu-Tsu is better known to the Christian world as Watchman Nee, a much-read author and one of many Christian martyrs to Chinese Communism. He was born in 1903 to Christian parents, and his grandfather had been a pastor. He made a personal commitment to the Lord when he was seventeen and took the name Watchman, believing God had called him to raise a warning call.

From 1920 until 1952, Nee preached and wrote, often living close to the poverty line and coping with numerous physical ailments. He had no formal theological training but based all his ministry on the Bible itself and a library of Christian books left to him by a missionary friend. He did not belong to or found a denomination, something that endeared him to many Christians and alienated others.

Nee's greatest book, still popular today, is *The Normal Christian Life*, which he based on Paul's letter to the Romans. The brief book *Sit, Walk, Stand*, based on Ephesians, is also popular. In these and other writings, Nee makes the cross of Christ the center of the Christian life.

The author who wrote about suffering knew it firsthand. In March 1952 he was arrested by the Communists who had seized power in China in 1949. Because of his founding of more than four hundred local churches, Nee was a high-profile Christian that the Communists wanted to make an example of. He spent the rest of his life in prison, allowed no visitors except his wife (who had taken the appropriate name Charity). Nee died in his prison cell on May 30, 1972. In the cell was a scrap of paper with these words: "Christ is the Son of God who died for the redemption of sinners and was resurrected after three days. This is the greatest truth in the universe. I die because of my belief in Christ. Watchman Nee."

Prayer: Lord, thank you for sharing in the sufferings of your holy ones. Amen.

Come and see what God has done, how awesome his works in man's behalf!

PSALM 66:5

1594: The Italian painter who died on this date was born Jacopo Robusti, but the world knows him as Tintoretto, Italian for "little dyer" or "dyer's son," for his father was a dyer of fabrics. Many of Tintoretto's contemporaries knew him as *Il Furioso*, the mad one, for he worked with great energy and was known as a "direct" painter, working directly on canvas instead of from preliminary sketches.

Born in Venice in 1518, he was eldest in a large family—twenty-one children. He was mostly self-taught, which is why his paintings resemble no one else's. Like most artists of the time, he painted religious scenes, and since St. Mark was the patron saint of Venice, Tintoretto did several famous pictures of the life of Mark. *Christ Carrying His Cross, The Agony in the Garden, Christ Before Pilate*, and *The Adoration of the Magi* were some of his great works. Like all Christian artists, he painted *The Last Supper*, but his version is much more dramatic than the familiar image of Leonardo da Vinci. Jesus is not seated but is standing and handing the cup of wine to the disciple next to him. An oil lamp in the room gives off smoke that takes the form of translucent angels—theatrical, but unforgettable. *Christ at the Sea of Galilee* is also dramatic, capturing the moment when Peter is setting one foot on the storm-tossed waters.

Tintoretto, when he was seventy years old, painted what is probably the largest religious painting ever done on canvas, *Paradise*, which measures 74 feet wide by 30 feet tall. It shows heaven, crowded with many people, with Christ at the center. Tintoretto could have named his price for the project but did not, for he had never been a greedy man. He told a follower that it was appropriate for a man his age to keep his mind fixed on heaven.

Prayer: Lord, thank you for people of talent who give us glimpses into the story of salvation. Amen.

JUNE

June 1 · MIND OF A MARTYR

Do not conform any longer to the pattern of this world, but be transformed by the renewing of your mind.

ROMANS 12:2

165: The saint known as Justin Martyr was born in the ancient city of Shechem, familiar to readers of the Old Testament. In Justin's day it was known as Flavia Neapolis because, like many towns in Palestine, it had been renamed following the Jewish revolt that the Romans put down so brutally. Raised in a pagan family, Justin knew Jews and Christians, but he sought his spiritual satisfaction in pagan philosophies, especially that of Plato. Like so many mentally restless men of his time, he found in Christianity something that was lacking in other philosophies, a human element seen in good men and women willing to suffer for their faith. This man who admired the martyrs became one himself on June 1, 165: he was scourged and then beheaded after he refused to sacrifice to the pagan gods.

Before following his Master to martyrdom, Justin wrote some *apologias* ("defenses") of the faith to reach out to those who were as he had been, in search of the Perfect Philosophy. In the *First Apology* Justin showed that Christianity was not contrary to reason—in fact, the Logos that so many philosophers spoke of was Christ, described as the Logos (Word) in John's gospel. Point by point, Justin looked at parts of the Bible that the pagans found hard to believe and observed that the pagan myths were much harder to accept and often contradicted each other. Perhaps the most appealing statement in the *Apology* is "never was the crucifixion imitated in any of the so-called sons of Zeus." Justin had hit upon the core of the gospel: a son of a god—rather, the one Son of the only God—gave himself up, the innocent suffering in place of the guilty. In his writings and in his martyrdom, Justin was a shining example of how so many Christians out-thought, outlived, and out-died the pagans.

Prayer: Father, let our lives and our words light up this dark and selfish world. Amen.

June 2 · PRINCE AND SIMPLE FOLK

"See that you do not look down on one of these little ones."

MATTHEW 18:10

1537: In 1534 the Catholic Church had a new pope, and at first he did not seem to be an improvement over his predecessors. His name was Alessandro Farnese, born into a rich, ambitious, and immoral Italian family, and he had fathered four illegitimate children before becoming pope. Taking the name of Paul III, the new pope made two of his grandsons—both teenagers—cardinals. He oversaw the completion of the opulent Farnese family palace in Rome and of Michelangelo's magnificent painting of *The Last Judgment*. He commissioned one of the other great artists of the time, Titian, to paint his portrait. In short, Paul III, like so many of the popes before him, seemed more interested in living like a prince than a saint.

And yet, he did not ignore the spiritual issues of the day—such as the Protestant Reformation which had broken huge chunks of Europe away from the Catholic Church. He summoned a council to deal with the Reformation, and its first session began at Trent, Italy, in 1545. Paul also gave some thought to an issue an ocean away: how the European colonists should treat the native peoples of America. On June 2, 1537, he issued the decree *Sublimus Deus* in which he prohibited Catholics from making slaves of the Indians. While it was obvious that the Indians were primitive in many ways, the pope declared that they were human beings with souls and that they were to be treated as objects of God's love and, when possible, converted to Christianity.

The same man who made two of his grandsons cardinals also appointed some worthy men to the post, and some genuine reforms did take place while Paul III was pope. The church had to pray for future popes to be even less worldly and more spiritual.

Prayer: Lord, turn our gaze from the enticements of this world to the souls of those in need of salvation. Amen.

June 3 · ANTIOCH, CHRISTIAN AGAIN

Be strong in the Lord and in his mighty power.

EPHESIANS 6:10

1098: In the book of Acts, the city of Antioch in Syria is one of the centers of Christian belief, and "the disciples were first called Christians at Antioch." In the year 636 the Christian city fell to Arabs professing the new religion, Islam. Muslims lost control a century later, but in 1084 the Muslim Turks took the city. The Muslims' conquest of Palestine provoked Pope Urban II in 1095 to call for a holy war, a crusade to return the lands to Christian control. Why, the pope wondered, should the knights in Christian Europe spend all their energy fighting each other while Christians were being harassed by the Muslims in sacred places such as Antioch and Jerusalem? In 1098 a force of 300,000 Crusaders besieged the city for seven months, capturing it on June 3. Some believed they had been aided by the finding of the Holy Lance, supposedly the spear that had pierced the side of the crucified Jesus.

This was the first big victory for the Christians in the First Crusade. Another was in July 1099 when they captured Jerusalem and set up a Christian kingdom. This small realm was constantly being whittled away by the Muslims who resented the presence of the "infidels." Most of the later Crusades were efforts to recapture Jerusalem, and probably, if the Europeans had been more committed (and less prone to fighting among themselves), they could have held the Holy Land permanently. But because they could never maintain a consistent, unified effort, the Muslims who never gave up their goal of inhabiting the area would retain power in the region.

Not all the men who went on the Crusades cared who controlled the Holy Land. Many Crusaders were motivated by the love of adventure, plus there was the pope's promise that fighting in a holy war would wipe out their sins. But no doubt many Crusaders were sincere and eager to return the land to its Christian inhabitants. What a pity that both religions found war more attractive than peaceful coexistence.

Prayer: Father, grant us courage but also wisdom enough to pursue the path of peace. Amen.

June 4 · REVEREND SPEAKER

I do not conceal your love and your truth from the great assembly.

PSALM 40:10

1801: The first U.S. Speaker of the House grew up speaking German as his first language and received most of his education in Germany. He was Frederick Muhlenberg who was from a family that made a name for itself in both religion and politics. His father, Heinrich Muhlenberg, was born in Germany, studied for the ministry there, settled in Pennsylvania in 1742, and is known as the father of Lutheranism in America. (Like many German immigrants, he anglicized his first name and is generally referred to as Henry not Heinrich.) During the Revolutionary War Heinrich tried to remain neutral but was mildly pro-American. One of his sons was more dramatically pro-American: Peter, a pastor in Virginia, announced from the pulpit one Sunday that the time for battle had come. In his robing room he took off his clerical gown, put on a uniform, and proceeded to muster a German regiment, beginning with the men in his church. He eventually became a general and was with George Washington when the British surrendered at Yorktown. Afterward he served several terms in Congress.

Frederick Muhlenberg, his brother, was pastoring a church in New York City when the war began, and though he did not join the army, he did serve in the Continental Congress. After being elected to the first U.S. Congress, his colleagues elected him the first Speaker, and he served four years in that post. While he was Speaker, a bill came before the House to publish some of the federal laws in German, since so many Americans spoke German as their first language. The bill was defeated, and Muhlenberg voiced the sentiment that "the faster the Germans become Americans, the better it will be." He also became the first man to sign the Bill of Rights, the first ten amendments to the Constitution. Frederick died on June 4, 1801, after an active life of serving God and his country.

Prayer: Father, make us good citizens, worthy of your kingdom and a transforming presence in this world. Amen.

June 5 · Thor's Nemesis

They will tell of the power of your awesome works, and I will proclaim your great deeds.

Psalm 145:6

754: The man known as the "Apostle to the Germans" was born in England with the name Wynfrith. In the year 719 when the pope gave him the assignment of evangelizing the Germans, the native religion of the Germans was paganism, worship of the gods Thor, Odin, and Balder. Most Germans were not attracted to Christianity with its story of the Son of God dying as a criminal, but Boniface converted some of the German chieftains, and by the custom of the times, a whole tribe would follow its chief into the new faith. Wherever he went, Boniface established churches and monasteries. He also tore down pagan idols, which was risky business, but he was protected by Charles Martel, king of the Franks (and, later, grandfather of the great king Charlemagne).

One of the great episodes in the history of missions was the confrontation in 723 of Boniface with some pagans at the town of Geismar. An enormous oak tree there was known as the "oak of Thor," and the pagans worshipped it. Presumably Thor, the god of thunder and power, protected it. Boniface had it cut down and its wood used as timber for a church he was building. If the pagans expected Boniface to be struck dead, they were disappointed. Respecting power, they deduced that the God Boniface served was more powerful than mighty Thor. Word of this remarkable event spread widely and made Boniface's task easier.

But not all the pagans were in awe of Boniface and his God. On June 5, 754, after a long, active, and productive life, Boniface was attacked by a band of pagans. His companions were willing to defend him with their swords, but Boniface would not allow it, saying that evil must be overcome with good. Boniface was murdered that day. The cathedral in Fulda, Germany, has his tomb—and also the dagger with which he was murdered.

Prayer: Father, we praise you as the God of awesome deeds, none more awesome than the transformation of the human heart. Amen.

June 6 · FELLOWSHIPS IN URBAN BABYLONS

Let us not give up meeting together, as some are in the habit of doing, but let us encourage one another.

HEBREWS 10:25

1844: In London, twenty-three-year-old George Williams started the Young Men's Christian Association. At the time England was undergoing a rapid transition from rural to urban, and young men from the country or small towns often abandoned their religious upbringing when confronted with the temptations of large cities. A typical young man ended his work day by visiting a tavern or brothel—or both. Williams, a farm boy himself, knew there had to be a better alternative. Appropriately, the original group consisted of twelve men.

Interestingly, when the YMCA began, no one could have predicted that the "C" in the name would ever be neglected (or forgotten), and that mention of "the Y" would make people think of swimming and other physical exercise. At its founding, the group professed itself to be for "the spiritual improvement of young men." The men engaged in Bible study and attended lectures and religious discussions, although physical exercise in time became part of the program. The Earl of Shaftesbury, a noted Christian statesman, gave the Y much encouragement. YMCAs were founded in various other countries, including the United States, and a World Alliance of YMCAs was established in 1855. Future evangelist Dwight L. Moody found warm fellowship at the Y when he moved to Boston at age seventeen. Another notable who spent some time at the Y was former baseball player Billy Sunday who gave lectures on "Christian manhood" and later became a noted evangelist. Y members were active in providing relief work during both World Wars.

Williams was, incidentally, knighted in 1894 by Queen Victoria. In centuries past, monarchs bestowed knighthood on men who proved themselves skilled in shedding blood. By Williams's day, the Queen had a clearer idea of what sort of men made England a better place.

Prayer: Father, in a world that spreads so many temptations before us, guide us to places of spiritual shelter and fellowship where brothers and sisters in the faith can gather for mutual nurture. Amen.

Because you are my help, I sing in the shadow of your wings.

PSALM 63:7

1872: From Internal Revenue Service agent to singer on the evangelistic circuit . . . the lives of Christians take curious turns. The great singer-composer Ira Sankey, the music director for evangelist Dwight L. Moody, left his job with the IRS after meeting Moody at a YMCA convention. He and Moody were in a revival meeting when the Great Chicago Fire broke out in 1871, and the two, who barely escaped with their lives, ended up observing the fire from a rowboat in Lake Michigan.

A few months later, on June 7, 1872, the two began a successful tour of Great Britain. Moody considered the music an indispensable part of his ministry. When a pastor asked Moody what the role of a song leader was, Moody replied that "if we can only get people to have the words of the love of God coming from their mouths, it is well on its way to residing in their hearts." He might have added that Sankey's solos also prepared the congregation to receive Moody's message of salvation.

Sankey's output of hymns was astounding; he wrote well over a thousand. Many became popular in America and after the 1872 British tour, in Britain also, since they were often sung at the huge Metropolitan Tabernacle, the home church of the great preacher Charles H. Spurgeon.

The most famous story connected with Sankey's hymn-writing concerns a poem by Elizabeth Clephane, "There Were Ninety and Nine That Safely Lay," based on Jesus' parable of the lost sheep. Sankey saw it in a magazine and kept the poem in his coat pocket. At a revival meeting in Scotland in 1874, in a packed hall Moody asked Sankey to sing a solo, and Sankey composed the tune as he sang the words—a curious case of instant inspiration. It became his most famous tune, widely used in evangelism from then on.

Prayer: Lord, let the talents of speakers, singers, and songwriters draw more of the lost ones to you. Amen.

June 8 · PLUMBER EMPOWERED

Has not God chosen those who are poor in the eyes of the world to be rich in faith?

JAMES 2:5

1859: When Smith Wigglesworth married at age twenty-two, he could not read. His wife taught him to read the Bible, and he claimed it was the only book he ever read. One of the best-known English preachers of his day, he was barely literate which did not hold him back at all.

Wigglesworth was born on this date to a poor family and spent his youth picking turnips and working in factories. Later he made a living as a plumber. Though illiterate in his youth, he learned about the faith by attending Methodist and Anglican churches, was baptized in a Baptist church, learned much from the Plymouth Brethren man who taught him plumbing, married a Salvation Army preacher, and began speaking in tongues while attending a Pentecostal meeting. His was, to put it mildly, a richly diverse religious background.

Wigglesworth recalled that "I can never recollect a time when I did not long for God." His preaching ministry was based on his belief that all people needed fellowship with God. He was devoted to converting those who did not know Christ, and he claimed that he could not let a day pass without bringing someone to the Lord.

After God healed him of a ruptured appendix, Wigglesworth began a healing ministry, and many people claimed they were healed at his meetings. During his long life he experienced various ailments but never sought help from doctors. His fame as a healer brought him to the United States in 1914 and 1922 and to India and Ceylon in 1926, where he drew enormous crowds. The Angelus Temple, Aimee Semple McPherson's huge church in Los Angeles, hosted him in 1927, there his "morning feast" Bible studies were well attended.

He died in 1947, aged eighty-seven, having touched many thousands of lives. The working-class man who read only the Bible had done phenomenal things for God.

Prayer: Lord, you accomplish your will through all sorts of people. Teach us to see them not through the world's eyes, but through yours. Amen.

June 9 · FLAMBOYANT CRUELTY

The LORD watches over the way of the righteous, but the way of the wicked will perish.

PSALM 1:6

68: The Roman emperor Nero came from a seriously dysfunctional—and disgusting—family. His mother, Agrippina, had married her uncle, Emperor Claudius, and poisoned him with mushrooms. Nero became emperor at the age of seventeen, and eventually he had his domineering mother assassinated. He idled away his time in useless pleasures, allowing his tutor, the philosopher Seneca, to run the empire, which he did reasonably well. Eventually he forced Seneca to commit suicide and took charge of the empire himself, to everyone's horror.

Nero is most famous for launching the first imperial persecution of Christians. A great fire destroyed much of Rome in the year 64, and many believed Nero had caused it himself, wanting to clear areas for rebuilding. Fearing a rebellion, he blamed Christians for the fire, and there was enough anti-Christian feeling in the city that the populace applauded the ways that Nero contrived to kill the Christians, such as having them torn apart by wild beasts in the arena or crucified and set on fire to light up his pleasure gardens. The Roman historians Tacitus and Suetonius recorded the persecutions in gory detail, and though neither writer liked the Christians, they admitted that the Romans had seen so much bloodshed that eventually they began to sympathize with the Christians. Some of the later emperors proved to be even worse persecutors than Nero, but Nero's bloodletting stuck in people's memories. Tradition has it that the apostles Peter and Paul were both martyred by Nero, Paul by beheading, Peter by crucifixion.

Nero made a fool of himself in public, trying to impress people with his songs and poetry. His tyranny turned everyone against him, and a rebellion ensued. Knowing he was doomed, Nero cut his own throat on June 9, 68, at the age of thirty, lamented by no one. The "superstition" he tried to exterminate lives on.

Prayer: God of mercy, we trust in your promise of the final triumph of the good. Amen.

The word of God is living and active.

HEBREWS 4:12

2005: In 1972 *Time* magazine ran an article titled "A Plowman's Bible?" It was referring to one of the most amazing phenomena ever in Bible publishing—the best-selling nonfiction book in both 1972 and 1973. This was *The Living Bible*, a paraphrase done by Kenneth N. Taylor, the father of a large brood of children who was aware that those children (not to mention millions of adults) had trouble understanding the beloved (but dated) King James Version. Finding no Christian publisher interested in publishing a paraphrase, Taylor did the obvious thing: he started his own publishing house. In 1962 he published *Living Letters* with the Tyndale House imprint—William Tyndale being the first man to translate the Bible into English so that the common people could have access to the Word of God. Promoted by Billy Graham's crusades, *Living Letters* was followed by *Living Prophecies* (1964), *Living Gospels* (1967), and other portions of the Bible, until finally *The Living Bible*, complete with its distinctive green cover, was published in July 1971. Millions of readers loved it, and by 1974 it accounted for 46 percent of U.S. Bible sales. Even as late as 1977 it still outsold other versions.

And yet, as a sign of how out-of-touch secular media were with religion in America, the 1972 and 1973 best-seller lists in the *New York Times* and other secular publications failed to list *The Living Bible*—despite its being the top nonfiction seller for two years running. (In fact, the *Times* best-seller list was based not on actual number of books sold but on a cursory polling of large urban bookstores.) The success of *The Living Bible* gave a resounding "Yes!" to *Time*'s question, "A Plowman's Bible?" Plowmen—and millions of others—were eagerly reading the Bible.

Kenneth Taylor, a humble and saintly man, died on June 10, 2005, having given so many readers a Bible they could comprehend.

Prayer: Lord, as we read your words and try to put them into practice, we thank you for those who labored to put those words on paper, people who communicated clearly and faithfully. Amen.

June 11 · THE OPEN BOOK MINISTRY

The word of the LORD is right and true.

PSALM 33:4

1970: Literacy is not required to enter heaven, but Christians have always agreed that believers should familiarize themselves with the Word of God, so missionaries have often served as teachers of reading. One notable missionary was dubbed "Mr. Literacy" by *Time* magazine and also called the "Apostle of the Illiterates." He was Frank Laubach who died on this date after a life dedicated to literacy but also dedicated to the Lord.

In 1915 Laubach went as a missionary to the Philippines at first teaching in a seminary in Manila. Then he went to the southern part of the Philippines to teach the Maranao tribe who were Muslims and also suspicious of white foreigners. He won their affection by creating an alphabet for their language which had never been written down before. His experience with the Maranao was the beginning of his "Each One Teach One" method with a newly literate person teaching another, thus requiring fewer paid teachers.

Laubach became a literacy consultant for the world, advising governments, missions, and private charities on the most effective ways to teach reading. In 1955 he established Laubach Literacy which has helped to teach reading to millions of people in America and thirty-four other countries. He often spoke of the "silent billion," the illiterate or barely literate whose lives could be enriched if they learned to read. In India, with its hundreds of languages, Gandhi became an advocate of Laubach's methods.

Although the world at large knew Laubach as Mr. Literacy, he did not neglect his calling to witness to his faith. He wrote numerous books and articles, including *Prayer: The Mightiest Force in the World* and *How to Teach One and Win One for Christ*. He also created a New Testament version for people who were new to English. He spent a fruitful life dedicated to words and to the Word.

Prayer: Father, make us people who are rooted in your Word and live out its truths. Amen.

June 12 · The Rugby Duo

Children, obey your parents in the Lord, for this is right.

Ephesians 6:1

1842: Christian parents try to pass on their faith to their children, but children can choose to reject it, as so many do. Some embrace the faith—but only partly. Consider the example of Thomas Arnold and his son, Matthew. Thomas was the most famous headmaster of an English school in the 1800s. A graduate of Oxford and an ordained minister in the Church of England, he became the head of Rugby School in 1828. The person who recommended him for the post said that he would "change the face of education" in England.

He did. He aimed to make Rugby a training ground for Christian gentlemen, and he achieved this, partly through his sermons in the chapel, partly by his own warm personality. He was that rare thing in the world of education: a man who genuinely seemed to like boys. Many of the Rugby graduates went on to establish schools of their own, so Thomas Arnold's influence endured years after his death on June 12, 1842. Appropriately, he is buried in the school's chapel.

His son, Matthew, is probably best known as a poet, the author of the poem "Dover Beach," in which he laments the "sea of faith" ebbing away. Matthew experienced what many intellectuals of his time did: they saw the beauty of their parents' faith but just couldn't bring themselves to embrace it. Arnold wrote about this quandary in his book *God and the Bible*. In it he stated that man can not do without Christianity but "cannot do with it as it is." Both Christians and agnostics criticized him, claiming he was trying to find a middle ground that did not exist. Matthew *lived* as a Christian—not surprising, since he graduated from Rugby. His problem was that he lived in an age when science was casting doubts on Christianity. What a pity he did not possess the certainty his father had.

Prayer: Lord, bless the parents, teachers, and all who work to mold the character of children. Amen.

He who finds a wife finds what is good and receives favor from the LORD.

PROVERBS 18:22

1525: On this date a former nun married a former monk. Such marriages were common in the 1520s when Protestantism was on the rise, and nuns, monks, and priests who turned Protestant no longer felt bound by their vows of lifelong celibacy. The ex-nun's name was Katharine von Bora. The ex-monk's name was Martin Luther. He claimed he was marrying to please his parents, who wanted grandchildren. To his great surprise, he ended up loving married life.

A clergyman with wife and children seems normal to us but not to the people of that time, and Catholics mocked Luther for marrying and fathering six children. He was, Catholics said, a "sensualist," a man who did not keep the vow of celibacy he made when becoming a monk. Luther had deduced from the Bible that it was fine for clergy to marry, and he and Katherine became the prototype for the Protestant parsonage. Catholic priests had become notorious for fathering children by their housekeepers, and as Luther saw it, it was far better to marry and bring up children in a Christian home. He came to believe that Christian marriage pleased God more than celibacy.

The Luther home was a full house with six children plus Luther's colleagues and admirers. Katharine, whom Luther sometimes called "Master Katie," proved to be a good household manager. She could be difficult at times (so could Martin), but as a whole, the marriage was a success. Luther wrote that the command to love one's neighbor applies doubly to a man's wife who is his nearest neighbor. He advised husbands, "Make your wife sorry to have you leave," and told couples that once the early "intoxication" of physical pleasure wore off, real marital love could begin. He also wrote that "union of the flesh does nothing. There must also be union of manners and mind." Certainly his own marriage was an inspiring model of that spiritual union.

Prayer: Father, thank you for Christian couples who are models of deep and abiding love. Amen.

June 14 · GLOBAL FAITH

"Go and make disciples of all nations, baptizing them in the name of the Father and of the Son and of the Holy Spirit."

MATTHEW 28:19

1910: The World Missionary Conference opened in Edinburgh, Scotland, in an assembly hall in the shadow of the city's famous castle. The delegates discussed the training of missionaries, promotion of Christian unity, relations with other world religions, etc. In effect the Edinburgh conference was the beginning of the world ecumenical movement with Christians from many denominations cooperating and emphasizing their common goals.

At the time of the conference, probably 35 percent of the world's people could be identified as Christian, whereas ninety years earlier in 1800, it was probably less than 25 percent—evidence that the 1800s had been a great age for missions, and this amazing success led to even higher hopes for the twentieth century. Mission-minded Christians had good reason to be full of confidence. They were unaware that brewing in Europe and elsewhere were totalitarian ideologies whose followers would also show great confidence—and would be willing to change the world by force not persuasion.

Although designated a "world" conference, most of the 1910 delegates were in fact from the United States and Britain. A century later the missions scene was dramatically changed with thousands of missionaries from Asia, Africa, and Latin America—some taking the gospel to their own people but some taking the word to an increasingly secularized Europe and United States. In June 2010 a centennial conference was held in the same assembly hall in Edinburgh, but this conference was truly a "world" conference with delegates from more than sixty nations. At the same time that many Christians in Europe and the United States lost confidence in their faith and wondered if it was "imperialistic" to "impose" the faith on people in other cultures, the new wave of missionaries from Asia, Africa, and Latin America seemed to have the same confidence that the American and British delegates in 1910 possessed.

Prayer: Lord, we thank you for the valiant and devoted saints who have spread your word to the nations. Let us not forget their zeal and their sacrifices. Amen.

Surely the nations are like a drop in a bucket; they are regarded as dust on the scales; he weighs the islands as though they were fine dust.

ISAIAH 40:15

313: On this date Roman emperor Constantine and his co-emperor Licinius issued the Edict of Milan, ending the persecution of Christians by revoking the anti-Christian laws passed under the notorious emperor Diocletian. The edict was written to promote "public well-being and security," and it did not mention any specific god at all, only "the highest divinity," a term that could appeal to anyone. All gods and goddesses could be freely worshipped. The edict stated that Constantine and Licinius "thought it right that the Christians should be given full liberty to follow the religion of their choice." Christians were given no special status or privileges, but, happily, they could live in peace.

Constantine had been converted in 312, attributing his victory over a rival emperor to the power of the Christians' God. Before the crucial battle Constantine had a vision of the cross with the words "In this sign you will conquer" written on it. Whereas previous emperors had seen Christians as subversive troublemakers, Constantine saw Christianity as a way of binding his diverse empire together.

Constantine has been accused of making Christianity the official religion of the empire. This is not so, but it is true that he favored the Christians and appointed many to high government positions. Sadly, this resulted in many insincere "conversions," as people hoping to climb the government ladder were willing to profess to be believers. Before the Edict of Milan, being a Christian often meant putting one's life on the line. After the Edict, being a Christian often meant paying lip service to the faith in order to obtain a government job. Still, Constantine deserves our respect for ending the brutal persecutions and for perceiving that people of faith were the best kind of citizens.

Prayer: Almighty God, keep us mindful of the many who endured persecution for their faith and also of the statesmen who wisely discerned that Christians are a blessing to any society. Amen.

The evil conceits of their minds know no limits.

PSALM 73:7

1752: Christianity seemed to be on the defensive in the 1700s, the age of Enlightenment. Some of the Enlightenment thinkers were outright atheists but more numerous were the Deists, those who believed in a God but not in his intervention in human affairs—in other words, not the God of the Bible. Atheism was still scandalous, and the Deists had the satisfaction of being modern and "progressive" but still believing in God—although not a God many people found very appealing.

The church did not lack for defenders of the faith. One of the most capable of these was Joseph Butler, a bishop in the Church of England and author of the classic answer of Christianity to Deism, *The Analogy of Religion Natural and Revealed*, published in 1736. Butler knew that the Deists claimed that we can know very little—for certain—about God but know a great deal about nature, and *nature* was a favorite term in the Deists' writings. Butler turned that argument on its head, observing that in fact we know relatively little about nature. The Deists also placed a lot of emphasis on the power of human reason, and Butler responded by claiming that reason does not contradict faith but supports it. God, Butler said, revealed himself through the Bible but also reveals himself in nature, and God gave man his reason. The best use of reason is to realize that reason has its limits.

Intellectual defenses of Christianity are referred to as *apologetics*—not "apologies" but "defenses" of the faith. Apologetics have a long history, dating from when the apostle Paul preached Christianity to the pagans in Athens. Whether such defenses convert many unbelievers to the faith is debatable, but apologetics do serve the very useful purpose of keeping some wavering believers within the fold. When Butler died on June 16, 1752, he was honored as one of the greatest defenders of a faith under attack.

Prayer: Father, thank you for a faith that not only fills up the heart but stimulates the mind to action. Amen.

June 17 · A COUNTESS FOR CHRIST

Many women do noble things, but you surpass them all.

PROVERBS 31:29

1791: England in the 1700s was a worldly place, and the upper classes were especially secular, enjoying the material pleasures of this world and giving little thought to the next. Most of the aristocrats belonged to the state Church of England which was spiritually comatose in this century. The middle and lower classes flocked to hear preachers like George Whitefield and John Wesley, but upper-class folk often turned a deaf ear to the evangelists and their message of repentance.

One who did not was Selina Hastings who had the formal title Countess of Huntingdon. Born in 1707 to an English earl, she married Theophilus Hastings, Earl of Huntingdon, and bore him six children, five of whom died young. But the countess became better known as a sort of spiritual mother.

In 1739 she joined Wesley's Methodist society, and after her husband's death in 1746 she devoted herself full-time to aiding the ministries of Wesley, Whitefield, and other evangelical preachers. Ordinarily her fellow aristocrats would have had no contact with such preachers, but she made her homes available to the evangelists, who even had some converts among the upper crust. More importantly, the countess used her wealth to establish dozens of preaching chapels throughout England and Wales. The Church of England authorities grumbled about these "rival" churches that attracted so many people, but as a countess she had the right to appoint as many "chaplains" to her household as she liked, and technically the preachers in her chapels were members of her household. Collectively the chapels were known as the Countess of Huntingdon's Connexion. When some Methodist students were expelled from Oxford, the countess founded a preachers' college at Trevecca in Wales.

The countess died on June 17, 1791, a rare and noble example of someone who could have spent her life in idleness and luxury but chose to use her wealth and influence to further the preaching of the gospel.

Prayer: Lord, bless all those who use their gifts in the building up of your heavenly kingdom. Amen.

June 18 · JIHAD AND ICONS

Some trust in chariots and some in horses, but we trust in the name of the LORD our God.

PSALM 20:7

741: The first Christian emperor who had to deal with an all-out jihad was Leo III, who in 717 began ruling the Byzantine Empire with its capital in Constantinople, the Christian city founded centuries earlier by Constantine. Leo's military ability brought him wide renown, and he put his skills to good use during an Arab attack on Constantinople in 718, which resulted in a yearlong siege of the city. The Arabs had a hundred thousand men and a huge fleet of ships, but the walls of the city were secure, and an exceptionally cold winter led to disease and starvation among the Arabs. Leo and his Christian troops drove the Arab ships away by the use of Greek fire, an incendiary naval weapon, and many of the Arab ships were wrecked by a fierce storm on the way home. Leo's defense of his empire kept the Muslims from penetrating farther into Europe, so in a sense he was the savior of Christian Europe.

Leo engaged in another long battle of a completely different kind. The Byzantine Christians were fond of icons—pictures of Jesus, Mary, and the saints—which were an important part of worship. In Leo's view icons were idols, and many Christians did treat them this way. In 726 he banned all icons, but the public became rabid, and Leo faced a revolution with the icon party attempting to set up a new emperor. Leo put down the revolt, then in 730 issued his ban again, and some who opposed him were persecuted. The quarrel is known as the *iconoclastic controversy,* and it was finally settled more than a century later with the pro-icon party winning.

Leo died on June 18, 741, honored for fending off jihad, less honored for his ban of the icons that were so much a part of church life in the Byzantine Empire.

Prayer: Almighty God, keep us secure in the knowledge that our destiny is in your hands. Amen.

June 19 · THE POISON OF POWER

Do you rulers indeed speak justly? Do you judge uprightly among men?

PSALM 58:1

1902: "All power tends to corrupt, and absolute power corrupts absolutely." That familiar quote was from the well-furnished mind of John Emerich Dalberg-Acton, usually known as Lord Acton, one of the great minds of the 1800s, who thought deeply and widely about history, religion, and politics. He never finished his *History of Liberty*, but he did deliver some lectures on freedom in ancient times and freedom in the Christian world. For someone who published very little, he is probably one of the most-quoted men of Victorian England, perhaps because so much that he said makes perfect sense.

Acton was from a prominent English family that had been Catholic for generations. In 1870 the Catholic Church decreed that the pope when speaking officially was "infallible." Acton was devoted to his church, but the decree bothered him (and many other Catholics), and his famous quote about power corrupting is from a letter concerning the decree about the pope. The statement applies to all types of power, of course. Acton had studied history and drawn some conclusions: freedom is a fragile thing, and there is always some person or group wanting to impose their will on others. No one person or clique should ever be trusted with too much power. It is a biblical view of power, for though the Bible counsels Christians to be good citizens, human power is presented "warts and all" in the Bible, and most rulers in the Bible were corrupt and dangerous.

Acton was close friends with a very powerful politician, William Gladstone, who served for many years as prime minister. Gladstone, a devout evangelical Christian, shared Acton's biblical view of politics. Considering that Catholics and evangelical Protestants usually kept their distance from each other in the 1800s, the Gladstone-Acton friendship is remarkable. No doubt each admired the other's willingness to carry faith into the political arena.

Lord Acton died on June 19, 1902, a respected figure who seems to gain esteem with the passage of time.

Prayer: Almighty God, make us wise as serpents and innocent as doves, as your Son told us to be. Amen.

June 20 · Back to Genesis 1

The heavens declare the glory of God.

Psalm 19:1

1966: Science is supposed to be "self-correcting"—a theory gets proposed, and later, if something proves the theory wrong, it is discarded. In the case of the origin of the universe, the original theory, found in Genesis 1, was discarded—and then reinstated.

Science came into its own in the 1700s, and though some of the great names in science were Christians (such as Isaac Newton), the overall effect of science was to cast doubt on the Bible. The universe seemed to function by "laws" that scientists discovered, and all seemed predictable with no place in the universe for a Creator or Sustainer. Scientists agreed that the world had existed for millions of years, as fossils proved, and it would presumably go on forever—no beginning, no end. Twentieth-century scientists, including Albert Einstein, held to this "Steady State theory."

One scientist who did not was Georges Lemaitre, born in 1894 in Belgium. He became a Catholic priest but also studied physics and math. In 1927 he published a paper proposing that the universe had a beginning and was expanding. In 1930 he gave a lecture in which he spoke of a "point" from which the universe began and expanded. Scientist Fred Hoyle who did not accept the notion, sarcastically named it the "Big Bang theory." It is a short name for an extremely complicated theory, but the upshot is the universe most definitely did have a beginning. Lemaitre referred to it as "a day without yesterday." When he died on June 20, 1966, he was one of the most respected scientists in the world, and most scientists accept the Big Bang theory, though most do not believe it was the work of God. To scientists who finally came around to accepting a beginning to the universe, the Christian might well say, "What took you so long?"

Prayer: Creator God, we praise you for all that you made and the wisdom that leads minds back to you. Amen.

June 21 · ONE LESS MARTYR

They will turn their ears away from the truth and turn aside to myths.

2 TIMOTHY 4:4

1633: The Italian scientist Galileo is a hero to many people, not so much because of his discoveries but because he was put on trial by the Catholic Church. The familiar myth is about Blind Faith (the church) versus Enlightened Science (Galileo). The real story is rather different.

The Polish scientist Copernicus published, at the end of his life, a book stating that the earth and planets revolve around the sun which was contrary to the old view that the planets and sun revolve around the earth. In 1616 the church made it illegal to teach this theory *as fact*, but scientists could discuss it as a "proposition." In 1624 the pope gave Galileo permission to discuss Copernicus, so long as he did not publicly commit himself to the view. Galileo published the book *Dialogue of the Two Chief World Systems*. Technically, Galileo presented the old view and Copernicus's view and did not take sides. But critics pointed out that in Galileo's book, the old belief was spoken by a character named Simplicio, meaning "simpleton," and the consensus was that Galileo was letting it be known that Copernicus's view was his own. So Galileo was put on trial as a heretic.

At his trial he flagrantly lied and said he had never taught Copernicus's theory. On June 21, 1633, he was found guilty of heresy and had to publicly "curse and detest" his past opinions. His "punishment," if it could be called that, was to spend five months under "house arrest" in the palace of a bishop. There was no dungeon, no torture rack, no execution, and Galileo died peacefully in his own bed in 1642. The pope at the time of his trial was a friend and admirer of Galileo, and Galileo's book had been hailed as a masterpiece all over Europe. Galileo did not spend one day of his life in a prison cell. Christians have done terrible things over the centuries, but there was no "martyrdom" of Galileo.

Prayer: Lord, give us discernment so that we may distinguish falsehood from truth. Amen.

From infancy you have known the holy Scriptures, which are able to make you wise for salvation.

2 TIMOTHY 3:15

1714: The great preacher Charles H. Spurgeon said that "every minister ought to read it through entirely at least once." He was referring to the *Exposition of the Old and New Testaments* or, to use its more familiar name, *Matthew Henry's Commentary*. Matthew Henry died on this date after a long and fruitful life as a pastor and author of one of the most-read commentaries ever.

Henry was born in Wales in 1662, the son of one of the many Puritan pastors who had been ejected from the state Church of England for not conforming completely. Having some money put aside, Matthew's father provided his son a good education, and Matthew studied for the law. Then he became a Presbyterian minister in Chester, England, a post he held for twenty years. While there he published the first edition of his *Exposition* which he later expanded to six full volumes, a truly awesome verse-by-verse commentary.

Although Henry was a capable scholar, he did not intend his commentary for only theologians but for all readers of the Bible, so his commentary has a devotional purpose, telling the reader not only what a particular passage means but how it can be applied to daily life. Pastors fell in love with the commentary immediately, and the great evangelist George Whitefield claimed he had read it through four times.

Henry's commentary is still widely read, although most modern readers probably own a one-volume version, much abridged from Henry's original six volumes. In fact, he never completed his commentary, only reaching the end of Acts, but friends were able to complete the commentary using notes that Henry left behind.

Henry wrote that "nothing can make a man truly great but being truly good and partaking of God's holiness." This was a truth that he lived as well as spoke.

Prayer: Lord, bless the memory of all those who have shed light upon YOUR HOLY WORD. AMEN.

June 23 · NEW WORLD, OLD TRUTH

You are not your own; you were bought at a price. Therefore honor God with your body.

1 CORINTHIANS 6:19–20

1978: "What was true yesterday is true also today." So said Pope Benedict XVI forty years after the very controversial document *Humanae Vitae* ("On Human Life"), issued by Pope Paul VI in 1968. *Humanae Vitae* is remembered by most people for stating the church's opposition to birth control. What a pity, since there is much more to it than that.

Paul VI issued his famous decree in the turbulent 1960s. The contraceptive drug Enovid, better known as "the Pill," went on sale in the United States in 1960, causing dramatic changes in sexual practices. As liberals proclaimed with glee, the Pill gave women—whatever their marital status—control over pregnancy.

Humanae Vitae told Catholics they should not use the Pill or any artificial methods of birth control. Science had made it possible to separate sex from pregnancy—and from love. But God's moral laws did not change just because science had devised a new way of preventing pregnancy. Many Catholics ignored the pope's words, believing he was living in a dead past. Paul VI saw nothing "dead" about the past—Christianity had a rich tradition of affirming marital love and the bringing of children into the world. The main problem of birth control was not that fewer babies were born but that the God-given link between sex and love was broken. Critics said the pope was "afraid of sex," but in fact he understood just how rich and fulfilling sex could be—*in the context of lifelong commitment.*

Paul VI reigned another ten years after *Humanae Vitae*. He was aware of how many people, including Catholics, had mocked his decree. Yet on June 23, 1978, a few weeks before his death, he addressed the cardinals and said that he stood by *Humanae Vitae*. Truth was truth, and, as the life of Jesus showed, truth that offends is still the truth.

Prayer: Lord, strengthen us to live decent and moral lives in a world that mocks decency. Amen.

June 24 · GOD IN A SMALL SPACE

He brought them out of darkness and the deepest gloom and broke away their chains.

PSALM 107:14

1542: Sometimes people find God, or draw closer to him, in prison. This was the case with Juan de Yepes, a Spanish saint better known as John of the Cross. Born on this date into a poor family, John joined the Carmelite order of monks and became a close friend of the Carmelite nun, Teresa of Avila. John taught the novices (apprentice monks) and, like Teresa, worked to reform the lax monasteries and make them centers of spirituality. Some of his fellow monks found him too strict and had him imprisoned for nine months in a tiny cell. There, with little room and little air, he found himself drawing closer to his Father, and to his Father he attributed his miraculous escape from prison. Later, some of his brother Carmelites compiled a list of grievances against him and tried to have him booted out of the order. When he died in 1591, his former foes were filled with regret, for no one could deny that he had been a model of holiness.

John would probably be forgotten had he not written several devotional classics. The most read is *The Dark Night of the Soul*, written shortly after his escape from prison. The key idea of this great work is that the soul must empty itself before it can be filled with God. As horrible as John's imprisonment was, the long confinement in his tiny cell taught him to forget himself—certainly a wise response to such suffering!—and to focus on God who is present no matter what the external circumstances. Like all the great saints, John did not find that giving himself up totally to God made him passive—on the contrary, he was a man of amazing energy, despite poor health that had plagued him his entire life. His earthly life was brief, but he influenced all he met, and his writings lived on to touch later generations.

Prayer: Lord, be with us in all our trials, and never let us forget your holy presence. Amen.

June 25 · GYPSY GEM

The kingdom of God is not a matter of talk but of power.

1 CORINTHIANS 4:20

1877: William Booth of the Salvation Army commissioned a young man with a colorful heritage to preach on this date: he was a gypsy, born in a tent a few miles north of London in 1860. Given the gypsies' reputation, it is no surprise that this man, Rodney Smith, had been in jail more than once, but at age seventeen he was converted at a gospel meeting, turning his life around completely. Rodney, who had no formal education, taught himself to read the Bible, and he felt the call to preach. William Booth believed Smith was ready, and Smith began preaching on street corners and mission halls. He made hundreds of converts and married one of them.

Soon "Gypsy" Smith, as he was called, became an independent evangelist and drew crowds all over Britain, America, South Africa, and Australia, and during World War I he preached on the front lines to Allied troops in France. He was a superb preacher and, true to the gypsy tradition, musically talented as well, and he would sometimes break into song at an appropriate point in his sermon. (Thanks to the Internet, recordings of his songs are readily available.) *Time* magazine ran a story on Smith in 1927, titled "Heart in Mouth," reporting that Smith had made many converts in Chicago's red-light district.

Few men ever entered the ministry with less education, yet no one could deny Smith's power in the pulpit. As he pointed out often, the way to Jesus was not through Oxford or Cambridge or Harvard but through Calvary. Also, "it's the message that's important, not the messenger."

In 1917 King George V bestowed on him the Order of the British Empire—a remarkable honor for an unschooled gypsy boy who had done time in jail. Smith died in 1947 at the age of eighty-seven, having crossed the Atlantic forty-five times, a true "gypsy" for the gospel.

Prayer: Father, raise up voices of power to preach your truth to the nations. Amen.

June 26 · A CLOUD THAT QUICKLY PASSED

You will die like mere men; you will fall like every other ruler.

PSALM 82:7

363: Tradition says that the last words of the Roman emperor Julian were, "You have conquered, O pale Galilean." In fact, those were not his dying words, but they did sum up his sentiments, for Julian, the last pagan emperor of the Roman Empire, detested Christianity.

Julian was the nephew of Constantine, the first Christian emperor. Constantine's son Constantius, Julian's older cousin, had Julian brought up as a Christian. Julian conformed, but secretly he had a deep love for paganism— not paganism as it really was but the dignified paganism of the literary classics and the beautiful temples. On Constantius's death, Julian became emperor and threw off the mask he had been wearing. He knew better than to launch a violent persecution against the Christians which would only create martyrs, so he chose more petty forms of persecution. He restored some pagan temples, appointed pagans to government offices, and revoked some of the Christian clergy's privileges. He started to rebuild the Jews' temple in Jerusalem, but a violent storm was taken as an omen that this was not wise.

He hated the "Galileans," as he called them, but admired their charity and smooth-running organization. He tried to create a new paganism with these same features, but Julian's system seemed like a pale imitation of Christianity, and his cult of the "Supreme Being" pleased neither pagans nor Christians.

Because he switched from Christianity to paganism, Julian is known to history as Julian the Apostate. His death on June 26, 363, after reigning only two years, was seen by Christians as a final judgment on paganism. But one thing needs to be said in Julian's defense: his contempt for Christianity was partly the result of watching Constantine, supposedly a Christian, having his enemies murdered—including his own wife and one of his sons. Christians in high places, like Constantine, sometimes forget that unbelievers are always watching, wondering if Christians' deeds harmonize with their words.

Prayer: Father, when your children are persecuted, give them eyes that see a brighter day ahead. Amen.

June 27 · A PLACE TO GROW A MIND

The LORD gives wisdom, and from his mouth come knowledge and understanding.

PROVERBS 2:6

2002 : If your local public schools are of poor quality or hostile to religion or both, what are your options? Private school is a good choice for families who can afford it, but what about families who can't?

Cleveland, Ohio, in the 1990s had terrible public schools with its students ranking near the bottom on standardized tests. The state set up a voucher program, known as the Pilot Project, granting to needy families a stipend that would help them send their children to private schools in the Cleveland area. A whopping 96 percent of parents accepting the vouchers chose to send their children to religious schools. Not surprisingly, the program horrified secularists, who tried to scuttle the program, claiming that the vouchers violated the principle of separation of church and state.

The case, known as *Zelman v. Simmons-Harris*, was decided by the U.S. Supreme Court on June 27, 2002. The U.S. Supreme Court ruled in favor of the Cleveland program. In the Court's written opinion, the vouchers were "neutral with respect to religion," and there was no evidence that the Cleveland school system was working to "establish" or favor any religion. The choice of schools had not been in the hands of any government entity but in the hands of families trying to rescue their children from a failing public school system. The program did not favor religious schools since parents were free to choose nonreligious private schools for their children. Justice Clarence Thomas pointed out that the program was of great benefit to minority families. Justice David Souter who did not side with the majority, insisted that the program was indeed a case of government support for religion.

The case was seen as a victory for school voucher programs and also as a blow against an aggressive secularism that is constantly working to diminish the role of religion in American life.

Prayer: Lord, let our children learn the most valuable of all lessons, that life without faith is no life at all. Amen.

Do not be carried away by all kinds of strange teachings.

HEBREWS 13:9

203: At the end of the twentieth century, readers became intrigued by the Gnostic Gospels. Most of these readers were not Christians but people who liked to believe that the "real" Christian writings had been suppressed centuries ago.

This idea would have greatly surprised Irenaeus who was the bishop of Lyons in Gaul (in what is now France). His most famous writings were against the Gnostics in a work titled *Against Heresies*. As he saw it, the Gnostic Gospels were suppressed for a good reason: they were false.

The Gnostics were a diverse group, but they agreed that Christ only *appeared* to be human (which meant his death on the cross was only playacting). They thought that matter was corrupt, that only spirit was important (which led many to believe that whatever they did with their bodies had no effect on their spiritual lives). They had no real interest in the Jesus of history except to use him as a mouthpiece for "secret teachings" that they wrote into their Gospels.

For the Christians, Jesus was the Son of God but also the fully human carpenter of Nazareth, and his words and deeds had been recorded faithfully in the four Gospels. The Christians knew salvation came through faith in Christ. The Gnostics had no interest in faith, for they were saved by *gnosis*, knowledge. They did not care about the Bible as a record of history, and they felt free to mix snippets from the true Gospels with bizarre myths of their own.

The Gnostics had one positive effect on Christianity: they led writers like Irenaeus to identify just which writings were sacred, worth including in the New Testament. The circulation of false Gospels led Christians to agree on the true ones. When he died on June 28, 203, Irenaeus left the world more certain about the basis of Christian belief.

Prayer: Lord, open our eyes to discern the true from the false. Amen.

June 29 · THE BIG TENT OF FELLOWSHIP

Let us consider how we may spur one another on toward love and good deeds.

HEBREWS 10:24

1875: Some Christians cast very long shadows—such as American evangelist D. L. Moody whose influence was global. One ministry that emerged in the wake of Moody's 1875 British crusade still exists: the Keswick convention, named for the village of Keswick in northern England's beautiful Lake District. On June 29 of that year, T. D. Harford-Battersby and Robert Wilson set up a large tent in Keswick in which four hundred people gathered for a prayer meeting that lasted several days. It's motto: "All One in Christ Jesus."

Over the years the Keswick conventions attracted some great speakers, such as the missionary Hudson Taylor. Billy Graham attended Keswick in 1946 and wrote warmly of the experience in his autobiography, *Just as I Am*. John Stott was one of the featured speakers in 1965.

In 1969 Keswick was extended from one week to two, giving attendees more leisure time to enjoy the local scenery. In 1975 Billy Graham was present—not as attendee this time but as the featured speaker at the Keswick centennial, which drew fifteen thousand people by the shore of one of the lovely lakes. In 1987 the new Keswick Convention Center was opened, incorporating the familiar tent that is part of the tradition.

In this new century Keswick continues, running for three weeks in late July and early August, with the focus on in-depth study of the Bible during the day and various seminars and meetings in the evenings, with special programs for children, teens, the deaf, and the learning-disabled. Amazingly, there is no admission charge—Keswick is operated strictly by donations.

Ministries and conventions have their day and pass away, but Keswick is a rare example of a ministry that has continued to bless thousands over many decades, adapting to changing times yet adhering to its God-centered mission. Perhaps one key to its longevity is that it has centered not on an individual minister but on Christ.

Prayer: Father, help us find loving fellowships to enrich our faith. Amen.

June 30 · THE MISREMEMBERED BISHOP

The wisdom of this world is foolishness in God's sight.

1 CORINTHIANS 3:19

1860: "Christianity can be condensed into four words: admit, submit, commit, and transmit." So said Samuel Wilberforce, a bishop in the Church of England, the son of the great Christian social activist William Wilberforce who helped abolish slavery in the British Empire. Samuel inherited his father's charm as well as his zeal for the faith.

Unfortunately, Samuel is mainly remembered—or *mis*remembered—for his appearance at a debate on June 30, 1860, in Oxford, England. The subject: evolution. The main opponent: not Charles Darwin who was too ill to attend but the man known as "Darwin's bulldog," Thomas Huxley who was very cantankerous in contrast to the meek Darwin. Hearing that the English statesman William Gladstone, a Christian, opposed the theory of evolution, Huxley responded, "I really cannot use respectful language about this intrusion of an utter ignoramus into scientific questions." Gladstone was not an ignoramus, but Huxley, like many of Darwin's supporters, had no respect for men of faith, regarding them as a holdover from a pre-scientific age.

At the 1860 debate, held at the Oxford Museum of Natural History, the story goes that Wilberforce asked Huxley if he was descended from a monkey on his grandmother's or grandfather's side. Huxley supposedly replied that he was not ashamed to be descended from a monkey, but he would be ashamed to be a man like Wilberforce, using his gifts to obscure the truth. In fact, Wilberforce never asked the monkey question, though it has been endlessly repeated. Wilberforce, like many Christians, was not bothered much by whether men might have descended from monkeys but was more bothered by the fact that Huxley and others saw no place for God in the universe.

The debate—which was conducted with courtesy—settled nothing, and neither of the two participants changed his mind. It was a kind of preview of the next century when the battle would continue, but without the politeness of that 1860 debate.

Prayer: Creator God, give us wisdom to see things clearly and courage to maintain faith despite opposition. Amen.

JULY

July 1 · THE ONE ABOUT THE TRAVELING SALESMEN

I have put my hope in your word.

PSALM 119:81

1899: For a change, here is a *clean*, even *inspiring* story about a traveling sales-man—two salesmen, actually. In 1898 Samuel Hill and John Nicholson had to share a room at a crowded hotel in Wisconsin. Finding they were both Christians, the two had their daily devotionals together. They met again months later and discussed forming an organization for "Christian commercial travelers," and on July 1, 1899, the Gideons were formed with three members: Hill, Nicholson, and Will Knights. It was Knights who suggested the name Gideons, based on the story in the book of Judges of Gideon, a man of humility who acted exactly as God asked him to do. The familiar clay jar logo on Gideons' Bibles commemo-rates the torches Gideon used in Judges 7.

In 1908 the group, much larger by then, adopted "the Bible Project," the goal being to place a Bible in every hotel room in the United States. The Superior Hotel in Superior, Montana, holds the distinction of receiving the first Bibles from the Gideons. Distribution later expanded beyond hotels to military bases, hospitals, nursing homes, and prisons. The Gideons went global long ago and are active in more than 190 nations.

In the past Gideons often visited public schools during regular hours to dis-tribute Bibles to children, but federal courts have ruled that doing so violates the separation of church and state. Not to be dissuaded, the Gideons have taken to distributing Bibles before and after school hours and from sidewalks adjacent to but not on the school property.

Skeptics may ask: Do the Gideon Bibles in hotel rooms really serve a pur-pose? The Gideons say definitely yes and have compiled numerous testimonies of people who accepted Christ after turning to a hotel Bible. In some cases they had gone there with the intention of committing suicide. We should never underes-timate the power of the Word.

Prayer: Lord, thank you for your sacred Word and for those who send it out to those who do not yet know you. Amen.

Your wisdom and knowledge mislead you when you say to yourself, "I am, and there is none besides me."

ISAIAH 47:10

1778: A man who died on this date was someone we would today call "sensitive" and "in touch with his feelings." He himself used the word *sensibilité*. He was Jean-Jacques Rousseau, a French-speaking Swiss writer who shaped the modern world in a powerful way. Living in the time of the Enlightenment, a movement that emphasized logic and reason, Rousseau instead emphasized feelings, and he used a lot of ink analyzing his own. In his *Confessions* he wrote that "I am not made like anyone I have seen. . . . If I am not better, at least I am different." He also wrote that "my idea of happiness is . . . never to have to do anything I don't wish to do." He tossed aside the Christian duty to neighbor and duty to God and substituted a new virtue: being true to oneself. While Christians had for centuries stressed the importance of faith, Rousseau made a virtue of sincerity.

He also tossed aside the Christian view of sin and said that "the first impulses of nature are always right. There is no original perversity in the human heart." He believed that if people are evil, it is the fault of a corrupt society not their own hearts. Individuals do not need saving, but society needs a powerful government to do the "general will" of all people.

Man in his original state was, Rousseau said, promiscuous and happy. There was no private property and no monogamy—the word *mine* had done great harm. Rousseau himself kept a mistress, fathered several children by her, and abandoned all of them in a foundling home—and he said he did so "cheerfully," while the mistress "groaned but obeyed."

In short, he was a supremely selfish man, as everyone who knew him agreed. What a pity that he wrote well and that his ideas have had such influence.

Prayer: Father, when our minds are fogged by the foolish notions of this world, let your Spirit draw us back to you. Amen.

July 3 · SHUTTING OUT THE RELIGION OF DOUBT

Guard the good deposit that was entrusted to you.

2 TIMOTHY 1:14

1907: "I was born poor, I have lived poor, I wish to die poor." So said Pius X who did not find his nickname the "peasant pope" offensive. When an earthquake struck Italy in 1908, he opened his palace in the Vatican to refugees. He decreased some of the luxury in his court and refused to appoint his relatives to high office. He sometimes handed out candy to poor urban children.

From the time he was elected in 1903, Pius made resisting modernism one of his main goals. Many priests and laymen had been affected by the skepticism of the 1800s embodied in the popular *Life of Jesus* by Ernest Renan, a book depicting Jesus as a wise and compassionate man but not the Son of God. Also, both Catholics and Protestant scholars were engaging in "scientific" study of the Bible and casting doubt on its divine origin. Pius saw a danger here to the laymen in the pews: if Catholic priests and teachers doubted the Bible, what would happen to the faith of the laymen?

On July 3, 1907, Pius issued the decree *Lamentabili Sane* in which he said that the modern desire to probe into the origins of all things had resulted in doubts about the Bible and Christian belief. The decree listed numerous errors that scholars had fallen into. In 1910 he published a sacred oath that all Catholic teachers and clergy had to swear to, affirming their commitment to traditional teachings and the inspiration of the Bible. Critics called Pius a "reactionary" who opposed "progress." As Pius saw it, progress was possible in the material world but not in the spiritual. There were no "advances" to be made in morals and religion. Christians had the truth they needed as they had had it for centuries. The task was not to update the faith but to live it in the modern world.

Prayer: Lord, strengthen our faith and dispel our doubts. Make us good soldiers of the gospel. Amen.

July 4 · COLD WAR, WARM COUNTRY

Open the gates that the righteous nation may enter, the nation that keeps faith.

ISAIAH 26:2

1953: Did you know that a U.S. president was named for an evangelist of the 1800s? The president was Dwight Eisenhower, named for Dwight L. Moody, probably the best-known and most-traveled American evangelist of his day. Eisenhower's parents were devout members of a German Mennonite group known as the River Brethren. His father taught himself Greek so he could read the New Testament in the original tongue. As a child Eisenhower learned the Bible from his parents and could quote it at length. The River Brethren were pacifists, meaning they did not condone or participate in war—which is ironic, considering Eisenhower's later career as a general. They also did not condone drinking, smoking, or card playing—and as an adult, Eisenhower did all three.

For someone who abandoned so much of his parents' religion, Eisenhower has been identified with a particularly religious period in American history. Elected president in November 1952, he designated July 4, 1953, as a national day of prayer and penance. But Eisenhower himself spent the day fishing, golfing, and playing bridge. Was this hypocrisy—or did he sincerely believe that with atheists in charge of both Russia and China, America had a duty to acknowledge and honor God?

Perhaps he was aware that during the 1950s church attendance reached an all-time high in America, and many religious books became bestsellers. Crime rates were low, divorce was rare, as were out-of-wedlock births and abortions. As a whole, the nation was prospering, and unemployment was low. On the surface, at least, it was a fine time for Christianity in America. The country seemed to have confidence in itself and in God. In the decade that followed, so full of strife and change, people would look back on the 1950s with affection. It is a human trait not to count one's blessings until those blessings are gone.

Prayer: Father, thank you for the many blessings you have bestowed on us. Make us good citizens while we remember that our ultimate allegiance is to you. Amen.

July 5 · JESUS FOR MEN

News about him spread through the whole countryside.

LUKE 4:14

1967: What do Betty Crocker and Jesus of Nazareth have in common? Both were important to an advertising executive and congressman named Bruce Barton who created the advertising icon Betty Crocker and in 1925 published one of the best-selling books of the century, *The Man Nobody Knows: A Discovery of the Real Jesus.*

Born in 1886, Barton in 1919 founded an advertising agency in New York which he headed until his retirement in 1961. He also served two terms as a congressman. He was a prolific writer, and in 1925 published his best-known—and most controversial—book in which he aimed to show that the Jesus of the Gospels was the greatest salesman who ever walked the earth.

The Man Nobody Knows opens with a description of a small boy in Sunday school, unimpressed by the meek and gentle Jesus he sees in his church's artwork. He finds some of the Old Testament heroes, such as the vigorous David, very inspiring, but he has only been exposed to an effeminate Jesus. Barton was on to something: Christian art has emphasized Jesus as the meek sufferer, yet the men who followed him—tough, working-class men like Peter—had to have seen something vital and inspiring in the man before they called him Master. Barton paints Jesus as a thoroughly masculine man, physically strong, forceful, a "salesman" in the sense that the message of God's kingdom had to be "sold" to a world in need of salvation.

Critics, including many Christians, said the book was self-serving, that Barton the ad huckster had created a Jesus in his own image. Perhaps there was some truth to this. But the huge sales of the book suggest that Barton had struck a chord with many readers who were moved by the image of a Jesus who overflowed with charisma.

Barton died on July 5, 1967, having influenced both the advertising world and the religious world.

Prayer: Father, teach us to read the Gospels with open hearts and minds, to see your Son as he truly was. Amen.

July 6 · BOHEMIAN BACKBONE

Precious in the sight of the LORD is the death of his saints.

PSALM 116:15

1415: One of the great martyrs of the Middle Ages was John Huss of Bohemia (the area today known as the Czech Republic). Ordained as a minister in 1401, Huss taught at the Charles University in Prague and also preached in the nearby Bethlehem Chapel. Like most sensitive Christians of his day, he was offended at the wealth and immorality of the high officials in the church, including the popes themselves. Many of his fellow priests were worldly, but Huss took the Bible seriously and preached accordingly. Not surprisingly, such preaching offended the pope who put the entire city of Prague under an interdict—meaning, in effect, that the whole city was excommunicated—until Huss ceased preaching in the city. So Huss left and continued preaching outside the city where he drew huge crowds.

In 1414 he was summoned to a church council in the city of Constance and told he would have to defend his teachings publicly. The Holy Roman Emperor, Sigismund, promised him safe conduct—a promise he had no intention of keeping, and Huss was arrested as soon as he arrived. At the council Huss made his position clear: no bishop, pope, council, or emperor could override the clear truths of the Bible nor did any Christian have to obey a church official who commanded what was contrary to Scripture. He told the council, "I would not, for a chapel full of gold, recede from the truth."

On July 6, 1415, the council condemned him as a heretic and burned him at the stake. But his teachings did not die, and a Hussite church arose in Bohemia, called the *Unitas Fratrum* ("Unity of the Brethren"), despite the many efforts of the popes to stamp it out. In the 1500s the Hussites welcomed the Protestant Reformation.

Prayer: Almighty God, you call upon some of your servants to make the ultimate sacrifice. Thank you for men like John Huss, a betrayed and persecuted man unflinching in the face of death. Amen.

Fear of man will prove to be a snare, but whoever trusts in the LORD is kept safe.

PROVERBS 29:25

1647: The history books give a lot of space to the English Puritans who settled Massachusetts, which they deserve, but the other New England colonies had some remarkable personalities of their own, none more so than Thomas Hooker. Born in 1586, he was a graduate of Cambridge University, the center of the Puritan movement in England. He became a pastor, but because he did "unlicensed" preaching at times other than Sunday mornings, he ran afoul of the Church of England establishment. To escape arrest he fled to Holland, then in 1633 settled in Massachusetts. He and followers, known as "Mr. Hooker's Company," founded a new town on the Connecticut River, Hartford, in 1636. There he could preach to his heart's content, and to the great admiration of his flock, with no fear of harassment by the restrictive Church of England bureaucrats.

Hooker has a place in the political history of America—in fact, of the world. Part of the reason for his move from Massachusetts was that he and his followers had, a contemporary historian said, grown "very jealous of their liberties"—that is, they wanted to live where there was freedom. Hooker was way ahead of his time in 1638 when he spoke before the Connecticut general court and claimed that "the choice of public magistrates belongs unto the people by God's own allowance," and the people also have the power to "set the bounds and limitations of the power and place" of public officials. Some say Hooker deserves the title "Father of American Democracy." The sentiments he expressed were like seeds planted in the American consciousness with the desire for political freedom growing alongside the desire for freedom to worship God as one wished.

When Hooker lay dying in his home at Hartford, a friend said, "Mr. Hooker, you are now going to receive your reward." Hooker replied, "I go to receive mercy."

Prayer: Lord, we thank you for the freedoms we possess. Train us to use them for your glory. Amen.

July 8 · UNHEARD-OF FREEDOM

. . . Now the body is not made up of one part but of many.

1 CORINTHIANS 12:14

1663: "Rogue's Island" was the nickname of Rhode Island not because there were criminals there but because the colony attracted religious mavericks, those who had been booted out of or chose to depart from other colonies for religious differences. The Puritans of Massachusetts had left England to find religious freedom, but "freedom" was in the eye of the beholder, for the Puritans had their own code of conduct, and those not willing to conform to it moved on.

One who was forced out of Massachusetts was Roger Williams who sailed from England to Boston but did not stay long due to religious differences with the locals. Not wanting to return to England with its intolerant state church, he wandered south in the middle of a cold winter and found unoccupied land which he purchased from the Indians. There he started a new colony, calling it Providence. It attracted people like himself, Christians who had no desire to impose their own form of Christianity on others.

There was no established church in the colony, and there was complete separation of church and state. The government could maintain civil order but could not interfere with religious matters. So the colony which came to be known officially as Rhode Island and Providence Plantations attracted Baptists, Quakers, independents, and even Jews.

Williams himself was a Baptist for a while, building in Providence the first Baptist church in America. Never one to fit under any label for long, he left the Baptists and called himself a "seeker" with no denominational connection. However, he preached to both colonists and Indians, asking no pay. Though opinionated by nature, he stuck to his belief that government should not coerce in matters of religion.

"Rogue's Island," a colony for mavericks and misfits, was given its royal charter on July 8, 1663. No one knew then that the separation of church and state would someday apply to an entire nation.

Prayer: Father, teach us to respect and love fellow believers and to overlook the things that do not matter. Amen.

July 9 · HEAVENLY BLISS

It is good to praise the LORD *and make music to your name, O Most High.*

PSALM 92:1

1838: Born in a log cabin on this date, Philip Paul Bliss is one of America's greatest hymn-writers. Raised in rural Pennsylvania, young Philip worked in lumber camps and sawmills and at age twelve became a Christian at a revival meeting. A composer urged him to pursue a career in music, and he moved to Chicago in 1864, where he began composing religious songs, also taking to the road to conduct singing schools and music institutes. He was gifted as both a singer and speaker, and in 1874 he became the music director for evangelist D. W. Whittle. Bliss compiled a collection of gospel songs for use in revivals, and he merged his collection with that of evangelist D. L. Moody's music director Ira Sankey, the result being *Gospel Hymns and Sacred Melodies* which was used for decades in revival meetings worldwide.

Bliss and Sankey had learned that many of the hymns found in church hymnals were not suitable for evangelism and revivals since they tended to be too impersonal. The gospel songs Bliss and others wrote were more personal and emotional and often contained a call for conversion. Gospel songs became an indispensable part of any crusade.

If you thumb through any hymnal, you will notice that words and music are usually by different people, but Bliss was gifted at writing both words and music, and many of his hymns have become classics, including "Wonderful Words of Life" and "Man of Sorrows, What a Name."

In 1876 he and his wife were traveling by train through Ohio. A bridge collapsed and several train cars tumbled into a ravine and caught fire. Bliss extricated himself from the car but realized his wife was still trapped inside. He went back to rescue her, and both perished in the fire. Bliss not only sang as a Christian and composed as a Christian but also died as a Christian.

Prayer: Father, we thank you for music and its power to move the soul. Amen.

July 10 · The Yeshua Controversy

Rabbi, you are the Son of God; you are the King of Israel.

John 1:49

1957: *The Nazarene* was one of the best-selling biblical novels of the twentieth century. It made its author, Sholem Asch, very famous and very wealthy—and very hated by his many Jewish fans. Asch, born in Poland in 1880, was a Jew, and his language was Yiddish. He gained fame among his fellow Jews as the writer of historical novels depicting the lives of Jews in eastern Europe, lives often marked by persecution. He was admired by Jews worldwide, regarded as the greatest Yiddish writer of the century.

But after settling in the United States and becoming a citizen, Asch did something that horrified his fans: he wrote a novel about Jesus—or, as Jesus is called in *The Nazarene*, Yeshua. Written in Yiddish and translated into English, it was among America's top ten bestsellers in 1939 and 1940, and thousands of readers who had never heard of Asch's earlier works lined up to buy this compelling novel. But one Jewish newspaper lamented that Asch had "gone off the rails," and most Jews agreed. There was even more of a fuss in 1943 when he published another bestseller, *The Apostle*, the story of Paul. In time, many of Asch's Jewish friends no longer spoke to him.

A Christian reader inevitably asks: Had Asch become a Christian? It is not an easy question to answer. For Asch, there was no "switching" of faiths—he saw Christianity and Judaism as "one culture and one civilization" and said he could not think of them separately. His critics claimed he wrote his New Testament novels strictly for money and for the acclaim of a wider audience. His defenders observed that while he was writing *The Apostle*, he was also writing stories about the plight of Jews in Nazi Germany.

Asch died on July 10, 1957, before he could complete a novel on the story of Jacob. Many Christian readers lamented the passing of this gifted—and misunderstood—Jewish author.

Prayer: Father, thank you for all gifted storytellers who make your sacred Word come to life. Amen.

July 11 · Old Man Eloquent

Serve wholeheartedly, as if you were serving the Lord, not men.

Ephesians 6:7

1767: John Quincy Adams, born on this date, is remembered as the sixth U.S. president, but his spiritual life is more interesting than the four years he spent as president. He may have been the first president who was genuinely Christian. Washington, Madison, and Monroe were technically Episcopalians but rarely attended church, and Thomas Jefferson was considered a Deist. John Adams was a Unitarian, but his wife, Abigail, was a Congregationalist Christian, and John Quincy Adams leaned more to his mother's faith than his father's. He was blessed to have two very moral, intelligent, Bible-reading parents.

In his long career of public service, John Quincy Adams was ambassador to the Netherlands, Portugal, and Russia; senator; secretary of state; president; and finally, for many years, congressman. In those long years he kept a diary, and it reveals a man with many quirks and foibles but also a rock-like faith. Unlike many intellectuals of his time, Adams could not accept a Christianity without miracles, and he understood that if you accept one miracle in the Bible, you may as well accept them all. His Unitarian father was content to regard Jesus as merely a great teacher, but for John Quincy, Jesus was his personal Savior and Redeemer. For many years he delivered the lecture "Faith" which was his response to the Transcendentalists, the "New Agers" of the time, who spoke of "the God within" and the "World Soul." While secretary of state he served as president of the American Bible Society and took a great interest in its work.

Adams had a cerebral hemorrhage on the floor of the House and died in the Capitol on February 23, 1848. Despite the sour face he showed in his official portraits and his often stiff manner, the statesman known as "Old Man Eloquent" was a decent man of integrity and faith, a rare thing in the political world. Of such men we need reminding.

Prayer: Lord, teach us to reverence the heroes of our heritage, and to learn from both their failings and their achievements. Amen.

July 12 · A Good Man Dying Young

To me, to live is Christ and to die is gain.

PHILIPPIANS 1:21

1739: Young David Brainerd was "walking in a dark thick grove" on this date and had a sensation of God's unspeakable majesty. "I continued in this state of inward joy, peace, and astonishment till near dark." The words are from Brainerd's diary which proved to have more long-term influence than the events of Brainerd's own short life.

Born in Connecticut in 1718, Brainerd had a temperament that we would today call "depressive" but was called "melancholic" in those days. His conversion experience in 1739 gave him a sense of purpose and energy which sustained him through many difficulties.

He went to Yale in 1739 to study for the ministry. This was the period of the Great Awakening, a religious revival aimed at converting lukewarm Christians into zealous ones. Yale made a rule that students who criticized any professor as "unconverted" would be expelled. Brainerd did, and the expulsion meant he could not be licensed to preach—but he could go as a missionary to the Indians. His diary records in great detail the difficulties in being a frontier missionary. He slept for awhile in a wigwam and confided to his diary that "I have no comforts of any kind." Some Indians were friendly to missionaries; others were hostile. Worse, Brainerd was slowly dying from tuberculosis, yet he refused to rest from his labors. He made some converts among the Indians after learning their language and translating the Bible, prayers, and sermons.

His health worsened, and he spent some time in the home of the great preacher Jonathan Edwards whose daughters tended the dying missionary. He died in October 1747, age twenty-nine. Thanks to Jonathan Edwards publishing his diary, Brainerd influenced many people after his death. John Wesley, the founder of Methodism, insisted that all of his preachers study Brainerd's diary. Many missionaries and evangelists have claimed that Brainerd's story of his physical and spiritual trials has given them hope.

Prayer: Lord, you give your servants strength to endure many sorrows. Let their stories inspire us to endure. Amen.

July 13 · Faiths Collide

Put on the full armor of God so that you can take your stand against the devil's schemes.

EPHESIANS 6:11

1949: Communism was and is a religion or at least a substitute religion. One who understood this clearly was Pope Pius XII who on this date told Catholics they had to make a choice: be a Catholic, or be a Communist—but not both. Catholics who "enlist in or show favor to the Communist party" would be excommunicated, cut off from the Catholic Church.

It sounds severe, and it was meant to be. The world had recently been through a horrible war where two forms of totalitarianism (Nazism and Communism) had fought each other. The Communists in Russia had been on the winning side, allied with the United States, Britain, and France—but the Communists were not "the good guys" just because of that temporary alliance. Since the war's end they had lowered their "iron curtain" over most of Eastern Europe and were working to elect as many Communists as possible to political office everywhere, including Italy, the pope's homeland.

In the same year that the pope excommunicated Catholic Communists, China came under Communist control—only three years after Pius had appointed the first Chinese cardinal. The Communist government announced it would guarantee religious freedom but soon began persecuting all religions, especially those (like Catholicism) controlled from outside the country. Many Christians were declared "enemies of the people" and treated abominably. The pope's ambassador was expelled from China. Pius let it be known that a Chinese Catholic church independent from Rome would not be tolerated since it would inevitably become a tool of the government. He was correct: the so-called Chinese Patriotic Catholic Association aimed to "re-educate" Catholics and turn them into Communists, or at least sympathizers.

Before he died in 1958, Pius made Karol Wojtyla, a thirty-eight-year-old Polish priest, a bishop. Twenty years later, Karol would become Pope John Paul II, the first pope from a Communist nation. But he would live to see Communism fall in Europe.

Prayer: Father, bless those who suffer for your sake under unjust and oppressive governments. Amen.

May the words of my mouth and the meditation of my heart be pleasing in your sight, O LORD, my Rock and my Redeemer.

PSALM 19:14

1850: "The heart is the motivating force of theology." So said German author Johann Neander who died on this date. He was born in 1789 and named David Mendel by his Jewish parents, but in 1806 he was baptized as a Christian and took the name Neander, meaning "new man," for he saw himself as beginning a new life in Christ. He studied for the ministry but felt drawn to the academic world, and he spent most of his life teaching at the University of Berlin, influencing students not only with his vast knowledge but also by the warmth of his personality.

One of Neander's mentors was the theologian Friedrich Schleiermacher who emphasized the emotional side of Christianity and taught that there had been too much stress placed on correct belief—not that doctrine wasn't important but without a personal relationship with the Lord, beliefs were meaningless. Neander spent much of his career writing an enormous work titled *General History of the Christian Religion and Church* which he never completed. He was a careful scholar who did painstaking research for this book, but he combined intellectual rigor with an emphasis on the faith of individual believers. For him, personalities were more important than movements or groups, for it was in the individual's heart that salvation took place. The head mattered, but the heart mattered more. Without feeling, there was no theology which "can only thrive in the calmness of a soul consecrated to God."

In Neander's view of history, two powerful forces are at work: the Spirit of God and the spirit of the world, and their conflict is an important belief in the New Testament, especially in John's gospel and letters and in the letters of Paul. The life of faith involves being fully engaged with the Spirit and always striving to please God, not to please the world.

Prayer: Father, let our lives be centered in you, and teach us to do what pleases you. Amen.

He has made everything beautiful in its time. He has also set eternity in the hearts of men.

ECCLESIASTES 3:11

1606: In the Dutch city of Leiden, a miller and his wife had a new son who would become one of the great names in art, particularly Christian art: Rembrandt van Rijn. His parents were pious folk, and Rembrandt seems never to have read much except the Bible. This most skilled of artists devoted much of his long career to depicting biblical people and scenes, and the world's museums overflow with his masterworks: *Christ Appearing to Mary Magdalene, The Return of the Prodigal Son, Christ Before Pilate, The Raising of Lazarus, Peter Denying Christ*, and many others.

Living in Amsterdam, which had a large Jewish community, Rembrandt used local Jews as his models for biblical characters. He used street people as well, and the model for one of his paintings of King Solomon was a local beggar. While some artists depicted biblical characters as remote and superhuman figures, Rembrandt made them look like real people, on the assumption that the people of the Bible were flesh-and-blood just as his models were.

Like many great artists, Rembrandt could discern beauty behind the homeliest face—after all, aren't ugly people the creations of God? He produced numerous portraits of his own homely, pudgy face—an honest man painting what he saw. He could, it seems, see into his own soul, just as he saw into the souls of the people of the Bible and could bring them to life on canvas. In at least one painting, *The Raising of the Cross*, he included himself in the picture as one of the Roman soldiers raising the cross of Jesus, his admission that he, like all human beings, was responsible for the death of Christ. When he died in 1669, Rembrandt left a body of Christian art that no one has ever equaled.

Prayer: Father, you bless us through the many works of art that bring your sacred words to life. Make us like Rembrandt, able to see each person as part of the creation that you pronounced "good." Amen.

July 16 · CALIFORNIA SOUL

I will also make you a light for the Gentiles, that you may bring salvation to the ends of the earth.

ISAIAH 49:6

1769: Sometimes a brilliant student settles into academia and stays there for the rest of his life. This was not the case with Junipero Serra, a Spanish member of the Franciscan order. Though he was an excellent university lecturer, he left academia in 1750, feeling called to the New World as a missionary. In view of his reputation as a teacher, he found himself lecturing at a college in Mexico City, but he also conducted missionary work in the Baja California peninsula. Later he moved north into what is today California. The Spanish wanted to settle the area to prevent the Russians, who had established settlements on America's north Pacific coast, from doing so. Serra's concern was not the Russians but the unconverted natives of this land "untrodden by Christian feet."

On July 16, 1769, Serra planted the first of nine mission stations that stretched from San Diego to San Francisco. Establishing the missions was not easy, since the Indians were often hostile, and disease and hunger took their toll on the missionaries, including Serra, who was five foot two and always in frail health. In March 1770 he and his party gathered to say one last mass, expecting they were about to perish, but one of the men sighted a Spanish supply ship sailing into the harbor.

Serra not only took his faith to the Indians but also taught them to raise sheep and cattle and plant grains and fruits. Like Paul in the New Testament, Serra regarded converts as his spiritual children and was not afraid to stand up to the Spanish colonial officials if they seemed to be exploiting the Indians.

In the U.S. Capitol's Statuary Hall, Serra is one of two figures representing California. There is also a large statue of him in San Francisco's Golden Gate Park. The Apostle of California was a truly amazing man.

Prayer: Lord, thank you for stories that remind us that the age of apostles did not end with the New Testament. Amen.

July 17 · CHRISTIANIZING SONG

Rejoice, O earth; burst into song, O mountains!

ISAIAH 49:13

1674: From the very beginning Protestant churches were singing churches, and Martin Luther encouraged the writing of hymns and wrote some himself. But many Protestant churches were strict about what they sang—they would sing only *divine* songs, meaning the words of the Psalms, usually in rhymed form. While new hymns were being written by Lutherans in Germany, the Protestants in England and Scotland sang only rhymed versions of the Psalms. Some of these rhymed Psalms were well-written, but the problem was the Psalms, being part of the *Old* Testament, did not contain *Christian* material. Why not write Christian hymns? The old familiar answer: *We never did it that way before.*

Enter Isaac Watts, born on July 17, 1674. The son of a pastor, Watts became pastor of a London church in 1701. He also changed the course of English hymns. From an early age he had written Christian poetry. Now his congregation began singing some of these poems, using familiar Psalm tunes. In 1707 he published *Hymns and Spiritual Songs*, and English hymnody was never the same, for Watts's hymns spoke of Christ, the crucifixion, the resurrection, and the prospect of heaven—things the rhymed Psalms did not touch on. Later Watts published another collection, *Psalms of David Imitated in the Language of the New Testament.* He showed he too could write rhymed Psalms, but in his versions the Psalms became prophecies fulfilled in Christ.

Watts was not only a poet but a theologian as well, and like all the best hymn-writers, he could versify Christian doctrine and make it appealing. He gave the name "System of Praise" to the combining of his Christian hymns with Bible-based sermons.

And what a legacy he left us: "When I Survey the Wondrous Cross," "Joy to the World," "Alas, and Did My Savior Bleed," "O God, Our Help in Ages Past," and hundreds of others. As long as there are English-speaking Christians, the words of Isaac Watts will continue to be sung.

Prayer: Lord, thank you for those who have enriched our worship with song. Amen.

July 18 · The Shepherd Decree

Be shepherds of the church of God, which he bought with his own blood.

Acts 20:28

1870: In June 1846 Pope Pius IX began his reign which would be the longest of any pope. At the beginning of his reign he was universally lauded, but disturbing forces were loose in the world, such as secularism and nationalism. The Catholic Church needed to address these issues, and in June 1868 Pius called for a Catholic council to "discover the remedies against the many evils which oppress the church." It was long overdue, since the last Catholic council met in 1563.

Known as the First Vatican Council (or Vatican I), the gathering opened in December 1869. By a huge majority the delegates to the council voted to approve the doctrine of *papal infallibility*, meaning that the pope when speaking in his official capacity (*ex cathedra*) cannot err. The pope "by virtue of his supreme apostolic authority" can decree a doctrine and make it binding on the entire church.

The doctrine was made public on July 18, 1870, in the decree *Pastor Aeternus*, Latin for "Eternal Shepherd." Though the world and the Catholic Church itself had grown more liberal and more questioning of traditional authority, the Vatican Council went against the tide and sided with tradition. In a turbulent and confusing world, it was a comforting thought that the pope in Rome could speak with authority—*divine* authority.

Needless to say, not everyone was pleased. Many non-Catholics mocked the new doctrine, and some Catholics broke away to form a new denomination—called, oddly enough, the Old Catholics.

A new era had begun but not just because of the council's decree. For centuries the popes held political power over large sections of Italy. Now the pope's political power was at an end, for in September 1870 the new Kingdom of Italy left the pope in control only of Vatican City. At long last the head of a global church could concentrate solely on spiritual matters.

Prayer: Lord, remind Christian leaders that their kingdom is not of this world, that they must devote themselves to things of the spirit. Amen.

July 19 · WONDERFUL PLAN MAN

He has committed to us the message of reconciliation.

2 CORINTHIANS 5:19

2003: "The most important moment in anyone's life as a believer is the last breath, because the next breath is in heaven." So said Bill Bright whose "most important moment" occurred on this date, ending an earthly life of remarkable accomplishments.

Born in Oklahoma in 1921, Bright said he spent his youth as a "happy pagan." While running a successful business in the Los Angeles area, he began attending church and became a Christian in 1945. He began study at Fuller Theological Seminary but never took a degree, since he found himself immersed in ministering to students at UCLA. That ministry was the beginning of Campus Crusade for Christ, with hundreds of branches at college campuses worldwide. In the following years Campus Crusade expanded its ministries to include high school students, families, athletes, and adult professionals. *Money* magazine claimed that the huge organization was "the most efficient religious group" in the country.

Campus Crusade's 1979 movie *Jesus* has been used worldwide in evangelism, and the group sponsored the memorable "Here's Life, America!" campaign of the 1970s. Its "Washington for Jesus" rally drew a million people to DC in 1980.

Perhaps the most important item on Bright's resume is his creation of what was probably the most printed and most influential religious tract of all time, *The Four Spiritual Laws*, a small booklet that has left a large footprint. The laws can be summarized in this way: 1) God loves you and has a wonderful plan for your life. 2) Our sin separates us from God. 3) Jesus Christ is the provision for man's sin. 4) We must individually receive Christ as Savior and Lord. The booklet backs up each of the laws with Bible quotations. Critics have accused the booklet of simplifying the faith, but Bright never claimed that the four laws were all that a Christian needed to know, only that they were the key information needed to evangelize nonbelievers. The impact of this tract has been immeasurable.

Prayer: Father, make us all ambassadors for Christ, bearing the message of reconciliation everywhere. Amen.

He was a learned man, with a thorough knowledge of the Scriptures.

ACTS 18:24

1838: Sweden today is one of the most secular nations on earth, but it was not always this way. In the 1800s Christianity was a vital force in the country. One of the leaders among Swedish Christians was Paul Peter Waldenström, born on this date. He studied theology and ancient languages and was ordained in 1864. He did not serve as pastor for long because he began teaching religion, Greek, and Hebrew at a high school and did so for the rest of his life.

Although he never separated from Sweden's state church, he was not happy with its emphasis on doctrine and rituals. Waldenström encouraged small groups of Christians to meet together to pray and study the Bible. The state church encompassed (in theory) all citizens of Sweden, but the small groups were for those who took their faith seriously. For several years he edited a magazine, *The Pietist*, which encouraged Bible reading and prayer. For Waldenström, one of the great questions for the believer is "Where in the Bible is it written?" Answering that question should guide the church in its worship as well as guide the Christian in his daily life. Since he was a Greek scholar, he made a new translation of the New Testament into Swedish.

Waldenström was not liked by the state church hierarchy since he believed that churches should be free from any government interference. But he was admired abroad, and in 1889 Yale University awarded him a doctor of theology degree. Many of his Swedish admirers immigrated to America, and they formed a new denomination, the Evangelical Covenant Church, greatly influenced by his writings. Since America, unlike Sweden, had no state church, the new denomination could function as the "free church" that Waldenström approved of.

Waldenström died in 1917, a beloved figure in his homeland and to the rest of the world, a sign that Christianity was alive and well in Sweden.

Prayer: Lord, let us, in all things, be guided by the truths revealed in your Word. Amen.

July 21 · The Old Soldier's Last Battle

Rescue me from my enemies, O Lord, for I hide myself in you.

Psalm 143:9

1925: A famous (and infamous) trial that concluded on this date was the last public appearance of one of the great figures in American politics who also happened to be a devout Christian. He was William Jennings Bryan, three-time Democratic candidate for president, secretary of state under Woodrow Wilson, campaigner for Prohibition, and, at the end, crusader against the teaching of evolution.

In the small town of Dayton, Tennessee, a teacher named John Scopes had violated the state's law on teaching evolution. His 1925 trial has become known as the "monkey trial," and the media descended on Dayton, depicting the trial as a confrontation between science and backward religion. Bryan signed on as counsel for the prosecution, and the famous lawyer Clarence Darrow, an agnostic, defended John Scopes. The outcome of the trial was not in doubt: Scopes was guilty. What provided drama was that the crafty Darrow put Bryan himself on the stand, questioned him about the Bible and science, and made him look foolish. Bryan died within a week of the trial, and the catty journalist H. L. Mencken who had covered the trial was elated, as if the intellectuals had finally killed Christianity.

What a pity that the only thing most people know about Bryan is his role in the trial. He was a spellbinding orator, one of the stars of American politics, a powerhouse among the Democrats. His objection to the teaching of evolution was that he feared, with good reason, that it could be used to justify political oppression, not to mention undermining belief in the Bible and in God. A man who tried faithfully to apply his Christian principles to his politics deserves a better fate than being remembered as the foe of science.

Bryan, a gentleman and Christian to the end, offered to pay the hundred-dollar fine the court imposed on John Scopes.

Prayer: Lord, good deeds and good people are often mocked in this world, but they find their rest and reward in you. Amen.

July 22 · No King but God

The LORD is with you, mighty warrior.

JUDGES 6:12

1099: On July 15, 1099, an army made up of Christians from various nations achieved its goal: capturing the holy city of Jerusalem which had long been under Muslim control. The First Crusade, launched in 1095, seemed to have been a success. Taking the city was only the beginning, however, for a new government had to be set up to stabilize the region.

On July 22 the leaders among the Crusaders assembled in the Church of the Holy Sepulchre, built on the site of Jesus' burial place. They chose the knight Godfrey de Bouillon to rule over the new "kingdom of Jerusalem." Godfrey agreed to rule—but not with the title "king," for God alone was the king over this land, and Godfrey did not think it fit to wear a gold crown where Christ had been crowned with thorns. The only title he would accept was "Defender of the Holy Sepulchre."

Godfrey is described as tall, of muscular build with blond hair, humble, but also a bold warrior. He quickly found that as head of the new Christian government, his main task was to keep the Muslims from retaking territory. He died in July 1100, probably about fifty years old, having reigned barely a year.

Because of his upright character—very different from some of the other Crusaders—he is regarded as the great hero of the First Crusade, and the later Crusades regarded him as a saint and role model. He fascinated Christian Europe, and in the great poem *The Divine Comedy*, Dante described Godfrey as residing in a part of heaven reserved for "warriors of the faith." In the Middle Ages he was regarded as one of the Nine Worthies, nine noble warriors including Joshua, David, and Charlemagne.

Jerusalem was not in Christian hands for long, but later generations honored Godfrey as the Christian ruler of the city where Christianity began.

Prayer: God, endow your servants with courage and boldness, yet let us not forget your Son, the Prince of Peace. Amen.

July 23 · SPIRITED MEN

Since we live by the Spirit, let us keep in step with the Spirit.

GALATIANS 5:25

1993: On an average Sunday, a church will have more women than men—typically, six women for every four men, though in some churches it is seven women per three men. Are women basically more religious than men? Or does religion, or at least Christianity, seem like a feminine thing that many men wish to avoid?

Some men have chosen to answer that question with action not words. One such man was Demos Shakarian, a California dairy farmer whose family fled Armenia along with a large band of Pentecostal Christians. The band escaped the horrible slaughter of Armenians by the Muslim Turks, and Shakarian believed God had preserved his life for a purpose. A good organizer, he helped with the campaigns of several evangelists and could not help but notice that more women than men showed up for revival meetings. So in 1953 he founded the Full Gospel Business Men's Fellowship with one purpose being to find more men to give their testimonies at religious meetings. Evangelist Oral Roberts encouraged the group at its first meeting, and chapters were founded all over the United States and later abroad. In less than a decade the group had more than 100,000 members, aided by the growth of the charismatic movement among Catholics and mainline Protestants.

Full Gospel is a term used by Pentecostal and charismatic Christians to refer to the use of Christian gifts that are neglected in many churches, such as the gifts of healing or speaking in tongues. "Full Gospel" Christians believe, with good reason, that too many churchgoers lack the power of the Holy Spirit in their lives and do not seek the Spirit's gifts. Groups like the Full Gospel Business Men's Fellowship have contributed to a heightened interest in the Spirit and his gifts.

Shakarian died on July 23, 1993. A book about him and the fellowship he founded was aptly titled *The Happiest People on Earth*.

Prayer: Father, guide men to your truth, and show them that true manliness does not require a man to shun the life of faith. Amen.

July 24 · DISPENSING THE WORD

Take the helmet of salvation and the sword of the Spirit, which is the word of God.

EPHESIANS 6:17

1921: The author of the most popular study Bible ever, died on this date after a long, productive, and colorful life. Cyrus Scofield was born in 1843, and his family was living in Tennessee when the Civil War broke out. Cyrus joined a Confederate regiment, saw some action, and returned home. He settled in Kansas and became a lawyer and politician but ruined his marriage through heavy drinking. Then he became a born-again Christian and eventually a Congregational pastor who went to serve a small church in Dallas—though it did not stay small for long, for it grew mightily during his pastorate. His ministry reached beyond the church through his popular 1896 *Comprehensive Bible Correspondence Course*.

As the new century began, he commenced the work that made him famous: the *Scofield Reference Bible*, published in 1909 by Oxford University Press. Many of its notes and study helps reflect Scofield's *dispensationalism*, the belief that there are seven ages or *dispensations* in human history, and in each God deals with humanity in a distinctive way. If only dispensationalists had bought his Bible, it would not have been a huge seller, but millions of readers liked it simply because it provided helpful notes for the sometimes difficult King James Version. Scofield admitted to a friend that the dispensationalism presented in the notes and study helps was much less important than the key doctrines of sin and redemption.

When his *Reference Bible* became a bestseller, it was inevitable that critics would come out of the woodwork, trying to discredit him or dispensationalism or both. But the original 1909 *Reference Bible* still sells well, and modern editions with newer Bible translations are also available. He intended to create a Christian classic and succeeded.

Prayer: Lord, bless those who clarify your Word, and let us honor them and you by putting your Word into practice. Amen.

"You will be my witnesses in Jerusalem, and in all Judea and Samaria, and to the ends of the earth."

ACTS 1:8

1974: "Let the earth hear his voice" was the theme of the Lausanne Congress on World Evangelization which concluded on this date, having drawn more than two thousand leaders from more than 150 nations. One of these was Billy Graham who was the honorary chairman and a featured speaker. Other speakers included Corrie ten Boom and John Stott.

One of the lasting fruits of the conference was the Lausanne Covenant, a detailed statement of evangelical faith. The Covenant insists that Christians are called upon to evangelize the world, but this mandate does not rule out social or political action. Christians "should not be afraid to denounce evil or injustice wherever they exist." In the work of evangelism, "we who share the same biblical faith should be closely united in fellowship, work, and witness." The Covenant makes it clear that in reaching out to the world, Christians risk becoming worldly and that persecution is inevitable, but persecution must not keep them from their task.

One notable feature of the Covenant is that each of its fifteen articles is followed by a set of Bible references, showing that the articles were based solidly on Scripture. This was important to those attending the Congress since they were aware of how many modern churches gave little thought to whether beliefs or practices were based on the Bible. Liberal churches had mostly abandoned evangelism for social and political action, and "missions" for liberal churches could mean almost anything except trying to actually win converts. The Covenant made it clear that evangelicals had by no means given up on Christ's mandate to preach the gospel everywhere.

The world still has billions of people who have never been exposed to the gospel of Christ, and the Lausanne legacy is to reach those people and let them know God desires them.

Prayer: Lord, you have commanded us to carry the message of salvation everywhere. Help us to make this duty into a pleasure. Amen.

I have fought the good fight, I have finished the race, I have kept the faith.

2 TIMOTHY 4:7

1833: Three days before his death, English statesman William Wilberforce received wonderful news: the thing he had fought for over forty years, the abolition of slavery in the British Empire, had been enacted by Parliament. The great man, one who was not ashamed to carry his faith into the political arena, died on July 29 knowing his work had not been in vain.

Wilberforce was elected to Parliament in 1784 and at that time was not religious. His friend Isaac Milner led Wilberforce to think deeply about faith. Wilberforce did, experiencing a conversion. He asked friends, including the future prime minister William Pitt, if he should stay in politics or devote himself to some other field. Friends encouraged him to stay in Parliament, and he made the abolition of slavery his pet cause.

A London suburb known as Clapham was home to Wilberforce and several other Christian activists, and the group became known as the Clapham Sect. All of them opposed slavery, seeing it as a great sin for a nation that called itself Christian to buy and sell human beings as if they were property. A major victory was scored in 1807 when Parliament abolished the British slave trade. Full abolition of slavery had to wait until 1833.

Wilberforce was active in other causes and also found time to write the popular book *Real Christianity*, contrasting genuine, active faith with the indifference of the "professed Christians." He aided a number of charitable foundations, including the British and Foreign Bible Society and the Church Missionary Society.

It is worth noting that Wilberforce was considered one of the most witty, charming, and eloquent men of his time. His active life proved that being committed to political and social causes did not require being a humorless or self-righteous scold. He was a committed Christian who used his gifts, including wit and warmth, in the cause of his faith.

Prayer: Lord, bless all those who never tire of doing good, who fight the good fight. Amen.

"Go into all the world and preach the good news to all creation."

MARK 16:15

2011: At the age of ninety John R. W. Stott went to his heavenly home after a lifetime of preaching and writing that touched millions. The son of an agnostic father and churchgoing mother, Stott was drawn to Christ by Revelation 3:20: "Behold, I stand at the door and knock" (NKJV). The verse moved him from an intellectual acceptance of the faith to wholehearted dedication.

Stott had the satisfaction of serving as pastor to the church he had grown up in, All Souls Church in London. In the 1950s and '60s he became one of the most high-profile evangelicals in the Church of England, and, in a sense, all England—and the English-speaking world—became his parish. Evangelicals were (and still are) an endangered species in the Church of England, and many of them left for other denominations, but Stott remained within the church, a spokesman for biblical principles in a denomination that was becoming increasingly trendy and political. While many people regarded Church of England services as dry and boring, the pews at All Souls were usually full, and worship there was exhilarating.

Stott reached millions of people outside the Church of England, for he was a tireless writer, and his books were extremely popular, especially *Basic Christianity*, one of the classics of twentieth-century Christian literature. Despite his notoriety, the soft-spoken bachelor, known as "Uncle John" to acquaintances, maintained a low profile. Even so, in 2005 *Time* magazine included him among "the 100 most influential people in the world."

When he died in 2011, Billy Graham observed that "the evangelical world has lost one of its greatest spokesmen, and I have lost one of my close personal friends." Stott and Graham helped craft the 1974 Lausanne Covenant which in many ways defined the evangelical movement. Graham stated he looked forward to meeting Stott again in heaven, and no doubt many of Stott's readers share that sentiment.

Prayer: Father, we praise and thank you for those who minister through the printed word. Amen.

The time will come when men will not put up with sound doctrine.

2 Timothy 4:3

1881: Stick with tradition (the conservative side), or change with the times (the liberal side)? This was the burning question for Christians in the early 1900s, and one of the defenders of the conservative side was Bible scholar J. Gresham Machen, born on this date. Machen graduated from Princeton Theological Seminary and shortly afterward began teaching there. Princeton had a reputation as one of the best (and most conservative) seminaries. Machen sensed that liberal views were creeping in, and in 1923 he published his most famous book, *Christianity and Liberalism*. In it he insisted that liberal Christianity was not one type of Christianity but an altogether different religion, one not rooted in the Bible. Machen stated that liberals did not believe that man's salvation was due to Christ's death on the cross nor did liberals believe man really needed saving. In Machen's view, the liberals used Christian words and symbols but no longer held to the core beliefs.

In 1929 the Presbyterian Church which controlled Princeton Seminary, appointed two liberal professors to the faculty. Machen and some other Princeton faculty left and formed a new seminary, Westminster. Fearing that Presbyterian missions were being tainted by liberalism, Machen set up an independent Presbyterian mission board. The Presbyterian authorities booted Machen and his colleagues out of the ministry, a "de-frocking" that made front-page news. In 1936 Machen and his friends formed a new denomination, the Orthodox Presbyterian Church.

Machen died in 1937, having predicted that the size of government would increase and that in time public schools would become hostile to religion.

His chief contribution to the liberal-conservative battle (which is still going on) is that he made the conservative side intellectually respectable. Liberals liked to portray conservatives as backward, uneducated hicks, yet Machen and his associates were clearly intelligent men, defending their faith with eloquence. His classic *Christianity and Liberalism* is still readable, and most of it applies to the theological battles of today.

Prayer: Lord, bless all those who have defended sound teaching and who use their minds in your service. Amen.

July 29 · FORCEFUL FAITH

The LORD has made his salvation known and revealed his righteousness to the nations.

PSALM 98:2

1030: Norwegians celebrate July 29 as *Olsok*, a holiday in honor of one of Norway's most famous kings and a key figure in the history of Christianity in the country. He was Olaf II, but Norwegians often refer to him as *Heilag-Olav*, Olaf the Holy. He was born in 995, a descendant of Harald I, the first king of Norway, and he was raised as a pagan, spending much of his youth as a lawless pirate. Sometime around 1010 Olaf visited the country of Normandy (today part of France) and was so impressed with its duke's Christianity that he had himself baptized. He saw it as his duty to rule over a united nation, so he returned to Norway in 1015 and brutally subdued the various chieftains and ruled as sole king. His admirers recorded that Norway "converted" to Christianity under Olaf's rule, but the truth is that he *forced* the Norwegians to be baptized and put aside their pagan practices.

The chieftains called him "Olaf the Fat" and did not like him or his religion, so they rebelled against him, and for two years he lived in exile in Russia. Appropriately for a man of violence, he died in battle against the rebels on July 29, 1030. The church of Norway soon declared him a saint, an honor based not on his life—which was far from saintly—but on his making Christianity the national religion and basing his law code on Christian principles. His tomb was visited by Christian pilgrims, and he was referred to as "Olaf the Holy" and "the Eternal King." Norwegian Christians chose to focus not on Olaf the blood-stained warrior but on Olaf the man who paved the way for a more peaceful—more *Christian*—form of Christianity in his country.

Prayer: Lord, much violence has been done in your name. Fill us with the desire to be peacemakers, and may your saving gospel spread through zealous preaching and gentle persuasion. Amen.

July 30 · HOLY EXPERIMENT

The body is a unit, though it is made up of many parts; and though all its parts are many, they form one body. So it is with Christ.

1 CORINTHIANS 12:12

1718: In 1682 William Penn landed in America in what is today New Castle, Delaware. Penn belonged to the religious group known as the Society of Friends, better known as Quakers, a group frequently persecuted in England. The English king owed a large sum of money to William Penn's father, and the debt was paid off when the king granted young Penn the right to establish a new colony in America. Penn intended that the colony, Pennsylvania, would be a "holy experiment"—a place where there was no one established church and no harassment or persecution of Christians of different denominations. It would be a safe haven for Quakers and for other oppressed Christians—not just from England but from across Europe. Among those attracted were German-speaking Amish who came to be called (somewhat mistakenly) the "Pennsylvania Dutch." Appropriately, the first city established in the tolerant colony was named Philadelphia—Greek for "brotherly love."

Though the colony encountered problems (as all the English colonies did), the "holy experiment" was in fact a great success. Christians of different denominations lived together in relative peace. Earlier the Massachusetts colony had exiled and on occasion executed Quakers. There would be no such injustice meted out in Penn's colony, nor would there be any ill treatment of the native Indians, for Penn insisted that they be dealt with fairly and honorably.

When Penn died on July 30, 1718, could he have foreseen the day when people took it for granted that different religious faiths could live side by side in peace?

Prayer: Lord, we are taken aback by the sad stories of Christians persecuting other Christians. Keep us mindful of faithful men like William Penn, men who lived lives of deep faith and preached tolerance of others. Amen.

I heard the voice of the Lord saying, "Whom shall I send?"

Isaiah 6:8

1556: "Teach us, good Lord, to serve You as You deserve; to give and not to count the cost; to fight and not to heed the wounds; to toil and not to ask for rest." This prayer was composed by a former soldier of the Spanish army who became a soldier for Christ, Ignatius of Loyola who died on this date after forming a spiritual army known as the Society of Jesus, or Jesuits.

Ignatius was born into a wealthy Spanish family in 1491. Wounded in battle, he read a life of Christ while recuperating and committed himself to the Prince of Peace. He studied at the University of Paris and there made friends with the six men who would form the original band of Jesuits. They traveled to Rome and offered their services to the pope. In 1540 the pope gave his approval to the Jesuit order with the men agreeing to do whatever he commanded. As the pope saw it, the direst need at that time was to reconvert to Catholicism the parts of Europe that had turned Protestant. For him and for the Jesuits, this was not a matter of beating the competition but of saving souls, for Catholics of the time believed the Protestants were heretics who could not be saved unless they came back to the Catholic fold.

The Jesuits proved highly effective at converting Protestants. Some Jesuits went abroad as missionaries to Asia and to the wilds of America. Others established colleges, and the Jesuits became renowned as molders of the character of the young. The Jesuit order grew with young men inspired by the prospect of an active life dedicated fully to the church. Protestants naturally resented the Jesuits' activities but could not deny that Ignatius had founded a spiritual army of the highest order. Men willing "to toil and not ask for rest" can do amazing things.

Prayer: Lord, light a fire in our hearts so we may serve you as you wish. Amen.

AUGUST

———

August 1 · IMPERIAL ENERGY

O LORD, the king rejoices in your strength.

PSALM 21:1

527: On this day began the reign of one of the most dedicated, intelligent, and devout of the Roman emperors, Justinian I who over a long reign led the empire to become the mightiest realm on earth. Aiding him in his labors was his remarkable wife, Theodora, who in her younger days had been an actress, in a time when the line between "actress" and "prostitute" was very thin. Married to Justinian, however, she became a model wife and took as much interest as he did in religious matters.

One of Justinian's greatest projects is still standing: Hagia Sophia in Istanbul, today under the control of the Muslim Turks but for almost a thousand years one of the most stunning churches in the world. Hagia Sophia is Greek for "Holy Wisdom," an appropriate name, considering what a wise ruler Justinian was. Numerous other churches were built by this man who believed that luxurious buildings would convince people of the power and importance of Christianity.

Most inhabitants of the empire were Christian by the time of Justinian but paganism still lingered, so he decreed that no pagan could teach school, and he closed the ancient schools of philosophy. He also gave attention to the moral life of the church, banning clergy from attending the theater or horse races and from using bribery to rise to high office in the church.

Justinian has been credited—or blamed—with *caesaropapism*, the practice of the emperor dominating the church. When the emperor was a devout man like himself, this was not a bad thing, but in later years some very unspiritual emperors would impose their will on the church. By making the church a department of the state, he paved the way for serious abuses.

Contemporaries called Justinian "the emperor who never sleeps," for this vigorous man could go without food or sleep for long periods, losing himself in his many projects. He deserves his reputation as one of the greatest emperors.

Prayer: King of heaven, we pray that all earthly powers will rule with wisdom and compassion. Amen.

August 2 · SOME GAVE ALL

Consider him who endured such opposition from sinful men, so that you will not grow weary and lose heart.

HEBREWS 12:3

1643: In the book of Acts, we see the missionaries Paul, Barnabas, and Silas enduring great persecutions. The stories of missionaries in peril did not end with Acts.

Consider Isaac Jogues, born in France, a member of the Jesuit order whose dedicated men seemed to know no fear as they took the gospel abroad. In 1636 he sailed to New France (that is, Quebec) to be a missionary to the Huron and Algonquin Indians. In 1643 he and associates were traveling by canoe to visit the Hurons when the party was captured by the warlike Mohawks. On August 2 he and the others were tortured horribly. The Mohawks cut off some of Isaac's fingers and afterward kept him as a slave for more than a year. Amazingly, he made use of the time and tried to teach the Mohawks the basic beliefs of Christianity.

Ransomed from captivity by some Dutchmen from New Netherland (New York State), he sailed from Manhattan back to France. Those of a more timid nature would never have returned to America but Isaac did. In 1646 he and another Jesuit went into Mohawk country as peace ambassadors from the Hurons and Algonquins.

Curiously, the fact that Isaac had survived so many trials seemed to convince the Mohawks he was a sorcerer. They blamed a recent epidemic and crop failure on him (believing these were vengeance for the harm the Mohawks had done him), and they sent out warriors to capture him. When they found him, they slashed him with knives and beat him, and on October 18, 1646, he was tomahawked and decapitated, his body thrown into a river. The French later captured the man who had tomahawked Jogues, and before he was executed, he converted.

Born into a wealthy family, Isaac Jogues could have led a peaceful, comfortable life in France. But like so many others, he had a passion for the gospel.

Prayer: Father, when difficulties assail us, train our eyes to see opportunities and to live life boldly. Amen.

August 3 · A Fair Shake for Working Men

Honor the LORD with your wealth.

PROVERBS 3:9

1846: When a politician's nickname is "Golden Rule," you can bet he is no ordinary political hack. This was the case with Samuel Milton Jones, born on this date in Wales, famous as the reforming mayor of Toledo, Ohio. His large family (he was one of seven children) immigrated to the United States when he was three, and Jones received little education but held various jobs, most importantly working in the oil fields of Pennsylvania and saving enough to eventually own his own company. He moved to Ohio, established Ohio Oil, and became wealthy when it was sold to the giant Standard Oil Company. He then moved to Toledo and founded a company that made tools for the oil industry.

It sounds like a classic rags-to-riches story of which there were many in America at this time. Jones also happened to be a devout Christian, and he asked his workers to do as he had done: work hard, be honest, and follow the Golden Rule. He promised that if they did so, he would treat them fairly and pay them well. He was elected mayor of Toledo in 1897, promising to continue his Golden Rule policy in office. Anyone who was expecting him to favor big business and forget the little man was disappointed because Jones was a reform mayor through and through, helping improve conditions for working men and cleaning up the city government. His party was not happy with his crusading spirit and did not nominate him for a second term—so he ran as an independent and won anyway. He died in 1904 before completing his second term. To no one's surprise, he left much of his fortune to his employees.

"Golden Rule" Jones was a remarkable man, one who often expressed his indebtedness to the warm evangelical Christianity he had grown up in. He saw the world as God saw it: "little people" mattered, and a man with wealth had an obligation to help others.

Prayer: Lord, whatever our estate, make us people of integrity whose lives are rooted in you. Amen.

August 4 · QUEEN'S COUNSEL

Plans fail for lack of counsel, but with many advisers they succeed.

PROVERBS 15:22

1598: The story of Christianity contains many heroic episodes with brave missionaries and evangelists, some of them making the ultimate sacrifice for their faith. There is a quieter form of heroism that too often goes unnoticed, such as the politician who resists the temptations to bribery and corruption and emerges as that very rare thing, a Christian statesman.

One of these was William Cecil, also known as Lord Burghley, a title given to him by Queen Elizabeth I. The queen is regarded as one of the best rulers England ever had, but no ruler succeeds without wise advisors, and Burghley served her well as chief counselor. Earlier he had served under her half brother, Edward VI, and then under her halfsister, Mary I—the "Bloody Mary" who tried to turn England back to the Catholic Church and who sent many Protestants to the stake. Burghley, a Protestant, has been criticized for not taking a stand for his faith. He can be excused for this by understanding that he knew Mary's health was not good and that soon her sister, Elizabeth would take the country back to Protestantism. To his credit, he stood up for the property rights of Protestants who had fled to Europe.

Elizabeth was intelligent and crafty—and had a notorious temper and waspish tongue. Somehow this patient man formed a political partnership with this difficult woman. Burghley was at heart a Puritan, favoring a more thorough reform of the Church of England than Elizabeth would allow. Both of them agreed in their support for Protestants in Europe. It grieved him that Elizabeth executed many Catholics, but most of these were cases of treason, not religious differences.

As her chief counselor, Burghley was the most powerful male politician in England. Amazingly, his private life was exemplary, and he was a good father and faithful husband. When he died on August 4, 1598, England lost one of the finest public servants it ever had.

Prayer: Father and King, we thank you for wisdom and tact that allow human government to act compassionately. Amen.

August 5 · WAR WITH THE SONS OF WODEN

Thanks be to God! He gives us the victory through our Lord Jesus Christ.

1 CORINTHIANS 15:57

642: England in the 600s was divided into several small kingdoms, some ruled by pagans, some by Christians. Oswald, the son of the pagan king of Northumbria, fled to Scotland after his father was killed in battle, and on the Scottish island of Iona, Oswald became a Christian. Iona was famous for its monastery, and when Oswald came to power in Northumbria, he brought one of the Iona monks, named Aidan, to convert the remaining pagans to Christianity.

Before this, however, Oswald had to defeat Cadwallon, a pagan king who was ravaging Northumbria. Once this was done, Oswald was established as king of all the north of England. The region had a Christian king and, in Aidan, a dedicated Christian bishop who preached, cared for the poor, and ransomed Christians enslaved by pagans. Far from being a timid saint, Aidan was fearless in confronting Christian rulers when they sinned. Oswald and Aidan worked as a team, for Aidan did not speak the language of Northumbria, so when he preached, the king acted as his interpreter.

Paganism in England did not give in easily. The pagan king Penda of Mercia was notorious for his violence and his hatred of Christians. On August 5, 642, Oswald and Penda massed their troops at a site called Maserfield. Oswald was killed in the battle, and the victorious Penda had him dismembered with his head, arms, and legs impaled on stakes. It seemed at that moment that Penda's gods were more powerful than Oswald's God, but paganism's days were numbered in England, and the deeds of the saintly king Oswald of Northumbria were being spoken of when Penda was long forgotten. Pagans could, at times, outfight the Christians, but they could not defeat them in the spiritual world. Pagan kings like Penda claimed to be sons of the warlike god Woden, but the Son of God won the ultimate victory.

Prayer: Prince of Peace, give us strength and confidence and light in this world of darkness. Amen.

August 6 · HOUNDS OF HEAVEN

Whoever turns a sinner from the error of his way will save him from death.

JAMES 5:20

1221: Would you feel honored to bear the title *Domini Canis*, "dog of the Lord"? Thousands of men have, over the centuries. The religious order known as the Dominicans was actually named for its founder, Dominic Guzman of Spain, who made it his life's work to stamp out heresy—not by persecution but by preaching and persuasion.

Born in 1170, Dominic was horrified at the heresy known as Albigensianism which was sweeping through Europe, especially France. Thousands of people were attracted to it—partly because the Albigensians often had higher morals than Christians. Dominic saw a need for well-educated clergy who would lead exemplary lives and who would use their knowledge to preach to laypeople and turn them back to the faith. Dominic recognized a sad fact: despite every person in Europe being (in theory) under the care of a parish priest, many priests were extremely ignorant, resulting in a vast number of ignorant laypeople. Traveling about in pairs, the Dominicans could at least expose the people to correct doctrine.

Clad in their black cloaks (hence their common name, Black Friars), the Dominicans also ministered to the sick and dying, including victims of the numerous plagues. Centuries later, when Europeans began to settle in America, the Dominicans were active as missionaries. They were proud of being known as the *Domini Canes*, Latin for "dogs [faithful servants] of the Lord."

The sad part of the Dominicans' story is their connection with the Inquisition. This isn't surprising since one of the order's main goals was turning people away from heresy. The Inquisition's severity has been greatly exaggerated, but there is no getting around the fact that torture and executions occurred. Thirty years after Dominic's death on August 6, 1221, the pope approved the use of torture by the Inquisition and, sadly, some of the most notorious Inquisitors were Dominicans. What a pity that the order Dominic founded had become un-Christian in its methods.

Prayer: Lord, help us be both zealous and gentle as we strive to turn people away from false belief. Amen.

August 7 · FULLY ARMED

Though we live in the world, we do not wage war as the world does.

2 CORINTHIANS 10:3

1961: "When man obeys, God acts. When men change, nations change." So said Frank Buchman, an amazing American pastor who thought globally and acted individually.

In 1909 Buchman began a campus ministry at Pennsylvania State where, slowly but surely, some changes in students' behavior began to be observed. He had similar success at Princeton and Yale, but it was at England's Oxford University that Buchman's gatherings of Christian students grew so much that they had to be held in a hotel ballroom. While some newspapers mocked the "strange new sect" that met for prayer and confession, many young people were drawn to the movement that became known as the Oxford Group. Members not only met for worship and fellowship but also did charity work in the poorer sections of London.

This was all taking place in the 1930s when Germany was falling under the spell of Adolf Hitler and the Nazis. Buchman was an optimist: not only was the Oxford Group active in Germany but he hoped to meet Hitler—and convert him. Not surprisingly, the Group aroused the Nazis' suspicion. As the decade progressed and it appeared that war was likely, the Oxford Group changed its name to Moral Re-Armament. Buchman hoped to avert war through creating spiritual changes in nations. Some followers abandoned him, feeling the group had become too political. During World War II the group performed morale-boosting plays around the United States.

In the late 1940s and 1950s Buchman spoke of the menace of Communism and the need of the free world to resist it. He saw that young Communists were zealous for their cause and believed Christians should be just as zealous in theirs.

Buchman died August 7, 1961, active to the end. While some of his beliefs were open to criticism, there is no doubt that Buchman saw deep faith in God as the only solution to a troubled world.

Prayer: Almighty God, arm us with the zeal and confidence to minister as we should. Amen.

August 8 · To Worship Is to Copy

Be imitators of God, therefore, as dearly loved children.

EPHESIANS 5:1

1471: Thomas Haemmerlin, who probably died on this date, wrote one of the most popular books of all time, although no copy of it has his name on the cover. He is better known as Thomas à Kempis, his hometown being the German town of Kempen. It is likely, although not certain, that he wrote the amazing book *The Imitation of Christ* which has been translated into more languages than any other book except the Bible. We are fairly certain Thomas died in 1471 sometime in late July or early August, though the exact day is in doubt. He was born around 1380 and was a member of a group of lay Christians known as the Brethren of the Common Life, devoted to prayer and study of the Scriptures. Thomas had the duty of instructing novices in the spiritual life, and *Imitation* was probably a collection of books he wrote for that purpose. We know little else about the man. That is as it should be, because the book is more important than the author.

"In all things have regard for the end, and in what fashion you will stand before a strict Judge, to whom nothing is hidden." This is one of the key themes of the book and also of the New Testament: this world is a preparation for the next and less important than the next. "Keep yourself as a pilgrim and stranger upon earth." Another key theme is: don't trust people. This sounds a bit cynical, but it has a positive flip side: trust God. One chapter is titled "On Inner Fellowship" and offers the consolation that whatever humans do to us, we are never alone. Self-control is another key theme, and the book makes it clear that if we control our own bad impulses, we have less time to focus on the failings of others.

Perhaps the book's classic status is due to its being clear and simple. Like the Bible, alas, it is probably purchased more than it is read. And that is a pity.

Prayer: Father, in a world where people model themselves after sinners, teach us to model ourselves on your Son. Amen.

August 9 · TRANSPLANTED SCOT

The disciples went out and preached everywhere, and the Lord worked with them.

MARK 16:20

1883: Robert Moffat, who died on this date, is remembered as the father-in-law of the great missionary-explorer David Livingstone. In fact, Moffat had a long and productive ministry of his own and deserves to be better known.

Born in Scotland in 1795, Moffat was sent in 1816 to South Africa by the London Missionary Society, despite having almost no training to be a missionary. For years he accomplished little, but in 1824 he settled in the village of Kuruman near the Kalahari Desert which would be his home for almost fifty years. He traveled throughout the region and became familiar with the various tribes and gained their confidence. He learned the Tswana language well enough to translate the gospel of Luke and, in time, the entire Bible as well as John Bunyan's *Pilgrim's Progress*. While his chief aim was to convert the Africans to Christianity, and he converted many, he also instructed them in advanced methods of agriculture and raised their standard of living. Like so many missionaries, Moffat found it useful to be a jack-of-all-trades, developing skills in farming, carpentry, and printing.

Moffat had written that on a clear morning he could see from his home the smoke of a thousand villages that had not yet received the gospel. This statement inspired the young David Livingstone whom Moffat met in 1840. Livingstone in time married Moffat's daughter Mary with whom he had six children. Moffat expected his son-in-law would accomplish great things, and in this he was not disappointed.

In 1842 Moffat published *Missionary Labors and Scenes in South Africa*, a book that influenced many other believers to take to the mission field. They, like Moffat, were willing to uproot themselves from their homelands and live among those whose languages and customs they did not know—all for the glory of God. The 1800s was the great century of Christians stirred by the challenge to spread the good news everywhere.

Prayer: Lord, send your messengers everywhere and fill them up with untiring devotion. Amen.

David became more and more powerful, because the LORD Almighty was with him.

1 CHRONICLES 11:9

1951: The 1950s was the Golden Age of Biblical Movies, which was appropriate, given that it was also the decade when U.S. church attendance hit an all-time high. Director Cecil B. DeMille started the new wave of Bible movies with his *Samson and Delilah*, which premiered at the end of 1949 but made most of its profits in 1950. Hollywood saw that religious epics could make money, and every studio began production on movies based on the Bible itself or on popular religious fiction.

David and Bathsheba premiered on August 10, 1951, and holds the distinction of being the only biblical movie to be the top grosser in its year of release. It is easy to see why David is one of the most colorful characters in the Bible: his adulterous affair with Bathsheba is fascinating, and the movie starred two of the most popular and attractive stars of that time, Gregory Peck and Susan Hayward. Screenwriter Philip Dunne became fascinated with the character of David and as a result wrote an excellent script.

Like most biblical movies, this one took some liberties with the story. Bathsheba's guilt is almost condoned: she barely knew her husband, Uriah, when she married him, and when home on leave, he refuses to have relations with her. In seven months of marriage she had been with him only six days. David's own guilt is also minimized: we see him arguing with his wife, Michal, an acid-tongued harridan. The Bible—and, eventually, the movie—condemn David's adultery, but David and Bathsheba were portrayed so sympathetically that the audience does not want them punished.

The movie's success led Hollywood to make more of the same but strictly for profit not for religious motives. There was no great spiritual depth in the films, yet they pleased audiences at the time—and, by today's standards, are very clean and moral bits of entertainment.

Prayer: Lord, help us to carry the Bible in our hearts and minds so we may feed on it continuously. Amen.

August 11 · POVERTY AND PRAYER

Has not God chosen those who are poor in the eyes of the world to be rich in faith?

JAMES 2:5

1253: Francis of Assisi is one of the most beloved of the saints of the Middle Ages, but Clare of Assisi is also an appealing character. Born in 1194, she was pressured by her wealthy family to marry at age twelve. Instead she ran away and after hearing a sermon by Francis, devoted herself to the religious life. She and her sister took shelter in a convent, and though her father sent twelve armed men to bring the girls back home, they would not budge. In 1215 Francis put Clare in charge of a group of nuns, and this was the beginning of the Order of the Poor Ladies, usually known as the Poor Clares.

Like Francis, Clare insisted on a life of poverty, and when Pope Innocent III gave his approval to the Poor Clares, Clare insisted that the group never be allowed to own anything. Years later a different pope pressured Clare to allow the nuns to own land and buildings, but Clare would not change her mind.

Francis's male followers traveled about the countryside and preached. The Poor Clares did not do this but usually stayed in their convents and engaged in manual labor and prayer. It was a hard life yet one that attracted many women, and the order grew. Whenever a woman joined the order, she gave away her money and possessions to the poor. While some orders of nuns became notoriously lax, Clare resisted every effort to water down the strict regime of her convents. She nursed Francis, her spiritual brother, through his final illness. Clare died on August 11, 1253, and the Catholic Church declared her a saint two years later. A member of the Poor Clares, Mother Angelica, founded the Eternal Word Television Network.

Prayer: Lord, let our lives show the world that material riches are nothing compared to spiritual riches. Amen.

August 12 · CHANGE OF BOSS

Set me free from my prison, that I may praise your name.

PSALM 142:7

1973: The Watergate scandal of the 1970s has been credited with making Americans cynical about politics. While the scandal did a great deal of harm (especially to its key participant, President Richard Nixon), it produced at least one modern-day saint, Charles "Chuck" Colson.

Trained as a lawyer, Colson joined the Nixon staff in 1969, with the title Special Counsel. The media, which detested Nixon, detested Colson also, referring to him as Nixon's "hatchet man" and "evil genius." It was rumored that Colson claimed he would walk over his own grandmother if necessary to get Nixon reelected in 1972—which wasn't true, but the public believed it. Colson was one of several Nixon staffers indicted in connection with the break-in at the Democratic Party headquarters at the Watergate office complex.

A Christian friend had given Colson a copy of C. S. Lewis's book *Mere Christianity*. Colson read it, and he dated his conversion to August 12, 1973. He found peace with God—but not with the justice system, for he was indicted in March 1974. The media were, of course, cynical about his conversion and assumed it was a ploy to reduce his sentence or even to be acquitted. Colson pleaded guilty to obstruction of justice and was given a one-year sentence. He served seven months, and the cynics expected that after his release he would leave his Christianity behind.

Not so. Colson founded Prison Fellowship, a ministry to prisoners, and became one of the key voices in evangelical Christianity. He published his story, *Born Again*, in 1976 and wrote numerous other books and columns. In 1993 he received the Templeton Prize for Progress in Religion and donated the prize money to Prison Fellowship. Eventually his dedication silenced the cynics.

The former hatchet man for a president became a servant of the King. On April 21, 2012, Colson went home to his Master.

Prayer: Heavenly Father, you are a God of surprises, changing men's hearts, turning the ruthless into your servants. We praise you. Amen.

The teaching of the wise is a fountain of life.

PROVERBS 13:14

1667: One of the drawbacks of a state church is that it lacks spiritual vigor while exciting things happen *outside* it. This was the case with the Church of England in the 1600s and 1700s when a vital spirituality could be found among the Puritans, Baptists, Quakers, and Methodists with the Church of England almost in a coma. But there were some individual pastors within the state church who kept the flame of faith alive. Among these was Jeremy Taylor who died on this date.

Born in 1613, Taylor was a "golden boy," blessed with good looks, charm, and intelligence. After his ordination he met and deeply impressed the king Charles I who by royal decree bestowed a doctor of divinity degree on the young man. During the English Civil War of the 1640s, Taylor sided with the king and the Church of England, although he wrote the book *The Liberty of Prophesying* pleading for religious tolerance—something few Church of England clergy approved of at the time.

In 1650 Taylor published one of the world's great devotional books *The Rules and Exercises of Holy Living*, followed by its sequel *Holy Dying*. Living in a time of civil war, when many people died young and suddenly, he observed in *Holy Living* that "God hath given to man a short time here upon earth, and yet upon this short time eternity depends." Being of a generous and merciful nature himself, he could warn his readers that "if we refuse mercy here, we shall have justice in eternity." Taylor had a way with words and also a way with images, as when he compared sin to a grain of sand—although it is small, on the inside of a watch it causes great destruction, so there is no such thing as a "small sin."

Taylor was a lovable and loving man, and the Church of England rightly regards him as one of its most appealing saints.

Prayer: Lord, thank you for words and images that lodge in our hearts and guide us to you. Amen.

August 14 · A Place at the American Table

God is present in the company of the righteous.

PSALM 14:5

1932: A clergyman who hobnobbed with U.S. presidents was honored on this day with a massive statue, unveiled at the Shrine of the Sacred Heart in Washington. He was James Gibbons who died in 1921 after a long career as archbishop of Baltimore and also a cardinal. In his lifetime he saw the place of Catholics in American life change dramatically.

Gibbons was born in 1834 in Baltimore, the child of Irish immigrants. He was ordained as a priest in 1861, then in 1868 was made head of the Catholic Church in North Carolina, a predominantly Protestant state, which widened his perspective on Christianity in America. In 1876 he published *Faith of Our Fathers*, a bestseller in which he defended the Catholic Church. He became a popular preacher, and he personally met every U.S. president from Andrew Johnson to Warren Harding, and several of them sought his counsel. President William Howard Taft honored Gibbons in 1911 on the fiftieth anniversary of his ministry. In 1917 former president Theodore Roosevelt spoke of Gibbons as the most "venerated, respected, and useful citizen in America."

The Catholic Church had "arrived" in the sense that Americans no longer felt threatened by it. In the 1800s, waves of Catholic immigrants from Ireland, Germany, and other nations had led to a growth in anti-Catholic sentiment, and some Protestants felt that these people with their loyalty to the pope in Rome might not be loyal Americans. This attitude changed in time. The soft-spoken Gibbons appeared to be, and was, a pillar of respectability, and his presence on a podium beside a U.S. president gave American Catholics reassurance that they were very much part of a multidenominational and tolerant nation.

After Gibbons's death in 1921, the waspish journalist H. L. Mencken, no friend of Christianity, wrote in praise of Gibbons's wisdom, political sense, and upright character. Coming from a man like Mencken, this was praise indeed.

Prayer: Father, teach us to honor and respect people from all walks of life who put their faith in you. Amen.

August 15 · The Fellowship Colony

They were longing for a better country—a heavenly one.

Hebrews 11:16

1620: Two tiny ships sailed from England on this date, heading for Virginia. One of them, the *Speedwell*, began to leak, so both ships returned to England. The other ship left England again, alone, on September 6. This was the *Mayflower*, and most of the passengers were Separatists, Christians who wanted no part of the state Church of England and its persecution of nonconformists. They were seeking religious freedom, and they were traveling as families, not individuals—the first group of European settlers to do so.

On November 21 the forty-one heads of households signed what is called the Mayflower Compact, agreeing to "covenant and combine ourselves into a civil body politic" so as to create "just and equal laws" based on Christian teachings. It was a unique thing: not a contract between master and servant or between a king and his people but between likeminded people who called upon God as a witness to what they considered a serious undertaking.

The *Mayflower* reached land—not Virginia but, thanks to some rough seas, Cape Cod, several hundred miles farther north—on December 11. They called their settlement Plymouth, after the English port they had sailed from. One of the group's leaders, William Bradford, later wrote a history of the settlement and said of the people that "they knew they were pilgrims." In the past a pilgrim was someone visiting a sacred place. Bradford saw himself and the other settlers as pilgrims of another kind: not visitors to a sacred place but permanent residents of one, a place they would make sacred by their devotion to God and by their separation from the corruptions of England. The Spanish settlements to the south were for making a profit, and to some extent this was true of the English in Virginia. But the Pilgrims were something new and unique: Christian families seeking a place to live God-centered lives in peace.

Prayer: Father, thank you for the stouthearted men and women who braved an ocean voyage and many dangers in the quest for religious freedom. Amen.

August 16 · LAWYER FOR THE LORD

Give ear and come to me; hear me, that your soul may live.

ISAIAH 55:3

1875: In the 1800s a region of New York State became known as the "Burned-over District" because it had experienced so many religious revivals that people realized once the excitement of a revival died down not much remained. In fact, many people in the district became cynical about religion. This was the situation Charles Grandison Finney intended to change. Ordained as a Presbyterian minister in 1824, the former lawyer was determined to lead a real revival, with lasting results in the district. In doing so, he changed the way people think about revivals and evangelism.

Finney thought that previous revivals lacked organization. When he visited a town to preach, he had already contacted local ministers to organize prayer meetings and, after the revival, to counsel with new converts. This is all taken for granted today, and the "advance men" who go to a location and help organize are a crucial part of any evangelist's crew. But this idea was new in Finney's day, and it offended many who said that the preacher ought to rely on the Spirit not his own efforts. Finney did not deny the Spirit's role but insisted that revival also depended on organizing things properly for maximum impact.

Organization was only one aspect of Finney's success. He was a tall, striking man, and though he was not opposed to emotion, he spoke more like a lawyer pleading a case than a usual preacher. The congregation became in effect a jury, asked to render a decision on the question "Will you accept Christ?" Finney made thousands of converts, including, as he hoped, many in the "Burned-over District." His supporters built a church, the Broadway Tabernacle, for him in New York, and it became a center of a "permanent revival."

Finney died on August 16, 1875, and his ministry is remembered as the highwater mark of what historians call the Second Great Awakening.

Prayer: Lord, fill us with the zeal that energized the great preachers of the gospel. Amen.

August 17 · The Man of Many Tongues

Turn to me and be saved, all you ends of the earth.

ISAIAH 45:22

1761: Jesus was a carpenter, Paul was a tentmaker, Peter was a fisherman, and one of the greatest of all missionaries, born on this date, was William Carey, a shoemaker. The son of weavers, Carey was inquisitive about the world and highly intelligent, teaching himself Latin at an early age and, while apprenticing as a shoemaker, Greek as well. Eventually, while working at his craft, he taught himself Hebrew, Italian, Dutch, and French.

What need would a shoemaker have for languages? Plenty, as it turned out. Carey joined the Baptists, became a pastor (still earning his living making shoes), and was intrigued with the stories of the explorer Captain Cook, giving him the urge to carry the gospel to the unreached. Carey heard a pastor say that if God wanted to convert the heathen, he would do so without human help. Carey, thankfully, did not share this view. He and some friends formed a group that evolved into the Baptist Missionary Society. In 1793 he landed in Calcutta, India, and with his ability with languages, quickly learned the local Bengali tongue and began working on a Bengali New Testament. By 1800 he was printing it on his own press. He then learned the classical language of India, Sanskrit, since it was used among many of the intellectuals of India. Soon came a Bible in Sanskrit, and in Carey's lifetime Bibles or parts of it were printed in forty-four languages. Converts were made, slowly but surely.

Like all missionaries, Carey had his share of tribulations. His son died, bringing on his wife's mental breakdown from which she never recovered. A fire in his print shop destroyed irreplaceable manuscripts. Nonetheless the mission expanded, opening a college to train native Indians as missionaries.

Probably no figure in the history of missions is as admired as William Carey whose life was a living illustration of his motto: "Expect great things from God; attempt great things for God."

Prayer: Lord, teach us to expect great things from you as we attempt great things for you. Amen.

August 18 · MOTHER OF CHURCHES

May I never boast except in the cross of our Lord Jesus Christ.

GALATIANS 6:14

330: If you see a statue or painting of a matronly woman holding a large cross, that woman is probably Helena, the mother of Constantine, the first Christian emperor. Her connection with the cross is that her son sent her on a tour of Palestine to locate sites connected with Jesus and the apostles, and on this trip Helena supposedly found the cross on which Jesus died. In a sense she was the world's first archaeologist.

Helena was born probably around the year 250, and tradition says she was from a humble family, working as a stable hand or maid at an inn when she met the Roman general Constantius, who would later become emperor. She gave birth to future emperor Constantine around 272. Constantius divorced her to marry a woman of higher social standing, but she and her son were well provided for, and after Constantine became emperor, she was regarded as the very devout queen mother of the empire. Constantine was devoted to his mother and had her image stamped on many of the coins minted during his reign.

Constantine sent her to Palestine in 326, and one of her tasks there was to supervise the demolition of the pagan temple of Venus that had been built over the tomb of Jesus. In the excavation process three crosses were found, supposedly those of Jesus and the two thieves crucified with him. Constantine ordered the building of the Church of the Holy Sepulchre on the site. Helena also founded the Church of the Nativity in Bethlehem and the Church of the Ascension outside Jerusalem. On her return to Rome, she brought with her the cross of Jesus and also the nails that were presumed to have pierced Jesus' hands and feet.

Helena died on August 18, 330, honored for her generosity to the poor as well as her church-foundings in Palestine. Catholics and Eastern Orthodox Christians honor her as a saint.

Prayer: Lord, while we honor the places where the Savior walked, let the true place of honor be in our hearts. Amen.

August 19 · NOT TO BE MUZZLED

Perfect love drives out fear.

1 JOHN 4:18

1531: In the Middle Ages most churches in Europe, especially the great cathedrals, had relics of some saint—these could be teeth, bones, pieces of clothing, a sword or axe by which the saint was martyred, and so forth. Typically a relic was small and encased in a gold or silver container called a *reliquarium*. People were very superstitious about relics, and because they were used to inspire piety, there was a brisk trade in them, with large churches competing to obtain relics of the most important saints.

It sounds very silly to us, but to medieval Christians it was a part of church life they took seriously. Then in the 1520s a young English pastor began to preach against the cult of relics. His name was Thomas Bilney who, while he was studying for the ministry at Cambridge University, was struck by reading 1 Timothy 1:15: "Christ Jesus came into the world to save sinners—of whom I am the worst." Young Bilney was not the first nor last Christian to apply those words to himself. This marked his conversion, and soon he came to accept the new Protestant teachings of Martin Luther.

Like Luther, he opposed the ridiculous cult of relics. Cardinal Wolsey, England's most powerful church official, called Bilney in and ordered him to cease such preaching. Bilney complied but not for long. He began preaching Protestant views again, and one Sunday he was literally dragged out of the pulpit and imprisoned in the Tower of London for a year. The time in prison broke him, and he recanted of his views. But after his release, he realized he could not cease preaching the truth, and once again he taught Protestant doctrines—not in churches, since he was barred from them, but in the open fields. Because the church regarded him as a relapsed heretic, he was burnt at the stake on August 19, 1531, one of the first Protestant martyrs of England.

Prayer: Father, make us grateful for our spiritual forefathers who were valiant for the truth. Amen.

August 20 · GENTLE POWER

You kings, be wise; be warned, you rulers of the earth.

PSALM 2:10

1153: In the Middle Ages, a devout Christian might ask himself this question: Should I be a man of action in the world or withdraw to study and pray in a monastery? Many chose the second option and lived a quiet life, but some chose the second and had the first forced upon them by popular demand. One of the saints who was both man of action and studious monk was the famous Bernard of Clairvaux.

Born in France in 1090, Bernard, at age twenty-two, joined a strict monastery, expecting from that time on to have little contact with the outside world. Three years later he established a new monastery in a valley called Clairvaux. Bernard spent much time in his devotions, writing hymns to Jesus, including one found in many hymnals today, "Jesus, Thou Joy of Loving Hearts." Divine love was one of his key themes, and as he gained fame for his gentle spirit and wisdom, he became a sought-after spiritual counselor. He often played the role of mediator in religious and political disputes, including deciding between two rival popes. More than one ruler was deposed because Bernard backed his rival, and Bernard did not fear to scold a king who had behaved badly. He was also the driving force behind the Second Crusade. It has been rightly said that Bernard had all of Europe for his parish.

Somehow, despite all his activity in the rough-and-tumble world outside his monastery, he continued to write, including a book titled *Steps to Humility*. He wrote many Bible commentaries and claimed it was his goal to "penetrate hearts rather than explain words."

When Bernard died on August 20, 1153, it was said that during his life he had thought about everything—except himself. Totally devoted to Christ, he never gave a thought to his health nor did he fear the wrath of rulers he scolded. He is one of the most appealing men of the Middle Ages, and of all time.

Prayer: Father, instill in us a gentleness coupled with boldness and confidence. Amen.

August 21 · INTO THE ABYSS

They eat the bread of wickedness and drink the wine of violence.

PROVERBS 4:17

1849: In the 1800s missionaries often wore two hats: missionary and geographer. This was especially so in Africa where much of the continent had never been mapped accurately, a situation that was a hindrance to commerce as well as evangelism. One of the great missionary-geographers, George Grenfell, a native of Cornwall in southwest England, was born on this date. Raised a Baptist, Grenfell went as a missionary to Africa in 1875 and with a missionary partner began exploring the vast basin of the Congo River in central Africa. On board a steam-powered riverboat called, appropriately, the *Peace*, Grenfell made notes on areas no white man had seen before; one of the sights was later named Grenfell Falls in his honor. He made such careful observations that England's Royal Geographical Society awarded him a medal.

But Grenfell never forgot that his primary task was spreading the gospel. This was not easy, for many of the tribes of the region were hostile, and some believed that the men arriving on the noisy steamboat were fierce demons bent on conquest. Thus the *Peace*, with peaceful people on board, was often greeted by natives wielding spears. Grenfell let nothing deter him, not even the deaths of several missionary partners who succumbed to tropical diseases. (Africa in this period was often called "the white man's grave.") The region sorely needed the light of the gospel, for the tribes placed little value on human life, and when a chief died, several war captives and slaves would be killed also, in the belief that a chief must have attendants in the spirit world. Some victims were buried alive, others burned, some hacked to pieces. Superstition and witchcraft ran rampant, as did cannibalism, and the concept of mercy and forgiveness seemed unknown. And yet he persisted—and made converts. He died in 1906 and was buried in Africa, as were his wife and four children. The native Christians mourned for the loss of their beloved Tata, "Father."

Prayer: Lord, bless all those who sacrifice so much to carry the gospel to the unreached. Amen.

August 22 · THE OTHER SLAVERY

Blessed is he who has regard for the weak; the LORD delivers him in times of trouble.

PSALM 41:1

1861: Slavery is a horrible thing, but what about working conditions that are as bad—or worse—than slavery? That question was raised by Richard Oastler, an English Christian who was privileged as a child to meet John Wesley as a guest in his family's home. Oastler as an adult met a Christian textile manufacturer who expressed guilt over the working conditions in his factories, and Oastler wrote a famous letter, published in the local paper, about "Yorkshire Slavery," with its English citizens—including children—toiling away in working conditions worse than the black slaves in the colonies.

Oastler began to agitate for a working day of ten hours (in a time when the typical working day was much longer) and urged voters to elect members of Parliament who would pledge themselves to vote for a ten-hour day. When it was discovered Oastler was in debt to his employer (who detested Oastler's "radical" ideas), he was thrown into prison, where he remained for three years—never ceasing to write in favor of better working conditions. Since he was confined in the Fleet Prison, the writings from this period were published as the *Fleet Papers*. Friends formed "Oastler Committees" to raise money for the release of the man known as the "Factory Child's King."

In 1847 Britain's Parliament passed the Factory Relief Act, limiting to ten hours the working day for children in cotton mills. Not till after Oastler's death did another act apply to children in all factories, but the act was largely due to his relentless efforts.

Oastler, a large man with a powerful speaking voice, knew the importance of putting Christian compassion into action. He died on August 22, 1861, having worked for and witnessed the abolition of slavery in the British Empire and the improvement of factory working conditions. Manual workers both white and black owed him a great deal.

Prayer: Father, never let us forget the poor and the weak, for in serving them we serve you. Amen.

August 23 · Lowering the Walls

If we walk in the light, as he is in the light, we have fellowship with one another.

1 John 1:7

1744: The 1600s had been a time of persecution and killing of Christians—by other Christians. Denominations mattered in those days, and differences were taken seriously enough that people were willing to die, and kill, for them. By the 1700s things had simmered down considerably, and Christians were beginning to see that denominations might peacefully coexist—or, even better, work together.

A man born on this date was a great believer in interdenominational Christianity. His name was Rowland Hill, and he was schooled at England's Cambridge University. He began preaching around Cambridge without a license, so the state Church of England did not regard him kindly. It denied him ordination, and technically Hill was never licensed to preach in any denomination—but he spent his life preaching anyway. Inheriting some money from his father, he built his own church, Surrey Chapel, in London, with a deed stating it was tied to no denomination. A unique round building with a huge dome, it opened in 1783, and when Hill himself was not preaching there, he opened the pulpit to faithful preachers of different denominations. Though Hill insisted on sound preaching based on the Bible, he also thought music was a key element of worship and is remembered for his question "Why should the devil have all the good tunes?"

Hill stated that "I do not want the walls of separation between different orders of Christians to be destroyed, but only lowered, that we may shake hands a little easier over them." Surrey Chapel certainly contributed to some genial handshaking between Christians of different denominations. The church also ran several ministries, including Sunday schools and charities. Hill also encouraged his congregation to submit to a new medical procedure, vaccination for smallpox, an invention of his scientist friend Edward Jenner.

Hill died in 1833 and was buried, appropriately, beneath the pulpit at Surrey Chapel.

Prayer: Lord, let us reach out lovingly to all people who put their faith in you. Amen.

August 24 · Marriage and Carnage

Bring to an end the violence of the wicked and make the righteous secure.

PSALM 7:9

1572: "Kill them all!" was probably the most infamous royal quote of the 1500s because it was an order carried out with shocking brutality.

France in 1572 was a divided country with the royal family staunchly Catholic while many of the nobles and middle class had turned Protestant. The young king Charles IX became close friends with Coligny, the leader among the Protestants, a situation that irked his mother, the domineering Catherine de Medicis. Charles's sister was to be married to a Protestant prince, Henry of Navarre, and while Protestants flocked to Paris for the wedding, Catherine plotted to have Coligny assassinated. The plot failed, and Catherine feared a vengeful uprising of the Protestants. She pressured Charles to take swift action. Since all the Protestant leaders were in Paris, his order to "Kill them all!" made perfect—and horrible—sense.

The mass killing began early on August 24 which in the Catholic calendar is St. Bartholomew's Day, so the bloodbath is known as the St. Bartholomew's Day Massacre. Henry of Navarre, the Protestant who had married the king's sister six days earlier, was spared, but his entourage was slaughtered. Protestants were brutally murdered and their homes and shops pillaged. Catholic mobs took it on themselves to murder Protestants and so much blood was shed that the king finally ordered it stopped.

The king lied and announced the massacre was done because a Protestant plot against the royal family had been revealed. The massacre turned the surviving Protestants, who had mostly been peaceful citizens, against the government and made them willing to use force in the cause of their faith. The gory Wars of Religion would continue for another twenty years, ending when Henry of Navarre became king of France, turned Catholic, and extended toleration to the Protestants—but the path to peace proved long and bloody.

Prayer: Lord, teach your servants to fight with spiritual weapons, not the weapons of this world. Amen.

August 25 · SAINT KING

Endow the king with your justice, O God, the royal son with your righteousness.

PSALM 72:1

1270: The cathedral in New Orleans's Jackson Square may be one of the most photographed buildings in America, but few tourists know the church is named for a king of France, Louis IX, who—rather amazingly, for a king—is also considered a Christian saint.

In theory, everyone in medieval Europe was a Christian by virtue of baptism. In practice, people behaved badly and kings worse than most since their power gave them ample opportunity for sinning. Louis IX of France was an exception. He became king at the age of twelve in 1226, but for many years the government and the molding of Louis's character were in the hands of his remarkable mother, a strong and very devout woman who instilled in him the belief that he was accountable to God for his own soul and for his nation's welfare. Louis reigned with justice and tried to protect the poor from the greedy nobles of France. Not trusting royal officials to do their jobs right, he had a network of "investigators" to monitor their activity. Most kings would sign a treaty and then break it without troubling their consciences, but Louis was a man of his word.

Louis fought in the Crusades, the wars to recover the Holy Land from the Muslims. For many rulers, the Crusades were mostly a matter of public relations: a ruler would go to Palestine, fight in a few battles, and (if he survived) return home to be proclaimed as a warrior for the Lord. Louis was different: he really did want to recover the Holy Land for the Christians. He spent four years in Palestine, building up defenses and organizing the government. Louis died on August 25, 1270, while on Crusade.

America's federal government thought highly of Louis, for statues of him (honoring him as a law-giver) are found in the Supreme Court building and the House of Representatives.

Prayer: King of all creation, we praise you for statesmen who act with wisdom and fairness in this fallen world. Amen.

August 26 · BLOOD BROTHERS

Do not be surprised, my brothers, if the world hates you.

1 JOHN 3:13

2008: On this date Pastor Samuel Nayak stood at the entrance of his church in Orissa state, India, attempting to block the path of several hundred Hindu radicals. They slit his throat, left him for dead, and destroyed the church. This was one of several horrors occurring between August 25 and 28, 2008, a bloody wave of anti-Christian violence. Thirty-eight Indian Christians were killed, forty-one churches of different denominations destroyed, hundreds of houses and vehicles destroyed, and an orphanage burned. A few weeks later the radicals announced a large bounty for the killing of Christian pastors.

The rampage left fifty thousand Christians fleeing for their lives into nearby forests. A year after the carnage, many of these were still afraid to return to their home villages, having been warned by the radicals that if they came home, they would be forced to convert back to Hinduism—or die. For many of the refugees there were no homes to return to.

What prompted such hatred and violence? The short answer is: hatred of minorities and nonconformists, something found across the globe in all periods of history. The long answer: a noted Hindu swami was murdered on August 23, 2008, probably by Indian Communists, but many Hindus blamed his death on Christians and thus began the wave of violence. Christian and human rights groups worldwide condemned the violence, but those who closely monitor the world scene knew there was nothing new about anti-Christian violence in India. Though in the past Hindus were relatively tolerant of Christians—even though few Hindus actually converted—the twenty-first century has seen countless atrocities perpetrated, particularly aimed at Hindus who convert to the "alien" religion of Christianity.

The sad news is that, as Jesus foretold, his followers will suffer for his sake. The good news is that the gospel of love continues to spread in a world saturated with hatred.

Prayer: Lord, be with your children in their suffering. Arm them with love in the war against blind hate. Amen.

August 27 · NOVEL FAITH

You will be his witness to all men of what you have seen and heard.

ACTS 22:15

1877: Some successful authors, such as Charles Dickens, become famous when young. Lloyd Douglas, born on this date, did not write his first novel until he was past fifty. Born in Indiana, the son of a pastor, Douglas graduated from college, was ordained, and served churches in the Midwest and DC. While pastoring a church in Quebec, Canada, he began writing his first novel, *Magnificent Obsession*. It was published in 1929 and became a runaway bestseller, spawning two film versions and a television series. He published several more successful novels, all set in the present. Then a fan suggested an interesting subject: the story of the Roman soldier who received Jesus' robe.

Douglas set to work on this story that became his masterpiece, one of the most popular biblical novels of all time, *The Robe*. The soldier Marcellus believes Jesus to be innocent, and eventually he becomes a Christian, largely due to the influence of his Greek slave, Demetrius. At the end Marcellus dies by order of the mad emperor Caligula. The story of faith and sacrifice struck a chord when it was published in 1942, for America was caught up in World War II. *The Robe* sold 2 million copies and was the best-selling novel of 1943. It spawned a sequel, *The Big Fisherman*, telling the story of Peter.

Douglas died in 1951, so he never saw the lavish color movie version of *The Robe*, released in 1953 nor the movie of *The Big Fisherman*, released in 1959. Nor was he aware that *The Robe* was the best-selling novel in 1953 thanks to the release of the movie.

Douglas wrote, "If my novels are entertaining, I am glad, but they are written not so much for entertainment as for inspiration." After years as a pastor, Douglas was convinced that many people who would not subject themselves to a sermon or a religious essay might encounter the truth through fiction.

Prayer: Father, bless those who in any way help to spread abroad the truths of your Word. Amen.

August 28 · Homeless Heart

My soul finds rest in God alone.

PSALM 62:1

430: "Thou hast made us for Thyself, O Lord, and our hearts are restless till they rest in Thee." This familiar quote is from the opening of the *Confessions* of Augustine, a bishop, theologian and, for much of his life, a restless truth-seeker who finally found his peace with God.

Born in 354 in northern Africa, Augustine had a pagan father and a Christian mother. Though his mother tried to bring him up as a Christian, as a young adult he found himself captivated by pagan philosophers and the "cauldron of unholy loves" in the city of Carthage, where he kept a mistress who bore him a son. Augustine was unhappy about his sexual waywardness and would pray, "Lord, make me chaste—but not yet." For years he was a Manichean, a follower of a religion that was a serious rival to Christianity in those days, but it did not satisfy him. Living as a teacher of rhetoric in Italy, he came under the influence of the great bishop Ambrose. In 387 he was baptized, having found in Christianity the only true philosophy and the only source of righteous living.

In 391 the citizens of Hippo, a city in northern Africa, insisted that he be their bishop, and so history knows him as Augustine of Hippo. While pastoring his flock, Augustine found time to write, and he was embroiled in every religious controversy of the day. He wrote eloquently against his former religion, Manichaeism, and also wrote against Pelagianism, a Christian heresy teaching that people could save themselves by their own efforts. Augustine knew better: salvation came through the grace of God not human striving. In fact, theologians often refer to him as the Doctor of Grace.

Augustine died on August 28, 430, leaving behind a huge body of writings that still fascinate and influence theologians. For the non-theologian, Augustine's *Confessions* are one of the great spiritual autobiographies of all time.

Prayer: Father, we thank you for being our spiritual home in this world of unsatisfying beliefs and practices. Amen.

August 29 · UTTER DESOLATION

"Not one stone here will be left on another."

MATTHEW 24:2

70: On this day the Jews lost a treasure they never rebuilt and never forgot: the temple in Jerusalem. As Jesus predicted, the magnificent edifice was destroyed, the Romans' ultimate punishment for a Jewish rebellion that began in the year 66, when the temple's priests ceased offering sacrifices in the temple on behalf of the Roman emperor. This act of defiance didn't happen out of the blue, for there had been numerous violent confrontations between Jews and Romans. From 66 on, the violence would escalate.

Once the rebellion began, Roman soldiers released all their pent-up hatred for the Jews, people they despised and mocked for their customs of circumcision, Sabbath-keeping, and kosher food rules. The Jews likewise were fired up, having endured centuries of paying taxes to support immoral emperors and worthless layabouts in Rome. Emperor Nero sent General Vespasian to put down the revolt. When Nero died, Vespasian was called to Rome to be the new emperor, and he left his son Titus in charge of destroying Jerusalem. Holed up behind the city walls, the people of Jerusalem almost starved to death. The Romans' battering rams finally broke through the walls, and once the Romans were inside, they slaughtered the old and sick, sold the women and children into slavery, and sent the young men to work in the mines.

A soldier threw a firebrand in the temple, and Romans cut down the Jews trying to put out the fire. With the temple gone, so was the whole system of priests and sacrifices. From then on, the Jews' religion was centered in the synagogues, not the temple.

The emperor banned Jews from the city. Most of the Christians had already fled the city before Titus arrived. Henceforth their faith would be centered not in Jerusalem but in large Gentile cities such as Antioch and Rome. For both Jews and Christians, the temple of God would be the heart of the believer.

Prayer: Father, thank you for being with us, in all times and conditions, no matter what befalls us. Amen.

August 30 · God in Diverse Tongues

Exalt the LORD our God and worship at his footstool; he is holy.

PSALM 99:5

1971: "Mass Nostalgia" was the title of an article in the *Time* magazine issue on this date. The article referred to a major change in the Catholic Church that occurred in the wake of the Vatican II Council: the change from mass in Latin to mass in the vernacular languages. Clearly it had been the will of the Council, which claimed to represent the entire Catholic Church, that the people in the pews hear the words of the mass *in words they could understand*. But not all Catholics were pleased. Some began driving long distances to attend one of the few churches where a priest had been given special permission from his bishop to recite the mass in Latin. Change, as history proves, is always resisted. Is this just human stubbornness, or are there times when resistance is the right thing?

For many centuries the Catholic Church had conducted mass all over the world using the same words in the same ritual. Presumably the laity knew what all the words meant—but did they? There was no denying that a ritual conducted in an ancient language created an atmosphere of solemnity. After the switch to vernacular languages, some Catholics said the otherworldly feel of the mass was gone—and so were some of the worshippers. For many, the words of the mass spoken in everyday language didn't seem inspiring.

In 2007 Pope Benedict XVI, sympathetic to those who prefer the Latin rite, ruled that any priest willing to celebrate mass in Latin no longer had to have his bishop's permission. By this point, long after Vatican II, many of the older generation who loved the Latin mass had died off. But, amazingly, many *young* Catholics sought out churches with the Latin mass. *Time* spoke of "retro-Catholics," young people who in a secular, pop-music-saturated world love the dignity of traditional worship. The pope seems to have made a wise choice.

Prayer: Father, in all forms of worship, reach out to us, touch our hearts and minds. Amen.

August 31 · PILGRIM PRISONER

Here we do not have an enduring city, but we are looking for the city that is to come.

HEBREWS 13:14

1688: The English author, preacher, and convict who died on this date gave the world a book that at one time was found in the home of every English-speaking family, along with the Bible. It was *The Pilgrim's Progress from This World to That Which Is to Come*, by John Bunyan, a man with little schooling but immense courage and deep faith. By trade, Bunyan was a tinker, a mender of pots and pans; by divine calling, he was a preacher. He was a Dissenter, meaning not a member of the state Church of England, and like many Dissenters he endured persecution during the turbulent 1600s. His first imprisonment was in 1660, and not a man to waste opportunities, he began writing and penned his spiritual autobiography, *Grace Abounding to the Chief of Sinners.*

His masterpiece, however, is *Pilgrim's Progress*, published in 1678, telling the story of Christian, who flees the City of Destruction and journeys to the Celestial City, on the way encountering characters such as Worldly Wiseman, Hopeful, Ignorance, the Giant Despair, and Evangelist, passing through such locales as the Slough of Despond, the city of Vanity, and the Valley of the Shadow of Death, finally crossing the River of Death to enter heaven. As these names indicate, Bunyan was very familiar with the Bible but also familiar with his own soul and those of the people he preached to, and he had a knack for turning the Christian life, with all its adversities and pleasures, into a fine adventure story.

Bunyan wrote his masterpiece during one of his prison stretches. When he wrote in *Progress* about the persecutions and obstacles that Christian had to cope with, he was speaking as one who had himself suffered for his faith. Perhaps that is why the deep faith that shines through this classic seems so genuine.

Prayer: Father, when we find ourselves entangled in the cares and snares of this world, keep us mindful of our eternal home. Amen.

SEPTEMBER

In God I trust; I will not be afraid.

Psalm 56:11

1785: In 1846 Methodist preacher Peter Cartwright was running for Congress. He accused his opponent of not being a Christian. The opponent, who won the election, claimed, that though he had never joined a church, he believed the Bible. The opponent's name was Abraham Lincoln. It was better for both men that Lincoln won and Cartwright lost and also better for Christianity, for Cartwright was a better preacher than politician.

Cartwright was born on September 1, 1785, in Virginia and, like many Americans of the time, moved west, to Kentucky. He was converted at age sixteen, and shortly afterward the Methodists licensed him to preach. They gave him an extremely large parish, and Cartwright found himself one of the first circuit-riding ministers on the American frontier, traveling by horseback through all kinds of weather in sparsely populated regions still thick with wild animals and hostile Indians. At first preaching in Kentucky and Tennessee, he found slavery so distasteful that he moved to Illinois, where he served in the state legislature—in those days, a part-time job. He and Lincoln shared the dislike of slavery.

In his colorful *Autobiography* he recorded that his circuit in Illinois comprised almost two-thirds of the state, a huge area for a man on horseback. Cartwright could sometimes preach for more than two hours. The circuit-riding life could either kill a man or harden him—in Cartwright's case, it hardened, and no doubt some of the appeal of his preaching was that the preacher was obviously a man of great physical stamina. The rowdy men who often went to revival meetings with the aim of heckling the preacher were put off by Cartwright's toughness.

Peter died at age eighty-seven in 1872, having watched Methodism grow from 120,000 members in 1804 to more than a million. Although he lost an election to Abraham Lincoln, he had fulfilled his vow of "capturing the land for Christ."

Prayer: Father, preserve us in our trials as you have preserved your faithful servants for ages. Amen.

September 2 · In the Homeland of Atheism

The Lord is a refuge for the oppressed, a stronghold in times of trouble.

Psalm 9:9

1979: Christianity has never had an easy time in China. This was true when the country was mostly Confucianist and Buddhist and even more true after the Communists seized power in 1949. The country became officially atheist, and though churches were tolerated (but closely monitored), foreign missionaries were booted out. Things grew worse in 1966 when Chairman Mao launched his Cultural Revolution, when anything foreign, including Christianity, came under attack.

The Chinese church did not die under Communism. On the contrary, it had a certain vitality—but underground not publicly. House churches were nothing new—after all, they began with the book of Acts, and in times of severe persecution, they keep the faith alive.

Mao died in 1976, and there was a gradual diminishing of persecution. Something amazing happened on September 2, 1979: a church building in Shanghai held *public* worship with more than a thousand people attending. They met at the Mo En church, at one time a Methodist building, but this 1979 gathering was very much interdenominational. The atheist government seemed not to mind.

What is the situation today? China is still unapologetically Communist, but it is obvious to everyone, including the Communist bureaucrats, that Christianity is growing. There are Christian businessmen's clubs in most cities and house churches everywhere. As the new century began, China probably had more committed Christians than committed Communists. By 2050 it will likely have the largest Christian population of any nation.

Morally, the nation has serious problems. The infamous "One Child" policy has led to thousands of forced abortions—not surprising in a nation that officially recognizes no God and no authority higher than the state. Persecution of Christians is still being reported. Given the history of Christianity in the country, believers there know they should rely on God alone, not the favor of the government.

Prayer: Father, we pray that your holy gospel changes hearts everywhere, even in the nations that deny you. Amen.

September 3 · GREAT SERVANT

"Whoever wants to become great among you must be your servant."

MATTHEW 20:26

590: "Servant of the servants of God" was the title assumed by Gregory I who became pope on this date. Born into a wealthy family, Gregory gave most of his inheritance to the poor and turned his family homestead into a monastery. After becoming pope, he helped Rome deal with a pestilence that resulted from a flood of the Tiber River. The pope found himself in the position of being not only the highest church official in Italy but of taking charge of civil matters as well. Gregory proved himself an able administrator.

He was also a strict disciplinarian, and he cleaned up a great deal of corruption in the church, including monasteries where the monks lived like princes. Gregory enforced discipline, and idlers and troublemakers were booted out. He took missions seriously and sent Augustine off to England to evangelize the pagan Anglo-Saxons. He took music seriously also, and although he did not invent the Gregorian chant, it was named in his honor.

Somehow Gregory found time to write, and he penned a famous commentary on Job, titled *Moralia*. He also wrote a manual on how bishops should conduct themselves, and his sermons on the Bible were widely read. When he died on March, 12, 604, he was immediately declared a saint by the church and has since been known as Gregory the Great.

Despite his many achievements, Gregory erred in two matters that would affect the church. One was his advocacy for interpreting the Bible allegorically instead of sticking to the literal sense, and for almost a thousand years most commentators ignored the literal sense altogether. Gregory also erred in identifying the "sinful woman" who anoints Jesus' feet (Luke 7:36–50) with Mary Magdalene, leading to the belief (still common today) that Mary Magdalene was a prostitute, something the Bible never says.

Still, Gregory deserves his title "the Great," and he was a far finer man than many of the popes who followed him.

Prayer: Father, give us hearts for service and open opportunities for us to reach out in compassion. Amen.

September 4 · ABIDING ETERNALLY

"They will rest from their labor, for their deeds will follow them."

REVELATION 14:13

1847: In 1818 minister Henry Francis Lyte found himself in a curious position: he was giving comfort to a dying clergyman and found, to his shock, that the clergyman was unsure of his own salvation. Lyte was painfully aware that he himself was in the same position. Both men began to search the Bible, and both underwent a conversion. Lyte from that time on began to take his duties as a pastor more seriously.

The typical Church of England pastor of that time was content to baptize, marry, bury, and preach a brief Sunday sermon for which he had little enthusiasm. Lyte could not be satisfied with this: he became a devoted spiritual counselor to his parish in a coastal town in southwest England. He wore himself out for this church, composed of fishermen and their families, counseling with them, organizing Sunday schools, training teachers, and writing hymns, many of which are still popular.

The most famous of his hymns was written just a few weeks before he died. On September 4, 1847, Lyte took a walk along the seashore and contemplated the sunset. Returning home, he quickly wrote down "Abide with Me" with its memorable first lines: "Abide with me! Fast falls the eventide; / The darkness deepens; Lord, with me abide." The hymn was based on the scripture he had preached on earlier that day, Luke 24, the story of the risen Jesus encountering two disciples on the road to Emmaus. Luke 24:29 reads, "They constrained him, saying, 'Abide with us, for it is toward evening; the day is far spent.' And he went in to tarry with them" (KJV).

Lyte's health had been failing for several years, and it is possible that when he wrote "Abide with Me," he knew it would be his last hymn and that he would soon be abiding with the Lord forever. He died on November 20 that same year.

Prayer: Father, no matter what each day may bring, never let us forget that our destiny lies with you in eternity. Amen.

September 5 · EXPLOSIVE FAITH

The word of God spread, and the number of the disciples multiplied greatly.

ACTS 6:7 (NKJV)

2007: One of the best-known preachers in America was a former dance teacher at an Arthur Murray studio. He was D. James Kennedy who became a Christian in 1953 after listening to a radio evangelist and gave up teaching dance in 1955 to enter the ministry. In 1959 he founded Coral Ridge Presbyterian Church in Fort Lauderdale, Florida, serving there until his death in 2007. The church grew from the original group of 45 people (meeting in a school cafeteria) to the present building that seats 2,800. The church's services were broadcast weekly as *The Coral Ridge Hour*, and even after Kennedy's death on September 5, 2007, his sermons from Coral Ridge continue to be popular in syndication.

Kennedy not only pastored Coral Ridge but founded a school, Westminster Academy, and Knox Theological Seminary. But perhaps his greatest contribution to the church at large was Evangelism Explosion, a training program for Christian laymen, teaching them how to witness effectively to their faith. In his early days at Coral Ridge, Kennedy realized that a pastor alone could not grow a church, so in 1962 he started Evangelism Explosion. Coral Ridge grew tremendously, and in 1970 the Evangelism Explosion textbook was published. EE clinics were held in major U.S. cities, then spread to Canada and Europe, and in 1992 EE was established in Russia. Basic to EE is the concept of teaching laymen the essential Christian doctrines, key Bible verses, and communications skills in sharing the gospel with the unconverted. Kennedy wanted the contemporary church to be like the church in Acts which "multiplied greatly."

Kennedy was a dynamic preacher, and his sermons attracted thousands to his church. The various ministries he founded are a fine legacy for any Christian leader, but in creating Evangelism Explosion, he made Christians aware that church growth did not have to be pastor-driven, for God has called all his people to be witnesses to the faith they profess.

Prayer: Father, give us the boldness and the opportunities to witness to our faith. Amen.

September 6 · FUNDAMENTALLY SOUND

God is not a man, that he should lie, nor a son of man, that he should change his mind.

NUMBERS 23:19

1913: Say the word *Fundamentalist* and many people think of backward, uneducated, barely literate American Christians who oppose science and everything modern. This is curious because one of the original Fundamentalists was a well-educated college professor—living in Scotland.

He was James Orr who died on this date after a long career teaching religion at the college of his denomination, the United Free Church of Scotland. Orr had a master of arts and a doctor of divinity from the University of Glasgow. He taught church history and theology, but his area of expertise was apologetics, the intellectual defense of the faith.

When American layman Lyman Stewart and pastor A. C. Dixon decided to publish some booklets defending basic Christian beliefs, they enlisted pastors and scholars from both the United States and Britain. One was Orr who contributed four of the booklets that are known collectively as *The Fundamentals*, published between 1909 and 1915.

One of Orr's booklets defended the doctrine of Jesus' virgin birth—a core doctrine of the faith but one that had come under attack in modern times. Another booklet looked at the "higher criticism" of the Bible which cast doubt on its historical value. Yet another looked at the early chapters of Genesis—and Orr admitted that he did not think the "days" of creation in Genesis 1 were twenty-four-hour days, but that the basic truth of Genesis remained. In "Science and Christian Faith," he tackled head-on the issue of Darwinism and concluded that evolution "is coming to be recognized as but a new name for 'creation.' . . . It is, however, creation nonetheless." Orr knew his science and knew there were flaws and gaps in Darwin's theory. He also knew that even if evolution were true, God was not excluded from the picture.

Orr was a man devoted to the truths of the Bible. His writings deserve rereading, and the name "Fundamentalist" deserves reconsideration.

Prayer: Father, keep our minds rooted in your truths, and give us hearts to defend our faith. Amen.

September 7 · DIVIDED WE READ

All Scripture is God-breathed and is useful for teaching, rebuking, correcting and training in righteousness.

2 TIMOTHY 3:16

1559: Imagine trying to look up a Bible verse—in a Bible that wasn't divided into verses. Until 1560 no English Bibles had verse divisions. The Bible had been divided into chapters back in the Middle Ages, but verse divisions came later. An Italian scholar named Pagninus translated the Bible into Latin from the original Hebrew and Greek, and he divided and numbered the entire text into verses. This Bible was published in 1528, but, being in Latin, it was only read by scholars.

One scholar who read it was Robert Estienne, a French Protestant. Estienne published a Greek New Testament in 1551 and created his own verse divisions. He was friends with the English Protestants who were living in Geneva, Switzerland, and producing an English Bible. This 1560 version, known as the Geneva Bible, used Pagninus's verse divisions in the Old Testament and Estienne's in the New. For the first time an English-speaking Bible reader could look up "chapter and verse."

We take "chapter and verse" for granted today, but it was an amazing novelty in 1560. It wasn't the only one. The Geneva Bible was "portable"—not the bulky pulpit Bible found in churches but a handy size for the home or to carry on a journey. Another attractive feature was the type: plain Roman, the kind of type you are reading now, not the ornate but hard-to-read "black-letter" type found in pulpit Bibles. The Geneva also had thousands of explanatory footnotes. In short, this was the first genuinely "user-friendly" English Bible, and people responded enthusiastically, making it very much the people's Bible until the King James Version, published in 1611, gradually replaced it.

Robert Estienne died on September 7, 1559, before the Geneva Bible was published, but his verse divisions lived on in the Geneva and every later Bible in every language.

Prayer: Lord, so many people, known and unknown, have labored to unfold your Word to us. Let us not neglect it. Amen.

September 8 · LABORING IN JOY

In him you have been enriched in every way—in all your speaking and in all your knowledge.

1 CORINTHIANS 1:5

1783: How do you breathe life into a dead church? Nicolai Frederik Grundtvig, born on this date, answered that question by living eighty-nine years, writing fourteen hundred hymns and dozens of books, preaching constantly, and showing that the Christian life could be a joyous thing.

All this took place in Denmark which had a national church that, like most state churches, was spiritually dead. Grundtvig, the son of a pastor, became a pastor himself, but unlike so many pastors in state churches, he took his work seriously, preaching on the need for people to study the Bible closely and commit themselves to Christ. There was much more to the life of faith, he said, than being baptized into the church and attending now and then.

Grundtvig had an insatiable itch to write. He wrote poetry, hymns, history, and theology. While he loved the Bible and encouraged Christians to read it, he was also fascinated by the rich mythology of Denmark's pre-Christian days, and some of his poems retold these old stories. There was not only a revival of Christianity in Denmark but also a heightened interest in the country's colorful past.

He helped transform the country in another way: he encouraged new methods of cooperative agriculture and the founding of vocational schools to train the young people in practical subjects. He made Denmark richer not only spiritually but also materially.

Grundtvig struck most people as a joyous Christian, and he sincerely believed joy should be one of the marks of the life of faith. Despite his sunniness, he endured hard times, including seven years in which the church barred him from preaching because he had criticized a theology professor for saying the church existed to promote "general religiousness." Grundtvig knew there was much more than that to a truly Christ-centered church.

By the time he died in 1872, he had lived a productive, abundant life.

Prayer: Father, train us to be tireless and joyous workers for your sake. Amen.

September 9 · A Nation of Survivors

We are hard pressed on every side, but not crushed; perplexed, but not in despair; persecuted, but not abandoned.

2 Corinthians 4:8–9

439: The small nation of Armenia in the Middle East became Christian at an early date, and the old tradition that Jesus' disciples Bartholomew and Thaddeus took the gospel there may well be true. The Armenian king Tiridates was an ally of the Roman emperor Diocletian, a great persecutor of Christians. Tiridates, too, persecuted Christians, but in 301 he converted and made Christianity the national religion, so we might say that Armenia was the first Christian nation. Sadly, Armenia has had the bad fortune to be squeezed in between several large and usually hostile empires—Rome, Persia (Iran), Turkey, and Russia. The Christians of Armenia have clung to their faith tenaciously, despite persecutions launched by Muslims and Communists, and the Armenian genocide that took place during World War I is one of the horror stories of the twentieth century. The Armenians survived and so did their faith.

One of the heroes of Armenian history is Isaac the Great—or as the Armenians know him, Sahak. Born about 338, Isaac was orphaned at an early age but received a fine education. He was elected head of the Armenian Church during one of the few periods when the nation was independent. The country was soon divided between Persia and the eastern Roman Empire, and Armenia was in danger of losing its distinctive culture. Isaac and another Armenian saint, Mesrop, created an alphabet for the Armenian language and translated the Bible into Armenian. Isaac also founded Christian schools and helped rebuild churches and monasteries that the Persians destroyed. The Persian king who ruled part of Armenia booted Isaac from his post, but he eventually returned and died on September 9, 439 more than a hundred years old.

The Armenian Apostolic Church celebrated its 1700th anniversary in 2001 and paid homage to Isaac who, like the Armenian Church he worked so hard to promote, was a true survivor.

Prayer: Lord, give your people strength, remembering that your church is an anvil that has worn out many hammers. Amen.

September 10 · WAKING UP ENGLAND

Those who are led by the Spirit of God are sons of God.

ROMANS 8:14

1930: How can Pentecostalism with its emphasis on gifts of the Spirit such as speaking in tongues find a place in the Church of England with its emphasis on dignified ritual? It sounds like an unlikely match, and most Pentecostals in England have chosen to join denominations other than the state Church. But there have been a handful of pastors and laymen who were both faithful Church of England folk as well as enthusiastic Pentecostals. One of these was Alexander Boddy, the son of a Church of England pastor. Trained to be a lawyer, Boddy became involved with the Holiness movement and himself became a pastor. He heard of the Azusa Street Revival that began in Los Angeles in 1906 and was fascinated by this outpouring of the Spirit. He was equally intrigued by the Pentecostal revival taking place in Norway under the ministry of Thomas Barratt, and he traveled to Oslo to hear Barratt preach. Boddy then invited Barratt to his church to speak, and about thirty people were baptized in the Spirit.

This was in 1907. The following year, Boddy began publishing *Confidence*, the first Pentecostal magazine in Britain. The same year he hosted the first Whitsuntide conference of Pentecostals, drawing speakers from various nations. (Whitsuntide is the Church of England's name for Pentecost.) Many of those who attended the Whitsuntide conferences were leaders in the second wave of British Pentecostals.

Boddy had no desire to leave the Church of England but most of his fellow Pentecostals did, joining old denominations or forming new ones. The church authorities were never quite comfortable with speaking in tongues, especially since the secular newspapers liked to portray the practice as evidence of insanity. This is a familiar phenomenon in the twentieth century: an outpouring of the Spirit enriches the lives of some Christians, while church bureaucracies seem embarrassed or hostile, or both.

Boddy died on September 10, 1930, a pioneer of the Pentecostal movement in his native land.

Prayer: Holy Spirit, fill us with joy and with power as we spread the good news. Amen.

September 11 · A MIX OF BREEDS AND CREEDS

Salvation is found in no one else.

ACTS 4:12

1893: In the 1800s most Americans had never seen a Buddhist, Hindu, or Muslim in person. But the 1893 World's Fair in Chicago (technically, the World Columbian Exposition, honoring the four-hundredth anniversary of Columbus's voyage to America) drew visitors from all over the globe, and several "spin-off" fairs came into being, including the World Parliament of Religions which ran from September 11 to 27. Most of its speakers were Christians but among the others were Hindus, Buddhists, Muslims, Jains, Confucianists, Taoists, Shintoists, and Jews. One of the stars of the gathering was the Hindu teacher Vivekananda whose speeches were received with great applause.

Not everyone was pleased with the gathering. The archbishop of Canterbury, the head of the Church of England, made a protest, saying that Christians being part of a "Parliament of religions" suggested that the religions were equal. Similar protests came from various denominations, and, as a hint of future events, the sultan of Turkey, considered the chief spokesman for Islam, was outraged.

Another well-known figure who protested was evangelist D. L. Moody, whose base was in Chicago. Moody and his staff set up their own exhibit nearby, drawing people away from the Parliament. Under pressure from Moody and other Christians, the Parliament decided to close on Sundays.

The world we live in is different from that of 1893. Most Christians in those days—and most Jews and Muslims—did not see all religions as equal, and the traditional Christian view was that people of other religions should be converted if possible. In a sense the 1893 Parliament was a preview of the coming century, when tolerance and being nonjudgmental would be highly valued and would lessen the Christian missionary impulse. It is worth remembering that Jesus' apostles also crossed paths with people of different religions and felt no hesitation at all in seeking to bring them to salvation through Christ.

Prayer: Lord, in this world of many faiths, teach us a decent respect for others, but let us not neglect your mandate to save the lost. Amen.

September 12 · YOUNG AND CONSECRATED

Remember your Creator in the days of your youth.

ECCLESIASTES 12:1

1851: "Love and service" is the motto of Christian Endeavor, a worldwide Christian youth organization founded by Francis Edward Clark who was born on this date. Clark, a Congregational pastor in Portland, Maine, wrote in his diary the following entry for February 2, 1881: "The boys and girls take tea with us, about 35 of them, and we form a young people's society." (The "us" refers to himself and his wife, who had hosted the group in their home.) Two days later he wrote of the youth having a prayer meeting that was "very successful." These meetings marked the founding of the Young People's Society of Christian Endeavor, a result of his concern that young people often *heard* the word of God in church but were given limited opportunities to *practice* it.

Clark, like anyone who has spent time around teens, knew that young people have plenty of surplus energy, yet churches had shown little interest in harnessing that energy for constructive uses. He also understood the power of peer pressure and knew that outside the church walls plenty of unchurched teens assailed the church youth with temptations. Why couldn't such pressure work the opposite way—Christian teens gently pressuring each other to behave in ways pleasing to God?

The teens in Clark's church signed a pledge, committing themselves to acting out the Christian life—in other words, pledging to be something more than "Sunday morning Christians." They studied the Bible, learned to witness to their faith, and became, in the words of Clark's mission statement, "more useful in the service of God."

Within a few years Endeavor had gone international, and Clark was elected World President of the Christian Endeavor Union in 1895. By 1925 there were 4 million members worldwide. The *Portland Evening Express* commended Clark, stating that no Portland resident had brought the city more renown than this "great apostle of the Christian faith."

Prayer: Father, bless those who patiently work with youth, and bless youth who resist the world's temptations and find their chief pleasure in serving you. Amen.

"Enter through the narrow gate. For wide is the gate and broad is the road that leads to destruction."

MATTHEW 7:13

1321: A classic has been defined as "a book you wish you had read." That assuredly applies to *The Divine Comedy*, by Dante Alighieri, one of the greatest books ever written but more talked about than actually read. That is unfortunate because, unlike many classics, this one is a genuine pleasure to read, especially for a Christian, and many superb translations exist.

The poem is in three parts—*Inferno, Purgatorio,* and *Paradise*—hell, purgatory, and heaven. In *Inferno* Dante is taken on a tour through hell which is made up of nine concentric circles in the center of the earth. Each circle contains the souls of sinners progressively worse than the circle before. In hell are people from history, the Bible, and even mythology. Dante talks with some of these people who discuss their punishments and sins. At the bottom of hell, farthest away from God, is Lucifer, shown as having three heads and six bat-like wings, a sort of deformed Trinity.

In *Purgatorio* Dante is taken up a high mountain with seven terraces. In Catholic teaching, Christians are purged from their sins in purgatory, so the people he meets here are destined to enter heaven eventually, though they speak to him of their sins on earth. In *Paradiso* Dante's guide through heaven is Beatrice, a beautiful and virtuous woman he once loved. They encounter the apostles John and Peter, the medieval saint Bernard, and various other saints from the Bible and history. Dante learns that the saints in heaven are not equal, for those who were closest to God on earth are now closest to him in heaven. At the end Dante sees heaven as a kind of celestial rose unfolding before him, and he ends on a note of rapture—something difficult to communicate in words.

Dante died on September 13, 1321, having given the world something priceless.

Prayer: Lord, our souls are in your hands. Let us never forget the life beyond this life. Amen.

September 14 · RICH TARGETS

The love of money is a root of all kinds of evil.

1 TIMOTHY 6:10

407: A general rule about preachers: if they are not offending or angering someone, they are not doing their job. John of Constantinople was such a fine preacher that he was known as *Chrysostom*, Greek for "golden-mouthed," but his golden mouth angered as many as it impressed.

John was born around 347 in Antioch, one of the centers of Christianity in the book of Acts. He lived for a while as a hermit in a cave, but he returned to Antioch in 386 and became a noted preacher, famed for his sermons on the New Testament. In 398 he became patriarch (head bishop) in Constantinople, the capital built by Constantine (and today known as Istanbul, Turkey). There was much to preach against in this wealthy, luxury-loving city, and John did not hesitate to denounce the rich for their neglect of the poor. John practiced what he preached, living in simplicity and giving generously to charities.

He angered many of his fellow bishops by denouncing their lives of luxury. Some of them banded together in a council and ordered him sent into exile, but an earthquake persuaded them to revoke the order. Later Emperor Arcadius ordered John into exile, even though most people in the city supported John. Not willing to idle away his time while in exile, John wrote numerous pastoral letters. When some bishops pleaded for John's recall, the emperor sent him even farther away. John died in exile on September 14, 407.

When Constantine built Constantinople, he intended it as a Christian capital of the empire, and indeed it was full of magnificent churches. But any national capital is bound to attract the greedy and ambitious, including ambitious clergy. John did his duty: he called on the citizens of this supposedly Christian city to *behave* like Christians. The wealthier ones did not, and John paid a price for offending them. Saints find themselves at home in the next life, not in this one.

Prayer: Father, train us to listen with an open heart to those whose words sting us most. Amen.

September 15 · NEW WORDS, SAME GOSPEL

He opened their minds so they could understand the Scriptures.

LUKE 24:45

1966: *Gospel* is from the Old English word *Godspell*, meaning "good news," the same as the Greek word *evangel* in the New Testament. The American Bible Society published on this date a long-awaited New Testament translation called *Good News for Modern Man* with its cover made to look like world newspapers—not boring ancient history but "news" as fresh as the day's paper. It broke completely with the tradition of updating and revising the King James Version. Instead of a "new and improved" KJV, the public got a very fresh and readable version like nothing they had seen before.

It sold well, as almost any new translation of the Bible does. (The price was appealing: twenty-five cents.) Billy Graham endorsed it, as did the Southern Baptist Convention and several other denominations. Within three years it had sold over 12 million copies. But there were criticisms: many readers who had grown up on older versions were bothered that some familiar terms were not used. For example, "redeemed" was changed to "set free," and the "blood" of Jesus was changed to "sacrificial death."

Why? Because this version was based on a translation principle called *dynamic equivalence*—translating thoughts instead of words. The question guiding the translators was "How would an English-speaking person normally say this?" The American Bible Society which sponsored the translation was aware that many people who spoke English as a second language had trouble grasping older English versions. For that matter, so did many Americans and English with English as their *first* language.

In 1976 the entire Bible was published as *The Good News Bible: The Bible in Today's English Version*. Like *Good News for Modern Man*, it coupled a readable version with a very low price. It was still outsold by the King James Version, but Bible readers were learning to appreciate a version that was *not* the KJV.

Prayer: Father, your holy Word can be grasped by people in all times and places. Bless the diligent translators and their works. Amen.

September 16 · The Home As a Temple of God

I will sing to the Lord, for he has been good to me.

Psalm 13:6

1672: The first poet to be published in America was a very devout woman and a very contented wife. She was Anne Bradstreet, born in England around 1612, and, by the standards of those days, very well-educated. She married Simon Bradstreet when she was sixteen and sailed with him to New England in 1630, along with the many other Puritans who were hoping to establish a purer church in America.

Almost all American literature in the 1600s was religious. The Puritans were avid readers and writers, and their writings reveal people very conscious of God's presence in their daily lives.

Anne and Simon had eight children—not unusual for the time. Somehow in the busyness of rearing eight children and attending church frequently, Anne managed to produce poetry. A book of her poems was published in 1650 with the title *The Tenth Muse Lately Sprung up in America*. The nine Muses were the Greek goddesses of the arts and inspiration, and the title of Anne's book indicated that America was not some primitive backwater but was peopled with inspired authors.

Most of Anne's poems touched on familiar Puritan themes: awe of God, awareness of sin, belief that the next world was more important than this one. A family tragedy inspired her poem "Upon the Burning of Our House" in which she consoles herself that God still cares, despite the loss of material goods. Her devotion to Simon inspired her most familiar poem, "To My Dear and Loving Husband," thanking God for giving her such a wonderful life companion.

Curiously, Anne's book of poetry did not bear her name, only the indication that the poems were by "a Gentlewoman." It seems she thought that her poems' messages were more important than the name of the messenger. She died on September 16, 1672, a loved and respected woman.

Prayer: Lord, your saints feel your presence in the whole of life. May we do the same. Amen.

September 17 · THE PRIEST'S SON

We are therefore Christ's ambassadors, as though God were making his appeal through us.

2 CORINTHIANS 5:20

1575: Heinrich Bullinger was the son of a priest—at a time when all priests were, in theory, celibate. The celibacy rule for Catholic priests was frequently broken which is why Protestants did away with the rule and encouraged pastors to marry. Bullinger's father wanted him to enter the ministry, and when Heinrich began reading the works of Martin Luther, he converted to Protestantism. One of the more curious parts of Bullinger's story is that his father, the Catholic priest who had broken his vow of celibacy and fathered five sons by the same woman, also converted to the Protestant cause, which resulted in his losing his post.

Like Luther and other Reformers, Bullinger married a nun, and in time they had eleven children. His home became a model of the Protestant parsonage with the pastor, his wife, children, and an assortment of theological students and religious refugees—a biological family intermingled with a spiritual family.

Bullinger was a close friend of the Reformer Ulrich Zwingli, and after Zwingli died in 1531 (in battle against Catholic troops), Bullinger took his position as pastor in Zurich, Switzerland. On his first Sunday in the pulpit, many in the congregation were pleased that he "thundered" while preaching just as Zwingli had done.

Zurich took in Protestant exiles, especially from England where many fled the persecutions under the Catholic queen Mary. After her death the exiles returned to England with fond memories of Bullinger's preaching and, more importantly, copies of his *Decades*, a fine sermon series on the key Christian beliefs. Translated into many languages, *The Decades* were widely read and were required reading for Englishmen preparing for the ministry, so Bullinger was probably the most influential theologian for the Church of England at that time. Bullinger was also a tireless letter writer, giving advice and counsel to people from kings to farmers. He died on September 17, 1575, having made an immeasurable contribution to the Christian faith.

Prayer: Father, bless all faithful pastors and all who give spiritual counsel. Amen.

September 18 · CROSS CULTURE

Everyone who wants to live a godly life in Christ Jesus will be persecuted.

2 TIMOTHY 3:12

1598: The Japanese ruler who died on this date was known to his contemporaries as the "little monkey" and the "bald rat." His name was Toyotomi Hideyoshi, and he was the first—but definitely not the last—Japanese official to persecute Christians.

Europeans took the gospel to Japan in 1549, and by 1582 there were probably 150,000 Christians or, as the Japanese called them, *Kirishitans*. Hideyoshi was suspicious of this alien religion and in 1596 began persecuting Christians, crucifying several missionaries and converts. High government officials were forbidden to convert.

On February 5, 1597, Hideyoshi crucified several Christians in Nagasaki, a group that the Catholic Church honors as the Twenty-Six Martyrs of Japan. Among these was the saintly Paul Miki, a Japanese convert. Churches were destroyed, and missionaries that were not killed were deported. Hideyoshi's death in 1598 ended the persecution—temporarily.

In 1614 another bloodletting began. Over the next thirty years five thousand Christians were executed, always publicly. Many were crucified. Europeans were usually beheaded. Some Japanese were burned at the stake. Few were willing to renounce their faith, and this tenacity served to increase the persecution. Some Christians died slowly with boiling sulfur water poured into slits cut into their flesh. Some martyrs were suspended upside down until they eventually died. Persecution went on so long that some of the missionaries produced manuals, instructing Christians how to behave, urging them to harbor no evil thoughts against their executioners.

What is so amazing about this story is not the horror of the persecution but the steadfastness of the Japanese Christians. Once they accepted Christianity and determined to live their lives by its teachings, most of them accepted persecution. Missionaries marveled that the Japanese converted so easily—and became Christians in life not just in name. Historians have long wondered what Japan might have been like, religiously, if there had been no persecution and Christianity had spread through the entire population.

Prayer: Father, bless your persecuted children. Guide them safely to their final home. Amen.

He will take pity on the weak and the needy and save the needy from death.

PSALM 72:13

1905: Sometimes God changes the noblest of plans. That was the case with Thomas Barnardo who had intended to be a medical missionary to China but ended up as the founder of homes for poor children.

Born in Ireland in 1845, Barnardo was converted in his teens to a deep faith in Christ, and right away he began working with poor children in Dublin. Hearing missionary Hudson Taylor speak of the China Inland Mission, Barnardo decided to study medicine and then travel to China. While studying at a London hospital he became aware of the urban poor, especially children. Encouraged by some Christian friends, he gave up his plans for China and in 1870 opened the first of what would be called "Dr. Barnardo's Homes" in London. When he died on September 19, 1905, there were 112 of the homes in Britain, and more than 100,000 children had been rescued from the streets. The homes' motto was "the ever-open door."

London was full of orphans and "strays," children detached from families, and many of these often turned to crime (a story familiar from Charles Dickens's novel *Oliver Twist*). The Barnardo homes took in these children, fed them, clothed them, and prepared them for useful occupations. Barnardo owned a sixty-acre rural tract which he used to create a model village for some of the children, building cottages that eventually housed more than a thousand. Collectively his homes were known as the National Association for the Reclamation of Destitute Waif Children (which explains the briefer and more familiar name "Barnardo's Homes").

The homes emphasized religious instruction with provision made for two "faith traditions"—the established Church of England and the Nonconformists (Baptists, Methodists, Quakers, and others). As for the children's physical health, Barnardo found his medical training to be of great use.

Barnardo's is still an active charity in England, the legacy of a man who had a heart for the most vulnerable members of society.

Prayer: Father, let us never turn aside from the sight of suffering and poverty. Amen.

September 20 · COLONIZING IN BLOOD

It is fine to be zealous, provided the purpose is good.

GALATIANS 4:18

1565: The story of the European settlement of America is exciting—but sometimes saddening. From the very beginning there was competition, sometimes bloody, among the different nationalities. Spain, since it was first in the New World, was very protective of its territory which the Spanish thought included all of North America. When people from other nations built a settlement, there was inevitably trouble.

The oldest city in the United States is St. Augustine, Florida, founded by the Spanish. However, the French settled the area first. In 1564 a band of Huguenots (French Protestants) founded Fort Caroline at the mouth of Florida's wide St. John's River. The colony did not prosper, and the settlers were about to return to France in 1565, but a Spanish expedition landed nearby. Led by Pedro Menendez de Aviles, the governor of Florida, the Spanish killed all the men at Fort Caroline and sent the women and children off to captivity in Cuba. The slaughter which took place on September 20, 1565, was done, the Spanish said, not because the settlers were French but because they were "Lutherans," that is, Protestants, whom the Spanish Catholics regarded as heretics. The Spanish then built St. Augustine to keep other Protestants and other nationalities out of the region. Had Fort Caroline survived, it would have been the oldest French settlement in America—and the oldest Protestant settlement as well.

The saddest part of the story is the reaction of France to the slaughter at Fort Caroline: King Charles IX and his court showed no concern. After all, did it matter that the Spanish had killed off a handful of pesky Protestants? A few Frenchmen were angry enough that a revenge expedition was launched: on the very spot where the Fort Caroline settlers had been killed, numerous Spanish were killed. This was a violent age, and great crimes were done in the name of religion. Those who planted the cross on America's shores often forgot that Christ was the Prince of Peace.

Prayer: Lord, teach us the hard lessons of peace and mercy. Amen.

September 21 · INNOCENT POWER

The LORD foils the plans of the nations.

PSALM 33:10

1676: Sometimes to appreciate a person from history, we have to compare him with his contemporaries. Pope Innocent XI whose reign began on this date, compares—or rather, *contrasts*—very well with the most powerful king of the age, Louis XIV of France. Sparks were bound to fly in the conflict between a saintly but obstinate pope and an egotistical, pleasure-loving king with no scruples. Innocent saw himself as head of the Catholic Church all over the world. Louis saw everything in France as under his control—including the church. There was a threat of the French church separating from Rome—and the issue was still unresolved when Innocent died in 1689.

Then there was the matter of the Huguenots, the French Protestants. In 1572 the king of France had ordered a massacre of the Huguenots. The pope of that day reacted joyfully to the slaughter of the "heretics." Pope Innocent XI was a different kind of man. Louis's grandfather had issued the edict of Nantes, giving civil rights to the Huguenots, but the pope watched with annoyance as Louis heaped petty persecutions on the Huguenots and finally, in 1685 Louis revoked the Edict of Nantes. Louis gave the Huguenots these choices: convert to Catholicism, leave the country for good, or suffer the consequences. The pope was horrified. Though the Catholic Church technically still regarded Protestants as heretics, Innocent did not believe in using coercion to make people turn Catholic nor forcing good citizens out of the country. The day when a pope could smile upon the persecution of non-Catholics was past.

Two rulers did please Innocent: the Austrian emperor and the king of Poland, who with the pope's backing turned back a Muslim advance into Europe in 1683. This was one of the great achievements of his reign, along with his ridding the papal court of its corruption. Innocent did what so many earlier popes had failed to do: lived like a Christian.

Prayer: Lord, teach us to respect and honor those who use power in the service of good. Amen.

September 22 · THE SAINT AND THE DYNAMO

He guides the humble in what is right and teaches them his way.

PSALM 25:9

1791: It is always a pleasure to read of a working-class youth becoming world famous—and retaining his humility. Such was the case of Michael Faraday, born on this date, the son of an English blacksmith. Michael was apprenticed to a bookbinder and found himself fascinated by books of science. At twenty-one he became an assistant to scientist Humphry Davy who toured Europe and introduced Michael to many great scientists. Over time Faraday not only made new breakthroughs in chemistry and physics but was famed for fascinating youth with his lectures on science.

One of the great breakthroughs resulted from an 1822 item in his notebook: "Convert magnetism to electricity." In 1831 he had done so, demonstrating electromagnetic induction—that is, the electromagnetic motor that drives so many appliances. He also created the first dynamo. In his researches he coined or popularized many now familiar terms: *cathode, anode, anion, cation,* and *electrode*.

Throughout his life, Faraday was a devout member of the Sandemanian (or Glasite) church. Faraday never seems to have questioned his faith, and the idea of a conflict between science and religion never crossed his mind. In the years he was becoming a scientist of world renown, he was also serving as elder in his London church. He remained humble and declined a knighthood from the king. When England was fighting in the Crimean War, Faraday was asked to advise the army on chemical weapons, but he refused, saying he did not wish his scientific knowledge put to use harming others.

Prince Albert, Queen Victoria's husband, admired Faraday and had the queen award the scientist with living quarters at Hampton Court palace. He died there in 1867, after making it clear he did not wish to be buried in Westminster Abbey, the resting place of England's notables. Admirers later installed a plaque in the Abbey as a memorial to this humble Christian who happened to be a scientific genius.

Prayer: Creator God, may the understanding of your vast and intricate world teach us humility. Amen.

Teach me your way, O LORD, and I will walk in your truth.

PSALM 86:11

1800: Although Scottish immigrants to America were relatively poor, they put a high value on education—and on faith. No wonder so many Scottish Americans were notable preachers and teachers (and often both). One such immigrant was William McGuffey, born on this date. His Scottish parents instilled in young William their love of learning and the Bible, and at an early age William could quote large sections of the Bible from memory.

The American frontier needed teachers badly, and sometimes age was not a factor, so William was teaching at age fourteen. William worked six days a week and sometimes eleven hours per day, teaching in schools with no textbooks except the Bible. Eventually William earned a college degree and a post as professor of languages at Ohio's Miami University. Since he lectured often on moral and religious themes, a publisher asked him to create some reading textbooks for elementary-age children. In the 1830s he produced four readers, and the first two (for the earliest age levels) were the most popular textbooks of the 1800s, and every American family was familiar with the *McGuffey Readers*.

No one in those days believed that public education should be "values-neutral" or that religion should be avoided. On the contrary, as a Christian, McGuffey believed his *Readers* should instill moral lessons as well as teach reading, and in his lifetime most American families agreed. Probably 122 million copies of the *Readers* were sold. When McGuffey died in 1873, he had the satisfaction of knowing he had probably touched the minds of American schoolchildren more than anyone else. Later in the century the *Readers* were revised, and much of the religious material was removed.

Automaker Henry Ford was one of the countless students who had grown up using the *McGuffey Readers*, and in the 1930s he paid to have copies reprinted and given away to schools. The *Readers* were genuine American classics and so was McGuffey himself.

Prayer: Lord, thank you for writings that instruct the soul as well as the mind. Amen.

September 24 · A Man for the Long Haul

Preach the Word . . . correct, rebuke and encourage—with great patience and careful instruction.

2 Timothy 4:2

1759: Fifty-three years is a long time for a pastor to serve at one church, and that is how long Charles Simeon, born on this date, served at Holy Trinity Church in England's university town of Cambridge. Simeon entered the university in 1779, having been extremely worldly in his youth, but before taking Communion in the lovely chapel at King's College, he began to think seriously about his spiritual condition, and his conversion was the beginning of a long career as a dedicated pastor.

His ministry did not begin on a promising note. During his first sermons at Holy Trinity, some of the students seemed more inclined to heckle than to listen, but something about Simeon impressed them—not just the words, but something weighty and profound in his manner riveted their attention. Most of the hecklers quickly turned into devoted fans, and in time Simeon's preaching was so highly regarded that he published twenty-one volumes of preaching aids (including six hundred sermon outlines) and on Sunday evenings taught a preaching class that influenced hundreds of Church of England pastors.

Even so, there were many years when Simeon was, in the words of a friend, "by some adored, and by others abhorred." When Simeon began his ministry, it was rare to hear a Church of England pastor tell congregations that they needed to repent of their sins and be saved. Thanks to his influence, it became much less rare. He and other evangelicals brought an earnest and emotional quality to sermons, and the Church of England was transformed.

When Simeon died in 1836, huge crowds showed up for his funeral, and businesses in Cambridge shut down for the day. He had become a spiritual hero in England, having taught many that the life of faith led to both humility and unshakable joy: "Surely this is happiness: to taste the love of God, to find delight in his service."

Prayer: Father, raise up righteous and passionate souls to be shepherds of your flock. Amen.

September 25 · A Breathing Space

Since God so loved us, we ought also to love one another.

1 John 4:11

1555: Consider this rule: wherever you live, you have to adhere to the religion of the head of your government. That is exactly the principle that was worked out on this day in history.

Some background is helpful: in the 1500s the Protestant Reformation split Europe into warring camps. In the middle of Europe was the sprawling Holy Roman Empire, made up of several nations ruled by kings, dukes, or bishops. Over them all ruled Emperor Charles V, a staunch Catholic who regarded the Protestants as heretics. In theory, Charles controlled the whole empire—but in practice, the various rulers under him had a lot of independence, and some of those rulers turned Protestant and at times made war against the Catholic emperor. The king of France who was Catholic was happy to aid the Protestants in order to hurt Charles, his great rival. Adding to the muddle was the threat of a Muslim invasion on the empire's eastern border. Charles wore himself out fighting off enemies on his borders and "heretics" in his empire.

On September 25, 1555, a truce was reached, called the Peace of Augsburg after the German city where it was signed. The various rulers in the empire agreed to the principle of *cujus regio, ejus religio*—Latin that roughly translates as "the ruler's religion is the religion of his nation." So since the ruler of Saxony was a Lutheran, the people of Saxony had to be Lutheran—or sell their property and move to another country. The ruler of Bavaria was Catholic, so Bavarians had to be Catholic—or move. A few large cities allowed both Catholics and Lutherans to worship. Except for Lutherans, no Protestants were to be tolerated in the empire. It sounds like a bizarre agreement, and certainly it was not good news to Protestants who were not Lutheran. But it did end a long period of pointless bloodshed, and for a spell there were fewer Christians killing Christians.

Prayer: Lord, give us peace inside and the will to work for peace outside. Amen.

Administer true justice; show mercy and compassion to one another.

ZECHARIAH 7:9

1846: "Is it lawful to enslave the unconsenting?" That was the essay topic at Cambridge University in 1785. The essay was an intellectual exercise, testing students' ability to write good Latin and think clearly. For Thomas Clarkson it became more than a mental test. In preparation for the essay, he read all he could on the subject and talked with abolitionists. He concluded that "if the contents of the essay were true, it was time some person should see these calamities to their end."

Clarkson won the essay prize, and afterward translated the essay into English and had it published. The fame of the essay put him in contact with more abolitionists in Britain, most of whom were evangelical Christians. He joined a Committee for the Abolition of the Slave Trade and learned that slave traders were a powerful and influential group. Even so, Clarkson gathered evidence about the slave trade, collecting manacles, thumbscrews, and leg shackles and interviewing thousands of sailors who worked in the trade. He wove these interviews into reports that were widely published, and slowly British opinion began to change.

War with France in the 1790s took the British public's mind off slavery for several years. When the war ended, Clarkson resumed his abolitionist crusade, and in 1807 Britain's Parliament passed the Slave Trade Act. The poet William Wordsworth, a friend of Clarkson's, wrote a sonnet to honor both Clarkson and the ending of the slave trade with its last line referring to Clarkson as "firm Friend of human kind."

The slave trade had been eliminated, but slavery itself still existed in the British Empire. Clarkson continued his labors, riding thousands of miles on horseback. Finally, Parliament abolished slavery in 1833. His work was not over, for he was active in founding "free villages" for newly freed slaves in the Caribbean. Clarkson died on September 26, 1846, after a devout and active life.

Prayer: Lord, open our eyes for opportunities to work for justice and compassion. Amen.

September 27 · SISTER GOSPEL

Woe to me if I do not preach the gospel!

1 CORINTHIANS 9:16

1944: When other little girls were "playing house," young Aimee Kennedy was "playing Salvation Army," arranging her dolls and preaching to them. She was familiar with Salvation Army meetings through her mother's involvement with the group. When she grew up, Aimee married a young Pentecostal preacher, Robert Semple, and the two went to China—where Robert died, leaving Aimee a young widow with a daughter. Aimee remarried, gave birth to a son, then took to the road as an evangelist, known for her "Gospel Car." Her revivals in major cities sometimes lasted for weeks.

Settling in Los Angeles, she and her followers built the Angelus Temple, an enormous domed church that seated 5,300 with services held seven days a week, sometimes with three services per day. Dedicated on January 1, 1923, the Temple drew local residents and Christians visiting the area. In time the megachurch became the mother church of its own denomination, the International Church of the Foursquare Gospel. The church published a monthly magazine and had its own radio station, KFSG ("FSG" for Foursquare Gospel), and the LIFE Bible College.

"Sister Aimee" was one of the best-known religious figures of her time. She was also the center of a national controversy in May 1926. She disappeared, supposedly while swimming at a local beach, and was presumed drowned. The engineer at KFSG, a married man, disappeared at the same time. But Aimee appeared in Arizona in June that year, claiming she had been kidnapped. Many people were skeptical, believing it was all done for publicity or that Aimee and the engineer had a brief fling. Aimee's vague explanations caused her to be charged with obstruction of justice, but charges were dropped.

On September 27, 1944, Aimee's son found her dead in a hotel room. She had led a colorful life, one in which she touched many thousands with her preaching as well as the charitable work of the Temple. The truth about her "kidnapping" may never be known. Like all God's workers, she was human.

Prayer: Lord, we your servants are human and liable to fall. Keep our feet on the straight path. Amen.

From now on we regard no one from a worldly point of view.

2 CORINTHIANS 5:16

1573: One of the greatest creators of Christian art was no Christian in his life-style, being a violent, promiscuous, vain hedonist who did his work purely for money. Even so, his paintings have a depth and power that few other artists have ever matched.

Born on this date with the name Michelangelo Merisi, he is known to the world as Caravaggio after his birthplace. Since there was money to be made in art for churches, Caravaggio painted such familiar subjects as *The Supper at Emmaus* and *The Raising of Lazarus*.

He used a technique known as *chiaroscuro*, Italian for "light-dark," a contrast between well-lighted figures in the picture and a shadowy background, somewhat like characters on a stage with a spotlight shining on them. This created drama which he combined with extremely realistic human figures. Like Rembrandt, who lived a generation later, he picked people from the streets as his models of apostles, prophets, and saints, painting them "warts and all" but with compassion. There is nothing "pretty" in his religious paintings, but there is drama and depth, as in *The Entombment* where we see the agony of Mary and the others as Jesus is placed in the tomb. With most artists, we feel like we are looking out a window at a scene, but Caravaggio's paintings draw the viewer in, as if we are literally present at the scene.

One of his most famous works is *The Conversion of St. Paul*, showing the blinded Paul lying on his back on the road to Damascus with a divine light shining on him. The scene has been painted countless time, but no one did it better than Caravaggio. Though Caravaggio did not *live* as a Christian, something in him *felt* and *thought* as one. This very worldly man could, at times, see people and events through the eyes of faith.

Prayer: Lord, even the worldliest of people have been moved by the stories in your word. Let their works continue to inspire. Amen.

September 29 · THE ROCK BISHOP

We do not preach ourselves, but Jesus Christ as Lord, and ourselves as your servants for Jesus' sake.

2 CORINTHIANS 4:5

440: What a pity no one had a video camera at the meeting in 452 of Attila the Hun and Leo the bishop of Rome. Leo persuaded Attila not to attack Rome, and the army of Huns withdrew. It was a high point for Leo, a man who had a lofty view of his office.

Leo became the bishop of Rome on September 29, 440. At that time the idea of "pope" as the head of the whole church hadn't fully been formed. By the end of Leo's reign in 461, it was much clearer. Matthew 16:15–19 is the famous episode in which Peter says to Jesus, "You are the Christ, the Son of the living God," to which Jesus replies, "You are Peter, and on this rock I will build my church. . . . I will give you the keys of the kingdom of heaven." Tradition says that Peter was the first bishop of Rome, and Leo believed that all the bishops of Rome were Peter's successors and entitled to head the whole church not just the church in Rome. He saw himself as the "rock" on which the church was founded, and since he had the "keys of the kingdom of heaven," he had the right to dictate to all Christians what they should believe and how they should act. In his reign of twenty-one years, he was such a capable administrator and theologian that many Christians—though certainly not all—accepted his high view of his office.

The Catholic Church refers to Leo as "the Great" and regards him as a saint. He had great power and mostly used it for good purposes, but, sadly, Leo could not have known that in times to come, unspiritual and immoral men would vie for the office, coveting the power and forgetting that Christ and his apostles practiced humility and had no use for worldly power.

Prayer: Father, whatever power we possess, let it be used not for our own glory but for yours and for love of our neighbors. Amen.

September 30 · MAKER OF A TRUE CLASSIC

How sweet are your words to my taste, sweeter than honey to my mouth!

PSALM 119:103

420: One of the most brilliant and least lovable of Christian saints, the scholar Jerome, the man responsible for the Vulgate, the translation of the Bible from Greek and Hebrew into Latin, died on this date. The Vulgate was something unique: a Bible translation in wide use for over a thousand years, the official Bible of the Catholic world, and, until the twentieth century, the only version that could be used as the basis for Catholic translations.

Jerome was living in Rome, an aide to Pope Damasus. Fewer and fewer people in western Europe could read Greek anymore, and the Latin translations of the Bible were of poor quality, so Damasus commissioned Jerome to do a definitive Latin Bible. Jerome chose to do the task not in Rome but in Bethlehem where contact with Jewish scholars convinced him that his Old Testament translation needed to be based on the Hebrew originals not on translations from Hebrew.

When he completed the Vulgate (sometime around 404), it was not immediately accepted by all Christians, since some churches feared Jerome had given them a "Judaized" Bible. But in time Jerome's Latin translation became the official Bible of the Catholic Church. Sadly, over time Latin became a "dead" language, used only by scholars, yet the Catholic Church prohibited any Bible but the Vulgate, so for most laity, the Bible was a closed book. Not until the Reformation in the 1500s would scholars revert to Jerome's own principle: translate from the original Hebrew and Greek.

It would be pleasant to record that this dedicated scholar was a lovable character. However, he was anything but. His writings reveal him as bitterly sarcastic, mean-spirited in debate, and taking a dim view of marriage and family life. Nonetheless, he was an amazing man. God can use difficult, disagreeable people to accomplish his will.

Prayer: Lord, you call people of different temperaments to your service. Teach us to accept each other's faults and to appreciate the better qualities that each brother and sister possess. Amen.

OCTOBER

October 1 · An Earnest, Honest Man

He who oppresses the poor shows contempt for their Maker, but whoever is kind to the needy honors God.

PROVERBS 14:31

1885: London's famous Piccadilly Circus district is so hectic that most tourists overlook the aluminum statue of a young winged man shooting an arrow. Though the statue is often called "Eros" (the Greek god of love), in fact it is the Angel of Christian Charity, a monument to one of England's greatest reformers, Anthony Ashley Cooper, also known as the Earl of Shaftesbury.

Born into the English upper class in 1801, Cooper was not close to either of his parents, but the housekeeper was a woman of deep faith, and Cooper considered himself fortunate to have a model of Christian charity in the home. When he was elected to Parliament in 1826, Cooper took his faith with him and worked to improve conditions for factory and mine workers and also for the mentally ill who at this time were treated like animals in the brutal asylums. He was active in the Society for Prevention of Cruelty to Children and also gave his support to the Young Men's Christian Association. Charles Dickens, who depicted the English slums so vividly in his novels, hailed Cooper as a political hero.

Cooper told his biographer that a man's religion, "if it is worth anything, should enter into every sphere of life, and rule his conduct in every relation." Several political figures of the 1800s shared this view with Cooper, people whose political actions were shaped more by faith than by ambition. The 1700s had been a century of cynicism and corruption in British politics, and though these were still to be found in the 1800s, something had definitely changed, and members of Parliament no longer provoked snickering when their speeches alluded to the Bible or Christian principles.

Politically active well into his eighties, Cooper died on October 1, 1885, a fine example of a well-lived life.

Prayer: Heavenly Father, touch our hearts and minds so that we may carry our faith into every aspect of our lives. Amen.

Righteousness exalts a nation, but sin is a disgrace to any people.

PROVERBS 14:34

1803: We have been exposed to so many scandals about philandering politicians that we are tempted to shrug our shoulders and say that a politician's private life is his or her own business. Samuel Adams, one of our Founding Fathers, did not see things that way: "He who is void of virtuous attachments in private life is, or very soon will be, void of all regard for his country." As Adams saw it, a man who would break his marriage vows could certainly break other promises.

Among the Founders, Sam Adams was probably the one who took his Christianity most seriously. A cousin of John Adams, Sam was born in Massachusetts in 1722 and was involved with many episodes in the American Revolution, including the Boston Tea Party and the ride of Paul Revere. After the Revolution, Adams continued in public service, including serving as Massachusetts's governor—at a time when the governor's term was *one year*. Adams was a great believer in what we call "term limits," since he accepted the Christian belief in original sin and thought that the fear of being voted out every year would keep politicians on their best behavior. When the state of Massachusetts drafted a constitution in 1780, Adams was on the committee, and he insisted that the constitution's preamble refer to the "Great Legislator of the Universe," God.

Adams was friends with two Founders who were *not* orthodox Christians, Thomas Jefferson and Thomas Paine. Jefferson, skeptical about Christianity, admired Adams and called him the "patriarch of liberty." Adams's friendship with Paine soured as Paine became hostile to religion. In an exasperated letter to Paine, Adams asked him if he really thought the world would be better if people became atheists.

In his will Sam Adams commended his soul to God, "relying on the merits of Jesus Christ for a pardon of all his sins." Adams loved the new nation he helped to form, but his ultimate allegiance was to God.

Prayer: Father, may we live as loyal citizens while never forgetting that our true homeland is heaven. Amen.

October 3 · POOR BROTHERS

"He who is least among you all—he is the greatest."

LUKE 9:48

1226: It is hard to imagine a more appealing figure than Giovanni Bernardone, better known as Francis of Assisi. Born to wealth in Italy around 1182, he spent much of his youth as a playboy. Gradually the playboy became a compassionate visitor of the poor, including lepers. His father, thinking him insane, threatened to disinherit him. Francis responded by stripping off all his clothes, giving them to his father, and saying that henceforth he would serve only his Father in heaven.

Not everyone thought him insane. He drew people like a magnet by doing something people saw little of: acting like Christ, owning nothing, subsisting on what people gave him to eat, and preaching the love of God. His followers acted like Jesus' disciples, going about in pairs, preaching, speaking gently—and sometimes being insulted and pelted with mud.

Pope Innocent III saw that the group could be radical troublemakers—or, perhaps, a way to draw people back to the Church. He approved of the group which Francis gave the name Friars Minor—"minor" because Francis took seriously Jesus' words about humility. More commonly they were, and are, called the Franciscans.

Francis is famed for his love of nature for speaking of "brother sun and sister moon." He and his followers were known for their simple and direct sermons, poverty and humility, forgiveness of enemies, and confession of sins.

After a long and painful illness, Francis died on October 3, 1226. In his last years he watched the order he founded change, giving up the simplicity and poverty Francis insisted on. In fact the Franciscans have had numerous splits over the years, always with a breakaway group insisting on a return to Francis's ideals. Despite many internal battles, the Franciscans have made a huge contribution to the life of the church and are active in missions, charity work, and education. But the greatest legacy is Francis himself, a figure who is difficult not to love.

Prayer: Father, thank you for the shining example of those who serve you fully. Amen.

October 4 · DOCTOR TERESA

"I hold this against you: You have forsaken your first love."

REVELATION 2:4

1582: "Though we do not have our Lord with us in bodily presence, we have our neighbor, who, for the ends of love and loving service, is as good as our Lord himself." Those were the words of one of the most appealing of saints, Teresa of Avila, who died on this date after a lifetime of loving God and all people she met. Born in Avila, Spain, in 1515, Teresa was religious from an early age, and she entered a convent of Carmelite nuns. Finding the lifestyle of the nuns a bit too relaxed, she started her own convent for those who took their faith more seriously. Over time she founded sixteen other convents based on the strict rules she had drawn up. The Carmelites who followed her rules were known as the Discalced (barefoot) Carmelites, for their vow of poverty extended even to going without shoes.

What Teresa did to the Carmelites is part of a familiar pattern among Christian organizations: At the beginning the people are full of zeal and willing to exercise self-denial in serving God, but in time a new generation becomes more worldly and less zealous, so a reformer comes in to draw people back to the original ideals. Often the reformer is regarded as a troublemaker, and Teresa herself came under the suspicion of the Inquisition, but King Philip II of Spain protected her, seeing her as a sincere saint.

There was more to Teresa than strict rules. She penned a highly readable autobiography and also the devotional books *The Way of Perfection* and *The Interior Castle*. She combined intelligence and hardheadedness in managing convents but also great charm and the ability to draw close to God in prayer. She encouraged the nuns to pray and meditate but then to go and actively serve the Lord. In 1970 Pope Paul VI honored her as a "Doctor [teacher] of the Church," the first woman to be so honored.

Prayer: Lord, draw us back to our first love for you, and let us not flag in zeal. Amen.

October 5 · Mr. Epic's Swan Song

No prophet has risen in Israel like Moses, whom the LORD knew face to face.

DEUTERONOMY 34:10

1956: When the movie *The Ten Commandments* premiered on this date, audiences expected—and got—their money's worth. The director Cecil B. DeMille had a reputation for doing historical epics like no one else, and this time he outdid himself—literally, for he had made a black-and-white (and silent) version of *The Ten Commandments* in the 1920s. In December 1949 DeMille released *Samson and Delilah*, and it was so successful that the 1950s became the Golden Age of Biblical Movies. Surely it is no coincidence that the decade of biblical epics also happened to be the decade of America's highest church attendance.

Did DeMille have any motivation besides making a profit? According to his autobiography, yes. He grew up in a religious family and was familiar with the Bible. His 1927 biblical movie *The King of Kings* was not only popular but was widely used by missionaries around the world. As a Hollywood bigwig, DeMille lived lavishly, and though he loved his wife, he had several mistresses. Even so, his autobiography gives the impression that his biblical movies had a spiritual as well as financial motive. Like many Americans in the 1950s, DeMille feared atheistic Communism, and he hoped his movies would turn people's minds to religion. *The Ten Commandments* is not just the reenactment of a biblical story but, according to DeMille, a message to audiences that true freedom could be found only in obeying God. He made a wise choice casting the masculine, charismatic Charlton Heston as Moses, giving audiences a religious figure they could cheer for.

The Ten Commandments is one of the few old movies that is broadcast on network television year after year. Some people scoff at the dialogue and the sometimes hammy acting, yet there is no doubt that it is genuinely absorbing, a vivid reminder that whatever else the Bible is, it is certainly not boring.

Prayer: Lord, thank you for the people who over the centuries have presented the stories of the Bible in vivid and inspiring ways. Amen.

October 6 · Burning Bibles—and Translators

The word of the Lord spread widely and grew in power.

Acts 19:20

1536: At Vilvorde, a castle in what is today Belgium, William Tyndale an ordained minister from England was executed as a heretic—first strangled then burned at the stake. Tyndale was condemned for his Protestant theological writings, but his legacy to the world was his being the first to translate the Bible from the original languages into English. Receiving no encouragement from King Henry VIII or the English church authorities who were in fact hostile to the whole project, Tyndale moved from England to Europe where he worked on his translation of the New Testament from Greek into English. Printed in 1525, it had to be smuggled into England where it was extremely popular, despite the church authorities burning every copy they could get their hands on. (Consider the irony: church officials burning Bibles!) Tyndale then set to work translating the Hebrew Old Testament, beginning at Genesis and progressing as far as 2 Chronicles before he was betrayed by a supposed friend and imprisoned as a heretic, spending a year and a half in a clammy, gloomy cell before his execution. A touching letter survives in which Tyndale asked for a candle for his cell—and a Hebrew dictionary. Even in prison he hoped to complete his Old Testament. Tyndale's jailor admitted that Tyndale was truly a saintly man.

Tyndale can rightly be called the Father of the English Bible, and almost three-fourths of the King James Version is in fact the work of Tyndale who was not only a master at Greek and Hebrew but a writer with an amazing feel for clear, direct English—the rare gift of "ear" that made his translation stick in people's minds for centuries. Generations of English-speaking Christians owe a great deal to this amazing, dedicated man who believed the word of God should be accessible to all.

Prayer: Father, thank you for faithful men like William Tyndale who endured betrayal, prison, and the ultimate sacrifice to bring your sacred words to all people. Amen.

October 7 · MERCHANT OF FREEDOM

The LORD hears the needy and does not despise his captive people.

PSALM 69:33

1772: In his readable *Journal* John Woolman who died on this date recorded that as early as age seven he felt the moving of "divine Love." This is not surprising, considering that his parents were devout Quakers who instilled in him a love of the Bible. His *Journal* reveals one of the most appealing Christian personalities in colonial America.

Woolman was born in 1720 in what was then called West Jersey (later part of New Jersey). He was devout and industrious and took a job working for a Quaker merchant, and at one point his job required him to write out a bill of sale for a woman slave, which pained his conscience. (At this time slavery existed in all the colonies not just the Southern ones.) Unlike many later Christians who pressed the government for immediate emancipation of the slaves (by violence, if necessary), Woolman worked as a "quiet revolutionary," speaking gently to slaveowners, especially those who considered themselves Christian. Woolman published a book, *On Keeping Negroes*, laying out his case that keeping slaves was not Christian but that Christians who owned slaves should at least treat them humanely, freeing them if possible.

Woolman was no radical, and he knew that some masters were decent and caring toward their slaves. Part of what offended him about slavery was that it was a sign of luxury, and as a Quaker, he believed in living simply, keeping possessions (including *human* possessions) to a minimum. His own life was simple, and he wore undyed clothes since some of the dyes of that day were produced by slave labor. Making his living as a merchant, he would not deal in rum, sugar, or molasses which were products of Caribbean slave labor.

Woolman believed in applying the Golden Rule to all his fellow men, including black slaves and Indians. Before dying of smallpox in 1772, Woolman wrote an essay titled "On Loving Our Neighbors as Ourselves."

Prayer: Lord, as we strive to do your will, keep us aware of the power of gentle persuasion. Amen.

October 8 · THUNDERING GOSPEL

Lift up your voice with a shout, lift it up, do not be afraid.

ISAIAH 40:9

1936: Goforth sounds like the perfect name for a missionary, one who goes forth to spread the gospel, and Jonathan Goforth was indeed one of the great missionaries of the twentieth century.

Born in Canada in 1859, Goforth became a schoolteacher, but after hearing a missionary speak about China, he felt God calling him to that country. Like many future missionaries, he was fascinated by Hudson Taylor's story of his China mission. He studied at seminary, married a devout English girl who worked at a Toronto rescue mission (and who would bear him eleven children), and in 1888 he and his wife arrived at a mission in Henan, China, their journey funded by Jonathan's fellow seminary students.

The turn of the century brought the violent Boxer Rebellion in which all foreigners were under suspicion, and the family had to flee on foot for many miles. At one point Jonathan was attacked with a sword and almost beaten to death, but he survived. More than once the family was menaced by angry mobs of Chinese. The family spent a few years back in Canada before Jonathan grew restless and wanted to return to Asia, which he and his wife did in 1908. He proved to be a stirring preacher. He became a traveling evangelist instead of being settled at a single mission station, and hundreds of converts were made in China and neighboring Korea.

Jonathan wrote, "I love those that thunder out the Word." His preaching style was thunderous and emotional—and effective. Many of his converts became preachers themselves and modeled their preaching style on his. He and his wife became friends with a Chinese general who had converted to Christianity, and Jonathan made many converts among the troops.

Health problems took their toll as Jonathan aged, and he and his wife returned to Canada where he continued preaching until his death on October 8, 1936, after a lifetime of thundering out the Word.

Prayer: Father, in this spiritually deaf world, give us boldness to speak your words of salvation. Amen.

October 9 · LIGHT IN THE FOG

The path of the righteous is like the first gleam of dawn.

PROVERBS 4:18

1940: "The service we render to others is really the rent we pay for our room on this earth." So said Wilfred Grenfell who died on this date after a lifetime of putting his words into practice.

Born in England in 1865, Grenfell studied medicine in London and graduated in 1888. He had been to American evangelist Dwight L. Moody's revival meetings and was struck by the fact that some of the Christians on the podium with Moody were athletes he admired. The Moody encounter inspired him to a life of Christian service. In 1892 he began his long association with the Royal National Mission to Deep Sea Fisherman on the bleak coast of Newfoundland, Canada. He saw that the scattered, hard-pressed communities in Newfoundland badly needed medical aid and other assistance. In his first year of service he sailed along what was called the "starvation coast" and gave medical care to nine hundred people. The following year he had a larger ship available, and he continued trolling the foggy coast, giving medical aid, preaching, and distributing clothing. Seeing that the merchants who traded with the fishermen were notorious for price-gouging, he helped the fishermen form cooperatives. Though his work was at first limited to the fishermen and their families, he later reached out to the native Eskimos in the province.

Grenfell once encountered Moody at a Boston hotel and told him that fourteen years earlier he had put his faith in Christ because of attending a Moody meeting. Moody replied, "And what have you been doing with your life since?" Grenfell told him, and Moody seemed pleased with the answer. Moody asked him to attend a revival meeting that evening and give his testimony.

In 1927 he was knighted, becoming "Sir Wilfred." Though he was honored by this, he had his own definition of honor: "To say any man is a real Christian is undeniably the highest honor we can confer upon him."

Prayer: Father, let our lives of loving service light up this gloomy world. Amen.

October 10 · THE IRISH TEE-TOTALER

Since, then, we know what it is to fear the Lord, we try to persuade men.

2 CORINTHIANS 5:11

1790: In Ireland, a nation with a reputation for hard drinking, Theobald Mathew, a Catholic monk, started a campaign for temperance. Born on this date, Mathew (known as the "Apostle of Temperance") well knew the devastating effects of alcohol abuse. In 1838 he founded the Total Abstinence Society. He and sixty others signed a no-alcohol pledge. The group met twice weekly in a schoolhouse but later had to move to a much larger building. In only a few months twenty-five thousand people in the town of Cork had signed the pledge. He traveled throughout Ireland, giving his lecture on temperance, and thousands more signed the pledge. He took his message to Scotland and later to America.

Never did he push for nationally enforced abstinence—that is, prohibition by law. Instead, he encouraged "taking the pledge" for abstinence strictly voluntarily with no stigma attached to refusing the pledge. He never claimed that abstinence was necessary for Christians. He only claimed that more abstainers—or at least *moderate* drinkers—would make a safer and happier Ireland. This is exactly what occurred—not a complete turnaround in morals and public welfare but at least a 45 percent decrease in liquor consumption and, as police observed, a definite drop in crime. This was accomplished not through legislation but through preaching.

It is revealing to compare his methods with those of Americans who pressured Congress to pass the Prohibition Act that went into force in 1919. Prohibition did reduce alcohol consumption, yet in most ways it was a failure, leading many respectable citizens into contempt for the law. We can respect the Prohibitionists' intentions but not the method. It is tempting to use the tactics of modern pressure politics. Yet Theobald Mathew seems to have followed the wiser course: preach to individuals and groups; if their attitudes and behaviors change—voluntarily—then society will change.

Prayer: Lord, teach us to partner our zeal with the spirit of gentle persuasion. Amen.

October 11 · POWER FAILURE

The devil took him to a very high mountain and showed him all the kingdoms of the world and their splendor.

MATTHEW 4:8

1303: If Satan had tempted Pope Boniface VIII with his offer of worldly power, Boniface would have accepted—and some say he did. His reign from 1294 to 1303 was one unceasing scandal. His predecessor Pope Celestine was a decent man, and his death after a brief reign was attributed to poisoning by Boniface. Whether this was true or not, Boniface was a typical pope of the Middle Ages, loving the wealth and power of his office and being not even remotely spiritual. He had the bad fortune to lock horns with some secular rulers as powerhungry and unscrupulous as himself. The worst of these was Philip IV, the king of France. To finance one of his wars, Philip tried to tax the clergy. Boniface issued a decree saying this could not be done without the pope's permission. Philip countered by engaging in a propaganda war and by abusing of the French clergy. Boniface caved in.

A French bishop was giving Philip trouble, so Philip asked the pope to remove him from office so he could be punished. Boniface replied with the decree *Unam Sanctam*, claiming that the pope had power over both secular and spiritual realms, and any king who did not accept this could be deposed by the pope. Then the stinger at the end: "subjection to the Roman Pontiff [the pope] is absolutely necessary for the salvation of every human creature."

In response the French legislature met, and one of Philip's cronies convinced the delegates that the "very Christian king of France" should depose the "heretical monster," the pope. Philip had Boniface kidnapped and physically abused. Boniface returned to Rome but died broken on October 11, 1303. No one shed a tear. Like many of his predecessors, Boniface tried to play power politics—and failed. Like many of the others, he ignored Jesus' words: "My kingdom is not of this world."

Prayer: Lord, teach us to seek only after spiritual power and to serve only the kingdom that will endure. Amen.

October 12 · THE CRAZY SAILOR

Since we have such a hope, we are very bold.

2 CORINTHIANS 3:12

1492: The year 1992 marked the five hundredth anniversary of Christopher Columbus coming to America. This was not celebrated much since many people have become convinced that the European settlers who followed Columbus did only harm, exploiting the native Americans. That view is understandable but very unfair to Columbus himself.

Columbus had a crazy idea: he could reach Asia by sailing west, and so Europe could trade with Asia without making the dangerous voyage around the tip of Africa. We now know he was not crazy—it *was* possible to reach Asia by sailing west, except that North America happened to be in the way. Queen Isabella of Spain was so impressed by Columbus's sincerity and piety that she backed his voyage. If he succeeded, it would increase trade—and open up a new field for Christian missions. On the long voyage Columbus's crew came close to mutiny more than once, but Columbus believed God had told him to keep sailing till they reached land.

On October 12, 1492, he stepped ashore on what was probably one of the Bahama Islands off Florida, and he named the island San Salvador, "Holy Savior." He was convinced he had reached Asia. The islanders led a primitive existence and were obviously not the civilized Japanese or Chinese that Columbus hoped to encounter. The natives did possess some gold, and within a short time the Europeans decided that instead of trading they could mine for gold—and also convert the people to Christianity. Isabella made it clear that these new "subjects" were not to be enslaved or abused. Unfortunately, she had no way of enforcing this policy, and many of the Spanish settlers did treat the American natives shamefully. But missionaries also made the voyage. Despite the harm done by the colonizers, we can never forget that Columbus's voyages led to the evangelizing of two continents.

Prayer: Lord, we thank you for the brave souls who opened up new worlds in which to preach the gospel. Amen.

October 13 · Hearts and Hands

Greet Tryphena and Tryphosa, those women who work hard in the Lord.

ROMANS 16:12

1836: Christians still debate the issue of whether women should serve as ordained ministers, but there is no debating the fact that women have always played a vital role in the churches, as we see clearly in Acts and the letters of Paul. In the Middle Ages devout women often became nuns, and though some convents were places of idleness, most nuns spent their lives in selfless service to the sick and needy. Areas of Europe that turned Protestant did away with convents and monasteries, for Protestants believed the whole system was beyond reform. Unfortunately, this left Protestantism with no personnel to perform the tasks that nuns did in Catholic areas. Protestant women attended church, of course, and they prayed and read the Bible and (unlike nuns) were wives and mothers in Christian homes. But Protestant women who were single or widowed had few organized ministries.

This situation changed thanks to a German Lutheran pastor named Theodor Fliedner, a prison chaplain who walked many miles to reach out to prisoners and to help ex-convicts find their place in society. In 1833 he set up a halfway house for women ex-convicts and put a woman in charge of it. On October 13, 1836, he opened a deaconess training center for women committing themselves to serving the poor, sick, and young. Unlike nuns who made lifetime vows of poverty and chastity, the deaconesses could return to secular life if they chose. But many deaconesses were fully committed for life, and Fliedner eventually gave up his pastorate and devoted himself full-time to establishing more deaconess centers. By the end of the century there were over eight thousand deaconesses in Germany and many more in other nations. Among the women trained at the centers was Florence Nightingale, considered the founder of modern nursing. Thanks to Fliedner, women with a heart for others found a place to serve.

Prayer: Father, thank you for the countless dedicated women who put their hearts and hands to work in loving service. Amen.

October 14 · NEVER AT A LOSS FOR WORDS

This is what we speak, not in words taught us by human wisdom but in words taught by the Spirit.

1876: Children can be amazingly creative. Consider Harry Ironside, born on this date in Toronto, Canada. His family moved to Los Angeles, and eleven-year-old Harry, finding no Sunday school to attend, gathered some other children together and used burlap bags to create a large tent to accommodate a hundred people. Finding no adult to teach the people, he did it himself.

Two years later Harry was impressed at the crowds that evangelist Dwight L. Moody drew, and he hoped to do so himself one day. When he finished eighth grade, he decided he had enough schooling and began preaching at night at the Salvation Army. Later he became an itinerant preacher for the Plymouth Brethren and began to draw crowds. His lack of formal education did not hold him back from preaching—or writing either, for he published nearly a hundred books, including Bible commentaries.

Moody Church in Chicago invited Harry to preach for one year, and for most of his sermons the church was filled to capacity. "One year" turned into eighteen. He continued to tour as an evangelist and drew large crowds in England and Ireland, but despite being on the road for perhaps forty weeks out of each year, he usually managed to be back at Moody on Sundays. On most Sundays at Moody Church he made new converts. He died of a heart attack in 1951 while on a preaching tour of New Zealand.

By the world's standards, Harry Ironside should not have happened—how could a man with an eighth-grade education reach so many people in so many places through his sermons and books? Perhaps the explanation is *focus*: someone wholly dedicated to Christ can do impossible things.

Harry Ironside said that "time is given to us to use in view of eternity." It is a solid New Testament sentiment and a fine summary of his entire life.

Prayer: Father, we praise you for your Spirit-led proclaimers of the saving truth. Amen.

J. STEPHEN LANG · 301

October 15 · SIMPLE AND CLEAR AS SPRING WATER

*My message and my preaching were not with wise and persuasive words, but with a
demonstration of the Spirit's power.*

1 CORINTHIANS 2:4

1906: The Ryman Auditorium, also known as the Grand Ole Opry House,
exists because Thomas Ryman, a Nashville riverboat captain and saloon owner,
went out one night in 1885 intending to heckle evangelist Sam Jones. Instead,
Ryman became a convert, and he built the Union Gospel Tabernacle for Jones
to preach in when he was in town. The building, famed for its superb acoustics,
was renamed Ryman Auditorium after Ryman's death in 1904.

What about Sam Jones? He was one of the star evangelists of the late 1800s, a
time when there was no shortage of them. Born Samuel Porter Jones in Alabama
in 1847, he was from a family with several Methodist preachers, but Sam became
a lawyer, drank heavily, and lost his practice but reformed and converted when
his dying father asked him to stop drinking. True to the family heritage, he
became a Methodist preacher and was so good at it that he became a traveling
evangelist.

Jones was active at the same time as the great evangelist D. L. Moody, and
some called Jones the "Moody of the South," but in fact Jones preached all over
the country. His style was simple and direct, laced with wry humor. His familiar
call to convert was "quit your meanness." He told friends that one of the greatest
compliments he was ever paid was hearing a child tell his father that he understood everything Preacher Jones said.

Jones never actually prepared a sermon. He showed up to preach at the
appointed time and place, always with a treasury of Bible verses in his head and
would preach "off the cuff." Apparently this practice worked very well for him.

Jones died on October 15, 1906, returning from preaching a revival in
Oklahoma. So great was his fame that his body lay in state in the Georgia capitol
where thirty thousand people paid their respects.

Prayer: Lord, make our witness to the world simple and direct to glorify you not ourselves. Amen.

October 16 · SAINT OR DEMON?

A cruel man brings trouble on himself.

PROVERBS 11:17

1859: A troubled and troublesome man who had failed at everything found success at the end of his life. He was John Brown, a radical abolitionist who was certain God had called him to free the American slaves. In the 1850s when the Kansas Territory was called "Bleeding Kansas" because of the violence perpetrated by both pro-slavery and anti-slavery factions, Brown was a key player, brutally killing and mutilating pro-slavery settlers. He was hailed as a hero in the parlors of New England aristocrats who gave him support and believed him when he said he was acting on God's direct commands. Owning slaves created a state of war, Brown said, and so violence was necessary. His favorite Bible verse was Hebrews 9:22: "Without the shedding of blood there is no remission of sins."

On October 16, 1859, Brown and twenty-one armed men stole into Harper's Ferry, Virginia, late at night, intending to seize the federal arsenal, arm the slaves, and launch the great slave rebellion. In his fantasy Brown had drawn up a new U.S. Constitution and saw himself as the president of an America without slaves. But his wild plan had no chance of success. Some in his band were killed, the rest taken prisoner. Brown himself was convicted of treason and hanged. He refused to be visited by any clergymen at the end. Most abolitionists praised him as a martyr while others (including Abraham Lincoln) were horrified by his violence.

After a distance of many years we can now ask: Was Brown right in what he did? He considered himself a Christian doing the will of God, yet there was no place in his religion for mercy or love of enemies. Slavery in a nation that considered itself Christian and that valued equality was a sin, as Brown said—but was bloodshed necessary to change things? We have to leave the matter to the ultimate Judge.

Prayer: Father, endow us with mercy and give us eyes and minds to seek opportunities for peaceful resolution to all quarrels. Amen.

October 17 · Beastly World

"If they persecuted me, they will persecute you also."

John 15:20

107: The words of a man about to be executed are worth taking seriously. We are fortunate to possess seven letters written by Ignatius a bishop from Antioch on his way to Rome to be executed by order of the emperor Trajan.

Though Ignatius was under guard, he was allowed to meet with men from the Ephesian church while the guard was paused at Smyrna, and he sent a letter back with the Christians, warning the congregation against "strangers" who were spreading false teachings. The "strangers" claimed that Jesus was not fully human and only appeared to be suffering on the cross, but Ignatius assures his readers that Christ was truly man but also truly God.

Not surprisingly, in these letters Ignatius's mind is on martyrdom—not just on his own impending death but on the death of Jesus. At times he appeared to be eager for his fate which was to be torn apart by wild beasts in the Colosseum in Rome in front of thousands of pagans. He wrote, "I do not want to live any more on a human plane"—he knew his fate but no longer feared it, for he was following in the footsteps of his Master. He seemed more concerned that "wild beasts in human shapes," false teachers, would lead Christians astray. Again and again Ignatius told Christians to honor and obey their church leaders—but he also reminded them that the chief authority is the High Priest in heaven, Christ.

Six of Ignatius's letters were to churches, but one was to his friend Polycarp, a bishop in Smyrna. He told his friend to "stand your ground like an anvil under the hammer." In 156 Polycarp would indeed stand his ground and die as a martyr. As Jesus foretold, his servants would suffer persecution, yet the message of salvation would continue to spread. Ignatius died on October 17, 107, not the first nor last saint to make the ultimate sacrifice.

Prayer: Father, teach us to fear nothing but to face all trials certain that our souls are in your hands. Amen.

October 18 · "Most Christian King"

Our citizenship is in heaven.

1685: On this date Louis XIV, the king of France, proved how intolerant he was. He revoked the Edict of Nantes which his grandfather, Henry IV, had issued in 1598, granting toleration to the French Protestants (known as Huguenots). Henry had been a Protestant himself but had turned Catholic so as to govern France, a predominantly Catholic country. But he did not forget his Protestant friends, and the Edict of Nantes guaranteed them a certain measure of security.

Louis XIV's real religion was himself. The French court was turned into a Church of Louis with the nobles of France fawning over the egotistical king. Louis had one thing in common with his grandfather: he was notoriously promiscuous and fathered various children by his mistresses. Perhaps a sense of guilt made him zealous for the Catholic Church, and his government began a program of petty persecution of Protestants, forcing many of them to house soldiers in their homes and gradually whittling away at their rights. Under the persecution many Protestants fled to other countries, notably England, while the more halfhearted ones became Catholic. With the revoking of the Edict of Nantes in 1685, Protestantism was technically illegal, so more of the half-hearted converted, and most of the others immigrated. In a short span of time, more than 400,000 people left France. Not only was this a gross instance of religious intolerance, but economically and socially this was a disaster for France since the Protestants were respectable and industrious citizens. Pope Innocent XI heartily disapproved of Louis's action. Louis, ironically, held the title "Most Christian King."

Shortly before his death in 1715, Louis announced proudly that he had completely exterminated the Protestant religion in France. This was nothing to be proud of, and, in fact, it was not correct, for not all Protestants fled or converted. They clung to their faith and endured persecution as true believers have done for centuries.

Pray: Lord, when your children face persecution, fix their minds on the better country that awaits them. Amen.

October 19 · SALVATION SQUABBLES

Warn them before God against quarreling about words; it is of no value.

2 TIMOTHY 2:14

1609: "Once saved, always saved" is believed by many Christians but not all. Believers have been arguing over this for centuries, and, sadly, in the 1600s you might have been executed for your belief if your view happened not to agree with the church in your region. John Calvin, the great Reformation leader in Switzerland, definitely believed in "once saved, always saved," and he was a powerful influence on Protestants everywhere. He also taught that God's grace could not be resisted—that is, if you were one of the "elect" that God predestined to salvation, you would not (in fact, *could* not) resist the pull of grace.

One theologian who disagreed was the Dutchman Jacob Harmensz—or, as he is better known, Jacobus Arminius. He taught that a Christian could backslide and lose his salvation and that God's grace could be resisted. Arminius taught at a university in the Netherlands till his death on October 19, 1609, but Protestants argued over his views for many years afterward, the notorious Calvinism-versus-Arminianism quarrel. A council called the Synod of Dort in 1619 came down on the side of Calvinism, declaring that Arminians were heretics, and a few days later one of the Arminian leaders was beheaded.

Why should this old quarrel interest us today? For one thing, we should be thankful that Christians no longer persecute each other over such issues. Intelligent people, well-versed in the Bible, still disagree about predestination and backsliding, and the wise thing to do (which, sadly, did not occur to the Christians in the 1600s) would be to tolerate minor differences in belief. There have been fine Calvinist Christians and fine Arminians and many people who have never bothered to fret over such matters and simply trust in Christ to save them. It is pleasant to think that in heaven the divisive issues that seemed so important on earth will no longer concern us as we feast in a fellowship of love.

Prayer: Father, make us steadfast in our core beliefs, and make us charitable about nonessentials. Amen.

October 20 · GODLY STRICTNESS

As for me and my household, we will serve the LORD.

JOSHUA 24:15

1629: John Winthrop, an English lawyer and devout man, was chosen on this date to be the governor of a new colony to be planted on Massachusetts Bay. Winthrop, like most of the other settlers, was a Puritan, meaning he did not think the state Church of England was sufficiently Christian in practice. The Puritans known as the Pilgrims who settled in Plymouth, Massachusetts, were Separatists, ones who wanted no part of the Church of England, period. Winthrop did not want to separate from it but wanted to show, in America, just what a godly Church of England could be like. He wrote that "we shall be as a city set upon a hill, the eyes of all people are upon us."

In 1630 he sailed for America. He settled in Boston and lived there till his death in 1649, serving the entire time as governor or deputy governor. He was a cheerful man but also a firm one, and residents that seemed to him to be transgressing the Christian moral code would be told to move elsewhere. One of the beauties of America was that nonconformists had plenty of room to set up their own colonies. Those who did not move on might be punished—sometimes severely. Winthrop saw this as necessary, for a colony surrounded by a howling wilderness and often hostile Indians could not tolerate dissension. Thomas Morton a profane man who sold firearms and liquor (a lethal combination) to the Indians was sent back to England.

As governor, Winthrop tried to put into practice a sermon he preached while sailing to America. Titled "A Model of Christian Charity," it stated that "the end [goal] is to improve our lives to do more service to the Lord." The sermon used the word *community* many times and emphasized that if the people would collectively and individually honor God, the settlement would prosper—if not it would fail. It did prosper, and Winthrop died an honored man.

Prayer: Lord, thank you for godly politicians who bring their faith to the public arena. Amen.

October 21 · God and Country

It was said among the nations, "The LORD has done great things for them."

PSALM 126:2

1808: The tune for "My Country, 'Tis of Thee" is, in fact, the tune for Britain's national anthem, "God Save the King" (or "Queen," for the present). Samuel Francis Smith, born on this date, was not familiar with the British anthem but in 1831 stumbled upon the tune in a book of German songs. His friend Lowell Mason, the composer of hundreds of hymn tunes (and also of "Mary Had a Little Lamb"), challenged Smith to translate some of the German songs. Instead, thankfully, Smith felt inspired to write his own original song and within thirty minutes had written the words for the song that he titled "America." Mason liked the song, and it was first performed, appropriately enough, on July 4 that year, long before "The Star-Spangled Banner" had become the official U.S. anthem. The occasion was an Independence Day celebration at Park Street Church in Boston.

At the time Smith wrote the song he was a student at Andover Theological Seminary in Massachusetts. He graduated in 1834 and was ordained a Baptist minister; he taught languages as well and later became the editor of a Christian magazine. He was active with the Baptist Missionary Union and took many trips abroad to inspect the work of missionaries. He also, not surprisingly, wrote more than a hundred hymns, publishing them in a collection titled *The Psalmist*. The author Oliver Wendell Holmes Sr. was a friend of Smith and correctly predicted that "America" would have a very long life. Appropriately, it was sung at Smith's funeral in 1895.

Familiar as the song is, most people know only the first verse. The fourth and fifth verses mention God, expressing loyalty not only to the nation but to the God who had blessed it so richly. Smith's phrase "Let freedom ring" from the first verse is stamped on our memories, but we would do well to remember the fourth verse which credits God as the "Author of liberty."

Prayer: Heavenly Father, thank you for the freedoms we enjoy, and let our gratitude show itself in deeds of kindness. Amen.

Though an army besiege me, my heart will not fear.

PSALM 27:3

741: A man who died on this date saved Europe from conquest by the Muslims. He was Charles Martel, ruler of the Franks, governing the territory we today know as France. Charles, like all Europeans of his day, was horrified at how fast the Muslims conquered areas that had been Christian for centuries. Muhammad had died in 632, and by 635 his followers had conquered Damascus, by 638 Jerusalem, by 650 most of Persia. Worse, by 715 Spain had fallen, and the Muslims had crossed the Pyrenees Mountains into Frankish territory. The lion's share of the Christian Roman Empire was under the control of a religion that did not even exist a century earlier. Many Christians must have wondered if God was indeed on the Muslims' side.

The Muslim general Abdal-Rahman, based in Spain, led his armies north in 732. Charles Martel had his Frankish cavalry positioned near the city of Tours. In October of that year, Charles's Christian army beat back the Muslims. The battle is referred to both as the battle of Tours and battle of Poitiers.

No one celebrated much at the time because for all anyone knew the Muslims would soon attempt more invasions of Europe. But in fact they did not, and as time passed Christians began to recover some of their lost territory in Europe. The Muslims focused their energy eastward as far as India. Their later invasions of Europe would occur on Europe's eastern border. Western Europe would be safe, relatively, until another sort of invasion began in the late twentieth century. The Muslims have shown no indication that they will let up in the effort to conquer the *kafir*, the infidel.

When Charles Martel died in 741 he had no idea what his army had accomplished. His grandson the great Charlemagne would enlarge a Christian empire, pushing its boundaries into Spain, taking territory that had been held by the Muslims in his grandfather's day.

Prayer: Lord, give us courage in all our endeavors, and grant us inner peace no matter what befalls us. Amen.

Put on the full armor of God, so that when the day of evil comes, you may be able to stand your ground.

EPHESIANS 6:13

1456: Prison is a terrible thing to endure, but the list of people who turn to God while in prison is a long one. One notable example is John of Capistrano, born in Italy in 1386. Working as a lawyer and living a worldly life, John found himself in prison during one of the frequent wars in Italy. He gave his life to Christ during his ordeal and on his release joined the Franciscan order of men. In a short time he became one of the most noted preachers of the Middle Ages, drawing huge crowds when he urged people to repent of their sins. It is said that on one occasion he preached to 120,000, and in some towns business would come to a halt when he was preaching. He and some other Franciscan preachers were the movers behind a great spiritual revival in Italy.

John had given up his career as a lawyer, but he still possessed a power with words, and the popes often used him as a diplomat. He was also useful as a preacher and writer against the various heresies of the time.

In 1453 the Muslim Turks conquered Constantinople, and it was feared they would press on westward and conquer the rest of Europe. John's fervent preaching resulted in a Crusade to drive the Turks back, and though he was seventy years old, he traveled with the Crusaders to relieve the Christians in Belgrade, and he actually led a regiment into battle, earning the label "the Soldier Saint." The Christians won, and John survived the battle, but due to the unsanitary conditions of the time, he contracted the Black Death—the bubonic plague— and died on October 23, 1456.

John's tomb inscription refers to him as "a man worthy of all praise, defender and promoter of the faith, guardian of the church," and an "ornament to all the world."

Prayer: Lord, endow us with strength and courage to defend what is good and honorable. Amen.

October 24 · Stop the Bleeding

When a man's ways are pleasing to the LORD, he makes even his enemies live at peace with him.

PROVERBS 16:7

1648: The Peace of Westphalia, signed on this date, ended one of the worst wars in Europe's history, the destructive Thirty Years' War, fought from 1618 to 1648, affecting almost every country in Europe and mingling together religious and political motives.

In a way, the Thirty Years' War began in 1517 when Martin Luther launched the Protestant Reformation. Fighting between Catholics and Protestants began in the 1520s and continued off and on—mostly on—for decades. The religious wars were based on an old assumption: for a society to survive, it had to be unified in religion, and the Christians of the 1500s could not imagine a nation tolerating different forms of Christianity. And so, sadly, Christians of different sects killed each other, believing they were doing God's will.

The agreements signed at Westphalia in Germany showed that the Christians of Europe were taking a slightly more tolerant view of the situation. The Reformed Christians—those who followed the teachings of John Calvin—were finally given legal recognition in some areas. The sprawling Holy Roman Empire (Germany and nearby regions) still existed, but the old illusion of a unified Catholic empire was gone, and the emperor had a great deal of prestige but little power. Within the empire citizens could practice their own form of Christianity in private without fear of harassment.

From our point of view, the long destructive wars could have been avoided. Why couldn't the Christians of western Europe simply have tolerated each other and not tried to coerce—or kill—Christians with slightly different beliefs? The only answer is that Christians are human, and the desire for conformity and distrust of nonconformists lives in us all. Also, what we call "tolerance" the people of the 1600s might have called "not taking belief seriously." We can only trust that God will judge us all fairly.

Prayer: Father, give us hearts filled with compassion and minds that let us distinguish between the important and unimportant. Amen.

When he saw the crowds, he had compassion on them, because they were harassed and helpless, like sheep without a shepherd.

MATTHEW 9:36

1891: The U.S. Constitution guarantees freedom of speech and freedom of the press. But a man born on this date discovered there were limits on freedom. He was Charles Edward Coughlin, born in Canada to Irish Catholic parents, ordained a priest in 1916. He settled in Royal Oak, a suburb of Detroit, in 1923 and in 1926 began a weekly hour-long radio program, at first confining his broadcasts to spiritual matters. The Depression prompted him to shift to political and economic issues, and he spoke out boldly against Communism and Socialism—and against capitalism as well. The CBS radio network grew uncomfortable with Coughlin's broadcasts and dropped him, so he created his own network that reached millions of listeners.

He supported Franklin Roosevelt in the 1932 election and was an avid supporter of FDR's New Deal programs with Coughlin claiming that "the New Deal is Christ's deal" and the choice was "Roosevelt or ruin." But he grew disenchanted with FDR, seeing him as a tool of Wall Street capitalists, and the former FDR fan became one of his worst critics.

Some Catholics were uneasy with Coughlin's political broadcasts, but his superior, the archbishop of Detroit, supported him. Apparently the public did also, for he received thousands of letters per day. His supporters saw him as a faithful Christian, standing up for the common man against both Socialism and capitalism. However, FDR's administration pulled strings to deny Coughlin a broadcasting permit and curtail circulation of his magazine, *Social Justice*. In 1942 a new archbishop of Detroit ordered Coughlin to confine himself to the work of a parish priest. He served as a priest till his retirement in 1966 and died in 1979.

In the 1930s he was widely loved, and probably 4 million people tuned in each week to his broadcasts. Though often controversial, during the Depression he gave hope and comfort to the oppressed.

Prayer: Lord, give each of us a voice to speak out for the poor and downtrodden. Amen.

October 26 · AT WAR WITH A WORLD OF DOUBT

He who doubts is like a wave of the sea, blown and tossed by the wind.

JAMES 1:6

1928: Is the Bible really the inspired word of God, or is it just a collection of ancient writings of purely human origin? In the 1800s universities in Germany were believing the second assertion, creating a generation of pastors and religious scholars who no longer believed the Bible was the divine foundation of faith.

One alumnus of German universities who did not feel that way was Reuben Archer Torrey, an American preacher and writer who came down on the side of belief. Born in 1856, he went from attending school in Germany in 1883 to assisting American evangelist D. L. Moody in 1889. After Moody's death in 1899, Torrey took up his mantle as evangelist and from 1902 on, preached across the United States as well as Canada, Britain, Australia, China, and Japan. The great Moody who never attended college and Torrey who had earned several college degrees, saw themselves as equals in the work of evangelism.

Aside from preaching, Torrey wrote some of the booklets that are known collectively as *The Fundamentals*, a series launched in 1909 to defend basic Christian beliefs. Having been educated at Yale and at two German universities, Torrey understood the threat Christianity faced with the skepticism being taught in most colleges, and he used his contacts in America and Britain to enlist capable pastors and scholars to defend the beliefs that were under assault. His article defending the truth of Jesus' resurrection is one of the best in *The Fundamentals* series. Like a brilliant and eloquent lawyer in a courtroom, Torrey raised every objection to belief in the resurrection, then demolished them one by one. To those who doubted the Bible, Torrey affirmed that "this Book is the Word of him who cannot lie."

Torrey died on October 26, 1928, but his life was proof that being well-educated did not have to lead to doubts about faith.

Prayer: Lord, arm us with confidence as we carry your message of salvation into a world of doubt. Amen.

October 27 · AN EVERYMAN'S BIBLE—ALMOST

Your word, O LORD, is eternal.

PSALM 119:89

1978: Is it possible to publish a version of the Bible that *all* English-speaking people will embrace? It hasn't happened in the past century, despite several attempts to replace the beloved KJV (King James Version) with something modern readers can understand. The RSV (Revised Standard Version) published in 1952 sold well, yet the KJV continued to outsell it. The same was true for Today's English Version and the New English Bible—big sellers but not destined to become the "Common Bible" that the KJV had been.

Why did the RSV, so similar to the KJV, not succeed in replacing it? Partly because it had a reputation as a "liberal" version, mostly based on the rendering of Isaiah 7:14: KJV had "a virgin shall conceive," while RSV had "maiden." And in John 3:16, the KJV had "only begotten Son," while RSV had "only Son." The RSV never overcame many people's objections to its rendering of these two verses.

In 1965 a group of evangelical scholars met, agreeing to do a new version which would be called the New International Version. The New Testament was published in 1973 and was well received. The full Bible was published on October 27, 1978, with advance sales of 1.2 million, and the largest print run of any Bible ever. Isaiah 7:14 had "virgin," to many readers' relief. Psalm 23 retained the familiar phrase "valley of the shadow of death." In fact, one reason the NIV sold so well is that it stuck close to the KJV language while changing most of the outdated words. Millions of readers saw it as just the right balance of traditional wording and contemporary clarity. It became the basis for numerous commentaries and reference works. It was the best-selling Bible of the late twentieth century but has yet to become what the KJV was, the Bible of *all* the people. Even so, it has found a place in millions of readers' hearts.

Prayer: Lord, we thank you for all worthy translations of your Word. Let us show our approval by living by their teachings. Amen.

October 28 · CROSSING A CULTURAL CHASM

Say among the nations, "The LORD reigns."

PSALM 96:10

1646 : The first Bible published in North America was not in English nor Spanish nor French. It was in the Algonquin Indian language; the New Testament published in 1661 and the entire Bible in 1663. It was the work of a dedicated Massachusetts pastor named John Eliot. In theory, all the Christians who settled in America hoped to convert the Indians to Christianity. In practice, few of them made the effort. Eliot was one who did.

Eliot was born in England around 1604 and, like so many of his fellow Puritans, attended Cambridge. He worked for a while with Thomas Hooker, who would later found a colony in Connecticut. Eliot came to Massachusetts in 1631 where he became pastor in the town of Roxbury. He and two other pastors produced the *Bay Psalm Book*, the first book printed in North America.

On October 28, 1646, he preached for the first time to a group of Indians in their own language, beginning a ministry full of triumphs and frustrations. In a few years there were enough Indian converts to organize them into "praying towns," villages based on the assumption that the converts needed to be separated from their unbelieving tribesmen. It is estimated that possibly a fifth of the Indians of New England accepted Christianity, at least nominally. Unfortunately, the Indian-white conflict known as King Philip's War undid much of the work Eliot had done.

The sad part of the Eliot story is not that he failed in his mission but that so few others in the English colonies worked for the conversion of the Indians. Eliot's fellow Puritans had a low opinion of Catholics, yet they had to admit that the Catholics were much more active in reaching the Indians in the Spanish and French colonies.

Eliot, England's "Apostle to the Indians," had done his duty. In time, other English Christians would follow his example.

Prayer: God of all the earth, thank you for dedicated preachers and translators who carry your Word everywhere. Amen.

October 29 · LIVING LARGE

All over the world this gospel is bearing fruit and growing.

COLOSSIANS 1:6

1919: In the 1880s New York was the doorway that thousands of new immigrants passed through as they sought a better life in America. Many prospered as they had hoped, but many struggled. A. B. Simpson, a Presbyterian pastor from Canada, wanted to reach out to these "neglected peoples" with the "neglected resources of the church." Finding his denomination uninterested in this kind of outreach, he left his pastorate at a prestigious Presbyterian church and founded his Gospel Tabernacle in the heart of the city. Later he founded a school, which became Nyack College, for training people in outreach abroad and at home. Without meaning to, he founded a ministry that in time became a new denomination, the Christian and Missionary Alliance.

Born in 1843 on Prince Edward Island, Canada's smallest province, Simpson grew up in a strict Presbyterian home. He saw most churches as "associations of congenial friends" who gathered together once a week to listen to a sermon and some music. In his book *A Larger Christian Life*, he spoke of something more exciting, a church that would be "home to every form of help and blessing that Jesus came to give lost and suffering men." Simpson emphasized divine healing, having been miraculously healed himself, and he emphasized the necessity of evangelism and missions.

Simpson opened *A Larger Christian Life* with this invitation: "Let us consider the possibilities of faith." What were they? One was joy which he saw lacking in most believers. Another was growth—"enlargement" of the heart and of the whole life, brought on by a larger vision of the world and one's purpose in it.

"God is preparing his heroes," Simpson wrote. Surely he himself would qualify as one of them, a believer with a large vision who enlarged the worldwide church by making new converts and by leading lukewarm Christians into a heart-filling faith.

Prayer: Father, give us a holy craving for the abundant life that you promised to those who love you. Amen.

He put a new song in my mouth, a hymn of praise to our God.

PSALM 40:3

1807: The term *golden boy* would apply to Christopher Wordsworth, born on this date. The son of a notable minister-professor, Christopher attended Cambridge University and distinguished himself as both athlete and scholar. He was also well-connected: the great William Wordsworth, England's poet laureate, was his uncle, and it appears that a talent for verse ran in the family.

While serving as the headmaster at Harrow, one of England's finest schools, he conceived the idea of a hymnal with hymns tied to the church year: Advent, Christmas, Epiphany, Lent, Easter, Pentecost. In 1862 he published *The Holy Year*, in the hope that hymns would serve to reinforce the preaching and rituals of the church year. Like the great hymn-writers before and after him, Wordsworth believed hymns should not be just a pleasure to sing but be instructive as well. In his own words, "The first duty of a hymn is to teach sound doctrine, and thus save souls."

Many of his hymns in *The Holy Year* are still popular. "Sing, O Sing, This Blessed Morn" is a fine Christmas hymn, and in it Wordsworth incorporated the phrase "God of God, and Light of Light" from the Nicene Creed. The beautiful Easter hymn "Alleluia, Alleluia, Hearts and Voices Heavenward Raise" is theology turned into excellent poetry. His best-known hymn, "O Day of Rest and Gladness," is probably the finest hymn ever written in honor of the Sabbath. "Gracious Spirit, Holy Ghost" was written for Pentecost. All of Wordsworth's hymns are saturated with phrases from the Bible.

Wordsworth was a prolific writer, producing a commentary on the Greek New Testament, a history of the early church, and, not surprisingly, a biography of his famous uncle, the poet. But his greatest and most enduring contribution to the faith is *The Holy Year*, a delightful blending of the Bible, church ritual, and singable poetry.

Prayer: Lord, no matter what befalls us, keep us joyful; keep us singing in good times and bad. Amen.

Whoever is on the LORD's side—come to me!

EXODUS 32:26 (NKJV)

1517: If the printing press had not been invented in the 1400s, we would never have heard of Martin Luther. He was a German monk and university professor who began to question the Catholic Church's teachings about salvation, and on October 31, 1517, he posted a notice on the door of the castle church in Wittenberg, which served as a community bulletin board. The notice listed ninety-five "theses," topics for theological debate. They probably would have been long ago forgotten, but thanks to the printing press, they were reproduced all over Europe, and soon Professor Luther was seen as a brave man challenging the authority of the pope and the church's role as mediator between man and God.

Without meaning to, Luther had launched the Protestant Reformation. Soon, thanks to the printing press, all Europe would know of Luther's insistence that the Bible alone was the standard for Christian belief and that Christians were not saved by doing good works but performed good works because they were saved. The popes, Luther said, could be wrong in their teachings and so could church councils which in the past had executed reformers. The Catholic Church condemned him as a heretic and would have executed him, but the ruler of his native country, Saxony, protected him, hiding him away in a castle where Luther made good use of the time by translating the entire Bible into German, giving German speakers direct access to the Word of God. This set a precedent: Protestants would give people the Bible in their own languages so they could know what to believe and how to behave. The centuries when the Bible was available only in Latin, to be read only by scholars, had come to an end.

By the time Luther died in 1546, much of northern Europe had become Protestant. But his greatest contribution to Christianity was his emphasis on the individual believer, saved by faith and guided by the Bible.

Prayer: Father, when your children err in thought and deed, guide them back to the true faith. Amen.

NOVEMBER

November 1 · DIGNITY MEETS THE SPIRIT

You stiff-necked people . . . You always resist the Holy Spirit!

ACTS 7:51

1991: Prior to the 1960s you never heard the words *Episcopal* and *Pentecostal* in the same sentence. Episcopalians are known for their dignified worship style and (some would say) for being wealthy. Pentecostals with their emotionalism and the practice of speaking in tongues, were looked upon with suspicion by some Christians—and, let us admit, Pentecostalism was thought of as being lower-class.

Then a curious thing happened: on Palm Sunday 1960 Dennis Bennett, the pastor of an Episcopal Church in Van Nuys, California, announced that he and several members of the church had been baptized in the Holy Spirit and had spoken in tongues. An assistant pastor responded by throwing off his robe and resigning in disgust. Bennett's overseer, the bishop of Los Angeles, banned speaking in tongues in churches under his authority. Thanks to stories in *Time* and *Newsweek*, the incident became national news. One of Bennett's parishioners told *Time* that "we're Episcopalians, not a bunch of wild-eyed hillbillies."

Bennett resigned, but a bishop in Washington State invited him to "bring the fire" there, and he pastored St. Luke's Episcopal which grew into a two-thousand member congregation—to be precise, a *charismatic* congregation where people welcomed the baptism and gifts of the Spirit.

The line between "Pentecostal" and "charismatic" is thin—some would say nonexistent. Both groups believe in the same things, but "Pentecostal" has continued in use in the names of denominations, while "charismatic" usually refers to Spirit-led believers within mainline denominations. Bennett's revelation of being baptized in the Spirit suddenly made people aware that no longer were Pentecostals the only ones enjoying life in the Spirit. Mainliners—even the "dignified" Episcopalians—were being touched by the Spirit.

Bennett and his wife, Rita, founded two organizations: Episcopal Renewal Ministries and the interdenominational Christian Renewal Association. He died of a heart attack on November 1, 1991, and is remembered as a humble man who had never sought the notoriety he achieved.

Prayer: Lord, your Spirit moves where he will and takes us by surprise. Keep us open to his leading. Amen.

Who is wise and understanding among you? Let him show it by his good life.

James 3:13

1893: "When God has a work to be executed, he also chooses the man to execute it." The man who spoke those words was Daniel Payne who saw himself as God's man to improve the lot of black Americans, spiritually and mentally. Born in Charleston, South Carolina, in 1811, Payne was black—but *not* a slave. He was one of the South's free blacks, a minority within a minority. Raised by an aunt after both his parents died, Daniel was well-educated (mostly by his own efforts), and at the tender age of eighteen, he opened his own school. His plans for a lifetime as an educator got scuttled—temporarily—in the wake of the Nat Turner slave rebellion in Virginia in 1831, which led slave-holding states to restrict the teaching of all blacks, whether slave or free.

Payne left South Carolina to study at a seminary in Pennsylvania. He joined the African Methodist Episcopal (AME) church, the denomination started by freed slave Richard Allen, and he helped set higher education standards for it. In 1852 Payne became a bishop of the AME. The AME and the white Methodists joined together to found Wilberforce University in Ohio, named in honor of William Wilberforce, the Christian politician who helped end slavery in the British Empire. During the Civil War a Southern sympathizer tried to burn down some of the buildings, and the school encountered some financial stress, but Payne worked to keep the school solvent and in time became its president, the first black college president in America. When the war ended, he led a band of missionaries to the South to raise the spiritual condition of the newly freed slaves who badly needed guidance after years of having all their life decisions made for them, and the AME became a permanent part of the lives of Southern blacks.

Daniel Payne died on November 2, 1893, after a lifetime of tireless service, a vivid example of faith, hard work, and commitment.

Prayer: Lord, teach us to pursue wisdom and knowledge that will increase our faith. Amen.

"Love the Lord your God with all your heart and with all your soul and with all your mind."

MATTHEW 22:37

1723: A man born on this date would be very proud that the college he helped establish is one of the elite schools in America. He would likely be horrified that the school has, like the other Ivy League colleges, become aggressively secular.

His name was Samuel Davies, born in Delaware and ordained a Presbyterian pastor in 1747. He was called to serve Presbyterian churches in Virginia where the established church was the Church of England, and Davies became the first preacher licensed outside the established church. He convinced the colonial authorities that England's 1689 Toleration Act allowed for freedom of worship in the colonies as well as in England.

While he was pastoring in Virginia, a new college had been founded, the College of New Jersey, open to all denominations. The school persuaded Davies, an accomplished speaker, to travel to England to help raise money for the college. Davies wrote in his diary that it was "a most animating prospect" to be aiding an institution that would be "of extensive benefit to mankind." He and evangelist Gilbert Tennent raised enough money for the college to erect its first permanent building, Nassau Hall, in the town of Princeton. A few years after Davies's fund-raising tour, the college asked him to serve as its president. He died in 1761, aged thirty-seven, having accomplished much in a short life. Many years after Davies's death, the College of New Jersey would take its more familiar name, Princeton University.

Though he died before the American Revolution, Davies was a powerful influence on one of its key figures, the orator Patrick Henry, remembered for his "Give me liberty or give me death" speech. Henry as a child had heard Davies preach many times, and late in life he told his biographer that Davies had taught him what an orator should be.

Prayer: Father, give your church around the world leaders with minds and hearts grounded in unshakable faith. Amen.

November 4 · Ex-Radical Poet

I will praise you among the nations, O LORD; I will sing praises to your name.

PSALM 18:49

1771: James Montgomery was born on this date in Scotland, the son of a minister. His long and colorful career could be summed up as "poet, political radical, journalist, and poet." Although his poems would have been forgotten long ago if he hadn't published them as hymns, many are still sung today.

In Montgomery's youth, the French Revolution was in full swing, and like many young men, he sided with the Revolution—at first. In Britain this was risky, and he served time in prison for publishing a pro-Revolution poem in his newspaper. (Like many young radicals, he mellowed as he aged, plus the bloody excesses of the Revolution eventually turned the radicals against violence.) After running the paper for thirty years, he retired—or more precisely, gave himself to full-time Christian work, promoting foreign missions and working to end the slave trade and the abuses of child labor. Although he had distanced himself from the revolutionary politics of his youth, he was still zealous for social reform, and like many of his contemporaries, he never separated piety from charity.

The British churches had a long tradition of singing rhymed versions of the Psalms during worship, and in 1822 Montgomery published *Songs of Zion*, his collection of versified Psalms. But he broke away from the Psalm tradition and composed many hymns not based on the Psalms, and these were published in 1853 as *Original Hymns for Public, Social, and Private Devotions*. He had been writing poetry since age ten, and by the time he died in 1854, he had written four hundred hymns. Of these, several are still popular: "Prayer Is the Soul's Sincere Desire," "In the Hour of Trial, Jesus Plead for Me," "Hail to the Lord's Anointed," and the wonderful Christmas hymn "Angels from the Realms of Glory." How fortunate the church is that this man with a zealous spirit changed from political radical to Christian poet.

Prayer: Lord, bless all those whose love of neighbor is rooted in their love for you. Amen.

November 5 · DEFENDING INSPIRATION

"I will give you words and wisdom that none of your adversaries will be able to resist or contradict."

LUKE 21:15

1851: What do we mean when we say the Bible is "inspired"? That question, which for all Christians should be of great importance, engaged the mind of a man born on this date, Benjamin B. Warfield, one of the great theologians of the 1800s.

Warfield was well-connected. His mother was the sister of John Breckinridge, a U.S. vice president and, later, Confederate general (Warfield's middle name was Breckinridge). Born in Kentucky, he entered Princeton University in 1868 and graduated with high honors. In 1873 he entered Princeton Seminary. He pastored several churches but in 1887 settled into the job that made him famous, professor of theology at Princeton Seminary.

At the time Princeton had a reputation for having high intellectual standards, combined with a deep devotion to the Bible. Warfield had no love for the modernist theology coming out of Europe which was casting negative light on the Bible and claiming it was a purely human document, not a sacred one given by God to man. Warfield agreed that the Bible's human authors each had distinct personalities, but he insisted that God inspired the writers, not overriding the writers' individual styles but working with and through them. His book *The Inspiration and Authority of the Bible* is one of the classic texts defending the truth of the Bible.

Warfield criticized not only modernism but another "-ism"—revivalism which was a huge force in American Christianity in his lifetime. Warfield did not deny that people could find salvation at revival meetings, but he criticized the theology of revival preachers as "shallow." Oddly enough, he did not oppose the teaching of evolution but insisted that God was behind it and that belief in evolution did not require disbelieving in God.

Warfield was a powerhouse of American theology in the 1800s and early 1900s, influencing hundreds of preachers and thousands of readers.

Prayer: Lord, your Word stands firm. Bless those who use the intellectual energy to defend its truths. Amen.

November 6 · "The Most Hated Woman"

With God we will gain the victory, and he will trample down our enemies.

PSALM 60:12

1967: In 1963, in an 8–1 ruling, the U.S. Supreme Court declared it unconstitutional for public schools to require Bible reading, despite several states having laws mandating daily Bible reading and prayer in public schools. The infamous *Murray v. Curlett* ruling involved the most high-profile atheist in America, Madalyn Murray O'Hair who claimed her son, William Murray, had been "bullied" by classmates for not wanting to participate in his school's daily Bible reading.

Reveling in her newfound fame, O'Hair was profiled in *Life* magazine and on November 6, 1967, was the first guest to appear on Phil Donahue's television talk show. She criticized the televised reading of a passage from Genesis by the Apollo 8 astronauts on Christmas Eve 1968 and announced that she stood for total sexual freedom for not only adults but children as well. As head of American Atheists, she claimed she welcomed the ire of religious people and delighted in being the "most hated woman in America."

Ironically, in 1980 her son William became a Christian—despite his mother having said that she would have him committed to an insane asylum if that happened. William told his story in the book *My Life Without God*. What we learn about his troubled and troublesome mother is disturbing: she hated her father (she wanted William to poison him), William's father was not her husband but a married man with whom she had an affair, and she inflated the membership figures for American Atheists so people would think she was the head of a large pressure group.

She, her son Jon, and granddaughter Robin disappeared in August 1995. Later their dismembered bodies were discovered in Texas, the three having been caught up in a financial scam and an attempt to flee the IRS. They had been murdered not by the Bible-reading Christians she so despised but by shysters as unscrupulous as herself.

Prayer: Remembering your command, we pray for our enemies, as we also pray that your will be done in this troubled world. Amen.

November 7 · PAINTER TO THE KING

Let us fix our eyes on Jesus, the author and perfecter of our faith.

HEBREWS 12:2

1598: An artist born on this date had friends in high places. He was Francisco Zurburan of Spain, and at one point the Spanish king Philip IV placed his hand on the artist's shoulder and said, "Painter to the king, and king of painters." At that time he was one of the most respected artists in the world, and like most artists of that day, he devoted much of his time to religious paintings.

It was the time of the Counter-Reformation when the Catholic Church was encouraging dramatic and emotional artwork that would evoke a response in the viewer. Most of Zurburan's paintings are indeed emotional, such as *Christ and the Virgin in the House at Nazareth* which shows the boy Jesus and his mother. Mary looks on with a touch of sadness as the young Jesus plaits together a ring of thorns, an omen of what he will suffer as an adult. Zurburan painted many pictures of the infant Jesus with Mary and Joseph, and he broke with the tradition of showing Joseph as much older than Mary. In Zurburan's works Mary and Joseph are the same age, a young couple doting on—and in awe of—the holy child.

An old tradition says that Luke, the author of the gospel and Acts, was a painter, and thus he was regarded as the patron saint of painters. In *St. Luke as a Painter Before Christ on the Cross*, Zurburan depicts himself as Luke, his palette in his hand, gazing up in sadness and admiration at his crucified Lord. Besides painting familiar biblical scenes, he also painted numerous pictures of one of the favorite Catholic saints, Francis of Assisi.

Zurburan died in 1664, having been largely forgotten in his later years, but his reputation rose again later, and today he is regarded as one of the finest Christian artists, a man with the power to make religious figures both realistic and dramatic.

Prayer: Lord, give us eyes to see spiritual beauty, to see our fellow creatures through your eyes. Amen.

November 8 · MANY HATS, ONE GOD

Dominion belongs to the LORD and he rules over the nations.

PSALM 22:28

1920: "An office-holder who wants something other than to obey his King is unfit to hold office." The man who said those words held the highest political office in his country and throughout a long career tried to obey his King. What a pity this remarkable man, pastor-politician Abraham Kuyper, is not better known.

Born in the Netherlands in 1837, Kuyper studied for the ministry but found his faith deepened not by seminary but by the devout simple folk he served in his first church. As he became more conservative in belief, he had doubts about whether the state church of the Netherlands was genuinely Christian in practice. He was elected to the Dutch parliament in 1874, and in 1880 he founded the Free University in Amsterdam, a Christian school not affiliated with the state church. In 1886 he led the group that broke away from the state church and took the name Reformed Church.

In 1900 his party came to power, and Kuyper became prime minister of the nation. While in office he pushed for laws that would aid the working classes. He left office in 1905 but continued to be active in parliament. As a politician he looked after the interest of *de kleine luyden*, "the little people."

Kuyper did not believe in separation of politics from religion. Christians *had* to carry their beliefs into the political arena, for no aspect of a believer's life should be sealed off from God. He pushed for government policies that would put religious schools on an equal footing with public ones. He opposed Socialism and Communism and saw them as dangerous secular religions.

Known as "Bram" to friends and "Abraham the Great" to his many admirers, Kuyper died on November 8, 1920, after an active life in which he wore many hats—pastor, journalist, teacher, and statesman. No matter what he did, he did it for God.

Prayer: King of kings, bless those with courage to walk with faith into the political arena. Amen.

November 9 · Scotch Lion

The righteous are as bold as a lion.

Proverbs 28:1

1572: People have for centuries been intrigued by the colorful life of Mary Queen of Scots. The story of the man she considered her worst enemy is just as intriguing.

Born in Scotland probably around 1514, John Knox joined the rising Protestant movement in the 1540s, gaining fame for his sermons that combined intellect and emotion. He lived for a while in England, helping to guide its Reformation, but when the Catholic queen Mary Tudor took the throne, Knox lived in exile in Europe. The persecution of Protestants under Mary convinced Knox that the personal religion of a ruler should not be allowed to determine the religion for an entire nation.

Scotland had its own woes, its queen being a devout Catholic who tolerated the Protestants for a while but then decided to crush them. Queen Elizabeth I of England lent the Scotch Protestants an army, and the Protestants triumphed. Catholicism was banned in Scotland; a Scots Confession (creed) was drawn up, and the laity were given important roles in the new church.

Mary Queen of Scots, who had been living in France while all this took place, returned to claim her throne in 1561. As she was devoutly Catholic, she and Knox inevitably locked horns. They met together four times: Mary insisting that subjects had to obey their ruler and not make trouble, and Knox insisting that even though she regarded him as a commoner and heretic, he had a duty to speak on the people's behalf. Knox was one of the few human beings who was never manipulated by Mary's charm or tears. Mary foolishly lost her throne after conspiring to murder her husband and then marrying one of his murderers. Forced to abdicate, she fled to exile in England.

Knox, the "thundering Scot," and the Protestant party triumphed. On November 9, 1572, he ended his term as preacher at St. Giles's cathedral in Edinburgh. He died a few days later, and it was said at his funeral that he "neither feared nor flattered any flesh."

Prayer: Lord, give us more believers like John Knox, people whose zeal drives out all fear. Amen.

November 10 · REASON V. FAITH

"If the world hates you, keep in mind that it hated me first."

JOHN 15:18

1793: The beautiful and historic Notre Dame Cathedral in Paris was officially designated a "Temple of Reason," part of the attempted de-Christianization of Europe by the French Revolutionaries. On this date an opera singer, posing as "Liberty" with a papier-mâché mountain as a backdrop, bowed to the flame of Reason, symbolizing that Christianity had given way to something modern and "enlightened." Witnesses report that what followed resembled a pagan orgy, with these "enlightened" people taking delight in behaving immorally in a church. Around the same time, Paris streets bearing the names of saints were renamed. A new calendar was created and even a new week (of ten days) in the hope that all the familiar Christian holy days, and Sundays, would soon fade from people's memory. In times past, France's Catholic kings had worked to stamp out Protestantism. The Revolutionaries went further and tried to stamp out Christianity altogether.

The Revolutionaries assumed that Christianity and other "superstitions" would disappear in a short time. But the made-up religion of Reason had only a short reign, and, soon after, a religion of the Supreme Being was substituted. Neither satisfied the masses of the French people.

The Revolutionaries were gravely mistaken in predicting the imminent demise of the "superstition," Christianity. In fact, the horrors of the Revolution—especially the Reign of Terror in which thousands of people were executed by the guillotine—had the effect of turning many people back to Christianity, once they saw the bloodshed unleashed by the "religion of Reason" with France's armies trying to spread their "Enlightenment" all over Europe at the point of bayonets. In many ways the 1800s was Christianity's greatest century with missionaries carrying the gospel to the far corners of the globe—using persuasion, not force.

Prayer: Father, in a world that is more and more hostile to people of faith, keep our minds fixed on you, give us peace, and remind us that we will endure despite hostility and persecution. Amen.

November 11 · PRISON AND POLITICS

My comfort in my suffering is this: Your promise preserves my life.

PSALM 119:50

1821: Fyodor Dostoevsky, born on this date, is considered one of the world's greatest novelists, and like the other great Russian novelist, Leo Tolstoy, Dostoevsky was deeply affected by Christianity. Born into a well-to-do family in Moscow, he got caught up in radical politics in his younger days, and like many student radicals of the time, he found himself on the wrong side of a prison wall. In fact, he was sentenced to death but at the last minute was sentenced to ten years in cold, bleak Siberia.

Suffering widened his mind and heart and also purged him of his radical notions. He came to see that for the radicals of his day, politics was a religion. His novel *The Possessed* depicted the political agitators, one of whom makes the terrifying statement, "If God doesn't exist, then I am God." Dostoevsky foretold that Communism and the other radical "-isms" of the time would cause untold suffering if they were ever put into practice. The radicals' "compassion" was merely a cover for their hunger for power over others.

Although his mind was grounded in the Bible, Dostoevsky had some serious personal failings, notably his addiction to gambling. Living at the edge of poverty must have spurred his creativity, for he managed to produce the great novels *Crime and Punishment*, *The Idiot*, and *The Brothers Karamazov*. *The Idiot* looked at a nobleman who resolved to live as a Christian and found it very difficult. In *The Brothers Karamazov*, he gave the world one of its great fictional characters, the priest Father Zossima, a believable but inspiring example of Christian love. Dostoevsky believed that the world could be transformed not through political change but through the influence of people like Father Zossima.

Dostoevsky was a flawed and afflicted man who endured prison, epilepsy, poverty, a gambling addiction, and disillusionment. The suffering produced a better man and some masterpieces of literature.

Prayer: Father, teach us to learn from our trials, to have our hearts and minds widened as we learn to do your will. Amen.

November 12 · A Profitable Tale

If anyone is in Christ, he is a new creation.

2 Corinthians 5:17

1880: One of the most popular novels ever written, made into two of the most popular movies ever made, resulted from a chance conversation on a train. In 1875 Lew Wallace, who had been a Union general in the Civil War, chatted with Robert Ingersoll, a notorious advocate of atheism. The conversation made Wallace aware of how little he knew about Christianity and the Bible. He began reading as much as he could about the world Jesus lived in and also toured the Holy Land. His research was poured into the novel *Ben-Hur: A Tale of the Christ*, published on November 12, 1880. Joseph Harper, of the novel's publisher Harper and Brothers, said that the novel was "the most beautiful manuscript that has ever come into this house."

The novel became a publishing phenomenon, outselling every book except the Bible. Until *Gone with the Wind* was published in 1936, *Ben-Hur* was the top-selling American novel. Contributing to the book's success were many devout Christians who generally did not read novels. Pope Leo XIII actually gave his official blessing to the book, the first papal blessing bestowed on a novel.

Wallace licensed a stage version of the book and more than 20 million people saw it. Inevitably the book was made into a movie—or rather, two movies; the first, released in 1925 was one of the most successful silent movies. Among the crowds it drew were many Christians who ordinarily avoided movies completely. The spectacular 1959 movie version with Charlton Heston was the most popular movie of the year and one of the great movies of all time.

Behind all this popularity lies Lew Wallace's own spiritual testimony: "After six years given to the impartial investigation of Christianity as to its truth or falsity, I have come to the deliberate conclusion that Jesus Christ is the Messiah of the Jews, the Savior of the world, and my personal Savior."

Prayer: Father, bless all those whose creative works turn the thoughts of people to the story of salvation. Amen.

November 13 · MIND WARS

His unspiritual mind puffs him up with idle notions.

COLOSSIANS 2:18

2006: The issue of *Time* magazine bearing this date ran a cover story on "God v. Science," commenting on the "atheist literary wave," best-selling books insisting that God does not exist. Richard Dawkins's *The God Delusion* had just been published and was selling well. Sam Harris's *The End of Faith* also sold well as did Daniel Dennett's *Breaking the Spell: Religion as a Natural Phenomenon*. The article listed several more recent scientist-denouncing-religion books, including a posthumous collection of atheist writings by Carl Sagan.

According to the article, most Americans don't see science and faith as opposed. But obviously the scientists (or pseudo-scientists) who wrote the atheist books believe one excludes the other. The article included a debate between Richard Dawkins, atheist, and Francis Collins, respected genetic scientist *and* Christian. In the debate Collins made the point with which all Christians would agree: scientists are wrong to believe that nothing exists outside nature. He also made the point that he himself did not take the Genesis 1 story of the universe being made in six days to be literal nor did he deny evolution, but he insisted God is still Creator and that man is made in his image. Collins and Dawkins crossed swords over the Big Issue that has long divided scientists and believers: miracles. Neither, of course, changed the other's mind, though the debate was conducted with courtesy.

According to Collins, "Faith is not the opposite of reason. Faith rests squarely upon reason, but with the added component of revelation." Believing in revelation requires believing in God—and atheists are certain he does not exist. The debate goes on as it has for several centuries, although the atheists seem to forget that many great scientists of the past—Isaac Newton, Johann Kepler, and Michael Faraday, to name but a few—saw no conflict between faith and science. Perhaps the true battle is the atheists fighting God.

Prayer: Creator God, thank you for giving us a world to explore and hearts to praise its Maker. Amen.

November 14 · SMALL PEOPLE, BIG GOD

Set your minds on things above, not on earthly things.

COLOSSIANS 3:2

1990: Some celebrities eventually grow up and simmer down. One who did was English journalist Malcolm Muggeridge, born into a liberal family and, in his youth, fascinated by Communism, as were most liberals of his time. But an actual trip to Russia showed him not a heaven on earth but an oppressive totalitarian hell.

Muggeridge was for many years a notorious womanizer and heavy drinker. In the later part of his life he was scolding the younger generation for its "pot and pills" lifestyle. Though for a time he was head of Edinburgh University, he resigned in disgust at the students' wild habits.

Disillusioned by Communism and the new immorality, Muggeridge was also disillusioned by the celebrities he met through his work, finding that almost all of them were disappointing in person—not bigger than life, but smaller than life. One notable exception was Mother Teresa of Calcutta whose faith in action helped move Muggeridge from agnostic to believer.

In 1969 he published his first religious book, *Jesus Rediscovered*. His famous way with words that made him such a successful journalist were put to use in God's service. "Sex is the mysticism of a materialist society." "It is only the otherworldly who know how to cope with this world." "One of the most effective defenses against God's incursions has been organized religion." As the last quote shows, Muggeridge feared that the church was working against God instead of for him. Having reported on the modern world and its materialism and narcissism, he thought the church was the only spiritual force people could turn to, and yet the modern church with its attempt to keep in step with the times was losing its own soul.

Muggeridge, who died on November 14, 1990, titled his memoirs *Chronicles of Wasted Time*. His life from his conversion on was by no means wasted.

Prayer: Father, while people may disappoint us, we turn to you as the sole source of love and truth. Amen.

November 15 · Songs from a Fretful Soul

Out of the depths I cry to you, O Lord.

Psalm 130:1

1731: One of the world's great hymn-writers and poets, born on this day, lived much of life in fear of going insane. Born in England and trained to be a lawyer, William Cowper was so painfully shy that he attempted suicide while waiting to take a civil service exam. Afterward he was put in a lunatic asylum where he experienced a religious conversion, but even after release from the madhouse, he suffered from depression the rest of his life. A handful of Christian friends tried to lift his spirits and keep his mind occupied.

One of those friends was former slave trader John Newton, a pastor in the village of Olney. Cowper provided Newton some stimulating conversation, and Newton provided him with spiritual counsel. Newton saw that one way to help Cowper and the entire parish was to enlist Cowper's aid in compiling a hymnal. Published in 1779 and known as *Olney Hymns*, the book had 280 hymns by Newton, 68 by Cowper. The hymns were so good that the new hymnal became popular with hundreds of other congregations.

Unfortunately, the writing put such strain on Cowper's nerves that he lapsed into depression again. A friend nursed him back to health, and Cowper produced some of the best secular poetry of the late 1700s. Until his death in 1800, Cowper wrote poetry, tended his garden and pets, and socialized with a few trusted friends—never quite sure that his mind would not snap again.

Troubled souls can produce great hymns. Cowper produced some classics: "God Moves in a Mysterious Way," "There Is a Fountain Filled with Blood," "O for a Closer Walk with God," and many others—all of them filled with tranquility and trust in God, as if Cowper was trying to create in song something he didn't possess in real life. We hope this troubled, sensitive, and talented man finally found peace with God.

Prayer: Lord, we ask your blessing on those who cope with gloom and grief. Lift their spirits and let them find peace in you. Amen.

November 16 · BEAUTIFUL IN DEED

Charm is deceptive, and beauty is fleeting, but a woman who fears the LORD is to be praised.

PROVERBS 31:30

1093: In the Middle Ages a devout woman often became a nun. One, however, became a queen: Margaret of Scotland. The child of an English prince and German princess, Margaret was born in Hungary where her father was in exile. When she was twelve, the family settled in England where she lived at the court of the last Saxon king, Edward. In 1066 Edward died, and England was overrun by his cousin William of Normandy, better known as William the Conqueror. Margaret's family fled north to Scotland, and in 1070 she married the Scottish king Malcolm III. He married her for her beauty, but her character proved even more appealing.

Although she was raised among royalty, Margaret had lived much of her life as an exile and stranger, and she had a natural sympathy for the needy. As queen she gained renown not for maintaining an opulent court but for her kindnesses to the common people. Before her meals she would see to the distribution of food to poor widows and orphans, and at times she even washed the feet of the poor.

These were violent times, and King Malcolm did as kings were expected to do in those days, make war—he could also outdrink any of his soldiers. But the devout Margaret was a good influence on her husband, and she bore him eight children, including two future kings of Scotland. The court admired her genteel manners, and both the men and women became more civilized under her influence.

Margaret died on November 16, 1093, after hearing the news that her husband and oldest son had died in battle against the English. Ironically, her daughter Edith married Henry I of England, and so all the later rulers of England are descendants of Margaret of Scotland. The Scots had taken her to their hearts, and she has long been one of the country's patron saints.

Prayer: Father, give us an eye for inner beauty, to look upon the heart as you do. Amen.

November 17 · ACTS—THE SEQUEL

You do not lack any spiritual gift as you eagerly wait for our Lord Jesus Christ to be revealed.

1 CORINTHIANS 1:7

1997: Is evangelism merely *proclamation*—or does it also involve *demonstration*? John Wimber, who died on this date, was convinced that demonstration of spiritual power was an indispensable part of evangelism. Wimber was converted at age twenty-nine, having been a successful pop musician who chain-smoked and abused drugs and alcohol. Following his conversion, he pastored a church and taught part-time at Fuller Theological Seminary in California where his encounters with pastors and missionaries convinced him that the spiritual gifts described in the New Testament were by no means confined to the past and that the Spirit was just as active today. If Christians in the Third World were experiencing the Spirit's power, why couldn't Christians in America do the same?

Wimber began what he called *power evangelism*—proclamation and demonstration together with several healings occurring in his church. Where the Spirit's power is being manifested, churches grow. His church, located in Anaheim, California, grew to more than 5,000 members and expanded into more than 1,500 Vineyard Fellowships in the United States and abroad. Although Wimber was not the founder of the Vineyard Fellowships, he is the name most associated with this fast-growing network of churches where worship is informal and upbeat. The Vineyard churches are considered both evangelical and Pentecostal, but there is less emphasis on speaking in tongues than in more traditional Pentecostal churches.

Some Christians criticized Wimber and the Vineyard Fellowships, taking the view that the gifts of healing, prophecy, and speaking in tongues were part of the New Testament Christians' experience but no longer occur today. Wimber heartily disagreed: the gifts of the Spirit are for all Christians for all time, and the vibrant church life seen in Acts and the letters of Paul is not a thing of the past but a present reality. Reading about the Spirit's work in Acts is good but reading about it *and* experiencing it personally are better.

Prayer: Holy Spirit, awaken our comatose churches; fill them up with new life and confidence and joy. Amen.

November 18 · WOMEN EMPOWERED

Our people must learn to devote themselves to doing what is good.

TITUS 3:14

1874: "Home Protection" was one of the mottos of the Women's Christian Temperance Union (WCTU), founded on this date in Cleveland, Ohio. The WCTU saw overindulgence in alcohol as a major cause of domestic violence, the breakup of homes, and thousands of women and children left destitute. In those days when most women did not work outside the home, a father's addiction could mean his family would starve. Saloon owners had no scruples about locating taverns near mines and factories, so it was easy for a man getting paid on Friday to waste his week's pay before staggering home.

To remedy these ills, the WCTU sought to "Agitate, Educate, Legislate." Many of its members lectured to teens about the ills of alcohol. Members also pushed for laws protecting women and children from violence, and many also pushed for women's right to vote in the hope that laws restricting or prohibiting the sale of alcohol would be passed.

The WCTU was one of several organizations promoting abstinence from alcohol. Most of the organizations' members were Christians and saw their activism as a Christian duty. Since the Bible condemns drunkenness but does not tell people to completely abstain, a "two-wine theory" was proposed, the idea being that in many cases the "wine" in the Bible was in fact unfermented grape juice. This was not the case, and the push for abstinence was not rooted in the Bible but in the general Christian desire for happier homes and a more stable society.

In the early 1900s liberal and conservative Christians joined together in pushing for national prohibition, which became law in 1920. Prohibition created problems of its own, but the crusaders' motives were noble, and, as predicted, many of the ills resulting from alcohol did decrease when Prohibition was the law of the land.

Prayer: Lord, we ask your blessing on those who act on behalf of better homes and a better society. Amen.

November 19 · PITCHING THE GOSPEL

Boldly and without hindrance he preached the kingdom of God and taught about the Lord Jesus Christ.

ACTS 28:31

1862: Born in Iowa on this date was William Ashley Sunday, better known as Billy Sunday, one of the best-known and most colorful men of his time. Orphaned at an early age, Billy spent time in an orphans' home, worked on a farm, and then for eight years played professional baseball. Then he began working with the YMCA, giving lectures on self-improvement and "Christian manhood." From 1896 till his death in 1935 he was a traveling evangelist, staging revival meetings in major U.S. cities—probably more than three hundred revivals in all with an attendance of perhaps 100 million. Billy claimed that during his revivals a million converts "hit the sawdust trail," making their way down the aisles to shake the evangelist's hand and profess their changes of heart.

Sunday's revivals were never boring. He had served for a while on the team of evangelist J. Wilbur Chapman, but Sunday's revival meetings were much more exuberant than Chapman's. Lively music was led by Sunday's choir leader, Homer Rodeheaver (also a noted songwriter), but the real attraction was the energetic—indeed, *hyperactive*—Sunday himself, not a man to confine himself behind a pulpit and more of a vaudeville entertainer than a typical preacher. As a former professional athlete, he appealed to men as well as women; his sermons were laced with sports anecdotes, and he spoke the language of the common folk not of the seminaries. No doubt some of the people who came to his meetings were just there to see a consummate entertainer—but there is also no doubt this dynamo of fizzing vitality made many sincere converts. Critics sneered at his "buffoonery," but urban police chiefs knew that saloon brawls decreased and other crimes declined in the wake of a Sunday revival.

Prayer: Lord, you have used men of phenomenal vitality to spread your gospel. Thank you for such people, and may you raise up others around the world to show that faith is not a dead and boring thing. Amen.

November 20 · ROYAL MARTYR

Blessed is the man who perseveres under trial, because when he has stood the test, he will receive the crown of life that God has promised to those who love him.

JAMES 1:12

869: Kings have often been the persecutors of Christianity not the persecuted, but there are a few shining exceptions to that rule, and some kings paid the ultimate price for their faith. One of these was Edmund, king of East Anglia, one of the small kingdoms that England was divided into in the Dark Ages. Edmund was only fifteen when he was crowned king in 855, but he had wise and devout advisors, and he himself was deeply devoted to his faith. During one long spiritual retreat in his royal lodge, he memorized the entire book of Psalms and was afterward able to recite it by heart. Like any statesman, Edmund knew that being religious is not enough, for a king also has to be worldly wise, able to discern flattery and malicious gossip from the people of his court.

The biggest challenge of Edmund's reign was foreign not domestic. The great threat of that age came from Denmark with its seafaring plunderers, pagans who had no qualms about looting churches as well as castles. East Anglia lay on the coast, and Edmund led his armies to repulse the troops of two Danish warlords, but the Danes were soon back, and they captured Edmund, carrying him off in chains to their chieftain, Ingvar, who ordered him to renounce and curse his religion. Edmund claimed that his faith was dearer than his life to him. The Danes beat him mercilessly with cudgels, bound him to a tree, and lashed him with whips, but he would not renounce his faith. Finally the exasperated Danes shot him with dozens of arrows and beheaded him with a sword. His death occurred on November 20, 869, and English churches have for centuries observed November 20 as the Feast of St. Edmund the Martyr.

Prayer: Father, thank you for wise and faithful statesmen who value your kingdom above all earthly possessions. Amen.

November 21 · "ALMOST" BRETHREN

Make every effort to keep the unity of the Spirit through the bond of peace.

EPHESIANS 4:3

1964: From the beginning of the Reformation in the early 1500s, Protestants were considered "heretics" by Roman Catholics. Protestants were often persecuted and sometimes even executed by Catholics—and the reverse was also true. Certainly this was not Christian behavior, and the only thing to be said in favor of this extremism is that people did take their faith seriously. By the 1700s the hatred between Protestant and Catholics cooled, but technically Catholics still saw Protestants as heretics, and Protestants viewed Catholics as religiously backward and superstitious. Most Catholics were certain that Protestants, even if they led saintly lives, were destined for hell, and many Protestants felt the same about Catholics. Seldom did the two sides cooperate in anything.

A dramatic change came with the Vatican II council which opened in October 1962. The council on November 21, 1964, issued the statement *Unitatis Redintegratio* which begins, "The restoration of unity among all Christians is one of the principal concerns" of the council. The document does not refer to non-Catholics as "heretics" but as "separated brethren." In the past, "men of both sides" (Catholics and Protestants) were to blame for the divisions. Though the Catholic Church still officially teaches that the "separated brethren" are "deficient in some respects," they are part of God's plan of salvation. The Catholic Church asked forgiveness for its mistreatment of separated brethren and in turn forgave when it had been sinned against.

Perhaps the core of the statement is that the true unity of Christians is furthered when they "live holier lives according to the gospel." For the first time in its history, the Catholic Church was making behavior, not doctrine, a key element of being a Christian.

The decree did not satisfy everyone, and there was criticism from both sides. Nonetheless, most people saw it as a positive thing in a century when new secular religions such as Nazism and Communism proved dangerous to all forms of Christianity.

Prayer: Father, help us reach out in love to Christian brethren everywhere. Amen.

November 22 · THE OVERLOOKED OBITUARY

The mind of sinful man is death, but the mind controlled by the Spirit is life and peace.

ROMANS 8:6

1963: Think fast: Who died on this date? The world remembers the big news of the day, the assassination of U.S. president John F. Kennedy. Hardly anyone noticed that day that another celebrity—a far different man from Kennedy—had also died, the British author C. S. Lewis. Lewis was a shy professor of literature at Oxford and Cambridge who had, much to his own surprise, become an intellectual defender of Christianity, penning such Christian classics as *Mere Christianity*, *The Screwtape Letters*, *Miracles*, *The Four Loves*, and the autobiographical *Surprised by Joy*, the fascinating account of his very gradual conversion.

Spending much of his young life as a rationalist and atheist, Lewis slowly realized that God was "closing in on him," that the elusive Joy (he spelled it with a capital *J*) he sought could only be found in the Christianity he had so long rejected. Later in life the aging bachelor married a woman named—appropriately—Joy and found great happiness before losing her to cancer, a tragedy recounted in his book *A Grief Observed*.

Lewis's books for children, *The Chronicles of Narnia*, are still widely read, as is his science-fiction "space trilogy," and even in these fiction works he managed to incorporate Christian themes and symbols. But he is best remembered for *Mere Christianity* and the other books mentioned above, all brief and highly readable, from a master communicator who wrote as a committed layman not a preacher or theologian. Perhaps his most loved book for adults is the remarkable *Screwtape Letters* in which a senior devil instructs a novice devil on how to tempt the human soul to which he has been assigned. Lewis had a clear understanding of how the life of faith consists not so much in avoiding the "big" sins but in learning to say no to pettiness and selfishness hour by hour.

Prayer: Father, keep us ever mindful of saints who loved you with all their minds, people who thought deeply yet wrote clearly, to the great benefit of future believers. Amen.

November 23 · SCIENTIST WITH HEART

You will keep him in perfect peace him whose mind is steadfast, because he trusts in you.

ISAIAH 26:3

1654: "Inconstancy, boredom, anxiety"—these are the characteristics of life without God, according to Blaise Pascal. Man, Pascal said, is wretched without God and only happy with God. Pascal was one of the greatest scientists of his time, and all time. He applied his scientific mind not just to the physical world but to the human condition and reached a conclusion found in the Bible: men are self-deceiving and egotistical sinners who need saving.

Born in France in 1623, Pascal intended to write a book defending the truths of Christianity. He never wrote the book but instead left behind a collection of jotted-down fragments—some more than a page long, some of them no more than one sentence. After his death in 1662, these were published with the French title *Pensées* ("Thoughts"). No one will ever know how Pascal planned to organize these random thoughts, but even read individually they reveal the mind of a man who had thought deeply about man and God. Living in an age when many people were skeptical about religion, he stated that one of his goals was to show that faith was not contrary to reason. But he also stated that "the heart has its reasons that reason does not understand." He understood that reason, a gift from God, had its limitations. Reason might nudge man toward faith, but only love and awareness of his own need could make man embrace faith.

Included in the *Pensées* is Pascal's "Memorial," a piece of paper he wore sewn into his clothing. In it he recalls the "night of fire," November 23, 1654, when he felt flooded with "certainty, certainty, heartfelt, joy, peace" with "the world forgotten and everything except God." This brilliant and celebrated man of science knew that he, like everyone else, was a sinner whose sole happiness was in clinging to the God of love.

Prayer: Father, remind us that the greatest thing we can achieve in life is to be in fellowship with you. Amen.

The god of this age has blinded the minds of unbelievers.

2 CORINTHIANS 4:4

1925: A man born on this date said it was his mission to say "Stop!" to the twentieth century. He was William F. Buckley Jr. who believed that the key problem of the century was the loss of religious faith with many people turning to politics to give life meaning. In 1945 William went to Yale—founded in 1707 as a training school for ministers—where he found no respect for God or Christianity nor much patriotism. After Buckley graduated he published his first book, *God and Man at Yale*, firing the first shot of his lifelong war against liberalism in politics and religion. He saw traditional Christianity—despite its failings—to be worth preserving, and he felt the same about American democracy which in the past had given individuals a great deal of freedom. He had learned at Yale that people who toss aside religion often embrace politics as a substitute god—which in the Christian view of things is idolatry.

Buckley founded a conservative magazine, *National Review*, and from 1966 to 1999 was the host of the PBS series *Firing Line* in which he argued—good-naturedly—with liberals, displaying his quick mind furnished with a huge vocabulary. He wrote numerous books and also a syndicated column. One of his best books was *Nearer, My God*, subtitled *An Autobiography of Faith*, in which he observed, "If God is a given, then other data are arranged around that given"—if God exists, we must think and act with him in mind. He often addressed the criticism that Christians do not live up to their own standards, observing that "the man [Peter] whom Christ designated as the rock on which he would found his church sinned three times before the cock crowed."

Buckley claimed that one of the pleasures of Christianity was that Almighty God was also a Companion and Friend. He went to meet his Friend on February 27, 2008.

Prayer: Father, teach us to think clearly and find in you our richest pleasure. Amen.

November 25 · JIHAD AND THE LEPER CHRISTIAN BOY KING

You give me your shield of victory, and your right hand sustains me.

PSALM 18:35

1177: Muslims and Christians despised each other in the Middle Ages, but Christians did grudgingly respect the Muslim leader Saladin, for he was one of the most determined and successful of the Muslim foes. Saladin's name means "honor of the faith," and it was appropriate, for Saladin devoted himself wholeheartedly to Islam and to *jihad* against the "infidel" Crusaders.

When Saladin was born, the Crusaders occupied large parts of the Holy Land, partly due to their own fighting skills, partly due to Muslims fighting among themselves. He grew up determined to unite the Muslims and permanently expel the Christians, and he was ambitious enough to assassinate any rival leaders among the Muslims. He focused his attention on the city of Jerusalem which was in the hands of the Christians, though considered a holy city by both Christians and Muslims.

November 25, 1177, was a memorable day for both sides: the Christians scored one of their few victories against Saladin. Sixteen-year-old Baldwin IV who had the title "king of Jerusalem," learned of Saladin's plan to march on Jerusalem with a huge Muslim force. At a site called Montgisard, poor Baldwin, afflicted with leprosy and in great pain, knelt in prayer then led his men into battle with bandages covering his leprous hands. The small Christian force defeated Saladin's army of twenty-five thousand, and the Christians credited God with the victory. Saladin barely escaped with his life, and he returned to Egypt with only a tenth of his army. His official report (to the Muslims) was that the Christians had lost the battle.

The Battle of Montgisard was a high point in the history of the Crusades, but Saladin was not a man to give up, and in October 1187 his armies conquered Jerusalem. He was not the first nor last Muslim leader to demonstrate the stubbornness of men committed to *jihad*.

Prayer: Father, whatever befalls us in this life, let our hearts trust in you to give us the final victory. Amen.

November 26 · RULE OF FAITH

I have been very zealous for the LORD God Almighty.

1 KINGS 19:10

1504: From a religious point of view, Queen Isabella of Spain was one of the most important women in history. When she died on this date, she could look back on dramatic changes in her own country and the opening up of two continents to Christianity.

Isabella was very devout, and she turned to the equally devout Cardinal Cisneros to reform the church in Spain which he did with zeal. Aiding him in reform was the fact that the Christians of Spain had at long last driven out the Moors, the Muslim invaders who had conquered Spain centuries earlier. By 1492 all of Spain was under Christian control again, and a surge in religious feeling followed.

Also in 1492 Isabella and her husband, Ferdinand, ordered that all Jews in Spain either convert to Christianity or leave the country. Some did leave, and many of those who did not went through the formality of baptism, the "conversions" being sham. In 1502 the rulers commanded that the remaining Muslims in Spain either convert or leave. As with the Jews, most "conversions" were insincere. On the surface at least, Spain had lots more Christians and lots fewer Jews and Muslims. The Inquisition was set up to prosecute "converts" who still practiced their old religions in private.

One more important thing in 1492: with the backing of Isabella and Ferdinand, Christopher Columbus landed on American soil, claiming it for Spain. The Spanish formed the first wave of Europeans—and Christians—in the New World. Economic motives guided the colonization of America, but so did religious motives and Isabella was insistent that her new "subjects" be treated kindly and, if possible, converted.

Today we find some of the queen's actions horrible, especially the setting up of the Inquisition. Her zeal for the faith was pure, even if some of the methods were wrong.

Prayer: Lord, teach us to act with zeal and to temper zeal with love. Amen.

These people come near to me with their mouth and honor me with their lips, but their hearts are far from me.

ISAIAH 29:13

511: France was not always the land of culture, good food, and men afraid to fight. In the early Middle Ages it was a barbaric, violent place with bloodthirsty pagan tribes constantly at war. As it happened, one of the barbarian chieftains became a Christian through the influence of his devout wife. He was Clovis, and in 492 he married a princess named Clothilda, a Christian who took her faith seriously.

Some historical background: the area we know as France was for centuries the province of Gaul, part of the Roman Empire. When the empire ceased to exist in western Europe, Gaul was invaded by barbarian tribes known as the Franks. Clovis, a brilliant military strategist, managed to unite the Franks, and in 496 he was baptized as a Christian—he and his entire army of three thousand. Marriage to the saintly Clothilda had convinced him that Christianity was the true religion, especially when a battle turned in his favor after he prayed to Clothilda's God. The bishop who baptized Clovis hoped that this savage warrior might, in time, bring peace to the country and set an example of Christian life.

Clovis did unite the country, and historians regard him as the first real king of France. He was baptized at the cathedral of Rheims which from that time on was the site where all French kings would be crowned. And he selected a city for his capital: Paris which would grow to be one of the great cities of Europe.

Unfortunately, the baptism of Clovis's army set a bad precedent. Technically, baptism made the soldiers part of the Christian fellowship, but aside from baptism and attending church at times, nothing in their behavior changed. When Clovis died on November 27, 511, he left behind a country that was only superficially Christian.

Prayer: Father, help us spread your faith around the globe, and let it put down deep roots in men's souls. Amen.

November 28 · DELUDED PROPHET

They speak visions from their own minds, not from the mouth of the LORD.

JEREMIAH 23:16

1757: "The Old and New Testaments are the Great Code or Art." So said an extremely talented and extremely peculiar man born on this date and destined to be both artist and poet. He was William Blake, born in London, and as a child he thought he saw angels—and the prophet Ezekiel. He grew up on the Bible, and as an adult he created some beautiful and unique illustrations for the books of Job and Revelation and other sections of the Bible, as well as for the great Christian poem of the Middle Ages, *The Divine Comedy* and John Milton's epic *Paradise Lost*.

Despite his affection for the Scriptures and Christian poetry, Blake was not a conventional Christian, and he was noted for saying, "I must create a system or be enslaved by another man's." He saw Jesus as Savior in the sense that Jesus was both divine and human, and he believed that people found salvation in realizing that they themselves combined the divine and human. He thought the churches held people back from this goal, repressing man's creative and sexual impulses. He saw "good" as passive and "evil" as energetic and believed that in combining the two principles, people would find fulfillment. One of his poetic books is titled *The Marriage of Heaven and Hell*, expressing his belief that the "contrarieties" in life would eventually be resolved.

Blake died in 1827, not famous in his own time but rediscovered in the twentieth century as people drifted away from Christianity and searched for some "spirituality" which many found in his writings and dream-like pictures. In fact, Blake was a favorite writer of the 1960s crowd. What a pity this talented man so steeped in the Bible let his imagination run amuck, creating a mish-mash of biblical images and an incoherent philosophy of "liberation" that later generations found more appealing than the truths of Christianity.

Prayer: Lord, keep us from foolish and trendy "spiritualities" and let us find fulfillment in lives grounded in your Word. Amen.

November 29 · MISSION MISUNDERSTOOD

I hear the slander of many; there is terror on every side.

PSALM 31:13

1847: Narcissa Whitman and Eliza Spalding hold the distinction of being the first women to cross the North American continent. They were not alone but were accompanied by their husbands, Marcus Whitman, a doctor, and Henry Spalding, a minister, the four going to the Oregon territory to serve as missionaries in 1836. The goal was to convert the Cayuse and Nez Perce Indians and to minister to the white settlers in this rough country. They established a mission in what later became Washington State.

Narcissa opened a school for Indian children, and Marcus served as both doctor and teacher to the Indians, showing them how to build houses and mills and how to plant and irrigate. The white settlers brought diseases to the Indians, such as measles, that were not fatal to whites but often were to Indians. Ironically, Marcus, a doctor, got much of the blame for disease deaths among the Indians. It was thought he was using his "magic" to harm as well as to heal, a belief fostered by the fact that whites who were ill usually recovered while diseased Indians did not—something Marcus had no control over. As more white settlers arrived, the Indians became more hostile. Given the danger, Marcus decided that for the time being the missionaries should serve the white settlers and not try to convert the Indians.

On November 29, 1847, two Indians came to the mission, one of them claiming to be sick which got the doctor's attention. Marcus realized, too late, that the second Indian was the notorious Tomahas, nicknamed "the Murderer." He tomahawked Marcus. Seeing what happened, Narcissa tried to flee along with some of the white children, but she and twelve other whites were killed that day.

Whitman College in Washington State was named in their honor, and a statue of Marcus Whitman represents the state in the National Statuary Hall in DC.

Prayer: Lord, you alone see our hearts clearly. When we are misunderstood and slandered, remind us that you are the righteous Judge. Amen.

November 30 · MISSING PEACE

Give your servant a discerning heart to govern your people.

1 KINGS 3:9

1718: Imagine a king of Sweden who was handsome, athletic, brave, highly intelligent . . . and celibate. This was the remarkable Charles XII, a genuinely Christian ruler in a century that had few of them.

Charles became king at the tender age of fifteen when his father died. No one complained that Charles was too young to rule, for his father had groomed him to be both active and studious and to live an exemplary moral life. What a pity that Charles did not live in a peaceful age when he could have devoted himself to domestic matters. Instead, most of his reign was spent in the Great Northern War in which Sweden's chief enemy was Russia, ruled by the land-hungry, war-loving Peter the Great. Sweden was tiny compared to Russia, but Charles's troops were well-trained, and they had an exceptionally brave and inspiring leader.

Things turned in Russia's favor, however, and Charles found himself living in exile in Turkey. He managed, through couriers, to make his wishes known in Sweden even while absent. He returned to his kingdom in 1714, though the old quarrel with Russia remained to be settled. He amassed an army of sixty thousand men, but he was not destined to lead them for long. On November 30, 1718, to rally his men he exposed himself to enemy fire and was fatally shot in the head. His men, so inspired at having a king who would not lead them into danger unless he faced the danger himself, saw their beloved leader dead at age thirty-six.

Reared in an affectionate family, Charles had promised his court, "I'll marry when the war is over." The war outlived him. This man of amazing vitality, self-control, courage, and confidence rooted in his belief in God had to use his gifts in a defensive war hatched by other kings who were Christian in name only. Surely he found peace in a more enduring kingdom.

Prayer: King of kings, in this world of strife make the rulers' eyes open to the prospect of peace. Amen.

DECEMBER

December 1 · FUGITIVE PRIEST

Make every effort to live in peace with all men and to be holy; without holiness no one will see the Lord.

HEBREWS 12:14

1581: In 1581 an intense manhunt was taking place in England. The prey was Edmund Campion, a Catholic priest believed to be conspiring to assassinate Queen Elizabeth I. In fact, all Catholics in England at this time were under suspicion because the pope had decreed that Elizabeth, a Protestant, was not the legitimate ruler—and the decree did indeed lead many English Catholics to conspire against the queen.

Was Campion one of the conspirators? Probably not, but in those days politics and religion were hard to separate. Campion seems to have been a devout man. Raised as a Catholic, he turned Protestant in his youth and was ordained in the Church of England, and his brilliance and devotion to the faith impressed many people, including the queen. Had he stayed Protestant, he probably would have been made a bishop. But he turned Catholic again and, for safety, fled to Europe. But in 1580 the pope sent him and another priest back to England to work—underground—as Catholic missionaries. Naturally the Church of England regarded him as a turncoat. One of the government's many spies betrayed him, and he was imprisoned in the gloomy Tower of London. He was urged to become a Protestant again—and offered large bribes to do so, with the queen herself pleading with him. Campion would not renounce his faith, so he was tortured on the rack but still refused. On December 1, 1581, after assuring the crowd that he was not a traitor and was as loyal a subject as Elizabeth ever had, he was publicly tortured and executed.

Poor Campion! A good man, zealous for the cause of Christ, he had the bad fortune to live in an age when denominational differences could mean loss of life. Perhaps the many Christians executed by other Christians in this blood-stained century have found a fellowship with each other in a better world.

Prayer: Lord of love, give us wisdom to discern which differences matter and which do not. Amen.

December 2 · THE CRICKET PLAYER'S RESCUE SHOP

God did not give us a spirit of timidity, but a spirit of power, of love and of self-discipline.

2 TIMOTHY 1:7

1860: Not many world-class athletes are also Christian missionaries but such was the case of C. T. Studd, born on this date and renowned as one of the all-time great cricket players and a missionary to Asia.

Studd's wealthy father had been converted at a Dwight L. Moody crusade, and C. T. and his two brothers—all renowned cricket players—were converted while students at England's elite Eton school. C. T. recollected that "the Bible, which had been so dry to me before, became everything." When his initial zeal started to diminish, the near death of one of his brothers brought him face-to-face with eternity, reminding him that his fame as an athlete would not endure. The experience awakened his desire to carry the gospel abroad, and in 1883 he sailed for China, observing that "some want to live within the sound of church or chapel bell; I want to run a rescue shop within a yard of hell." He was one of the "Cambridge Seven," recent graduates of the university and all fully committed to Hudson Taylor's China Inland Mission. While serving in China, C. T. reached the age of twenty-five and was due to inherit part of the family fortune: he gave part to D. L. Moody, part to George Müller's orphanages, and the rest to other Christian ministries.

After a productive ministry in China, Studd founded the Heart of Africa Mission, telling his friends "Gentlemen, God has called me to go and I will go." For a time his health broke down in Africa, but he recovered and founded the World Evangelization Crusade which sent workers to South America, the Middle East, Asia, and Africa.

"Heroism," Studd wrote, "is the missing note of Christianity." He knew that one of the key problems of evangelism was that Christians are seen as "nice" but hardly "heroic." He himself lived as a true Christian hero.

Prayer: God of power, strengthen your people; make them bold and fearless witnesses. Amen.

December 3 · GOLDEN VOYAGER

Declare his glory among the nations, his marvelous deeds among all peoples.

1 CHRONICLES 16:24

1552: Francis Xavier, born into a wealthy family in Spain in 1506, was a "golden boy" seemingly destined for great things. Charming, attractive, and athletic, he was also intelligent and well-read. Rather surprisingly, when he went to the University of Paris he kept aloof from the student vices and seemed determined to use his many gifts for God. In Paris he met a fellow Spaniard, Ignatius of Loyola, and he would join Ignatius in founding a new religious order for men, the Society of Jesus, or Jesuits. Given approval by the pope in 1540, the Jesuits made themselves available to go wherever the pope would send them.

Francis was sent off to India, newly opened to trade with the Portuguese. The charming, amiable Francis found that the Portuguese (who supposedly were already Christian but acted like pagans) needed evangelizing as much as the Indians did, as did the growing number of Portuguese-Indian children. He turned the city of Goa into a base for Christian mission work and made thousands of converts among the pearl fishermen of India.

The Portuguese had also begun trading with Japan, and in 1549 Francis went there, learning the language and establishing a thriving Christian community, which later endured great persecution. This young man reared in wealth and comfort had no qualms about living among the poor and enduring harassment and deprivation.

Francis was fascinated by the Chinese, knowing they were the most numerous of the Asian peoples, and he dreamed of spreading the gospel among them, but he paid only one brief visit there before dying on December 3, 1552. In later years the Jesuits would fulfill his dream of taking the gospel to the Chinese as well as continuing his work in India and Japan. With good reason the Catholic Church made Francis Xavier the Patron Saint of Foreign Missions.

Prayer: Lord, instill in us the awesome dedication that we see in the lives of your saints. Amen.

December 4 · DEAD VILLAGE, NEW LIFE

All the believers were one in heart and mind.

ACTS 4:32

1637: In the 1500s England's king Henry VIII closed all the monasteries and convents in the land, and many people said, "Good riddance," since so many of the monks and nuns had led worldly (and sometimes scandalous) lives. But once these communities were shut down, people realized that they had in fact provided some useful services, such as education and ministry to the poor—and the less visible but important benefit of having some people always in prayer.

But people of faith do naturally flock together, not only to worship in church but to fellowship and minister in other ways. Nicholas Ferrar, an Englishman born in 1592, formed a unique Christian community that included his mother and his two siblings with their spouses and children. In 1626 they settled in a deserted village named Little Gidding, restored its vacant manor house and its church, and ministered to the local people in many ways, including setting up a school. At all times one member of the Little Gidding family was at prayer, since the community took literally the biblical command to "pray without ceasing." Worship was held three times daily (6 a.m., 10 a.m., and 4 p.m.), and the Bible was studied on a regular basis. The fellowship had some critics who sneered that the family was trying to create a new form of monastery in England. This was not the case at all: monks and nuns took lifetime vows of poverty, celibacy, and obedience to the head of the monastery, while Little Gidding was strictly voluntary with members free to leave if they chose—but none did, for it was a deeply satisfying fellowship.

Visitors to the community were impressed by the commitment of the members to live lives wholly dedicated to God and neighbor. When Nicholas Ferrar died on December 4, 1637, at age forty-five, he was regarded as one of the true saints of the Church of England.

Prayer: Father, in a world that is so often hostile to faith, help us to find warm and godly fellowship. Amen.

December 5 · BABYLON'S BOUNDARIES

Woe to those who call evil good and good evil.

ISAIAH 5:20

1965: In the 1930s the Hollywood movie studios agreed to abide by a code under which no film would "lower the moral standards of those who view it." This Production Code was often called the Hays Code, named after Will Hays, the respectable Presbyterian layman hired by the industry to head the Motion Picture Producers and Distributors of America. The Code banned profanity, obscenity, and nudity. It required that criminals always be punished, that adultery not be condoned, and that any form of evil not be made attractive. It also specified that clergy of all religions be presented respectfully and not as villains or buffoons.

The actual administration of the Code was the job of a devout Catholic layman named Joseph Breen who died on December 5, 1965 with the *New York Times* reporting the death of the "Watchdog of Movie Morals." Breen's office was in charge of enforcing the Code from 1934 until his retirement in 1954, and he took his work seriously.

What was the result? Two decades of movies that, by all standards, made up Hollywood's Golden Age. While directors and writers occasionally found the Code burdensome, there is no denying that many superb films were being made. Sex was "understood," of course, but the moviemakers in the Breen age assumed adults could "fill in the blanks" and not actually have to see sex or nudity on screen. Would *Casablanca* or *Gone with the Wind* have been better films with graphic sexual scenes? Surely not.

And aside from the sexual restraint, clergy (and Christians in general) were treated with respect not as fools or hypocrites. When the old movies depicted religion, it looked appealing, and one of the biggest money-makers of the era was *Going My Way* with Bing Crosby as a lovable priest. Under Breen's watchful eye, moviemakers had boundaries they could not cross, and the movies made within those boundaries managed to entertain without lowering the morals of the people in the audience.

Prayer: Lord, keep our minds and hearts pure. Lift them up to higher things. Amen.

December 6 · DIAMOND TEMPLE

The Lord added to their number daily those who were being saved.

ACTS 2:47

1925: The "megachurch" has become a fixture on the American landscape, a church with an enormous seating capacity, a huge membership, a large staff, a full calendar of programs for all ages, and a keen sense of mission. Long before the term *megachurch* was coined such a church existed, in large part due to the energy and dedication of its pastor, Russell Conwell.

A Civil War veteran with a law degree and a talent for writing and speaking, Conwell was ordained a Baptist minister in 1880 and in 1882 was called to pastor Grace Baptist Church in Philadelphia. With Conwell at the helm, the church quickly outgrew its original site, and the congregation relocated to a much larger building that became known as the Baptist Temple. Various ministries and groups evolved out of the growing church, such as the youth group known as Christian Endeavor which became a national organization. When Conwell discovered that an assistant pastor needed additional schooling, he founded Temple College which in time became Temple University, one of the major colleges in Philadelphia. The church also sponsored charity work for the city, as well as athletics, lectures, nurseries, and reading rooms.

Aside from the Baptist Temple, Conwell's other claim to fame is the sermon "Acres of Diamonds" which he delivered around the country an amazing six thousand times—possibly the most-preached sermon in history. In it he urged listeners to get rich—which hardly sounds like a Christian message, except that he believed those who prospered would naturally contribute to churches and charities and not use their wealth just for selfish ends. Conwell has been both praised and criticized for preaching a "prosperity gospel," but there is no doubt that his famous sermon did encourage many lazy and aimless people to try to improve their lives by working themselves out of poverty. Conwell died on December 6, 1925, having lived a spiritually profitable life.

Prayer: Father, endow us with the energy and ambition to do great things in your name. Amen.

December 7 · NOT SEPARATION, BUT ILLUMINATION

"You are the salt of the earth. . . . You are the light of the world."

MATTHEW 5:13–14

2003: In his youth Carl F. H. Henry was working for a newspaper, and when a female coworker heard him use "Christ" in swearing, she responded, "Carl, I'd rather you'd slap my face than take the name of my best Friend in vain." In time Christ would be the name of Carl's best Friend also. In 1942 Carl was one of the founders of the National Association of Evangelicals. Later he served as the first professor of theology at the newly founded Fuller Theological Seminary.

But perhaps Henry's greatest contribution to Christianity was his 1947 book *The Uneasy Conscience of Modern Fundamentalism*. In it he drew a distinction between fundamentalists and evangelicals. The two agreed on many things: the inspiration of the Bible, the virgin birth of Christ, the resurrection, Jesus' miracles, the necessity to live one's life by the moral teachings of the Bible. But Henry believed that fundamentalists had gone too far in their separation from the secular world and that evangelicals (of which he was one) should not only be concerned for the salvation of their own souls but also concerned for the societies in which they lived. Evangelism was essential, but social and political involvement were part of the Christian life as well.

He and his wife, Helga, made a significant contribution to evangelical involvement in the form of their son, Paul Henry, who went from being a professor of political science at a Christian college to being a U.S. congressman from 1985 until his death from cancer in 1993. In his honor, Calvin College, where he had taught for many years, established the Paul Henry Institute for the Study of Christianity and Politics.

Carl Henry died on December 7, 2003, after a lifetime of shaping the evangelical movement, watching it move from the sidelines of American culture into the thick of many challenging political and social battles.

Prayer: Lord, bless people of faith as they strive to be salt and light in a culture of decay and darkness. Amen.

December 8 · FAITHFUL SHEPHERD

Set an example for the believers in speech, in life, in love, in faith and in purity.

1 TIMOTHY 4:12

1691: "The Devoted Pastor" would be a perfect title for Richard Baxter who died on this day. Born in England in 1615, Baxter lived in a turbulent age when a person's religious views could land him in prison, deprive him of a job, or even end his life. Baxter saw his share of trouble, yet through it all he kept one goal firmly in mind: to minister faithfully to his congregation, with "ministering" involving more than just preaching, baptizing, marrying, and burying. Like most sensitive Christians of his time, Baxter found the established Church of England to be sorely lacking in spiritual vigor. Some who felt this way left the church completely (often risking persecution), but Baxter stayed within the church, believing he could turn his own congregation into an example of genuine Christian fellowship.

Serving in a small town called Kidderminster, Baxter was such a fine preacher that people came from miles around to hear him. Unlike most Church of England clergy, he emphasized conversion, and one of his many books was titled *A Call to the Unconverted*. To those who were already converted he preached the need to show in one's daily life that one was a child of God. Baxter and his assistant pastor visited often with each family in the parish, answering questions about spiritual concerns and counseling the people to lead a life worthy of Christ. People came from outside his parish for counsel, and he received letters from all over England. He reached thousands of people with his devotional books, including *The Saints' Everlasting Rest*.

Although his parish adored him, the Church of England always regarded him as a maverick, and in 1662 he lost his position. Not easily silenced, he preached wherever he could draw an audience and more than once landed in prison. When he died in 1691, he was one of the most respected men in the land.

Prayer: Father, thank you for the many faithful pastors past and present who have given selflessly to their flocks. Amen.

December 9 · THE BOOKWORM AND THE SERPENT

The LORD gives sight to the blind, the LORD lifts up those who are bowed down.

PSALM 146:8

1608: Born on this date, the English poet John Milton was a bookworm—the best kind, the kind who uses his intellect and knowledge to serve God. Milton's poetic career got sidetracked by England's Civil War in which Milton sided with Oliver Cromwell and his Puritans against King Charles and the Royalists. Cromwell tried to establish England as a Christian commonwealth, and Milton held a post in Cromwell's government. After Cromwell's death England reverted to a monarchy, and Milton lost faith in all human governments. In his youth he had thought of writing an epic poem about the great King Arthur, but he became so disillusioned with human rulers—and humans in general—that he decided to write an epic about the universal problem: human sin.

In the King James Version of the Bible in Genesis 3 the story of the fall of man is told in 695 words. Milton took that small amount of material and created the greatest epic poem in English, *Paradise Lost*, more than 10,000 lines of poetry. Milton did not confine himself to Genesis 3 but told of the fall of the rebel angels led by the angel Lucifer who takes the new name Satan and resolves to corrupt God's creation, man. The cast of characters includes not only Adam, Eve, and Satan but also the angels Michael and Gabriel, as well as the devils Beelzebub, Belial, and Mammon. With scenes in heaven, hell, and on earth, *Paradise Lost* is truly a cosmic poem.

Technically, Milton did not "write" *Paradise Lost* because by this time he was completely blind and had to dictate to secretaries. Blind to the external world, Milton had keen sight into spiritual matters. Though his poems are, by our twenty-first-century standards, difficult to read, they repay the effort. In our secular world, English-speaking people should be proud that the greatest English poem deals with God, man, sin, and salvation.

Prayer: Lord, thank you for men who use their intellects and creative powers for your glory. Amen.

December 10 · ONE MAN AND GOD

I thank Christ Jesus our Lord, who has given me strength, that he considered me faithful, appointing me to his service.

1 TIMOTHY 1:12

1561: Kaspar Schwenkfeld, who died on this date, was a unique individual, to put it mildly. Born into wealth, he embraced the Protestant Reformation when it came but was never quite comfortable with any of the Protestant groups, and though many people admired his writings, he made no effort to organize these followers into a denomination.

What did Schwenkfeld believe? His key idea was that Christianity was a matter of the heart more than of external acts. Conversion was important for him, and he agreed with the Anabaptists that baptism should be only for believers not infants. He also agreed that a "territorial church" consisting of all people within a certain area had no basis in the Bible. Instead, church had to be a voluntary association of committed Christians. He was a pacifist and believed the government had no right to force a Christian to go to war. Yet despite the many ways he agreed with the Anabaptists, he never joined them, and he spent much of his life on the move, never welcomed anywhere for long because his teachings were condemned by all Catholics and most Protestants.

Even so, he had admirers, and sometime in the 1540s a Schwenkfelder church was formed in Germany, the congregations calling themselves Confessors of the Glory of Christ. Disliked and persecuted, many of them immigrated to America in the 1700s, settling in Pennsylvania which welcomed all religious sects. A few Schwenkfelders still exist, and there is a Schwenkfelder Library in Pennsburg, Pennsylvania.

Schwenkfeld died on December 10, 1561, and because he had so many enemies, his place of burial was kept a secret. He is an interesting case of a Christian who never quite fit into any group or category, a spiritual loner who believed his one faithful Companion was God.

Prayer: Lord, when your servants feel isolated and friendless in a hostile world, bless them with your presence. Amen.

December 11 · SOMETHING BEAUTIFUL FOR GOD

Be rich in good deeds.

1 TIMOTHY 6:18

1979: You do not have to be beautiful to be famous. Consider the case of Agnes Gonxha Bojaxhiu, better known as Mother Teresa. This small woman's wrinkled face became one of the best-known faces of the twentieth century, for in that face people discerned a spiritual beauty lacking in most celebrities. Mother Teresa died on September 5, 1997, less than a week after another woman with a famous face, Diana, the former princess of Wales, a renowned beauty. Mother Teresa's death was almost overlooked in the outpouring of grief over Diana, but more discerning commentators observed that the death of Mother Teresa was a greater loss to the world.

Of Albanian heritage, Mother Teresa became a citizen of India, and it was there that in 1948 she founded her order of nuns, the Missionaries of Charity, ministering to the hungry, homeless, poor, and forgotten. English journalist Malcolm Muggeridge made a documentary film about her, titled *Something Beautiful for God*, and the film helped draw the world's attention to the work of these selfless nuns.

On December 11, 1979, Mother Teresa accepted the Nobel Peace Prize. Naturally she gave the prize money to the poor. As the focus of worldwide attention, she took advantage of her position to criticize abortion and to remind people who were materially comfortable that there was such a thing as spiritual poverty.

Shortly after taking office in 1981, Ronald Reagan almost died from an assassin's bullet. He survived, and Mother Teresa told him that God had kept him alive for a purpose and that his ordeal would make him more sympathetic to the world's suffering. In 1985 Reagan presented her with the Presidential Medal of Freedom.

In 1999 two years after her death, Mother Teresa was voted first in a Gallup poll of Most Admired People of the Twentieth Century. In a world obsessed with beauty and glamour, human beings are still touched by spiritual beauty.

Prayer: Father, thank you for the beautiful works of kindness done by selfless saints. Teach us to honor their memory by doing as they did. Amen.

December 12 · An Eagle of a Businessman

May integrity and uprightness protect me, because my hope is in you.

Psalm 25:21

1922: Department store mogul, U.S. postmaster general, philanthropist, and, last but not least, committed Christian—John Wanamaker of Philadelphia wore many hats.

Born in 1838, he opened his first store in his hometown in 1861. The store had two policies unique at the time: fixed prices on everything, and items could be returned for a full refund. The store prospered, and Wanamaker bought an unused rail depot and converted it into his second store. In 1910 he opened the twelve-story flagship store with President William Howard Taft present at the dedication. It was this store that had (and still has) the enormous bronze eagle sculpture in its grand court, and "Meet me at the eagle" became a Philadelphia catchphrase.

Wanamaker was appointed postmaster general by President Benjamin Harrison, and one of his legacies was ending the sale of lottery tickets by mail. He also pushed for free mail delivery to rural areas, though this was not implemented until after he resigned.

"When a customer enters my store, forget me. He is king." Such was Wanamaker's business policy, and it served him well. While becoming extremely rich, he was superintendent of the Sunday school at his church. For some businessmen, affiliating with a church is a formality, a means to look respectable in the world, but Wanamaker's faith was genuine, and he encouraged members of his Sunday school to commit themselves to Christ. He was a generous contributor to, and supporter of, evangelist D. L. Moody. He was active in the YMCA when its emphasis was on Christianity, not physical fitness, and he contributed some of his wealth to help the Y construct new buildings.

When he died on December 12, 1922, he was one of the most respected businessmen in America. Philadelphia has a statue of him in front of its city hall, a monument to a devout Christian who combined his faith with business savvy, risk taking, and genuine respect for customers.

Prayer: Lord, bless those who deal honestly and fairly with others. Amen.

December 13 · A Too-Late No-Compromise
Council

How good and pleasant it is when brothers live together in unity!

PSALM 133:1

1545: The one thing all Christians agreed on in the 1500s was this: the church needed reforming—badly. Many clergy were corrupt and unspiritual, offices in the church were bought and sold, and monasteries and convents were often nothing more than dens of idleness. Christians who believed the church ought to be a force for spiritual good had been pushing for a council that would address the issues and lead to reform. The Catholic Church finally summoned a council, which began on this date. Sadly, by this time Protestants had already broken away.

Known as the Council of Trent, it assembled at Trent in northern Italy. It would meet off and on until 1563, and for a council that was supposed to represent all of Christian Europe and deal with grave matters, attendance was scanty, probably because there had been talk for years of "reform councils," and nothing much had come of the talk. There was some pettiness, occasionally even fistfights, between delegates. The council's second session, which opened in 1551, was interesting because some Protestants attended. The Holy Roman Emperor, Charles V, had seen his empire split between Catholics and Protestants, and he still hoped to reach compromises, but neither side was willing.

The third session, which began in 1563, was productive—but it also built a wall, a permanent one, between Catholics and Protestants. Protestants were allowing clergy to marry; Catholics stuck with the old rule of celibacy. Protestants said there were only two sacraments, baptism and communion; Catholics stuck with the traditional seven. Protestants wanted Bibles in the people's languages; Catholics said the Latin Bible was fine. In Germany Martin Luther had predicted that the council would produce no compromise and no reunion, and he was correct. There were some steps toward making the clergy behave in a less worldly manner, but, sadly, the council only assured that several centuries would pass before Catholics and Protestants would again meet as brothers.

Prayer: Lord of truth, give us wisdom to know when to compromise and when to stand our ground. Amen.

December 14 · RADIANT, SINGING FAITH

Rejoice in the LORD and be glad, you righteous.

PSALM 32:11

1836: Frances Havergal, born on this date, had a conversion experience in 1851: "I committed my soul to the Savior, and earth and heaven seemed brighter from that moment." Educated in her native England and in Germany, she was fluent in Latin, Greek, Hebrew, French, and German and was also a talented singer and pianist with a charming personality and winning smile. Men considered her a "catch," yet she never married but instead devoted her life to evangelism, not by preaching in churches but by witnessing to people she happened to meet and performing songs at parties.

She also witnessed in her poetry which she distributed in the form of leaflets or ornamental cards. Every few years she published collections of these, such as *Ministry of Song, Loyal Responses, Life Mosaic,* and *Life Echoes.* She is remembered today because many of her poems were set to music and appeared in many hymnals.

Frances's first hymn was written in 1858 after she had visited a museum and seen a painting of the crucified Jesus with this inscription: "This have I done for thee. What hast thou done for me?" In a few minutes she had written the classic hymn "I Gave My Life for Thee." Over the years, until her death in 1879, she wrote many other hymns, including "Take My Life and Let It Be," "Who Is on the Lord's Side?" "I Am Trusting Thee, Lord Jesus," and "O Savior, Precious Savior." As the titles make clear, she did not think of God as some distant figure but as "up close and personal," and her hymns exude warmth and vitality and a sense that being committed to Christ is the greatest pleasure in the world. In her hymns, Christ's love is not for "the world" or "mankind" but for *me*, a deep love that demands a personal response. This was the rich and rewarding faith that she hoped to pass on to others.

Prayer: Dear Lord, light a flame in our hearts, and let the love of Christ radiate so that we warm everyone we encounter. Amen.

December 15 · GROWING VERSUS VEGETATING

The churches were strengthened in the faith and grew daily in numbers.

ACTS 16:5

1897: Donald McGavran, born on this date, spent much of his life with the School of World Missions at Fuller Theological Seminary. His book *Understanding Church Growth* was the foundation of the dynamic and influential Church Growth Movement. Curiously, he almost got derailed from his role in church growth after his reading one of the notable Christian authors of the twentieth century H. Richard Niebuhr who took the liberal view that whatever the church did outside its own walls was "mission"—education, health care, philanthropy, and world friendship. Niebuhr included evangelism in the list too, but most liberals ignore evangelism. McGavran had Niebuhr's view of mission in mind when he went as a missionary to India in 1923, but he soon returned to the traditional view of missions: converting unbelievers to Christianity is the main goal and education, medicine, and other activities are secondary.

McGavran went about the task of making converts in India—and proved to be very good at it. And he began asking: Why do some churches grow while others do not? What causes some to stagnate? His answers to these questions led to his being first dean of the School of World Mission at Fuller. He published *Understanding Church Growth* in 1970, and thousands of pastors responded to his thoughts on setting goals, utilizing the laity, overcoming barriers to growth, and tailoring the message to the audience without altering the core truths of the faith. He received some criticism, but many pastors and laymen responded warmly to the image of the pastor not just as the man who prepares sermons in his study and visits the sick in hospitals but as an active apostle for Christ, growing his own church and leading to the founding of new ones.

In a sense McGavran's valuable work is a rediscovery of something that all Christians should know from reading Acts: the church exists through growth just as a fire exists by burning.

Prayer: Lord, never let us be slack in praying for and working for the growth of your fellowship. Amen.

December 16 · A KINGLESS REIGN

He breaks the spirit of rulers; he is feared by the kings of the earth.

PSALM 76:12

1653: Oliver Cromwell is a controversial figure in world history. Many remember him as the English general who perpetrated a massacre of Irish Catholics. There's no doubt that in a violent age, Cromwell knew how to be violent. But he deserves our consideration for some better qualities.

One of these was religious tolerance—a rare thing in the 1600s. Cromwell was a Puritan, meaning he took Christianity seriously and believed the state-supported Church of England needed serious reform. The king Charles I and the archbishop of Canterbury William Laud persecuted the Puritans, seeing them as dangerous radicals. They ordered all citizens to conform to the Church of England—or else. A civil war ensued, the king and his supporters on one side, Cromwell and the Puritans of Parliament on the other. The Puritans won, and both Charles and Laud were executed.

England was declared a "commonwealth," and Cromwell on December 16, 1653, assumed the title Lord Protector—practically king, but he would not accept the title of "king." Some historians say England was an oppressive place during Cromwell's rule, but this was not so. In fact, he was tolerant of the many Christian sects which had been persecuted under the king's rule. Cromwell even revoked the centuries-old ban on Jews living in England. For Cromwell, if a person was a loyal citizen, he could believe as he wished and practice his religion without fear. It's true he did order the massacre of Catholics in Drogheda, Ireland, but it was due to their rebellion not their religion.

Cromwell, a decent and devoted family man, died on September 3, 1658. His rule had proved that a nation could exist without a king or a state church and that Christians of different denominations could coexist in peace. Sadly, within a short time the English restored the monarchy and placed Charles II, the son of Charles I, on the throne, and once again religious intolerance set in.

Prayer: Lord, you alone are our king, and you alone do we trust completely. Amen.

December 17 · A MULTIFACETED TALENT

There are different kinds of service, but the same Lord.

1 CORINTHIANS 12:5

1957: Fans of detective fiction know her as the author of the Lord Peter Wimsey novels. Readers of literary classics know her as a translator of Dante's *Divine Comedy*. Christians known her as a lay theologian, author of radio plays on biblical themes, and member of the "Inklings" literary set that included C. S. Lewis. Dorothy Sayers was, to put it mildly, versatile.

Educated in literature at Oxford, Sayers worked as an ad copywriter. On the side she began writing her popular detective novels. Although these were "secular" writing, she worked Christian themes into her fiction, as did her friend C. S. Lewis. Like Lewis, she wrote some very popular books on Christianity, notably *Creed or Chaos* in which she examines the Apostles' Creed and other classic creeds. The book's subtitle is *Why It Really Does Matter What You Believe.*

Sayers wrote radio dramas for British Broadcasting. The best of these, *The Man Born to Be King*, consisting of twelve episodes on the life of Christ, aired during World War II. *He That Should Come* was about the birth of Jesus. In these biblical plays, Sayers departed from "King James English," which struck many listeners as irreverent, but most people praised the plays for making biblical characters seem real.

Sayers, like all Christians, was human. She got over a broken romance by having a sexual fling—and found herself pregnant by a man who had no interest in marriage. Not wanting to shock her elderly parents (her father was a clergyman), she had her son raised by a cousin, something not revealed to the world till after her death. She provided for the boy who knew her as "Cousin Dorothy." Her marriage to writer Mac Fleming had its difficulties; since he became disabled, she had to support them both with her writing.

When she died on December 17, 1957, she had millions of fans worldwide, many of them Christians.

Prayer: Father, thank you for those gifted with words that bolster our faith. Amen.

December 18 · THE HEART CHIMING IN

My servants will sing out of the joy of their hearts.

ISAIAH 65:14

1707: Charles Wesley, born on this date, stands in the shadow of his more famous older brother John, the founder of Methodism. But Methodism would not have been the same without Charles nor would Christianity's treasure of great hymns.

Four years younger than John, Charles was the eighteenth child of Samuel and Susanna Wesley. Reared in their devout home, Charles went through a wild spell at Oxford, but later he and John formed a "Holy Club" at the university, meeting for prayer and Bible study. Both brothers were ordained and went as missionaries to Georgia but had little success there. On May 31, 1838, Charles had a conversion experience: "I now found myself at peace with God and rejoiced in hope of loving Christ."

Two days after Charles's conversion, he began doing what he became famous for: writing hymns. Though he joined John in preaching and ministering to prisoners, it was clear that Charles's supreme gift was putting the Christian experience into songs that would touch the heart. In 1739 the Wesleys published the first Methodist hymnal, *Hymns and Sacred Poems*. Thankfully, Charles's hymns became popular among all denominations.

Hard as it is to believe, Charles Wesley wrote more than six thousand hymns. While some have become dated, many have not. Consider only a handful: "Love Divine, All Loves Excelling," "O for a Thousand Tongues to Sing," "Hark, the Herald Angels Sing," "Christ the Lord Is Risen Today," "Jesus, Lover of My Soul," "A Charge to Keep I Have," "O for a Heart to Praise My God." As the titles show, Charles felt no shame in emphasizing the emotional side of faith. In a day when worship in the state-supported Church of England was cold and dull, it is no wonder that thousands were drawn to Methodism with its emotionally rich sermons and hymns. The brothers succeeded admirably in their effort to "spread Scriptural holiness throughout the land."

Prayer: Father, in our daily walk with you, warm and transform our hearts. Amen.

December 19 · A Guru for Christ

"Repentance and forgiveness of sins will be preached in his name to all nations."

LUKE 24:47

1903: A unique figure in Christian history, a real "maverick," was Sundar Singh of India. Raised in the Sikh faith, Singh studied under a Sikh guru but attended a Christian school in order to learn English. His mother died when he was fourteen, and full of despair and rage, he took out his anger on the Christians, interrupting their classes, throwing filth on his teachers, even burning a Bible page by page. He was on the verge of suicide on December 19, 1903, when he prayed that the true God would reveal himself. He had a vision of Christ with pierced hands and resolved to follow Christ forever, which infuriated his Sikh family who disowned him and almost succeeded in poisoning him.

Singh cut off the braided hair that all Sikh men wore and took to the road, witnessing for Christ. Aware that India's Hindus expected a guru to wear a yellow robe, he wore such a robe, but his message was Christian not Hindu. Owning nothing, he relied on food and shelter from people he met. He became known as the "apostle with the bleeding feet." Many people responded to his Christian message; others shunned him or harassed him.

In 1909 Singh enrolled as a ministerial student at a Church of England college, though he felt that the English Christians' rules about clergymen wearing European clothing and singing English hymns were unnecessary. He took to the road again, the lone evangelist, making more converts and enemies. His message was based purely on the Gospels not on anything he had learned from the English. He traveled to many parts of Asia and was last heard of in Tibet in 1929; presumably he died there. Perhaps this mysterious end is appropriate for this unique and solitary preacher of the gospel.

A happy footnote to the story: he was reconciled to his father and brother after both became Christians.

Prayer: Lord, thank you for the stouthearted men who accomplish great things with only you to aid them. Amen.

December 20 · BURNING WORDS

Were not our hearts burning within us while he talked with us on the road and opened the Scriptures to us?

LUKE 24:32

1899: Born on the verge of a new century was Martyn Lloyd-Jones of Wales, one of many superb preachers to come from that tiny nation. Lloyd-Jones trained to be a doctor but felt the call of God to preach. After serving a church in Wales for a time, he settled in London as the associate pastor of Westminster Chapel, a large evangelical church within sight of Buckingham Palace. He became the senior pastor in 1943 and drew thousands to his sermons on Sunday mornings and evenings, and though his sermons were sometimes as long as an hour, he held the congregation spellbound. Those who could not attend read the sermons verbatim in the church's newsletter. Many of his sermons were "serials" in which he would preach through a book of the Bible verse by verse, each sermon linked to the ones before and after it. His ability to mine a great deal of material out of the Bible is evident in his commentary on the letter to the Romans—fourteen volumes.

Lloyd-Jones spoke of his preaching style as "logic on fire." His sermons were intellectually meaty but at the same time possessed the "fire" that enables the words to touch the heart and transform lives. Though he was an excellent speaker, Lloyd-Jones almost never preached on television, feeling that the time constraint left no room for the leading of the Spirit.

A minor controversy erupted between Lloyd-Jones and another notable among British evangelicals, John Stott. Lloyd-Jones urged evangelicals to break away from liberal denominations, including the Church of England, while Stott urged them to stay. Most evangelicals within the Church of England followed Stott's advice, but the controversy did no permanent harm to the relationship between the two men.

Lloyd-Jones died on March 1, 1981, having proved that in an increasingly secular century, Christianity was still alive and well in Britain.

Prayer: Father, give us the words to speak and give us the fire that gives those words power. Amen.

December 21 · "I Once Was Lost . . ."

Christ Jesus came into the world to save sinners—of whom I am the worst.

1 TIMOTHY 1:15

1807: Some people's conversions cause immediate changes in their lives. Others are a little slow in letting their lives catch up to their beliefs. Such was the case of John Newton. In his youth he led a colorful (and immoral) life as a sailor on a slave ship where even the other sailors were appalled at his profanity. Newton had a change of heart in 1748 during a storm in which he feared for his life. Sadly, his conversion did not immediately end his connection with the slave trade—in fact, he became the captain of a slave ship on which he often held worship services. It took a long time for him to realize what to us is obvious: a Christian cannot be involved in the sale of other human beings.

Finally abandoning the slave business, he studied for the ministry, but the Church of England authorities were slow to ordain him in light of his disreputable past. They finally became convinced that the former slave trader was a true believer, and he was ordained in 1764 and became a pastor in the village of Olney, England.

At this time the spiritually dry state Church of England held little attraction for people of faith. This was not so in Newton's parish where the people came to love this man with a sinful past, a man who could really appreciate God's amazing grace. He and one of his parishioners, the poet William Cowper, collaborated on a songbook, published as *Olney Hymns*. It contained what may well be the most popular hymn ever, Newton's "Amazing Grace." *Olney Hymns* was used throughout England, and it became the unofficial hymnal of English evangelicals. The hymns embody Newton's motto: "Christianity is not a system of doctrine, but a new creature."

Newton died on December 21, 1807, but his hymns, particularly "Amazing Grace," seem destined to live forever.

Prayer: Father, thank you for your amazing grace which transforms even the worst of sinners. Amen.

December 22 · LIFEBOAT CAPTAIN

"This gospel of the kingdom will be preached in the whole world as a testimony to all nations."

MATTHEW 24:14

1899: History is full of surprises, such as the remarkable story of an uneducated shoe salesman, born into a poor family of nine children, becoming one of the world's greatest evangelists. This was Dwight L. Moody who died on this date after a stellar preaching career in America and abroad.

Converted in his teens, Moody settled in Chicago where in 1857 a financial panic led many businessmen to turn to religion. At one of their meetings no preacher was available, so Moody was called upon to preach—despite having no theological training nor much schooling of any kind. Clearly God had intended that Moody give up selling shoes to take on the greater task of selling the gospel. From his clumsy beginning in the pulpit, he grew more confident, drawing crowds to his Chicago church. When it was destroyed in the Great Fire of 1871, Moody quickly built another.

This buoyant, optimistic preacher was too dynamic to be confined to one city, and Moody preached throughout the United States. He was also too big to be confined to the United States, and his preaching tour of Great Britain surprised cynics who never expected the British to turn out in droves to hear an American evangelist. Living in a period when denominational differences were important to many people, Moody reached out to all denominations. He did not impress the theological sophisticates, but even they had to admit that in the wake of a Moody crusade, crime and drunkenness decreased. Business moguls like department store head John Wanamaker backed Moody's tours, knowing their employees became better workers after conversion.

Moody avoided social and political issues, and though he firmly believed in hell, he preferred to draw people to the Lord through an emphasis on love and eternal life. "God has given me a lifeboat and said to me, 'Moody, save all you can.'" Moody did.

Prayer: Lord, thank you for the tireless men and women who carry the gospel of salvation to the world. Amen.

December 23 · ARMY WITH HEART

He will rescue them from oppression and violence, for precious is their blood in his sight.

PSALM 72:14

1793: Thousands of Frenchmen went into battle on this date wearing a unique badge: a heart topped with a cross and the words *Dieu Le Roi*—"God the King," though some said it also meant "God and the King." These men were not professional soldiers but civilians resisting the antireligious government that ruled France following the French Revolution. The Revolutionary government learned that not all French people hated the king or the Catholic Church, and resistance to the Revolution was particularly strong in the Vendée region in western France. There the locals were horrified that church property was confiscated, women were attacked on their way to church, and priests who would not swear a loyalty oath to the secular government were imprisoned or exiled.

When the government ordered the drafting of all able-bodied men into the French army, the Vendée broke into armed revolt, so the government sent thousands of troops to "pacify" the region. The rebels had formed a militia calling itself the Royal and Catholic Army, and though they were badly outnumbered, they knew the local terrain better than the government's troops, and they could rely on the aid of local people. In spring 1793 the Royal and Catholic Army won victories, and Christians all over Europe prayed the victories would continue. But the government's well-trained professional regiments finally "pacified" the Vendée at the Battle of Savenay on December 23, 1793. Afterward, the troops followed a "scorched earth" policy, burning farms, looting homes, raping women, and killing men and boys.

Historians know these events as the War of the Vendée, a classic case of a secular government carrying out a policy of genocide against its own people whose only "crime" was being more loyal to God than to a political system. In the short run, France's secular Revolutionary government won. In the long run, the church continued on, outlasting the Revolution and other political changes.

Prayer: Lord, in the day of trial, give us courage to stand up for you and your children. Amen.

December 24 · WARM WORDS FROM THE COLD ABYSS

The highest heavens belong to the LORD, but the earth he has given to man.

PSALM 115:16

1968: On this date three men in a very distant locale had the world's ear. The three were Frank Borman, Jim Lovell, and Bill Anders who happened to be orbiting the moon. The Apollo 8 astronauts photographed the "earthrise," showing earth as a fluorescent blue ball, very appealing when contrasted with the black sky and the cold grayness of the moon's surface.

The year just past had been one many people wished they could forget: two high-profile assassinations in the United States, a Communist crackdown in Eastern Europe, the ongoing war in Vietnam, political radicalism, a generation gap that seemed to be widening. . . . Perhaps the previous months had made the broadcast audience on December 24 receptive to the image of a strikingly beautiful home planet—and also to the words the three astronauts spoke. Anders began: "We are now approaching lunar sunrise, and for all the people back on earth, the crew of Apollo 8 has a message that we would like to send you. 'In the beginning . . .'" The three, in turn, read the first ten verses of Genesis 1. At the end of the passage, Borman concluded with "a Merry Christmas, and God bless all of you on the good earth."

The broadcast was watched by more people in the world than any previous one. Gazing at the image of the world, looking isolated but beautiful in a vast black sea of space, perhaps people paused to think that the world, with all its strife, was a fine place, that it was, as God said at the beginning, "good." In a world where so many seemed to be forgetting God or disbelieving or thumbing their noses at him, it was comforting to hear that "in the beginning God created" his fine world.

Prayer: God of creation, thank you for the home you created for us, and let us seek peace on it. Amen.

"Be merciful, just as your Father is merciful."

LUKE 6:36

1868: On this date a political leader who grew up poor, had no formal education and was illiterate until his wife taught him to read and write, issued Proclamation 179 "granting full pardon and amnesty for the offense of treason against the United States during the late Civil War." The leader was Andrew Johnson U.S. president, a lifelong Democrat from Tennessee who was, amazingly, elected vicepresident in 1864 as the running mate of Republican Abraham Lincoln. When his home state (goaded by its slaveowners) seceded from the Union in 1861, Johnson stubbornly retained his seat in the U.S. Senate and for his loyalty was picked by Lincoln as running mate, in the hope of sending a message of reconciliation.

Only a few days after beings worn in, Johnson found himself filling Lincoln's shoes. The war was over; the forgiving and reconciling Lincoln was dead, and now the Republicans in control of Congress wanted Johnson to grind the defeated South deeper into the dirt. When Johnson showed signs of being merciful, Congress tried but failed to impeach him.

Johnson was not a particularly devout man nor did he quote the Bible as often as Lincoln did. But he agreed with Lincoln that the war between two Bible-reading, church-attending regions that prayed to the same God for victory was shameful. Johnson hated slavery and had no love for slaveholders, but by late 1868 he thought the defeated South had suffered enough. As his pardon stated, it was designed to "secure permanent peace, order, and prosperity throughout the land, and to renew and restore confidence and fraternal feeling among the whole people." All former Confederates were unconditionally pardoned—even president Jefferson Davis who had been chained in a damp cell since the war's end.

The Christmas pardon was Johnson's last presidential act of any importance. He received hundreds of letters and telegrams from pastors and Christian laity from the North and South praising it as the finest thing he had ever done.

Prayer: Father, as we honor the birth of your Son, let us think on mercy, healing, and reconciliation. Amen.

December 26 · CARDINAL CRIMES

Remember those in prison as if you were their fellow prisoners.

HEBREWS 13:3

1948: In 1991 the body of a man who died in 1975 was buried—rather, *reburied*—in the Catholic cathedral of Esztergom, Hungary. At the time he died, he was regarded as a criminal by the Communist government of Hungary. In 1991 a democratic government in Hungary took a different view.

Born in 1892, Jozsef Mindszenty became a priest in 1915 and was arrested by the Communist leader Bela Kun in 1917 for criticizing the government's take-over of Catholic schools, but he was released after Kun's fall later that year. He became a bishop in 1944 and the same year was arrested for not letting the government quarter soldiers in his home. He was made head of the Catholic Church in Hungary in 1945 then cardinal in 1946—and on December 26, 1948, was arrested once again, this time for treason and conspiracy against the new Communist regime in Hungary. Mindszenty at his sham trial confessed to all his crimes—but years later stated that he had been given drugs in his food, was deprived of sleep, and had been beaten mercilessly until he agreed to confess. He was given a life sentence—a case of the Communist regime wanting to tag a high-profile church leader as a traitor. The pope, Pius XII, excommunicated everyone involved in Mindszenty's trial.

During the anti-Communist Hungarian revolt in 1956, the cardinal was released, but only days later the Soviet Union intervened to restore Communist power. The cardinal sought asylum in the U.S. embassy in Budapest, and he remained there for fifteen years, unable to leave the site. (Certainly the embassy was better than a Communist prison cell.) In 1971 Pope Paul VI made a proposal: he would revoke the excommunication of the cardinal's persecutors if the Communists would allow Mindszenty to leave the country. He resided the rest of his life in Vienna, Austria, but traveled often to speak on behalf of Hungarian Catholics. Today most Hungarians, especially Christians, regard him as a hero of the faith.

Prayer: Father, fill the hearts of those who suffer for you with peace and assurance. Amen.

December 27 · DISCOVERING GOD

Lift your eyes and look to the heavens: Who created all these?

ISAIAH 40:26

1571: When the Soviet Union launched a man into space, the cosmonaut reported that there was no God "up there," so God did not exist. Such logic might have impressed the Communists in charge of the Soviet Union but not many other people. In fact, some of the greatest scientists have seen much evidence of God in the universe. The brilliant German astronomer Johannes Kepler, born on this date, was a devout Christian who expressed the wish that "I may perceive the God whom I find everywhere in the external world in like manner within me."

Kepler was brilliant even in his youth. When he graduated from college, he hoped to enter the ministry but was persuaded to teach mathematics. A friend and mentor exposed him to Copernicus's theory that the earth and other planets moved around the sun. Kepler knew Copernicus was on the right track, but there was something amiss in the theory. Copernicus taught that the planets' orbits were circular—after all, hadn't the great philosophers Plato and Aristotle taught that the circle was the "perfect" shape? But Plato and Aristotle were poor scientists. The more Kepler studied the planets, the more he became convinced that the orbits were not circles but ellipses—ovals. Modern astronomy was built on this, one of the greatest breakthroughs in science ever made.

Kepler had built upon, and improved on, Copernicus. He and Copernicus were both great scientists, and neither saw any conflict between science and faith. Copernicus had written that astronomy was a "science more divine than human." Kepler wrote that "through my work, God is being celebrated."

In Kepler's day there was no distinction between astrology and astronomy, and one of Kepler's duties was to cast horoscopes for his aristocratic employers. Christianity had never quite extinguished the old pagan belief that the stars influenced individual lives on earth. What a pity this intelligent and devout man had to waste his time on such trifles.

Prayer: Almighty God, we praise you for the beauty and order of your vast universe. Amen.

December 28 · LOVE AND FAITH IN TURBULENT TIMES

We love because he first loved us.

1 JOHN 4:19

1622: The 1500s and 1600s were bloody centuries in Europe with Catholics killing Protestants and Protestants killing Catholics. This is a sad part of Christian history, but we in the twenty-first century can take a more objective view of those times and realize that some fine writing and preaching was being done by Christians in all denominations. One of the best writers was Francis de Sales, a Catholic whose works can be appreciated by all Christians.

Francis was born into a well-off French family in 1567 and given a good education, and his father hoped he would find a lucrative government job. Instead Francis devoted himself to the church and was ordained in 1593. The pope gave him a post that existed "in name only": bishop of Geneva, a city that was thoroughly Protestant, having been the base of the great Protestant reformer John Calvin. Settling in a town near Geneva, Francis preached to the local people and persuaded many of them to return to the Catholic Church. His whole life was persuasive, for this man, raised in comfortable circumstances, lived very simply, and his Christlike character gained him many admirers. Whenever he traveled, people from peasants to kings flocked to hear his sermons.

Francis's legacies to the world are two great books, *Introduction to the Devout Life* and *On the Love of God*. The first book was so popular that during Francis's lifetime it was translated into almost every European language, and even in this time of intense hostility between Catholics and Protestants, many Protestants admitted it was a fine book. *On theLove of God* has touched many readers with its conviction that everything that exists flows from God's love.

Francis died of a cerebral hemorrhage on December 28, 1622. In 1923 the Catholic Church declared him to be the patron saint of writers. Because he developed a sign language to communicate with the deaf, he is also the patron saint of the deaf.

Prayer: Father, thank you for inspired words that reach us across the centuries and across denominational lines. Amen.

December 29 · CATHEDRAL BLOODLETTING

It is better to take refuge in the LORD than to trust in princes.

PSALM 118:9

1170: If you read Geoffrey Chaucer's *Canterbury Tales* in school, you might recall that the storytelling pilgrims in the tales were on a pilgrimage to Canterbury cathedral to visit the tomb of the "holy blissful martyr," Thomas Becket. Interestingly, Becket was buried on the spot where he was murdered.

In the Middle Ages the only people with any real education were clergy. For an intelligent man who wanted to move up the career ladder, the means to do it was to attend university, be ordained, and hope that your intelligence would attract the attention of a ruler who would make you an advisor. One unfortunate result of this was that many men who became priests were not even remotely religious.

One example was Thomas Becket who became the chancellor of England under King Henry II—second in command, in effect. He and Henry were bosom friends, both hard drinkers and womanizers. Henry made Becket the archbishop of Canterbury, head of the English church—and something shocking happened: Becket started to act like a Christian, which Henry never expected. Becket also claimed Henry did not have the right to bring clergy to trial in secular courts. (There were separate courts for clergy.) He and Henry patched up their quarrel but soon clashed again. The key question was: who controlled the church in England—the king or his archbishop? Something else was at stake: Henry felt betrayed and abandoned by his best friend, a man he had lifted to high office.

In the presence of some of his knights, Henry was heard to say, "Will no one rid me of the troublesome priest?"—meaning Becket. Four knights set off for Canterbury and on December 29, 1170, did something that shocked all of Europe: butchered Becket in his cathedral. Becket was almost immediately declared a martyr, and the king had to do public penance at Becket's tomb. Becket's much-visited tomb was a monument to the freedom of the church from government interference.

Prayer: Lord, in a turbulent world full of treachery, fill our hearts with your peace. Amen.

Hate what is evil; cling to what is good.

ROMANS 12:9

1906: Josephine Butler took on one of the world's chronic evils, the sexual exploitation of women. Butler lived in Victorian England, generally considered the pinnacle of propriety and restraint. But Victorian England had its seamy side. Prostitution ran rampant, particularly in port towns, and there was a thriving business in procuring young girls for the trade. (The age of consent was twelve.)

Butler lived in the seaside city of Liverpool, notorious for prostitution. She helped establish homes for the women, giving them a chance to pursue another way of life. Then she turned her attention to Britain's Contagious Disease Acts, passed in the 1860s. In theory, the acts aimed to control the spread of venereal disease by requiring the arrest and medical examination of women suspected of infection. But in effect, the acts led to a sort of government-sponsored prostitution.

Butler organized the Ladies' National Association for Repeal, dedicated to informing the public that the acts failed as health measures and contributed to the exploitation of women. She circulated petitions, debated anyone who cared to debate her, and supported Parliamentary candidates who promised to repeal the acts. She was successful: the acts were repealed in 1886. She also campaigned to raise the age of consent to sixteen; again, she was successful. This helped reduce the procurement of young girls as prostitutes.

Josephine Butler is a good example of Christians coping with the modern world. She worked on the individual-focused "street level"—establishing homes for destitute women, giving them an alternative to the life of prostitution—but also on the legislative level, working to change laws that encouraged exploitation. In her tireless round of public debates, influencing members of Parliament and enlisting the aid of sympathetic newspaper editors (the media moguls of their day), she is a fine example of a Christian working for social change. Her death on December 30, 1906, ended a life rooted in practical compassion.

Prayer: Father, your saints shine like beacons in a dark world. Give us the power to follow their example. Amen.

December 31 · AHEAD OF HIS TIME

Though I walk in the midst of trouble, you preserve my life.

PSALM 138:7

1384: An English minister named John Wycliffe seemed to have had a charmed life: he was in the thick of most of the religious and political controversies of his time, and the church regarded him as a dangerous heretic, yet he managed to die of natural causes. Forty-four years after he died, his remains were dug up and burned, but the ideas he turned loose on the world lived on.

Born around 1330, John Wycliffe took his duties as a pastor seriously. The church was full of ambitious, greedy, immoral leaders, men whose lives were clearly nothing like Jesus' apostles. The problem was the Bible was in Latin, and few people could read Latin. Those who could, like Wycliffe, knew the church badly needed moral reform. Wycliffe spoke out against the church's immorality and its superstitious cult of relics (reverencing a bone or tooth of a saint). He questioned whether the pope was really intended to rule the whole church and whether the pope should be living in luxury. In other words, Wycliffe was bringing up all the ideas that would motivate the Protestant Reformation in the 1500s. His followers, known as the Lollards, dared to translate the Bible into English so that Christians could have direct access to the Word of God.

And he got into trouble. A church council banned Wycliffe's writings, and Wycliffe himself would likely have been persecuted, possibly executed—except he had a friend in high places: the Duke of Lancaster, uncle of the king, Richard II. The king had married a princess from Bohemia, and thanks to this England-Bohemia connection, Wycliffe's writings trickled into Bohemia and from there to the rest of Europe.

Wycliffe died on December 31, 1384. In 1415 the Council of Constance commanded that the "heretic's" remains be dug up and burned, but this wasn't done until 1428 because almost everyone regarded Wycliffe as a saint.

Prayer: Lord, your faithful ones put themselves at risk for the sake of your Word. Let our lives honor their efforts and their memories. Amen.

INDEX

For topics or names that are covered on more than one date, the date in **boldface** is the key entry dealing with that subject or person.

Abolitionists, May 22,
  July 26, September 26,
  October 7, October 16
Abortion, **January 22**,
  January 30, December 11
Acton, Lord, June 19
Adams, John, July 11Adams,
  John Quincy, July 11
Adams, Samuel, October 2
African Methodist Episcopal
  church, March 26,
  November 2
Albright, Jacob, May 17
Alexander VI (pope), May 23
Alleine, Joseph, May 29
Allen, Richard, March 26
Alphege, April 19
Altizer, Thomas, April 8
Ambrose of Milan, **April 4**,
  August 28
American Revolution,
  February 15, October 2
Anabaptists, **January 21**,
  December 10
Anthony of Egypt, January 17
Apollo 8 mission, November
  6, **December 24**
Aquinas, Thomas, March 7
Arianism, May 2, May 20
Arminius, Jacobus,
  October 19
Arndt, Johann, May 11
Arnold, Matthew, June 12
Arnold, Thomas, June 12
Asbury, Francis, March 26,
  March 31, May 3

Asch, Sholem, July 10
Assemblies of God, April 2
Athanasius, May 2
Atheism, April 1, April 8,
  November 6, November 13
Attila, September 29
Augsburg, Peace of,
  September 25
Augustine of Hippo,
  August 28
Aylward, Gladys, January 3
Azusa Street revival, April 14
Bach, Johann Sebastian,
  March 21
Backus, Isaac, January 9
Baldwin IV, November 25
Baring-Gould, Sabine,
  January 2
Barnardo, Thomas,
  September 19
Barton, Bruce, July 5
Baxter, Richard, December 8
Becket, Thomas,
  December 29
Bede, May 26
Beecher, Lyman, January 10
Ben-Hur, November 12
Bennett, Dennis,
  November 1
Bernard of Clairvaux,
  August 20
Big Bang Theory, June 20
Bilney, Thomas, August 19
Blake, William, November
  28
Bliss, Philip, July 9
Boddy, Alexander,
  September 10
Böhler, Peter, April 27
Bonhoeffer, Dietrich, April 9
Boniface (missionary to
  Germans), June 5

Boniface VIII (pope),
  October 11
Boom, Corrie ten, April 15
Booth, Catherine, April 10
Booth, William, April 10
Boyle, Robert, January 25
Bradstreet, Anne, September 16
Brainerd, David, July 12
Breen, Joseph, December 5
Briçonnet, Guillaume,
  January 24
Bright, Bill, July 19
Brown, John, October 16
Bryan, William Jennings,
  July 21
Buchman, Frank, August 7
Buckley, William F.,
  November 24
Bullinger, Heinrich,
  September 17
Bunyan, John, August 31
Burke, Edmund, January 12
Butler, Joseph, June 16
Butler, Josephine,
  December 30
Calvin, John, **May 27**,
  October 19
Cambridge Seven,
  December 2
Campbell, Alexander,
  March 4
Campion, Edmund,
  December 1
Campus Crusade for Christ,
  July 19
Canute, April 19
Caravaggio, September 28
Carey, William, August 17
Carmelites, June 24,
  October 4
Cartwright, Peter,
  September 1

Carver, George Washington,
    January 5
Catherine de Medicis,
    August 24
Catherine of Siena, April 29
Cecil, William, August 4
Chalmers, Thomas,
    March 17
Chambers, Whittaker,
    April 1
Charismatic movement, July
    23, November 1
Charlemagne, January 28
Charles I (king of England),
    February 15, August 13,
    December 16, April 12
Charles II (king of England),
    February 6
Charles V (Holy Roman
    emperor), December 13
Charles IX (king of France),
    August 24
Charles XII (king of
    Sweden), November 30
Charles Martel, October 22
Chesterton, G. K., May 29
China Inland Mission,
    March 1
Christian Endeavor,
    September 12
Churches of Christ, March 4
Circuit riders, February 2,
    March 31, September 1
Clapham Sect, July 26
Clare of Assisi, August 11
Clark, Francis Edward,
    September 12
Clarkson, Thomas,
    September 26
Clephane, Elizabeth, June 7
Clovis (king of the Franks),
    November 27
Coke, Thomas, May 3
Colson, Charles, August 12
Columbus, Christopher,
    October 12, November 26

Communism, January 19,
    April 1, April 16, May
    8, May 30, July 13,
    August 7, September 2,
    December 26
Constance, Council of,
    April 22
Constantine, January 1, May
    20, **June 15**, August18
Contemporary Christian
    music, February 20
Conwell, Russell,
    December 6
Copernicus, Nicholas, June
    21, December 27
Coughlin, Charles,
    October 25
Countess of Huntingdon's
    Connexion, June 17
Coverdale, Miles, February 4
Cowper, William, **November
    15**, December 21
Cranmer, Thomas, March 30
Cromwell, Oliver, April 11,
    December 9, **December 16**
Crosby, Fanny, March 24
Crusades, June 3, July 22,
    August 20, August 25,
    November 25
Cyril (missionary to Slavs),
    February 14
Damian, Peter, February 22
Damien, Father, May 4
Dante, September 13
Darwin, Charles,
    February 12, June 30,
    September 6
David and Bathsheba
    (movie), August 10
Davies, Samuel, November 3
Dawkins, Richard
    November 13
Decius (Roman emperor),
    January 20
Declaration of Indulgence
    (1687), February 6

Defoe, Daniel, April 24
Deism, April 3, May 14,
    June 16
DeMille, Cecil B., August
    10, October **5**
Diocletian (Roman
    emperor), **March 12**,
    June 15
Disciples of Christ, March 4
Dissenters (from Church
    of England), February
    6, April 11, April 24,
    August 31
Divine Comedy, The,
    September 13
Dominic, August 6
Dostoyevsky, Fyodor,
    November 11
Douglas, Lloyd, August 27
Dow, Lorenzo, February 2
Dowie, John Alexander,
    March 9
Duff, Alexander, April 26
Durer, Albrecht, April 6
Dwight, Timothy, May 14
Edersheim, Alfred, March 16
Edmund (English king),
    November 20
Edwards, Jonathan, May 14,
    July 12, **March 22**
Eisenhower, Dwight,
    July 4
Eliot, John, October 28
Elizabeth I (queen of
    England), April 18,
    August 4, November 9,
    December 1
Enlightenment, March
    2, June 16, July 2,
    November 10
Erasmus, Desiderius,
    February 1
Estienne, Robert,
    September 7
Evangelism Explosion,
    September 5

Evolution, February
   12, June 30, July 21,
   September 6, November
   5, November 13
Faraday, Michael,
   September 22
Ferdinand (king of Spain),
   November 26
Ferrar, Nicholas, December 4
Finney, Charles G., May 22,
   August16
Fliedner, Theodor, October 13
Fort Caroline, September 20
Four Spiritual Laws, July 19
Fox, George, January 13
Foxe, John, April 18
Francis de Sales, December 28
Francis of Assisi, August 11,
   October 3
Franciscans, July 16,
   October 3, October 23
French Revolution, January
   12, February 28,
   November 4, November
   10, December 23
Freud, Sigmund, May 6
Friends, Society of
   (Quakers), January 13,
   May 1, May 21, October 7
Fry, Elizabeth, May 21
Full Gospel Business Men's
   Fellowship, July 23
Fuller, Charles E., April 25
Fundamentals, The,
   September 6, October 26
Galileo, June 21
Geneva Bible, January 14,
   September 7
Gerhardt, Paul, January 7
Gibbons, James, August 14
Gibson, Mel, February 25
Gideons, July 1
Gladiators, January 1
Gladstone, William, **May
   19**, June 19, June 30

Gnostics, June 28
Godfrey of Bouillon, July 22
Goforth, Jonathan,
   October 8
Good News for Modern Man,
   September 15
Gordon, Charles "Chinese",
   January 26
Graham, Billy, March 3,
   May 15, June 29, July 25,
   July 27
Graham, Franklin, May 15
Great Awakening, January
   11, February 5, March 22,
   July 12
Great Ejection, May 28
Great Disruption, March 17
Great Schism, April 22,
   April 29
Grebel, Conrad, January 21
Gregory I (pope), September 3
Gregory VII (pope),
   February 21
Grenfell, George, August 21
Grenfell, Wilfred, October 9
Grundtvig, Nicolai,
   September 8
Gutenberg, Johann,
   February 3
Haldane, Robert, February 28
Handel, George Frederick,
   April 13
Harnack, Adolf von, May 7
Harris, Howell, May 25
Hastings, Selina, Countess
   of Huntingdon, May 25,
   June 17
Hauge, Hans, March 29
Havergal, Frances,
   December 14
Hays Code, December 5
Helena (mother of emperor
   Constantine), August 18
Henry IV (emperor),
   February 21

Henry VIII (king of
   England), **January 27**,
   February 4, February 7,
   March 30, October 6,
   December 4
Henry of Navarre (Henry
   IV of France), August 24,
   October 18
Henry, Carl F. H.,
   December 7
Henry, Matthew, June 22
Henry, Patrick, November 3
Herbert, George, April 3
Hill, Rowland, August 23
Holiness movement, May 1,
   September 10
Hooker, Thomas, July 7
Hooper, Edward, February 9
Huguenots, August 24,
   September 20, October 18
Humanae Vitae, June 23
Huss, John, April 22,
   July 6
Huxley, Thomas, June 30
Icons, June 18
Ignatius of Antioch,
   October 17
Imitation of Christ, The,
   August 8
In His Steps, February 24
Indulgence, Declaration of
   (1687), February 6
Innocent III (pope), October
   3, **January 8**
Innocent XI (pope),
   September 21
Inquisition, April 29, August
   6, November 26
Irenaeus, June 28
Ironside, Harry, October 14
"Is God Dead?" (*Time*
   magazine cover), April 8
Isaac the Great, September 9
Isabella (queen of Spain),
   October 12, **November 26**

Mindszenty, Jozsef,
December 26
Moffat, Robert, August 9
Montgomery, James,
November 4
Moody, Dwight L., June 7,
September 11, October 9,
October 26, December 2,
December 22
Moral Re-Armament,
August 7
Moravians, April 27,
May 9
More, Thomas, February 7
Mott, John R., January 31
Muggeridge, Malcolm,
November 14,
December 11
Muhlenberg, Frederick,
June 4
Müller, George, March 10
Murray v. Curlett,
November 6
Murray, Andrew, January 18
Murray, William,
November 6
Muslim persecution of
Christians, March
11, April 17, June 3,
September 9
Nantes, Edict of, September 21,
October 18
Navigators, March 3
Nazism, March 14, April 9,
April 15
Neander, Johann, July 14
Nee, Watchman, May 30
Neesima, Joseph Hardy,
January 23
Nero, June 9
New International Version,
October 27
Newton, Isaac, March 20
Newton, John, November
15, **December 21**

Nicea, Council of, May 2,
May 20
Nott, Henry, March 5
Novak, Robert, February 26
O'Hair, Madalyn Murray,
November 6
Oastler, Richard, August 22
Olaf II (king of Norway),
July 29
Orr, James, September 6
Oswald (English king),
August 5
Paine, Thomas, October 2
Papal infallibility, July 18
Paradise Lost, December 9
Parham, Charles, January 29
Parris, Samuel, January 15
Pascal, Blaise, November 23
Passion of the Christ, The
(movie), February 25
Paul III (pope), June 2
Paul VI (pope), **June 23**,
December 26
Payne, Daniel, November 2
Penn, William, January 13,
July 30
Pensées, November 23
Pentecostals, January 29,
March 9, April 2, April
14, July 23, November 17
Philip III (king of Spain),
March 6
Pietism, May 9, July 20
Pilgrim's Progress, August 31
Pilgrims, **August15**,
October 20
Pius IX (pope), July 18
Pius X (pope), July 3
Pius XI (pope), March 14
Pius XII (pope), July 13
Polycarp, **February 23**,
October 17
Poor Clares, August 11
Praying Hands, April 6
Prison Fellowship, August 12

Production Code (movie
industry), December 5
Prohibition, October 10,
November 18
Quakers (Society of Friends),
January 13, May 1, May
21, July 30, October 7
Ramabai, Pandita, April 5
Ramsay, William, April 20
Reducciones, March 6
Relics, cult of, August 19
Rembrandt, July 15
Renan, Ernest, July 3
Revised Standard Version,
February 11, October 27
Reynolds, John, January 14
Ridley, Nicholas, April 18
Robe, The, August 27
Roberts, Oral, July 23
Rodeheaver, Homer,
November 19
Roe v. Wade, January 22
Rogers, John, February 4
Rousseau, Jean-Jacques,
July 2
Rowlandson, Mary,
February 10
Russian Revolution,
January 19
Ryman Auditorium,
October 15
Saladin, November 25
Salem witch trials,
January 15
Sallman, Warner, April 30
Salvation Army, April 10
Sankey, Ira, March 24, July
9, June 7
Savenay, Battle of,
December 23
Savonarola, Girolamo, May 23
Sayers, Dorothy, December 17
Schaeffer, Francis, January 30
Schleiermacher, Friedrich,
February 8, July 14